Praise for
Liberating Motherhood

Liberating Motherhood is an important contribution to a vital debate of our times. Vanessa Olorenshaw speaks with warmth, wit and clarity, representing lives and voices unheard for too long.

Shami Chakrabarti, author of *On Liberty*, former director of Liberty and formerly 'the most dangerous woman in Britain'

Lucid and riveting, this book sweeps you along to a realization that we are at a turning point in history. That even feminism hasn't asked big enough questions. Our humanity depends on re-elevating the nurture of young lives to our most primary purpose. Olorenshaw speaks for a generation of young women who are refusing to have their hearts numbed and their yearnings suffocated for corporate greed and a feedlot existence. This is The Female Eunuch of the 21st century.

Steve Biddulph, international bestselling author of *Raising Boys* and *Raising Babies*

Through her eloquent way of phrasing modernist questions, Vanessa is propelling herself forward as the symbol of the ultimate phase of the women's liberation movements . . . Read Liberating Motherhood from the beginning to the end and you'll appreciate the talent Vanessa has developed in phrasing inevitable new questions.

Michel Odent, obstetrician and author of *Birth and Breastfeeding*

A fierce and funny new voice — exploding with revolutionary verve. Olorenshaw puts motherhood firmly on the map. Bravo!

Dr Oliver James, Sunday Times bestselling author of *Affluenza*, *They F**k you Up*, and *Not in Your Genes*

Vanessa Olorenshaw's stimulating and timely book gives centre stage to both motherhood itself, and our confusion over it. And not before time . . . Women and men, left and right, should pay attention: mothers truly are our future.

Alison Wolf (Baroness Wolf of Dulwich), author of *The XX Factor*

While feminism has freed many women from domestic subservience, it has inadvertently cast a negative spin on personally delivered parenting. Olorenshaw reminds us that stay-at-home mothering is a damn good way to raise a child. Cogent and well-researched, it provides a much-needed corrective to distorted views of women's liberation.

Dr Shari L. Thurer, author of *The Myths of Motherhood*

Liberating Motherhood is a call to a revolution in thinking by all human beings … Olorenshaw is to be heartily congratulated on producing the opening salvo of the campaign to put mothering on the map so that sanity may return to the policy agenda of humanity.

**Dr Frances Hutchinson, author of
*What Everybody Really Wants to Know About Money***

Sharp, uncompromising and witty, Liberating Motherhood relocates maternal experience at the centre of feminist praxis, offering a rallying cry for mothers — and daughters.

Glosswitch, *The New Statesman*

Liberating Motherhood is a breath of fresh air in a culture deadened by the soulless grip of the money machine. Olorenshaw's call to mothers to honor the mysteries of pregnancy, birth, breastfeeding and childrearing, brings joy to the heart of this old feminist. Read Liberating Motherhood, pull on your purple stockings and join the revolution.

Naomi Ruth Lowinsky PhD, author of *The Motherline*

Vanessa Olorenshaw's call for a Purplestockings Movement is feminist, long overdue and urgently needed.

Mariam Irene Tazi-Preve, author of *Motherhood in Patriarchy*

An intelligent, well-researched book. It is an essential read for mothers, daughters, fathers, husbands, anyone who has children or is thinking of becoming a parent, and anyone who works with women. Thank you Vanessa for exposing the neglect mothers tolerate and for starting a movement that will create mother-honouring, mother-friendly policies.

Rosjke Hasseldine, author of *The Silent Female Scream*

Liberating Motherhood explores the need for a seismic shift in policymakers' priorities, examining why our systems are failing to secure a better and fairer world for our sons and daughters. Olorenshaw encourages readers to focus their energies on challenging a socio-economic system that is not fit for purpose and which leaves so many families impoverished, marginalised and without a voice. It reminds us that what counts in life can't always be counted.

Marie Peacock, Chair of Mothers at Home Matter

The erosion of respect for women to take care of their children should disturb everyone, not only mothers. Liberating Motherhood explores how the choice and right to work outside the home has to co-exist alongside the choice and right to care for our children. Vanessa tackles the 'mother issue' from the point of view of our bodies, our emotions and our work — but reminds us that love and humanity are a necessary part of the business of motherhood, too.

Laura Dodsworth, photographic artist and author of *Bare Reality*

Mothering is, perhaps, the most unappreciated and despised work of our time. Vanessa Olorenshaw's Liberating Motherhood is a hearty manifesto that tackles this hatred head-on.

Trista Hendren, author of *The Girl God* series

Vanessa is passionate about putting motherhood in to broader politics, activism and feminism. It's time — for the sake of all women's rights — to take motherhood out of the dusty corners and in to contemporary political and feminist discourse.

Rebecca Schiller, CEO of Birthrights and author of *All That Matters*

Liberating Motherhood is an important and heartfelt analysis of the misogyny underpinning Western culture and our disastrous devaluation of the maternal: read it.

Antonella Gambotto-Burke, author of
Mama: Love, Motherhood and Revolution

Vanessa's words of alarm are important. They are spoken and thought by every thinking woman from every generation. The time has come to stop history from repeating itself. The time has come for these words to merely call up memories of the past . . . for them to no longer be the present and future realities of motherhood.

Shannon Hayes, author of *Radical Homemakers*

How we raise our children and who will nurture them is one of the biggest issues facing society today. Thank you Vanessa for your contribution to the debate, your book is a real 'cri de coeur'!

Frances Scott, founder and director of 50:50 Parliament

Olorenshaw is immersed in her subject, impassioned but without anger, and oozing compassion and respect for mothers and children alike. Her exploration of maternal feminism is inclusive and compelling. She reveals the vulnerability of tenderly holding family life within an unforgiving economic climate and bothers not to dress up the betrayal of maternal freedoms as anything other. If you want to be reminded of why your mothering is beautifully but strangely revolutionary, read this book.

Michelle Mattesini, Attachment Parenting UK

A witty and forensic discussion of the politics and economics of motherhood. Olorenshaw goes beyond both the religious fetishisation of mothering and the 'feminist' fetishisation of jobs to build a solid case for an economy built around care — for ourselves, each other and the world we live in.

Barb Jacobson, Basic Income UK

This ground-breaking book is essential reading for anyone who cares about women and children. With passion, wit, intelligence, righteous anger and scrupulous research, Vanessa Olorenshaw lays bare not only the truth about how our society is deliberately shaped to require the exploitation of female unpaid caring and domestic labour, but the truth about the power, strength, skill, dedication and joy of mothering too.

Esther Parry, founder of All Mothers Work

Olorenshaw calls for a reinvigorated feminism that challenges all of us to think bigger — to understand that liberating women, liberating all of us across race, class and gender, requires not just opening opportunities for well-educated women to work in the marketplace, but redesigning that workplace, rethinking outdated policies, and finally honouring and valuing the care traditionally done by women that not only makes work possible in the economic marketplace, but is what ultimately gives work — and life — meaning. There is a better way. And Liberating Motherhood outlines a cogent strategy for getting there.

Brigid Schulte, author of *The New York Times* bestselling *Overwhelmed: Work, Love & Play When No One Has the Time*

Liberating Motherhood

BIRTHING THE PURPLESTOCKINGS MOVEMENT

Vanessa Olorenshaw

WOMANCRAFT PUBLISHING

Copyright © 2016 Vanessa Olorenshaw

Typeset and design by Lucent Word, Co. Cork, Ireland

Published by Womancraft Publishing, 2016
www.womancraftpublishing.com

ISBN: 978-1-910559-192 (Paperback)
ISBN: 978-1-910559-208 (Kindle)

A percentage of Womancraft Publishing profits are invested back into the environment reforesting the tropics (via TreeSisters) and forward into the community: providing books for girls in developing countries, and affordable libraries for red tents and women's groups around the world.

Womancraft Publishing is committed to sharing powerful new women's voices, through a collaborative publishing process. We are proud to midwife this work, however the story, the experiences and the words are the author's alone.

Ladder

Mothers' Voices
and the Falling Tree

his book is for my family, most importantly my daughter, my mother, my sister, my nieces and my grandmothers; my son, my husband, my father, my brother and my grandfathers. It is for any woman who is, or wishes to become, a mother.

Virginia Woolf spoke of A Room of One's Own. Well, if not a room, perhaps we all need **something** of one's own. This book is certainly that — it is for myself, past, present and future. If it speaks to you I hope it becomes something for you.

Maybe this book will make a noise. Perhaps it will echo amongst mothers and beyond — and it's about time. After all, those of us who are mothers at home are like the proverbial tree in the rainforest. When our words fall, if nobody listens, are we really here? Do we make a sound?

I found that 'invisible' and 'muted' feeling — in the work we do as mothers, in our voices that are kept silent and hidden from the public sphere, destined never to be heard — painful before I started on all this. Not so much now that I know I am not alone in feeling the way I do. We exist. The time for a mother-movement has arrived. It is not just sisterhood, but **motherhood**, which is powerful.

Thank you for reading. I am very grateful that you are hearing my falling tree.

Thanks and Acknowledgements

I am profoundly and humbly grateful for the help, support and encouragement which my family, friends and fellow mothers have given me in writing this book. I struggled for a long time with my right to write — the vulnerability and the emotional toil took me by surprise. By the time it was written, I started to liken it to a very long pregnancy and a birth with passionate and intense transition, calling for sheer physical and emotional stamina to push it through. Thank you to all those who held my hand while I birthed this book.

My husband showed patience. Thank you. You are an example to your children of what a man can be: affectionate, caring and decent.

My children showed enthusiasm for the idea of 'Mummy's book' while remaining my passion, my motivation and my inspiration; my brother and sister continue to scratch their heads about how I remain a bookworm after all these years; my nieces will read all about neoliberal capitalist patriarchy and be forewarned and forearmed; my dad gets his wedge for the table leg; and my mum now has that love letter — all 300-odd pages of it — from her daughter.

For my mother-in-law: You are something my own father's mother had been — adored by her son, and loved as a most wonderful grandmother. Thank you for your encouragement in my journey as a mother and in writing this book.

I owe word-midwife and writer Lucy H. Pearce heartfelt thanks, not only for believing in my voice and my book, but for inspiring me through her own book, *The Rainbow Way*, to share my words and harness determination in the face of insecurity and anxiety. Two qualities I now know I share with other writers. Turns out *page* fright is not so uncommon. Thank you, Lucy, for helping me turn my first draft into a book we are both proud of and excited to share with the world. I am beyond grateful to have connected with a publisher with whom I could share my voice and my vision, and to have *both* heard and embraced. The process, and you, taught me a great deal. Thanks to the team at Womancraft Publishing, and fellow Womancraft authors, who were inspiring and encouraging of my journey, too.

My heartfelt thanks to Naomi Stadlen, who provided such warm support and encouragement in my journey not only as a writer but (earlier, and unknowingly) as a new mother. Naomi, the solace and confidence I found in your words, the recognition of the value of *What Mothers Do* and *How Mothers Love*, will stay with me and generations to come, in my family and countless others. Your words and your message are important and your support of mothers in the work you have done for decades is admirable and inspirational. I am honoured and privileged that you agreed to write a Foreword for my humble book — thank you, and much love.

In campaigning circles, Marie Peacock and Lynne Burnham of Mothers at Home Matter, thank you both so much for everything you do, your tenacity and the tireless work you do for families: without women like you, the political scene would have no heart. The time is now! On a personal note, you have given me such support and shown huge solidarity from before the days of the *The Politics of Mothering* pamphlet through to the publication of this book. I don't think I could have got through some of it without your warm encouragement. Much admiration and gratitude, too, to Heather Ticheli for your tireless work over a number of years to push for the issue of maternal feminism and women's unwaged labour to form the basis of a panel at the Feminism in London Conference. What a wonderful event, and what fabulous women. Thank you Julian Norman and Lisa-Marie Taylor for platforming mothers at the Conference and for organising such an important event on feminism with such inspiring speakers and workshops. Thanks, too, in particular, to Kerry Hedley, Alexandra McVicar, Mel Tibbs, Imogen Thompson, Claire Paye, Karem Roitman, Esther Peacock and all committee members and members of Mothers at Home Matter, for their work and enthusiasm on the campaign. You are all very inspirational women. Alex, I don't think I will forget that evening of feminist 'variety' in a hurry!

To Mother-Sister of All Mothers Work, Esther Parry, thank you for your solidarity and support. I have massive admiration for your infectious passion for the cause. Your voice is an important, inspiring and tenacious one in modern political feminism and I am honoured to have shared a platform with you at Feminism in London Conference.

To all fellow campaigning mothers and members of Mothers at Home

Matter and All Mothers Work, it has been a privilege to spend time with you in person and online. How wonderful that we can create the village we so need as mothers, and as women of words and activism. Thanks, particularly, for encouragement, support, inspiration and more to Denise Sumpter, Teika Bellamy, Tiffany Bray, Barb Sheppard, Melissa Mallows, Hannah North, Erika Edwards Decaster and Carolina-Kawika Allen.

Great thanks to Selma James, Nina Lopez and Kim Sparrow, of Global Women's Strike, for solidarity and support and such warm conversations during my foray into campaigning in this field. Thank you for welcoming me to speak at the International Women's Conference. An important event and an important message.

Thank you Frances Hutchinson for introducing me to the economics of love and *The Machine Stops*, and for your generous support and time in conversation and correspondence. One thing I have felt since starting my campaigning is just how much common ground we can have with other women, including other mothers, despite generational and geographical divides. Your encouragement is much appreciated.

Many thanks to Rosjke Hasseldine. Not only for your time and our wonderful Skype conversations, but for your support, solidarity and encouragement. Your words in *The Silent Female Scream* and in our conversations helped me regain my confidence in my right to write: we all do have the right to speak and to be heard. Your work is valuable and you are inspiring. Thank you.

Thank you to Sophie Walker, leader of the Women's Equality Party, for inviting me to contribute to the policy working group on parenting. This is democracy. We can expect disagreement and we should encourage healthy debate. As is often the case, the strongest dissidents in a party are those who had the highest hopes and I am certainly guilty of the last bit. The motherhood issue was always going to be more challenging and complex than could be adequately dealt with in a matter of a couple of months of policy development. This book fills some significant gaps that were inherent in the process and I remain optimistic that the party will take the issues on board — after all, WEP wants to do things differently. Here's your chance.

Finally, thanks and gratitude variously for encouragement, inspiration, permissions, endorsements, counsel, support, and friendship to: Steve Biddulph, Antonella Gambotto-Burke, Milli Hill, Beverley Beech and the Association for Improvements in Maternity Services, Martha Fineman, Kathleen Lynch, Alison Wolf, Sue Tibballs, Nancy Folbre, Victoria

Smith, Stephanie Davies-Arai, Laura Dodsworth, Sophie Christophy, Michelle Quashie, Vicky Jordan, Lucy McGilchrist, Rebecca Cluett, Laura Macnamara, Lindsay Gorrill, Barb Jacobson, Shelley Macnaughton, Edwina Shaw, Susanna Blake, Catherine Gray, Nadia Mohammed, Judith Brook, Rosie Redstockings, Chrissy Chittenden, Nina Finbow, Marie-Thérèse Groarke, Claire Shaw, Finn Mackay, Sue Scott, the women of Red Tent Medway and Red Tent Sevenoaks, fellow mothers, fathers and grandparents of the school run, the playgroups, the preschool, breastfeeding support meetings, and social media, and, finally, those women who stand their ground, show solidarity and harness their social conscience for good and for all. Inspiring women. Inspiring voices. Love and thanks.

Mothers of the world, unite!

#LiberatingMotherhood #Purplestockings

Foreword

by Naomi Stadlen

his book is a call for justice — justice for mothers. It is a call long overdue.

Vanessa Olorenshaw has worked as a lawyer and in legal publishing. When she became a mother and started looking after her two children, she realised that she was doing something important. She found she was contributing to humanity and to our society in a way that she hadn't professionally. Yet our society, she explains in *Liberating Motherhood*, sees mothers who care for their children as 'not working'.

"We could say," she writes, "that a mother's place today is on society's naughty step." With this brilliant image, Vanessa conveys the assumption that many people make: that taking time to be a mother is 'naughty', indulgent and unproductive. Just as children are often ordered to sit on the 'naughty step' without getting a chance to explain their actions to their irate parents, so mothers are frequently judged without being heard. But now mothers have an advocate in Vanessa.

Some feminists might protest: Haven't we fought to liberate mothers from motherhood? Yes, replies Vanessa. She is grateful to earlier feminists and is aware that not every woman wants to be a mother. But she challenges the idea that women's liberation has to mean enabling women to join the culture of paid work. Liberation, she says, can mean freeing ourselves from the wrongs of that culture. "For me," she writes, "mothering my children has been a liberating experience."

The goal of *Liberating Motherhood* is not to liberate every woman *from* motherhood. Rather, it is to liberate every woman who wants to be a mother for motherhood. Many mothers want to spend more time with their children but cannot afford to. Vanessa wants us to recognise that it is our *society* that has to change, not mothers. She wants to see mothers supported, and to be given both social respect and better financial options.

Vanessa uses the simple word 'love' (rather than 'bonding' or 'attachment'

— can't we forgo these?) to express how mothers feel for their children. She frequently refers to 'humanity' too. This word describes the best qualities of being human: our awareness of others, our sensitivity to differences, our ability to be compassionate and understanding. And humanity, says Vanessa, is exactly what mothers develop and then bring to society. At present, our society rewards behaviour motivated by selfish values. The humane contribution of mothers, Vanessa keeps reminding us, is much needed today.

Vanessa is determined to see justice done. Hers is a search for fairness. She has practical suggestions too. But her strength lies in her courage. She refuses to remain silent over all the wrongs she has witnessed that are attributed to mothers. Mothers, she contends, are "society's paradoxical scapegoats sat on a pedestal."

If we acknowledge the truth of her words, I don't think we can be bystanders. Vanessa is inviting mothers to join her. She wants to see changes in our society. Mothers need to be heard. And I like her proposal that we wear purple stockings (or tights). We need to be able to recognise one another. There is a good deal to discuss.

In one respect, we need to move forward with caution, and Vanessa agrees with me over this. There is a strange advantage in being disrespected as mothers. Because people are so busy urging us 'back into work', we have been left free to mother our children in our different styles. We may disagree with one another, but we enjoy the precious freedom to differ. Once mothering is recognised as genuine work, isn't it only too likely that someone will draw up a plan to finance us – and then to regulate us?

I marvel at Vanessa for completing *Liberating Motherhood*. She had two children under five years old when she did all the research and wrote it. After long days with them — when most of us would be ready to collapse into sleep – she would stay awake, reading, thinking, making notes and writing.

The result is the book that you hold in your hands. It is a sharp spur to action. "The workplace," says Vanessa, "increasingly encroaches on family life." If we value family life, we need to speak up for it. As individuals, we may be ignored. But collectively, mothers can develop a powerful voice.

Naomi Stadlen is a mother, grandmother and author of *What Mothers Do* and *How Mothers Love*.

Introduction

A MOTHER'S STOCKINGS

A Mother's Stockings

Women's liberation must be mothers' liberation
or it is nothing.

Germaine Greer, *The Whole Woman*

WOMEN'S LIBERATION, MOTHERS' LIBERATION

Mater, Mama, Maman, Mutter, Mummy, Mommy, Mother. Me. You. Us.

If it is true that there have been waves within the women's liberation movement, then mothers' rights are the flotsam left behind on the ocean surface of patriarchy. We are currently experiencing a tsunami of 'fourth wave' feminism yet, for mothers who want to care for their young children, little seems to have improved. Many mothers remain alienated from feminism,[1] feeling that it still doesn't speak for us or recognise our lived reality. We see, too, that politics and economics seem to have no place for maternal care. Well, with that in mind, we need to get onto dry land and make the women's movement an earthquake to shake the foundations of our culture to its core. And to get there? I have often reflected that, as women, we can rock the boat but we are not allowed to build a new one. Well, sisters, we really do need a better boat. *The Mother Ship*, to take us to the Motherland. Or something.

We have the right to stand up for ourselves and our families, and we deserve a society which takes on board our rights *as mothers*. Because the reality is that, in all, the right of women to care for our own children on our terms is diminishing, along with any recognition that *care* is valuable and necessary work. When it comes to *maternal* care, we are socially and financially penalised for nurturing our families, despite the fact that care is crucial for the benefit of the human race and society as a whole. Many of us are forced away from our babies and young children against our wishes —

1

financial pressures leave us little choice but to find paid work to put food on the table and a roof over our heads. Our bonds of motherhood are being replaced with binds to the market and wage slavery. We are in bondage — and not in a 50 Shades way.

When we stop to see where we are now, it is clear that we are witnessing a silencing (bordering on contempt) of mothers who wish to provide loving maternal care to their children: those of us who choose to care are becoming sacrificial lambs at the altar of equality, economics and neoliberal* selfishness. Our sisters who are compelled to be separated from their children against their wishes, who are thereby relieved of the 'burden' of care under capitalist patriarchy, have been betrayed. We are supposed to be grateful for this, yet many women are treading water financially or drowning under immense pressure.

As Western women we occupy an interesting time. We have been liberated from the edict that a woman's place is in the home: it is now *out* of the home. Whether she is a mother or not. Regardless of her own needs and inclinations or those of her children. It is understandable that feminists have traditionally spoken carefully about matters of the womb. After all, a woman's biology and reproductive powers have been used to keep her down over the course of patriarchal history. The problem is that elements of the women's movement, in cohorts with neoliberal individualism, have effectively alienated us from motherhood or from caring for our families. Yet women's liberation never was, nor ever should be, about liberation *from motherhood*: it's about liberation from *oppression*.

For many women, myself included, becoming a mother and mothering our children can be a liberating and sacred experience. It can *connect* us to something and someone: to love, spirituality, meaning, our children, and our maternal ancestors. It can free us *from* something, it can free us *to* something. There is *something* about motherhood.

From the power of our bodies to create life and give birth, to the nurturing of our children we, as mothers, touch something outside the 'machine' of modern economic existence. We know the value in what we do, and it goes far beyond basic economics. But to publicly address such 'soft' subjects as maternal care and motherly love is seen as too risky by feminists and politicians in our world where GDP is as God.

* I will explore the meanings and implications of 'capitalism' and 'neoliberalism' in later chapters and the glossary at the end. For now, think 'rampant selfishness' and 'dog eat dog'. That should do it.

We know that when mothering takes place in conditions which allow us and our children to flourish, it can be one of the most precious times of our lives. Motherhood need not be an institution of inequality or self-sacrifice, if our culture had the will and decency to honour it for what it is: the active continuation and nurture of the future members of the human race. We can celebrate mothering, too, without reducing it to sentimentality or idealisation. We need to speak about the joys, the benefits and the satisfaction in mothering our children, as well as the challenges; and we need society to value what we do and respect us in our work. When mothering is on our terms, it can be a *liberating* motherhood. We know it when we live it, when we feel it and when we see it. It is what we will remember on our deathbed: life, love and little people.

For me, mothering my children has been a liberating experience: I finally saw and understood the power of women. I knew I was doing something important that contributed to humanity and to society in a way that my work in the legal profession hadn't. I know I am not alone in feeling like this. But our society doesn't see it this way. It sees caring for our children as *not* working or, worse, as being somehow parasitic or exercising a privileged choice. Of course, I'm not supposed to say any of this. None of us are. We are supposed to go out to work like good little girls and be grateful for what we've got. Well, that wasn't what got the women's movement rolling — we need to summon up our strength and resist what is happening and demand change. We need to demand the right to frame our lives with autonomy and self-determination.

Many mothers feel immense social and economic pressure to 'get a job' and face financial penalties for caring for their children, or feel the strain of working outside the home on top of everything. We know this from our own experience, our family, our friends, and social media. Mothers in Western culture are effectively forced to return to employment to reduce their financial and personal vulnerability. There were, after all, good reasons for seeking economic autonomy and greater rights in the workforce for women. However, for many women, working our jobs comes at a high cost — the sacrifice of time and the opportunity to care for our own children, and immense domestic pressure at home. Something has to give.

When I talk about *liberating motherhood* then, it is also with a second meaning: how can we ensure that a mother is free of constraints which prevent her from mothering her children? What are these barriers? How can she be free of conditions which render her without economic security or public standing if she chooses to care for her family? In other words, how can she enjoy both the authority and means to direct her own life, and the respect for her wishes and the choices she makes? How can we make sure that we do not penalise women for making the choice of caring for their families? What could we do to support and empower our sisters who want to care, but are currently compelled to 'get back to work'? How can we make sure mothers have the chance to take time out of the workforce to care for their children, if that is what they want to do, and ensure that they are not penalised when they try to get back to the workplace? Because it needn't be forever. It just has to be for the time that is right for *us*. And the next generation we are raising.

The problem is, for all the talk of women's liberation, when it is predicated on liberation *from* motherhood, it is no liberation at all. When feminism is based on ideas of equality which ignore the actual reality of her life, her deep wish to care for her children, and deny the value of caring, a mother is in chains. We need to get going on liberating *motherhood*. We can say, loud and clear that: "I don't need liberating *from* motherhood: motherhood needs to be liberated from a system which devalues it, devalues us and devalues our children."

So what are the barriers which work against mothers? What do we need liberating from? Well, for starters, despite decades of feminism, Western culture *remains* sexist. I will talk about a little something called 'patriarchy' and a big something else called 'misogyny'. For seconds, we have a cute system called 'capitalism', and its heavyweight contingent called 'neoliberalism'. All these combine so that a mother's price for caring for her family is the sacrifice of full citizenship and financial safety. And the cure under patriarchal neoliberalism? The workplace. Often in low-paid, low-security, low-status jobs. With the second shift[2] of housework and childcare on top. Which, despite some improvement[3], still falls heavier on the shoulders of women. That ain't no liberation, sisters. When it comes to mothers, we have to do better for those of us who *want* to work outside the home, as well as those who would *prefer* to care for their children. It's the least feminism can do: value mothers, the majority of women.

The problem is, despite the average mother's predicament within motherhood, there is no *sisterhood*: the agenda is now driven as much by a privileged class of women as men. They are those women who, instead of trying to dismantle the master's house[4], moved in and shut the glass door behind them. The power of women to grow babies, birth babies and nurture them from the breast and beyond is becoming as taboo as the needs of our children to responsive family care, particularly in the early years. The priority is the 'market' and our ambition is supposed to be 'self-sufficiency'. And neither of those honour our wishes, love, our wellbeing, humanity or family life.

The fundamental point is that when it comes to mothers, our culture refuses to honour its responsibility to the very reproducers of the human race. And when we try to order our lives in a way to survive and flourish, we are damned if we do and damned if we don't.[5] We could say that a mother's place today is on society's naughty step.

Consider the fact that today's mother is expected to be educated, ideally before becoming a mother. But then motherhood is considered a waste of this education. She is expected to give birth naturally, but within a medical situation which tends to interfere with natural childbirth. She is expected to breastfeed, but within a culture still reeling from institutionalised formula milk promotion and loss of skills, expertise and normality of nurturing at the breast and frequent sabotage of her efforts. She is expected to mother her child, but return to work outside the home for long hours. She is expected to be more than a mother, to be a self-fulfilled gender-neutral individual worker-consumer in a capitalist postfeminist world which places the wellbeing of human beings very low indeed. In the midst of this, she is expected to raise healthy, well-adjusted, high-achieving children. If she chooses to care for her children, she is at the mercy and charity of a partner, cast down into the 'private sphere'[6] in which she is utterly marginalised. Mothers who wish to care for their children are reduced to caricature: the 'stay at home mother', the 'homemaker', the 'housewife',[7] or just plain 'lazy' and 'unambitious'. We are retrograde, unfashionable, smothering of our children, wasting our talent and 'human capital',[8] and failing society by 'not contributing'. Welcome to twenty-first century motherhood.

WHERE ARE WE NOW? A MOTHER'S-EYE VIEW

Women have been freed of the expectation of domestic *subservience* by dint of their *sex*. Hurray! Put that feather duster down with pride! Yes, things have changed. A bit. Feminism has achievements to be found here and there: we can now *talk* about sexism as well as *experience* it; we can demand access to careers or jobs yet are also practically *obliged* to check in;

we can talk about pay gaps in the over-forties without creatively finding ways of rebalancing the books or reframing the debate to talk 'income' rather than 'pay'; and we can still argue amongst ourselves about what to do to improve the lives of girls and women around the world. We now know we can be educated alongside men. At least, in Western culture we can. In some regions it can earn a girl a bullet to the head. We know we can enter the professions, but have to fend off sleaze in professional social networks. We have the vote, just no party that represents us. We know we can secure a safe abortion, sometimes, if we are not shot outside Planned Parenthood or living in a Catholic country. We can demand equal pay, and perhaps get it so long as we behave as an unencumbered economic male with no care responsibilities and with limitless enthusiasm for overtime.[9] But when you become a mother it becomes clear how little freedom you really have. Where once I was a feminist, I am now a Feminist with a capital F, since becoming a mother. It became vivid and real to me just how women are devalued when they dare to connect to their female body and power. If feminism is for the rights of women but does not reflect or fully support the rights of a woman *as* a mother, then it's letting women down. It is failing to see a huge part of the picture. We are buying tickets for the main show but leaving after the compère. It is not enough to talk work/life balance, childcare, sharing care, flexible working or the pay gap. *Everyday Sexism*[10] is the tip of the iceberg. If our culture remains misogynistic and premised on patriarchal economics, mothers will have to play by the rules they didn't write and which fail and exploit them. Sisters, our right to care for our children *without sacrificing full citizenship or financial safety* is a right yet to be won.

One could argue that childhood is a recent invention, that parents today invest more time and emotional energy in their children than previous generations, and that our parents and their parents and beyond turned out alright. But we could open our eyes and ears and see a history littered with war, with domestic violence, rape and murder, with neglect and abuse of children, with poverty, with adults with the emotional range of a gnat, with misery and with conflict. We could open our eyes and see patriarchal history, replete with domination and Empire[11] and the oppression of women. We could hope for better for our children. Surely that comes with a greater need for humanity, love and care. Without it, our human futures are going to be pretty miserable.

So, sisters, feminism *must* embrace mothers if it is to embrace women.

After all, the old feminist phrase got it only half right: the personal is indeed political. *But so is the maternal.* It sometimes seems that "at the place where feminism and motherhood intersect the fires still burn".[12] Yet, the rights and needs of mothers are a necessary and central force in feminism, if feminism is going to serve women and our humanity and lead to necessary and fundamental social and economic change. It is time for a progressive new movement of women: an energised, humanist, maternal feminism. One which puts humanity at the heart, and remembers to call mum — because, for years, feminists have fought to free women *from* motherhood . . . but we are still having to fight to free motherhood itself. For the benefit of mothers *and* society as a whole. Because we are all born to a mother: every human being was grown inside a mother's body.[13] It is a universal shared experience within our humanity. As Patrice DiQuinzio writes, "being a mother and being mothered are both imbued with tremendous social, cultural, political, economic, psychological, and personal significance".[14]

The problem in the twenty-first century is that our perspective as a class — women — has fundamentally changed. We are unaffected by maternity for longer than our ancestors ever were. So by the time the *mother* problem becomes *our* problem, we're so mired in it that any action we can agitate for is too little, too late. For us. The average age for first-time mothers in the West is increasing. It is now into our thirties. What does that mean, in reality? It means feminism is becoming *remote* from mothering. Becoming a mother later in life brings with it a greater sense of shell shock: we have lived a large proportion of our lives as autonomous, relatively carefree, adults of a 'post-domestic' age. We taste economic autonomy, we live equality. Then a baby comes and screws it all up.

We have had, what, thirty-plus years of child-free feminism to live and preach. No room for nappies. No room for thinking about 'non-economic' contributions to society. No room for remembering that while a woman can do anything a man can do, there are three big things a woman can do that a man can't: create life, give birth, and breastfeed. We need to proclaim that power rather than be ashamed. We have internalised the message that we do not matter and that these things are inconsequential, or make us weaker, or are things to be 'offed'. We live identity not bodily reality; our experiences may well be ethereally gender-neutral until a human being makes his way down our vagina and attaches to our breast, covering us in amniotic fluid and connecting us with the life-creating and birthing process of generations of women before us. We have sneered at work (breastfeeding) when it is something only a woman can do, disqualifying it from the very definition of 'work' (tell that to those of us who are doing it 24/7 for months on end), seeing formula milk as liberation. We devalue work (child-rearing) when it is work traditionally done by women. We have failed to protect and support mothers or value women's life-creating power and life-sustaining work. Sisters, we must demand greater support and flexibility for that — not simply the liberation *from* it.

As Daphne de Marneffe observes, "every woman's feminism is a love letter to her mother."[15] Indeed, in modern feminism, 'mothers' feature (especially for the younger and child-free variety) often only in relation to our *own* mother, to be dreaded, hated, adored or feared. Those who are not mothers, or not yet mothers, do not need to address their minds to what it means, and what the variety of needs might be for those women who *have* children. There is a lack of solidarity, of common ground and respect, within feminism in the twenty-first century. So, the sister lives the dream, albeit within a sexist society which pretends the feminist fight is won. She fights the battle on the feminist front but leaves mothers in the trenches. Because the thing is, she is not, contrary to her noble ideals, Everywoman. She is not her sister, her cousin, her mother. Women are diverse: the concerns of women vary according to our experience, our class, our race, and more. Her concerns and activism can never speak for all women. Add race, sex, sexuality, disability and education and other factors to the mix and you have an intersectional[16] soup of needs, desires and struggles. And the most infuriating part of it is that it is usually only the Feminist the Younger, or Dissatisfied-with-Mothering-Woman or Capitalist-Woman or Journalist-cum-Politician who is heard, lauded, respected, published, elected and heeded.

The reality is that many women dream of a life where they could be free from the chains of bondage to the workplace, even for a short time, and retain standing and economic security. Many women who are well-educated and working in the professions might well, at one point, sit down and think, "That's it, I've had it, there is more to life than this". Traditional feminist thought implies that women are put down and kept down by reason of patriarchy and their sex. As much as I agree with that one, its brother, capitalism, has its fingers in mum's apple pie and is the Iago in the ear of feminist politics. And it whispers "work till you drop".

Yes, it is an uncomfortable fact for many, inconvenient but nevertheless true, that women can, and do, bear and breastfeed children. As many families will know, sometimes — if not often — only mummy will do. Like I said, inconvenient. But ask a hundred mothers who their baby cries for, who their toddler cries for, who their preschooler cries for. Even a grown man dying on the battle field whispers, in his last breath, for "mother". We lived in her. She is not insignificant. This is not to say that sex is destiny. Feminism has been there, and done that. But somewhere along the line, the rightful protest that we are *more* than mothers and more than our wombs has led to a failure to remember that we are, still, *mothers*. We can dissect 'sociological this', and rebut 'anthropological that', but as human beings we have evolved, and I want to believe that we have evolved for decency, responsibility, joy and love. Mothers remain an important part of that outlook, and it has to have a feminist lens. Maternal feminism[17] in purple stockings, reminding the world to remember the need for love and humanity, and which places mothers at the heart, rather than in the margins.*

The political and economic system must start to reflect this reality and the reality of what many, *many* women want: to have their work as mothers respected, valued and supported. For their return to employment to be of a time of their genuine choosing, rather than compulsion. We have a long lifespan. With that in mind, we can do better than forced workforce participation for our *entire* adult lives. For the set-up of a mother's employment to be based on her wishes and her family's needs, including flexible or home-working and greater opportunities for fathers to work flexibly and take dependency leave. For a mother's choice (if that is what she decides) to shun employment but to run the home and care for the children instead, to be supported and for socio-economic policies finally to cut mother-women some slack.

We talk about choice. We look at careers. We look at education. We look at employment rights. We look at maternity and paternity rights. We encourage the separation of mothers from their babies, toddler and preschool children. We deride women who stay at home when their children are at school. The only choice we are supposed to make is: combine motherhood with employment *outside* of the home. There is no other

---

* 'Maternal feminism' in this context is *not* the socially conservative kind advocated in the eighteenth century, related to the 'cult of domesticity', or discussed by, say, Christina Hoff Sommers in *Freedom Feminism*. It is *not* about celebrating inherent feminine qualities, patriarchal family and capitalist society. It is a bit more radical than that.

way. No other framework within which to protect mothers' interests (for example, state stipends, a carer's income, universal basic income, readjusted pay on return to the workforce to allow for the time out, funding for retraining, investment in community projects and services for the family at home) is tolerated or explored. Choice? What choice?

MY JOURNEY

I was a woman: a professional. Then I became a mother. And things changed. I found myself *needing* to communicate with other mothers about what is going on in our culture. I couldn't be the only one, surely, who winced every time mothers at home mentioned that they 'didn't work'. The implication being that we are doing nothing. We know this is unfair and untrue: I know it now and I knew it when I hadn't slept for more than a two-hour stretch, had kept a baby alive and growing on my milk alone, whilst managing to keep a toddler happy, fed and safe, preparing three meals a day, and two loads of laundry before every.other.thing.I.had.done. I knew I couldn't be alone in wondering why the work of mothers is seen as a lifestyle choice equivalent to keeping poodles.[18]

I started my activist and writing career in the snatched moments between a toddler at the breast, tantrum calming, sibling negotiations, moment-to-moment care, reading, phonics, baking, loving, with a particular agenda: to discuss, in a professional manner, *The Politics of Mothering*.[19] That was the name of the 2015 political pamphlet I wrote, taken from a chapter of a first draft of this book. It was well-researched yet careful. In it I was to remain cautious, fearful of appearing judgemental, worried about offending anyone, and astute to use acceptable English prose at all times. After all, I had been schooled in the law, tutored in decorum and raised as a female — to know my place.

However, humble and polite requests only get you so far. I researched the issues, talked to varied groups of activists, campaigners, feminists, academics, psychotherapists, volunteers, writers and mothers and realised that I needed my book to speak to *mothers* first and foremost. Because, at times, we can feel like we are on the sidelines, listening to political discussion *about* our lives and shaking our heads because it simply doesn't speak for *us*. I had to lay it on the line: I couldn't face this becoming a book gingerly tiptoeing around the issue, apologising for the message out of fear of causing offence. Women do enough of that, already.

As I wrote this book, I found myself blogging, writing, speaking at the Feminism in London Conference and the "Caring, Survival and Justice v The Tyranny of the Market", International Women's Conference in 2015. In between, I became involved with the Women's Equality Party UK (WEP) as a founding member. I contributed to a policy working group in which I headed a sub-team of myself, Global Women's Strike and Mothers at Home Matter. We advocated on behalf of the many women who would like to see greater recognition and support for their desire to look after their children. We needn't have bothered. Instead it demonstrated through its policy launch that it was the Women Employee's Equality Party (and did I WEEP). "Some women are more equal than mothers" might have been an accurate strapline.

So when I talk of mothers at home (or mothers who want to be) being *personae non grata*, I can tell you that I experienced that feeling first-hand in my subsequent dealings with the party: I had had the *cheek* to talk about the economic vulnerability of mothers who want to care for their children and about the injustice facing women who were deprived of the opportunity to. I had spoken heresy in the house of capitalist equality.

This demonstrated to me just how urgent the need *is* for a radical shift in the way in which motherhood, child-rearing and family life are viewed in Western culture and how, as a result, they are treated socially and economically. It requires fundamental change. Because what will the world be like without motherhood? We are starting to see already . . . Our culture is separating the reproductive function of *mother* from the caring, nurturing aspect of *mothering*, which the state insists can be performed more *efficiently* and *expertly* by paid carers thus adding to GDP by paid services to childcare-workers. It frees up the 'wasted labour' of well-educated mothers as well as the 'cheap labour' of less educated women. Call me cynical. Turns out rebellion now resides where my placentas had once been.

#NOTALLWOMEN #NOTALLMOTHERS

It's important we get a few things clear, before we continue.

First off: not all women need be mothers. Not all mothers need care for their children either full or part-time. Not all mothers should be forced out to work in the labour force. No two mothers are the same. Some will relate to what I write, others will not. While I speak of mothers as a class, I do not suggest that mothers are some kind of homogenous mass with identical needs, values, ambitions, personality or talents. That is, actually, my very point: a feminism and a politics which assume we are all itching to delegate care of our children fails us. Nor do I mean any offence or insult to women who, for whatever reason, cannot have children. We know that many women feel a loss for not being able to have children. We can and must support, empathise with, and respect them in their own journey. Consideration and respect must go, too, to those women who choose not to have children: they are not lesser women — although they may be rebels against patriarchy and as such have received some almighty flack over the years. They are entitled to respect and understanding for their decision. Although only women bear children, it does not follow that only *real* women bear children. #WomenOfTheWorldUnite

Such subversive ideas! My goodness, it's almost as though I have just said that women should be respected in their *diversity*! A woman's place must be wherever she wants to be, and where it suits her and her family. Not just the capitalist state. And not just patriarchal heteronormative* standards (you know, that world view that promotes heterosexuality as the normal or preferred sexual orientation). After all, many women become mothers before or within same-sex partnerships, or become a lone parent out of choice or compulsion. A fundamental part of a humane feminism and society is that women's choices, loves, lives and personal relationships are a matter for her, and her alone. She should be entitled to respect and support, no matter the set-up, her sexuality, her marriage status, her class, her colour and more besides. We have to shed ideas about 'deviant mothers' and recognise that a woman must be empowered to mother without a man, if that is her wish and her choice, or *not* to be a mother at all. A 'conservative family values' approach to children and mothers is not what this is about. It is about a motherhood in which we are free from stereotype and discrimination. It is about valuing care and valuing mothers: we needn't have chains to a man to be deserving of this fundamental right.

Second: yes, yes, being a mother does not *define* us. But it's the elephant in the birthing suite. We cannot ignore it any longer. The treatment of mothers politically is predicated on *continuous* workplace participation[20] to the detriment of many women, children and their families. A mother

---

* If this term is new to you, you will find a short definition in the glossary. Just think: Me Tarzan, You Jane, as the law of the jungle.

who wants to stay home with her babies and toddlers might well want to share the care down the line, to reflect the differing needs of the children at different stages of their development. Yet there is no recognition of this in public policy and economics or in society at large. Many would wish to have a chance of exercising *choice* about how to set up family life. If family life and the work of care and nurture were to be valued, elevated and respected (as well as funded, for the job is an important one which somebody's got to do) then we would be on our way to a fairer society, a more feminist society and one which stops worshipping the dollar as though we can take it with us.

Third: mother does not equal victim. There are many, many, families that, during a particular stage of life, would like the mother to take time out of the workforce to care for her children. This is not the same as saying she is, or should be, destined to 'domesticity' or 'housewifery' for the rest. of.her.life. Women tend not to have a baby every two years for fifteen years, nowadays. Thanks to feminism, we have moved beyond the bogus love affair with the twin tub and twin sets. It is simply recognising that, at a particular time in her life's journey, she is on a different track (not the mommy track[21]), doing caring family work instead of employed or professional work.

At heart, the reproductive effect on the division of labour and discrimination against women in the workplace has little, in reality, to do with the *few* years a mother might want to take out of the labour force. It is about misogyny and sexism against women; it is about the refusal of the economic system to reform the workplace to recognise that women and men have lives and family outside of the workplace; and it is as much to do with our refusal to value the work a mother has done and the skills she can bring back with her when she does. It is centrally about our workplaces failing to honour the family responsibilities of mothers and fathers. It is about "the maternal wall"[22]: the penalties mothers who want to do market-work face by reason of the care which it is presumed falls to *them*.

Fourth: who do I mean by mothers? There are extensive nuances in feminist debate when it comes to motherhood, birth and reproductive creation. I nod to the intense emotions which can arise in this field (and if we think they are intense in this chapter, wait till we start talking *lactation*). Some women do not give birth at all, out of choice, frustration or inability. My focus, for example, on biological mothers in some chapters does not suggest that an adoptive mother is not a mother, or is less of a mother.

Whilst I speak of birth, I do not neglect the fact that one can become a mother by adoption. By choosing to love a child, to mother that person, and to raise that being as their own flesh and blood. To become a mother is such a precious thing that the very fact that women desperately seek to become one (whether biologically or adoptively) is testament to its importance. Its status. Its worth. To choose to become a mother to a child already born takes commitment. Nothing I say in this book takes away from the bond an adoptive mother has with her children.

Fifth: just as not all mothers are primary carers of their children, not all carers are women and not all carers are mothers. I recognise this at the outset because it is important for our culture and socio-economic systems to start to value *care* and *carers*. This is so whether the carers are men or women, whether parents or paid professionals, or other relatives, such as grandparents or even children. Indeed, in the UK, there is a significant number of children who care for their parents or siblings. It is important. When I argue for valuing care it is with *all* carers — of the young, the sick, the disabled, the elderly, and the dying — in mind. That said, I write from a mother's perspective and as a mother, to add to the wider debate about care and the need for feminism to recognise that many mothers want to care for their children for the time and balance of their choosing.

During the writing of this book I corresponded with academic and economist Nancy Folbre, whom I much admire. She told me that she focuses on *care*, not on mothering, "because I think care is a bigger, broader, more inclusive issue. Also, my experience in the US (which is a very different political and cultural environment than the UK) is that many men who are active fathers or elder caregivers feel like a 'mother mother mother' emphasis reinforces traditional gender roles. Adding an occasional sentence or phrase acknowledging men doesn't necessarily solve this problem". I understand and respect Folbre's perspective. I would like to see the work of more men in this area, to champion the need for care, such as the Payday Men's Network in the US, with a view to collaboration and partnership for the need to value care. I agree, as a feminist, that we have to challenge gender stereotypes and expectations, including embracing the fact that many fathers do and want to provide loving, responsive care. However, as Folbre knows, I personally focus on mothers. I do so because it is increasingly rare for mothers to feel able or entitled to speak our name. With that comes increasing difficulty in advocating for our rights and needs. That is a feminist issue: the naming of women; the naming of mothers.

Sixth: Women are often policed in our views or our language. It is a traditional and effective way to silence women. So I say at the outset that I make no apology for framing the book and terminology in the way I do, from the issues of love and care, to feminism and patriarchy, and from capitalism to social justice. To the issue of mothers and children, many people bring their own insecurities. Yet you will neither find judgement of other mothers nor suggestions that to be a 'good mother' requires being a primary carer. You will find no suggestion that mothers who do not care *for* their children full-time, doing the care-work, do not care *about* them. There is physical care-work; and then there is emotional labour and caring about our families. The sensitivities of those who might take umbrage at the cheek of a woman daring to talk about maternal care do rather demonstrate my point that mothers face significant barriers before them in seeking to discuss or promote their rights and needs.

And, finally, I speak about mothers and our reproductive bodies because the majority of the female population will become mothers at some point in their lives. It is not insignificant. I am speaking for and to women who want to care for their children or who cannot do so because their role as mother and the work of care are insufficiently valued. They may even fear to speak about their female bodies, given that talking about biology can be surprisingly contentious in the era of identity politics. What I see is that many women who are mothers are not being heard or respected. And so *I* focus on them. In sisterhood. In *motherhood*.

So on every count: #NotAllWomen #NotAllMothers. Let's march onwards, shall we? #Purplestockings

FEMINISM 101

Just as we mustn't fear talking about our needs* as women, and mothers, we needn't fear talking about feminism. We are women. We are mothers. We might well have daughters. Just think about the wisdom of Maya Angelou when she said, "I've been a female for a long time now. It'd be stupid not to be on my own side."

Feminism is not dead (rumours of its demise are always exaggerated). So before I go on, perhaps a short iteration of what feminism is and what it is not. One of the biggest challenges is the fact that so few people seem to agree about what feminism *means*, what it is seeking to achieve, and what it must do.

First things first, feminism is certainly *not* a system or a theory which wants to see the obliteration or oppression of men. Rather it illuminates the fact that our 'history' is a censored, photoshopped, patriarchal history of 'Man'. The reality is that women have to live, work and love within a culture and under the rules of the Father, the Son, the Husband, the Male, the worship of the masculine, and the prioritising of destruction over creation of life.[23] Hey, nobody said this was going to be about unicorns. To quote Andrea Dworkin, "I'm a feminist, not the fun kind."[24]

Feminism is about a quaint notion: that women are people too. And with that understanding, that women should have basic human rights, the right to autonomy and self-determination, freedom from inhumane treatment, oppression, gender stereotype, and all the rest. The thing is, much of the human rights message has been lost in translation. Equality became the buzzword: which is interpreted by many to mean 'the same'.[25] Equality is, in truth, a massive red herring. The overwhelming preoccupation with 'equality', to quote academic Eva Feder Kittay, "misses the importance of the symmetries and differences that are unavoidable and even desirable in human intercourse".[26] The debate about 'special treatment' has been raging for long enough. Time for some *humane* treatment: the recognition of a diversity of needs and the acknowledgement of discrimination and exploitation of women by virtue of their becoming mothers. The

---

* Although I speak directly to mothers throughout the book, don't worry, you have a place here, reading these pages, even if you are a man or not a mother. Just see it as a virtual eavesdropping of a subversive mothers' meeting. You would want to know what is being said, wouldn't you? What is being *exposed*? The mother issue and the Purplestockings Movement affects *you* as well. Really. It does.

standpoint[27] of mothers cannot be minimalised in feminism any longer. We are a beating heart. We are strong arms. And we need to march our way into politics, feminism and economics. We need to *demand* that the persistent and institutional discrimination against mothers is exposed and levelled with creativity and humanity.

There are numerous 'schools' of feminism[28], and tensions between them, ranging from liberal, Marxist, socialist and radical. We also have a de facto corporate feminism which is predicated on 'more women at the top'.[29] Come on now! That ain't feminism: it is capitalism. And under it, there will always be women at the bottom. Then there is a feminism which is clear that what is between our legs is irrelevant — it's how we *identify* that matters.[30] Clearly, feminism has many shades.[31]

Personally, I agree with Rebecca West's sentiment in 1913 that "I myself have never been able to find out precisely what feminism is: I only know that people call me a feminist whenever I express sentiments that differentiate me from a doormat . . ." And a doormat I ain't. The rights and challenges of women are central to my feminism. I will also address the needs of children. I am very clear that mothers are important to their children, and that our children — our flesh and blood — are important to *us*. If a feminist mother cannot say this, we are in trouble, aren't we?

However, when it comes to mothers, some schools of feminism seem to evoke *My Fair Lady* and Professor Higgins' lament "why can't a woman be more like a man?"[32] sung to a minor melody of "Capitalist Patriarchal Neoliberalism". I will discuss this poxy trinity, and the meanings of its components throughout the book, but for the time being 'money, men and selfishness' will probably give a good enough idea of what these mean.

Feminism was the movement that was supposed to free us from patriarchy and lead us to the promised land — not necessarily *Herland*,[33] but one where we could enjoy human rights, equality of opportunity and dignity. But somewhere along the way it got lost and confused. It has become seen as, and is, for some women: "I want what men have".[34] In reaching for that, we have lost touch with what *women* have (or could have). The baby has been thrown out with the feminist bathwater and, in doing so, some women have indeed got what men have: power over other women.

If we struggle to speak of the issues that remain for all women under patriarchy, we are even more bound when we try to articulate the mother issue. There is an awkwardness about women's reproductive and mothering experience. They are seen as more private and personal. In her work, Jean

Bethke Elshtain explored issues surrounding the 'private sphere': why do we devalue the 'private' over the 'public'? Why is a 'public' role effectively seen as more worthy and a marker of citizenship than private, family or community work? Why do we continue to deny broad differences in the lived experience of men and women? To quote Elshtain, "To recognize that women as a group experience their social worlds differently from men as a group complicates feminist thinking, deepens female self-awareness, and calls attention to the complexity and richness of our social experience and relations".[35] There is an unspoken rule that one may not engage in biological essentialism* or exploration of difference. In *Motherhood in Patriarchy, Animosity Toward Mothers in Politics and Feminist Theory — Proposals for Change*, Mariam Irene Tazi-Preve calls this the "taboo of physicality".[36] As Patrice DiQuinzio frames it, "the dilemma of difference and its resulting paradoxes are most salient and most difficult to resolve at the site of mothering".[37] She talks of the "problem of maternal embodiment".[38] Mothers are the square peg in the round hole. A reminder that individualism has its limits and that denial of difference fails to reflect substantial issues relating to mothers and motherhood.

When it comes to politics, socialist feminism has become somehow old-fashioned, talking as it does of redistribution of wealth, capital and accumulation, when nobody talks like that any more. In fact, some feminists resemble the pigs in Orwell's *Animal Farm*: it is hard to tell them apart from the patriarchal capitalist farmer.[39] And in our farm, some women are more equal than others. Indeed, as I have said, some women are more equal than *mothers*. Two legs (individualism) good — four legs (mum's two and little un's two), bad. The "occupational elite"[40] — those who, quite frankly, seem to live in a different world, immune to the issues facing many families today — are wilfully blind to the everyday existence of women outside their domain.

Our modern feminist and political dialogues obscure the desires and needs of the majority of mothers: those unimportant ones reproducing the human race and raising them to be decent future citizens. This tension leads many women on the ground to think that feminism is irrelevant

* See the glossary for further definition. For now, biological essentialism is about bodies. Feminism has traditionally argued that women are more than what is between our legs. Under some schools of feminism today, what is between our legs is irrelevant. Somehow, the point in between, namely, we are bodies, minds *and* worthwhile human beings all at the same time has been missed.

to their lives or their struggles. As Ann Crittenden writes in *The Price of Motherhood*, "changing the status of mothers, by gaining real recognition for their work, is the great unfinished business of the women's movement".[41] Well, sisters, time to finish the job. Time for a movement in our language: The Mother Tongue.

THE BIRTH OF A MOVEMENT

So what on earth is this 'Purplestockings' business? Well, you may have heard of the terms 'Bluestockings' to describe a collection of educated, intellectual, women in the eighteenth century; or 'Redstockings' to describe women's liberationists.[42] In the tradition of those sisters, I decided on 'Purplestockings' to signify a maternal feminism, as a nod to the Suffragette colours, to invoke the nobility of mothering, and because it aptly combines the hue of its two predecessors. We have to know our history as well as what we want in the future: the stockings movement has a worthy heritage to take us forward.

As former director of Liberty, Shami Chakrabarti, said at the Feminism in London Conference in 2015, sometimes it's worth remembering that Martin Luther King didn't say, "I had a nightmare". We must allow ourselves some measure of hope and optimism. We can imagine "better worlds".[43] We can have a dream. And mine is one in which our children enjoy fruitful and decent humanity, where mutual love and care abound, responsible society and ethical behaviour are the norm. Mothers can be respected for the work they do as mothers, *as well as* any work they do outside the home. Whether in combination or in a sequence. I can dream, can't I? It's not going to happen, is it? Well, if we had the will, it could . . . and it should. So rather than give up before we've begun, shouldn't we try to do something about it?

When it comes to women and mothers, we can do something *now*. Our task, and something which must urgently enter into feminist consciousness, is the attempt to balance and bring justice to the scales of judgement against mothers, to support mothers in the important work they do and to ensure that isolation, poverty and other struggles faced by mothers are alleviated. It is an injustice, cleverly camouflaged, that the work of mothers can be sabotaged by society or blighted by hurdles they face financially and socially, and yet mothers get the blame. It's a con trick. And women are sick of being the mark.

The problem is, when it comes to mainstream feminism and politics, there has been an abject lack of "nerve and imagination"[44] to push for equitable social and workplace conditions or labour and income redistribution. We rightly address the injustices of women losing their jobs or suffering discrimination in their jobs or career during pregnancy or after becoming a mother, but we forget those who want to step out of the workforce to be with their family. We talk about equality, but we forget fairness: equity. We talk about pay gaps, but we no longer talk about "redistribution of wealth". We talk about full employment, without reimagining labour rules and workplace structures which respect family life for mothers, fathers and children. Instead of liberation, we have witnessed strands of feminism becoming footsoldiers of capitalism[45] — itself patriarchy's recent incarnation.[46]

The problem is, there is no escaping the cold hard reality that, throughout the world, girls and women are at risk of being, or have been, emotionally, physically and/or sexually abused. By men. For me, there is no forgetting some of the horrific cases I saw during criminal practice and, later, as a law reporter. They were the proof I wish I had never seen that we indubitably live in a misogynistic culture.

This is the context in which a mother seeks to raise her family.[47] This is the context in which a mother seeks to improve her conditions of life, mothering and work, and her status and safety. And that of her children. This is the context that a mother has to stride. This is the context in which she does something explicitly and necessarily female (pregnancy, birth, breastfeeding) or something traditionally connected to women. She is mothering in the midst of *misogyny*: within a culture that dislikes and distrusts women. To quote the RadFem Collective, "our oppression as females is closely linked to and bound up in our roles as the bearers of new life and male hatred of our female reproductive power".[48] It is all connected: motherhood and feminism cannot and should not be separated.

The reality is that we cannot expect feminism to succeed until we embrace all women. And that includes mothers. We cannot treat women as being of value and worthy of respect only where they disavow or sideline matters of motherhood. We cannot exile mothering from feminism. We need a triad of human rights, women's rights and mother's rights within a prism of social responsibility.

Just so you know, this ain't no backlash.[49] There were never any good ol' days: feminism hasn't "gone too far". Actually, it didn't go far *enough*.

Patriarchy has had its *own* triad of capitalism, technology and male domination[50] for far too long. And within it, there is still little room for women, for mothers, certainly not a room of their *own*.[51] We need to start thinking about politics, economics and social policy, despite a potential knee-jerk reaction to groan. We have to connect to those fleshy things: our bodies. And those dangerous things: our minds. We need to take in issues of "sameness and difference"; the place of motherhood and whether we all want women's responsibility for children to be turned over to delegated childcare, or shared care with men; whether caring for children is part of a significant number of women's actual desire, rather than a social construction or result of conditioning; how to "create a society in which caregiving is not penalised"; and the diversity amongst women.[52] We need to retain that crucial thing: our heart.

This is before we even *begin* to factor in race and class struggle: factors which can bring profound difficulties and raise significant barriers for women.[53] As a woman of working-class upbringing, I heard both my grandmothers' stories of cleaning people's houses, working to the bone, working in factories and other things which it is not my place to share. I saw my mother struggle with three children, a full-time job and the second shift on top. Consequently, I have long questioned just *how far* the frustrations of a privileged class of white middle-class educated women can legitimately speak for those women whose struggles in respect of class, race and disability bring a different slant to the issue of motherhood. Their experiences of mothering may well be completely different in terms of social support, satisfaction, and prestige.[54] Betty Friedan's frustrated, isolated housewives, whom she depicted in *The Feminine Mystique*, for example, were not those women of colour who had strong support networks from female relatives but who were exploited in market-labour of low status and low pay, or Asian women who retained the culture of close extended family, or working-class women who lived in built-up areas with thriving solidarity amongst women in their terraced houses and low fences but who did double shifts of factory *and* home. *Their* struggles were rarely articulated in the movement, so preoccupied with the assumptions that white privileged feminism spoke for all, and that oppression under patriarchy was the principal source of oppression for *all* women. In terms then of priorities for the women's movement, opportunity, education and the freedom to flourish in the public realm, the arts, the professions and industry, are important. They are crucial aspects of women's liberation and empowerment. But *compelled* employment, low-status and low-paid jobs and zero-hour contracts versus impoverishment for unwaged work? No. We need to restructure the workplace and market-work on the one hand and the freedom to care, without penalty, on the other. We need the 'private realm' to be liberated from being somehow 'second class'.

Within the dominant ideology of twenty-first century Western cultures, it often feels that no one is actually listening to what mothers would prefer. Certainly not our politicians and policymakers anyway. There are clear (and fairly persistent) divisions amongst women as to what they would prefer: some would like to work full-time; others part-time; others to care exclusively for their families.[55] We all have different personalities and inclinations, after all. Yet, when politicians *do* hear women's preferences, they have a terrible habit of reformulating the answers to meet their own agenda and suggesting that we all want to combine market-work with care-work or to work full-time.[56] So it is that we face insidious ideological attempts at social engineering and a failure to reflect our true choices. The reality is stark: mothers — as a class — are, in gradual steps, losing the rights, freedom and economic ability to raise their own children, within the patriarchal and capitalist project.

If current trends in social and economic policy are anything to go by, there will be greater and greater barriers against our ability to care for our own families. And conditions may well become so intolerable owing to lack of money, security, support, respect, freedom and autonomy (or exhausting second shifts) that we, and the next generations of mothers, will struggle; but the blame will be placed on *motherhood*. Not politics. Not economics. Not patriarchy. Not neoliberal pathological market-driven environmental and social destruction. Not misguided attempts by some feminist camps to eradicate mothering. But *becoming a mother*. And that script is being written right now with the sanction of women, female politicians, and of course, patriarchal neoliberalism. We may not speak our own line: that being a mother by desire is, for many women, one of the most precious experiences of our lives.

When it comes to the popular script that we need liberating from care and children, it comes down to 'she who shouts loudest wins prizes'. It is no stretch of the imagination to see a link between the occupation of the public arena, fought for and won by women as a result of feminism, and the accompanying privilege of having a voice that is heard and respected. However, just because a voice grabs the mic doesn't mean that it is either right or in the majority: a woman at home raising her family, happily or not, will not have her voice heard. Democracy, eh? She will be conveniently ignored, her silent scream about the lack of recognition of her work will ring in her ears alone.[57] Social media can only go so far: yes, we can blog, we can chat on Facebook. We can even meet other like-minded mothers in real life at baby and toddler groups. But ultimately, there has to be a political, visible, active, in-yer-face movement. We need to move beyond a 'feminism of uncertainty'.[58]

I am not alone in my calls for the feminist movement to embrace this issue of mothers. In writing this book, I corresponded with many women who are writing, speaking and raising consciousness on this topic. One was academic Martha Fineman, the author of *The Neutered Mother: The Sexual Family and Other Twentieth Century Tragedies.* We discussed the tireless work which feminist academics have been doing for decades on the subject of women, care, the family and the sexual division of labour. I will be referring to this and other insightful work in this field that has been pushing the issue of motherhood and care into public debate, and which provide some extremely important and necessary perspectives on the issue. If you are looking for further primers on motherhood and feminism, you could start with *Maternal Theory*, edited by Andrea O'Reilly of Demeter Press and the Motherhood Initiative for Research and Community Involvement.[59] During the final stages of production of *Liberating Motherhood*, I caught an announcement (and I cheered!) from Demeter Press about a forthcoming book, *Matricentric Feminism: Theory, Activism, Practice*, from Andrea O'Reilly. Although academic in tone, I'd say the book's message is likely to be in the Purplestockings tradition. O'Reilly "argues that the category of mother is distinct from the category of woman and that many of the problems mothers face — socially, economically, politically, culturally, and psychologically — are specific to women's work and identity as mothers. Indeed, mothers, arguably more so than women in general, remain disempowered despite forty years of feminism. Mothers, thus, need a feminism of their own, one that positions mothers' concerns as the starting point for a theory and politic of empowerment". Yup. That'll do it. O'Reilly calls this "matricentric feminism".[60] Maternal feminism. Matricentric feminism. Mother-centric feminism. Justice and fairness for mothers. We are women and we are mothers. How can we tolerate our culture, feminism and socio-economic policy continuing to deny and neglect a core part of our identity, a huge range of our needs and the importance of what we do?

The more voices we raise the better, and we need our sisters to join us: it's our lives and the lives of our children. What can be more important than that? There is a wealth of skilful research, theory and analysis out there. Do read it. And add your voice.

Because it matters. Not just to us as individual women, but to our culture, our species and the quality of human existence.

Carl Gustav Jung, the father of analytical psychology, famously talked about the "unlived life" of parents. Whatever one's view of Jung's attitudes towards mothers (about right, questionable, blaming or pernicious, say[61]), we cannot, nowadays, avoid the suggestions that a "happy mother = happy child"[62] and that we must have our "own lives". Yes, parents are people, too — we all have loves and interests to explore which have nothing to do with our children. However, the biggest lie, which so many commentators, politicians and policymakers have perpetuated, is that value, self-worth and fulfilment for women can *only* come from paid employment outside the home,[63] even when their children are young. The message sent and received is that to be raising one's children is *not* to be living one's life, as though the two are discrete, separable and antagonistic. This has fed into another message: that only work performed in exchange for money is worthy of recognition as 'work' and that it is practically every mother's duty to 'get out to work'. Both of these messages are absolutely wrong. Both contribute to perpetrating unfairness, inequality and vulnerability in mothers. Yet feminism, the liberal and corporate varieties especially, is failing to see this injustice or, if it does, is resisting it. Because mothers are, even in feminism, bottom of the heap, less important than the bottom line.

It is also important to note at the outset that when I talk about life-creating power, biology and difference, I am not saying that one type of human being is *better*. It is not a matter of supremacy or dominion over another. That is the whole problem of patriarchal culture: its preoccupation with dichotomy, domination and destruction.[64] I'm talking about *humanity*: respect for difference, service to others, the cultivation of happiness and wellbeing, and respect for life rather than destruction of it. We have to begin to prioritise humanity. When I speak of difference, I am also talking about differences between individuals *within* the sexes. We are women and we are mothers, yet, at heart we, like all others, are *human*. And that is where we have to go, in feminism and in our societies. We need to discover humanity and put it at the heart of our society, our relationships and our economies.

I will introduce and advocate a progressive, humanist, maternal feminism and politics which puts the interests of human beings first in policy. We must push for economic and social change, moving away from neoliberal capitalist inequalities and exploitation and environmental destruction. As Julie Stephens argues, "actively remembering the bodily and emotional aspects of nurture, including the physical demands of birth, lactation and the postnatal experience, will pave the way for more just social policies for women and families".[65] It is this need for appropriate social policies for mothers and children, extending throughout the family life cycle, which lies at the heart of the Purplestockings Movement.

This feminism and politics must value mothers, the life-givers, the creators of human beings, in the unwaged work of family that they have done for generations, while recognising the changing family life cycle and a mother's individual humanity. It must push for a society in which women are liberated from barriers to full participation in society on our own terms and status as worthy human beings. We face more than "economic exploitation"[66] — our challenge extends to our politics, our society, and our culture.

In this book, I dare to suggest that we could begin to restructure our societies and revalue our priorities. We could insist that fathers contribute more to family life, whilst demanding that market-work frees up more time to family life too by restricting how much of our lives are taken over by the machine of economic workplace productivity and exploitation. Joan Williams has some very interesting points to make in *Unbending Gender, How Work and Family Conflict and What to Do About It*. She advocates a "reconstructive feminism" which doesn't try to fit mothers into a system that is predicated on "ideal workers" (read: men with no caring responsibilities and an abundance of overtime capacity and dedication to the job). Rather, a reconstructive feminism would seek changes to the structure of market-work. Because the fact is that the modern set-up in Western economies requires mothers work as though without family responsibility (or are penalised for having caring responsibilities which are presumed to be solely theirs) and that mothers face tremendous strain doing it all, never mind having it all; or mothers are expected to care for their families without financial support or recognition. And when something goes awry, we get the blame.

As things stand in Western capitalist patriarchy, mothers are held accountable on the one hand yet ignored and devalued on the other. Our work as mothers is deemed unimportant and delegable to the market;

yet it is elevated to the crucible in which our children's happiness and wellbeing are forged. We are in a double bind. We are hostage to unrealistic expectations; to a punitive economy; to unattainable standards; tied to the modern stake of moral judgement or, worse, decisions of (mostly secretive) family courts which are failing to do justice by women.[67]

So we need to demand it ourselves. Not quietly. Or politely. But loudly and with grit. We are mothers. We have it in us.

I have felt frustration, hopelessness, resignation, powerlessness and anger about the situation that mothers face. I know that many women share these feelings: ordinary mothers at home or in jobs they resent, not just campaigners and activists. But then, as mothers, our feelings rarely get top priority, do they? The question is: how can we harness this anger and this need for change with the positive traits of motherhood? How might this spark a storm? This is the aim of *Liberating Motherhood*. We need to put on those purple stockings and release our thunder.

THE PURPLESTOCKINGS SONGSHEET

That said, it's not enough for me to talk about what is wrong with the system. We have to have some concrete ideas about what would *improve* the lives of women who are mothers, and, indeed, society as a whole. And these need to be ideas which go beyond 'universal childcare'. However, I don't like the word 'manifesto'. It's either reminiscent of a Communist one or a political pledge that is used to court votes but is bound to be broken. But I do like a sing-song. And I know that I am singing from the same songsheet as many mothers out there. I hope we can start to join our voices and raise the roof. As bell hooks writes, mothering is "significant and valuable work which must be recognized as such by everyone in society, including feminist activists. It should receive recognition, praise, and celebration within a feminist context where there is a renewed effort to rethink the nature of motherhood; to make motherhood neither a compulsory experience for women nor an exploitative or oppressive one; to make female parenting good, effective parenting, whether it is done exclusively by women or in conjunction with men".[68] Simple. So, sisters, what are we for?

Value and Respect

Mothers to be valued in the work they do and the contribution they make to society. This requires an end to the suggestion that women do nothing productive when they look after their children and bring no skills back to the workplace after caring for their family. We must respect the lived experience of mothers.

A reassessment of what is valuable in our society: life creation, life giving, care and nurture should receive the respect they deserve.

Society and Services

If mothers were valued, our society would invest in public services and community projects to support families and neighbourhoods on the ground, including investment in maternity services and skilled breastfeeding support as a basic right. We would recognise that mothers require care *themselves* in order to care for others without strain.

We cannot continue with the expectation that all adults must work to the bone outside the home, being exploited by capital, with little time for living and leisure or family and love. Our workplaces must reflect the humanity of our citizens: neither men nor women need choose *between* care and paid work; families must be free to organise the care of their children in the way which suits their preferences — whether shared, full-time, part-time or exclusive childcare. We must pursue workforce structures which respect our needs.

Given that, for mothers and fathers at home, our communities and societies are our office, we need to invest in community and social structures which *enrich* our office, for our benefit and for the benefit of those we care for. Libraries, community centres, communal areas such as parks and the countryside, must all benefit from investment and preservation.

Economics

We cannot and must not tolerate financial sacrifice and greater risk of poverty in women because they raised their family for the benefit of society. The answer to the 'mother question' and the 'feminisation of poverty' cannot in all conscience continue to be "get her earning a pittance outside the home when she would prefer to be with her children".

Mothers must be supported socially and economically to mother their children and do the work of the home if that is what they wish to do.

We would push for fair tax policies (including transferrable tax allowances) and welfare policies that adequately reflect the care-work performed in the home. Mothers must be supported to exclusively care, delegate care, or share care *and* participate in the workplace on *their* terms.

Mothers to have money in their pockets. A universal basic income or a living wage for carers to provide economic autonomy and security to women who care for their families exclusively or predominantly. Exploring creative financial ways to reflect the important work done by mothers to support the family and to reduce their financial and personal vulnerabilities within relationships.

Radical, right?

Well, that'll be the Purplestockings for you. 999 Denier. Our song is about love; it's about mothers; it's about life; it's about time.

In our conversations during the writing of this book, Antonella Gambotto-Burke, the author of *Mama: Love, Motherhood and Revolution*, said to me that the cultural shift in our societies from matriarchal to masculine had been:

> . . . *based on fear: fear of sensitivity, fear of what men identify as 'weakness' (vulnerability to the feminine), fear of mutability, fear of chaos, fear of intimacy. Female high-achievers are now expected to not only distance themselves from their children, but are regarded as unserious if they do not. We are expected to express disdain for mothering and, concomitantly, for the tenderness and devotion that mothering entails.*
>
> *As television pundit Katie Hopkins wrote in 2014, "Full-time mummy is not an occupation. It is merely a biological status". Her use of the word 'merely' is interesting: she prides herself on her aggressive self-interest and intolerance. If you can't be loved, be feared, right? Far from subscribing to that antiquated ideal, we need to triumph in our tenderness and sensitivity. As a culture, we need to recognise that devotion to our children does not entail weakness — the very opposite, in fact. Love is the greatest power on this earth. Parenthood and everything it entails needs to be recognised and celebrated for what it is: a revolution.*

I couldn't agree with her more. In her book, Antonella calls for a Revolution. I'm with her; put on your purple stockings and join us.

A GUIDE TO THE RUNGS:
THE STEPS WE NEED TO TAKE

So where will this book be taking us? How high can we go to see everything on the ground? It's a question of body, mind and labour. With our hearts still beating, demanding to be heard.

In Part One, **A Mother's Body**, I discuss the bodies of women as a commodity under patriarchy and women's bodies as they relate to reproduction: menarche, menstruation, pregnancy, birth, breastfeeding, our vaginas (vaginae? If not a word, then maybe it should be) and the menopause (proof that the Old Woman is a witch: truly hideous, no longer 'fully a woman'). A mother's flesh. A mother's blood. A mother's body. What a collection of words. It is strange to see them, isn't it? Rare to read them, rare to talk about them. Yet we must be able to speak them.

As for birth, there is no doubt that it is, and should be, a feminist issue. The medical model of childbirth, from the indignity that is unnecessarily strapping women to monitors, legs akimbo, to increasing rates of caesarean sections, is a clear demonstration of the lack of trust in women's ability to birth their babies safely and without fear. Birth and breastfeeding can be seen as the pivotal moment where a woman who has become a mother is either rendered in awe of the power of her body or risks experiencing a sense of loss, grief or failure. However, maternity is relatively neglected politically (indeed wholly, by the Women's Equality Party, at the time of writing) more concerned as it is with women in the boardroom than mothers in the birthing room.

I also address the ages of woman and how women without children are often incapable of conceiving adequately the feminist struggles of mothers. Many successful politicians and feminists are not mothers. They don't have that 'M' sewn in red on their chests. This is *relevant*.[69] The 50:50 Parliament campaign for greater balance in representation of the sexes is important, to remove the male bias inherent in the process as it stands. Yet it is a fallacy to believe that more women in power will necessarily and of itself promote the rights of all women, especially mothers who prioritise family life. For starters, we might remember how wonderful we knew we would be as a parent before we *actually* became one; how unchanged we knew we would be before we and our babies became attached in love. Women who see mothering as incidental to their professional successes and needs may well tend towards derogation or dismissal of their sisters who enjoy and value mother-work. The idea of class struggle has given way to individualism: sisterhood has become personhood. And personhood is free to embrace a selfhood which is detached from bodily reality as well as the bonds of love, connection and care. We must reclaim our bodies.

In Part Two, **A Mother's Mind**, I examine **Maternal Thinking, Maternal Feeling**, the former being a concept explored by philosopher Sara Ruddick.[70] The truth is, our outlook can undergo a radical transformation when we become mothers, the positive aspects of which are often overlooked. When we talk or read about mothers, we are presented with the message that mothering is an obstacle to be overcome, a hurdle to be passed, a battle to be won, with 'control' the elusive prize. 'Baby brain' is considered a well-deserved lobotomy for the trespass of caring for our children in the age of employment. Indeed, when we talk about mothers' minds, we may risk being drawn only to the 'mental health' aspect of the debate, namely, postnatal depression and anxiety. This risks perpetuating the 'pathologising' of women and mothers rather than recognising the skills and emotional growth a mother can experience through motherhood.

I call out the promotion of so-called maternal ambivalence: the purported continual conflict between feeling love for our children and, at times, feeling negativity ranging from irritation to anger and hostility. There has to be *some* room for good old-fashioned maternal love and joy, surely?

I also discuss the woeful provision for postpartum support of women. Many of us may feel isolated, disempowered and penalised when we become mothers, especially if we choose to provide the care. It goes beyond political and economic policies pursued by legislatures (although the policies prop up and support the patriarchal structure) and goes directly to our need for society, community, support and sisterhood. "It takes a village," so they say: yet women are expected to mother, practically unsupported, in conditions which assault their self-esteem and their confidence in their ability to mother their children. They are expected to see to the needs of others: problem is, nobody is taking care of them.[71] So, although I write about mothers, do not think for one moment that I believe the way things are set up is hunky dory. They're not. Change needs to happen. Just not change which is predicated on workplace-economic emancipation from motherhood within a strained society which has no community or humanity. We need to value care. We need to value mothers. And what a *difference* that one step would make to women and society at large.

I also discuss the culture of 'mother-blame' in media, psychology and society generally. I explore how this is toxic to mothers: we blame our own, we blame ourselves and, in the end, *we too* are blamed. A mother's place is always in the wrong, it seems. It is quite liberating to reflect on the myths and lies that are pressed upon us about what makes a 'good mother' or a 'bad mother' and what our expectations are of our own and other mothers. However, in all this, it is crucial to remember that mothers do have an impact on our children: we are important, and most of us are good enough. It is an injustice that women are simultaneously blamed, yet their mothering work devalued at the same time.

How we mother is subject, too, to "the gaze" of others,[72] our fellow mothers, the 'experts', our families, the school system and beyond. I discuss how the mothering work we do is forever under scrutiny, invariably found wanting, and rarely supported or valued. The increasing drive to encourage families to use paid childcare for ever younger children is accompanied by the narrative that there are huge benefits to it. However, this is not borne out by the evidence,[73] particularly in families where the parental care is 'good enough'. Which is the majority of families. Who is going to stand up for women who want to mother? Allies are disappearing as fast as you can say 'pay rise'.

In Part Three, I address **A Mother's Labour** to give due respect and recognition to the work of mothers. I hope to bring together the job of mothering, the tasks, the fun, the joy, the privilege of seeing our children grow, and the relationship we build when we have the time and presence to be with our children. I remind those feminists who prize the manicure over the mess, or control over connection, that raising human beings and caring for the sick and the elderly involves 'sanitary work'. It requires immersion into the bodily reality of ourselves and others. Whereas our society and feminism seem to sanitise our existence, encouraging us to aim for the stars and reach for the 'top jobs', it forgets that there is the bodily work — snot, poo, wee, vomit — of human beings to do too.

Crucially, given the almost universal view that mothering — the work of raising our children — is oppressive, I discuss how this is in itself an insult to women who *want* to mother their children, and who find immense satisfaction and gratification in doing so. The social conditions and our culture might well be oppressive, given that mothers are devalued and rendered economically dependent if they choose care-work over market-work; but the work of mothering — the loving, the nurturing, the day-to-day raising of our children — *is* 'real work', and not *in itself* oppressive.

When a mother happily and willingly devotes her time to mother-work, that mother is not, in raising her children, a *victim*. She is not being *deprived* of better, more productive, more important things. Many mothers want to be with their children and would relish flexibility over time to recognise the shifting nature of mother-work over the child's lifetime. Only when this message is understood by policymakers who continue their assumption that 'childcare' and escape from the children is what *every* mother is yearning for, and that only market-work is productive work, will mothers even begin to start to get a better deal.

I take on the taboo subject of children's needs, attachment theory, disputes about maternal separation and group daycare. We can spit on these ideas, proud of our place as women of the twenty-first century. But the need for responsive care and time with our loved ones has not disappeared along with the cassette player. The nurture of children was never a fad. It is never dispensable, to be usurped by some iChild programme.

A theme which runs through is 'time as money' and how women are short of both. Time is not a universal commodity. We all have twenty-four hours in a day, yes, but there is serious inequality in the number of hours one is permitted to have for living rather than grafting for the benefit of the 1%. There is an agenda, folks. Get women into the workplace, get the kids into childcare ... and *screw you*. What, you thought there was some benevolent ideology of respect for women and mothers? Sorry to disappoint. Even countries where workplace participation amongst women is extremely high, there remains a significant gender division in the workplace in terms of pay and occupation. There is no equality utopia, if by that we settle for low-pay and low-status gendered occupations by women, a culture which smarts at the view of a child in public during the daytime, and high rates of anxiety in teenagers.[74] Ooops, did I mention that there might be a downside to practically compelled universal childcare, which does not allow for decisions to be made in the individual family for care of the unique child by a mother, or at the very least a father? Arrest me now, the heretic that I am.

In terms of economics, I look at mothers and the invisible hand that rocks the cradle and how it truly isn't ruling the world. I discuss feminist economics, the Wages for Housework Campaign, universal basic income debates and the way in which feminism has been sleeping with the neoliberal enemy. Once we have established, as I hope we will, that the value system of capitalist, patriarchal, Western culture has no place for mothers save as a receiver of a paycheck (and a small one, at that) I discuss how, whereas once women were seen as 'Other'* it is now Mothers who are Other, with a Capital M.[75] If a woman's place is wherever she wants to be[76] and if feminism is about women, the same freedom must apply to a mother. After all, to echo bell hooks and Sojourner Truth[77], ain't *she* a woman?

Lastly, I look at the politics of mothering, maternal politics and my involvement in the Women's Equality Party UK. I examine how the political class is as keen to suppress and devalue the power of mothers as ever. I show how mothers who want to mother their children and care for their families are disenfranchised from the political process. That self-worth and fulfilment can only come from paid employment outside the home is necessarily the message sent by a government when each and every decision they make about the family and children discriminates directly against any family which chooses for childcare (particularly of babies, toddlers and preschoolers) to be undertaken by the mother.

In Part Four, **A Mother's Heart**, I talk about love. Because it's at the core of what we do. And this love (not money) makes the world go round. The sooner we remember this as a culture, the better.

So, thank you in advance for reading my take on the world faced by women of the mother variety in Western culture; my book that, in amongst the toil of motherhood, got written and sounded the call for a progressive humanist, maternal feminism to get moving. It's the stuff we don't talk about enough. The gold thread left on the cutting-room floor of equality and mainstream politics. Things you might well recognise, sister. Or brother. I'm inclusive like that.

* See the glossary for further definition: for now, just think 'non-male', lesser, inferior and subordinate. The tinsel to the male Christmas tree.

Part 1

A MOTHER'S BODY

Flesh and Blood

*The woman's body is the terrain on which
patriarchy is erected.*

Adrienne Rich, *Of Woman Born*

OF WOMAN BORN

Shakespeare wrote about the 'Seven Ages of Man'.[78] There was not then, nor has there been since, any celebrated literary reflection on the Ages of Woman. So let us take a moment to reflect on the life journey we take. We are babies. We are children. We are teenagers. We are students. We are young women. We are workers. We are pregnant women. We are mothers. We are nursing mothers. We are workers. We are menopausal women. We are post-menopausal women. We are grandmothers. We are elders. We are crones. That's quite a few ages right there. I'm sure we can all add some more of our own, depending on our outlook and experience.

But the message is: all the world's a *man's* stage, so take your Ages of Woman and be off with you, wench.

In *Je, Tu, Nous,* feminist theorist Luce Irigaray (a proponent of the importance of recognising sexual difference) discusses the ages and stages of women's lives, recognising that women's lives are marked by "irreversible events that define the stages of her life".[79] In the light of these changes and milestones in women's lives, I agree with her that treating *ageing* as though the process were just a question of getting *old* is to forget "what an opportunity it is to have been born female".[80] We can experience significant spiritual development and changes as women. As mothers we touch something outside of ourselves by connecting to someone we brought to life *from* ourselves. Yet, fundamentally, our conception of age is based on years, not events; on seasons, not life's stages; on time, rather than on our growth and development as human beings.

Wouldn't it be radical, refreshing, brave, to acknowledge this very basic metaphysical fact: nothing stays the same. We grow. We change. Inside and out. Our interests change. Our skills improve. Our strengths alter. And that which others see on the outside is not all there is.

When it comes to the creation of life, it's humbling to stop and reflect on it. We lived inside our mothers. Our children lived inside us. We were, after all, to echo Adrienne Rich in *Of Woman Born*, all born to a mother and we all share that "unifying, incontrovertible experience", namely, the "months-long period we spent unfolding inside a woman's body".[81] All human life on the planet is born of woman. We must ask the question: how can we be Other when we make up half the world? How can we be powerless when every human being on the planet. Ever. In the whole of our history. Grew within a woman?

Despite this amazing fact, our culture's treatment of issues surrounding our bodies demonstrates the nature of society's true regard for human beings of the female kind: abysmal. Patriarchal culture has, for its entire history, deliberately cultivated shame and hatred of the female body and of women's being. Women suffer for our bodies emotionally, physically, financially and, potentially, sexually; we are disempowered; we are marginalised. Nancy Hartsock refers to the "series of boundary challenges inherent in the female physiology".[82] We can relate to this, can't we? As women, as mothers.

Modern liberal feminism hasn't fared too well in confronting all this, regarding the female body as a minefield and ending up afraid to move. If we assert difference, it's a free ticket to oppression based on our bodies and reproductive potential (what Julie Stephens calls the "shadow of essentialism, whether biological, cultural or ideological").[83] If we pretend that our bodies do not matter or are not powerful, we sell ourselves short. We play into patriarchal gender rules and stereotypes. We shut our eyes to the oppression of women based on our reproductive bodies. And we risk being unable to *name* that oppression. As Mary Daly lamented, we have had the power of naming taken from us.[84]

We would do well to remember Adrienne Rich's sentiment that "female biology — the diffuse, intense sensuality radiating out from the clitoris, breasts, uterus, vagina; the lunar cycles of menstruation; the gestation and fruition of life which can take place in the female body — has far more radical implication than we have yet come to appreciate".[85] Indeed, being a woman is certainly not *all* about getting pregnant and giving birth, but a critical mass of it involves our bodies and reproductive potential:

pregnancy, birth, breastfeeding, and disempowering experiences relating to our menstrual bodies and fertility; violence, discrimination, rape and sexual assault; and increased risks of poverty in our old age.

As UK feminist and writer, Glosswitch, says, "We all know that most of the forms of oppression associated with patriarchy — rape, forced marriage, reproductive coercion, economic exclusion, FGM — can be linked to the broader objective of controlling female sexual and reproductive agency. We know all of this. And it harms women to tell them they cannot say it ... Everyone knows reproductive difference exists. It's not something feminists create just by pointing it out."[86] Wise words, Glosswitch. We occupy an interesting time culturally in our freedom to speak about biology and our bodies. Identity politics reverses the old feminist objection about women being reduced to our bodies: whereas under traditional patriarchy women had to be bodies so that men could be minds, now under *fluid* patriarchy, women have to be states of minds so that males can change their bodies. What impact might the biology and body barricade have on women's freedom and ability to identify and promote their rights? These are important questions.

Our ability and power to create life and give birth is wondrous. And feminism has to honour that. Before we are reduced, in the name of liberation or equality, to growing babies in external synthetic uteruses[87] — the stuff of dreams or nightmares, depending on your point of view.

If our society demands that we resemble a bodily-neutral ideal worker floating in our cloud of self-fulfilment, what a wake-up call we get when our female bodies bring us down to earth. When it comes to our flesh and blood, our children and our place as mothers, we would do well to remember that *patriarchy* is fluid. It has adapted, it has survived, and it continues to exploit women's flesh and draw our blood. And so it is clear, that without fundamental structural and societal change, women as a *class* will continue to suffer; and that means that mothers, women who have created life, the majority of women worldwide, will continue to be oppressed, devalued, overworked, stereotyped, underpaid, unrecognised, and marginalised.

A CONVERSATION WITH MY FATHER: #NOTALLMEN

All this talk of mothers … what of the father? Well, patriarchy is the *rule* of the father. It is an oppressive system which has become so engrained in our sense of reality that we cannot easily see it for what it is.[88] In her preface to *Patriarchy and Accumulation on a World Scale*, Maria Mies defines patriarchy as: "an overall social, cultural and economic and political system which determines a woman's life from birth to death". In other words, it's all around you, and in Mies' words, "is still flourishing today in spite of 'modernization and development'".[89] When Mies speaks of exploitation of women it is in three distinct ways: in the workforce, as housewives and as human beings.[90] It is within a sexist society that women make their way and navigate their terrain as girls, women, mothers, grandmothers, employees, carers, partners and wives. Many women have happy relationships and lives, whether mothers or not, straight or gay, employed or not. Yet, they nevertheless remain in a system which is formulated to keep the majority of women down, which infiltrates their personal relationships and creates power imbalances within the home: the rules were not written with the rights of women in mind. How, I wondered, has patriarchy come to be accepted as the *only* possible historical or current way of living and organising our lives?

However, my husband's words often rang in my ears when I ventured to write this chapter. "You have a son," he reminded me. Well, yes, that's true. And I love him to the stars. I also have a father, a husband and a brother. All of whom I am very keen on, see. I am alive to the suffering of men in our societies and history: in Empire, in class struggle, in war and more. Many men suffer under gender stereotypes too of course. As Andrea Dworkin said, "I've read Hamlet* … I know men suffer".[91] To speak of women's struggles does not detract from that, just as the existence of men's struggles should not silence women's voices when we raise them. The suffering under Empire, class struggle and war (for example, the use of rape as a tactic of conflict) applies, too, to women and girls. So yes, I have a son. And I want for his safety and happiness. But I also have a daughter, for whom I wish the same.

I am mindful of the fact that many of us mothers, feminist or not, might well be in happy heterosexual relationships. We may well prefer not to

---

* I too have read Hamlet. Twenty-odd years ago, and it is still covered in highlighter and notes in the margin. I can't help but think that Ophelia suffered just a little bit more, though, you know? #ButAlwaysWhatAboutTheMen?

visualise our menfolk as forming part of a patriarchal project: we need allies if we are to struggle to improve our situation, and we need to collaborate. The problem is, feminism has been collaborating with the capitalist patriarchy for long enough, and it has not improved the lives of women. Allies yes, but masters, no. We may question Catherine Mackinnon's dominance theory,[92] or debate whether addressing the power/oppression issue is productive for future discourse between men and women. We can bear in mind that we needn't be hostile to men, despite the fact that the vast majority of women are not hostile anyway: 'Man-hater' conjures a convenient straw woman. The problem is that being honest and plain-speaking about the predicament of many women globally, or of the history of man and the law of the father, or of discrimination against women, is *interpreted as hostility*. We risk being shamed, silenced or silencing ourselves. Yet, to quote Mary O'Brien, "we will never liberate ourselves as women until we develop a systemic theoretical analysis of the roots and grounds and development of male history and male philosophy".[93]

With all this in mind, I thought I'd ask my personal patriarch, my father, about patriarchy and domination. After all, as he would be the first to admit, he is something of a man's man; he doesn't shy away from acknowledging honestly and freely that men can be right gits. He told me such, growing up: beware of the boys.

"So, Dad, I talk about something called patriarchy in my book. It's the law of the father, the rule of the father, the domination of women as a class by men. You know what I'm talking about, don't you?" *crosses fingers*

"Absolutely right. Men have always dominated women. Get a group of men together and you should hear what goes on."

"So when I talk about men as a class historically oppressing *women*, you would agree?"

"I'll make you right about that".

Why thank you, Dad. My husband chipped in that men dominated women "because they are physically stronger". Cliché, man, what cliché! Has he *forgotten* the pure physicality of pushing two people out of my vagina while he came out in hives with worry? Has he *forgotten* my mental and emotional strength in keeping it all together in the midst of exhaustion? Ah, he means *muscular* strength. Easy mistake to make. It is the go-to patriarchal 'male dominance is natural' response, critiqued for generations by countless feminists before me. In volumes on shelves.[94] In his own home. Turns out feminism doesn't work by osmosis.

I put it down to his reading too much Bernard Cornwell and Danish sword-wielding brutes, instead of exploring matriarchal and matrilineal cultures, Goddess worship, life-creation, respect for Mother Nature and 'pre-history'. I put it down to the fact that our educational curriculum in Western culture is dominated by male narrative and figures. I put it down to the fact that women's history, artefact, art, and narratives (when not conveyed in traditional oral fashion) have, through patriarchal culture, been suppressed or destroyed.[95] After all, they didn't just burn women, you know: patriarchy burned our history.[96]

Andrea Dworkin wrote, in *Our Blood: Prophecies and Discourses on Sexual Politics*, that "many women, I think, resist feminism because it is an agony to be fully conscious of the brutal misogyny which permeates culture, society, and all personal relationships".[97] We cannot discuss the predicament of women — mothers — if we do not discuss the rule of the father, the domination of women by men throughout patriarchal history, including even recent laws which severely curtailed the rights of women to involvement or responsibility in respect of her children. *Pater familias*: the inability to own family property; the risk of losing contact or residence with one's own children. Changes in the law were fought for by women; we have hardly begun to enjoy them; we must continue the struggle; and we must caution against complacency.

It's hard, though. "Not all men", of course, one might say. #NotAllMen #NotAllMen #NotAllMen Speaking of Twitter — online anonymity has given a rather illuminating illustration of the unedited vitriol many men are capable of spewing about, and to, women. A hefty proportion of men in our society are misogynists — they've just learned to keep it more undercover than in the 1970s. A sizeable number of men are busy terrorising their wives, girlfriends and children. Men kill two women a week in the UK or 1,269 *per week* worldwide, at least. With numbers like those, perpetrated almost exclusively by a particular class of person (man*), we should realistically be talking about terrorism against women and femicide.[98] It brings to mind Sylvia Walby's distinction between "public and private" patriarchy[99] and this is something to keep well in mind: the battle of the sexes starts, like charity, at home.

My mother witnessed my short conversation with my dad and my husband; she listened. She *knows*. She knows the power of women's bodies and the utter strength of women in creating life, reproducing human

* Yes, I know, men suffer too. And men kill other men, too.

beings, facing death in the room at the moment of bringing life, and of working, struggling and surviving as a woman in a man's world. She knows the persistence of the rule of the father, of the unequal division of labour, of the unequal distribution of power and means, and of the societal reflection of the power dynamics within personal relationships. She, like most experienced women, knows that two of patriarchy's greatest successes have been the silencing of women and the suppression of women's power.

It is this knowledge that has to be transformed into action. As Gloria Steinem said, "we have to move beyond words".[100] But this can only start once women start to articulate, without fear (especially in the modern technological Inquisition of the Internet) *what* they know.

At heart, however, it is sufficient for the moment to introduce you, if you are not already familiar, to the fact that human beings did not always live and organise under patrilineal and patriarchal standards and values. It was not always the father and the son.[101] We did not always valorise destruction, colonialism, domination and individualism as we do under patriarchal systems. We did not always experience male domination in society, personal relationships, laws, rule-making, authority, story-telling, narrative and aggression. Once, our human societies respected and valued the creation of life (within nature) and the creators of life (women). Once, our human societies organised themselves cooperatively, or we would not have survived. Once, the mother-daughter bond was rightly respected as a powerful force. Once, our human societies valorised women and mothers. Once, power, status and participation in the fullness of society, family, kin and community was not denied to women and mothers; we were part of it, central to it, and important human beings. The Goddess, the creation and nurturing of life and wisdom, were central to our human societies. But, instead, what we get on the history shelves are books about war, business, politics and patriarchal religion. Books about the Goddess are to be found in esoteric New Age shops, you weirdo.

As sociologist Dorothy E. Smith wrote in *The Everyday World as Problematic, A Feminist Sociology*, the women's movement discovered that "as women we had been living in an intellectual, cultural, and political world, from whose making we had been almost entirely excluded and in which we had been recognized as no more than marginal voices".[102] When we stop to look at politics, economics, social policy and history from the standpoint of women, rather than "from the standpoint of men located in the relations of ruling our societies", very different pictures emerge and very different priorities are raised.[103] It is this need, for a *maternal* standpoint, in feminism, economics and politics, which lies at the heart of the Purplestockings Movement.

Over time, the envy of women and their power to create life led men to desecrate not just the notion of the Goddess, but women and nature themselves; the Father and the Son replaced the Mother and Earth; destruction and domination replaced cooperation and preservation; and life creation became a source and cause of the oppression of women, rather than respect and worship. In *The Myths of Motherhood, How Culture Reinvents the Good Mother*, Shari L. Thurer explores the history of mothers and motherhood. She states that "the idea of woman as mother endowed all women with respect. But as men realised their contribution to procreation and seized control, organising much of what we know as mainstream history, the mother has been dehumanized, that is, either widely idealized (with mothers becoming prisoners of their own symbolic inflation) or degraded (with others viewed as brood mares)".[104] The end of herstory brought the beginning of history.[105] The womb as a symbol of life creation gave way to the symbol and imagery of the phallus and patriarchal control: a penetrating, dominating ideology. The patriarchal project began in attempts to metaphorically displace the life-creating power and social power and importance of mothers: it will end with the creation of extra-bodily artificially grown babies, fed on milk powder, cared for in facilities and, finally, the destruction of life itself whether through war, environmental destruction or disease. Happy times, right?

In the light of our history, we can reflect on where patriarchal destruction will eventually take humanity. Because feminist activism is not, and should not be, just about 'pay gaps' or 'the glass ceiling'. It is about life; it is about women as a class; it is about humanity and our environment.[106] It is impossible and blinkered even to try to dissect the political and social predicament facing mothers today without taking in the historical, political and religious contexts of patriarchal culture and the treatment of women over generations. We have to expand our understanding of the nature of the society in which we live now. When it comes to mothers, any woman who claims to be a feminist but who expresses disdain for mothers is acting as patriarchy's mouthpiece. They are ultimately advocating, as patriarchy has designed, the oppression of mothers and the end to woman's power of the creation of life itself.

Ultimately, it is impossible to be truly pro-mother if one is simultaneously beguiled by patriarchal culture and seduced into playing by its rules. Mothers will never be respected, empowered or justly valued until patriarchy loses its grip on society. After all, the end game of patriarchy is the annihilation of mothers[107] and the oppression of women, the degradation of our flesh, and the spilling of our blood. In the meantime, we are scrutinised and under surveillance. We live under the male gaze.

MALE GAZE, FEMALE BODY

Naomi Wolf wrote about *The Beauty Myth* back in 1990 — but things are no better now: they are manifestly and objectively worse. The Internet, pornography, body shaming, sexism and trolling have all taken aim at women and hit the bulls-eye. In the early years of the twenty-first century we may well have reached *peak* male gaze. Modern technology has spiked the debate because it has simultaneously revealed sexism as still rife and *increased and expanded* its prevalence by adding a new platform: social media.

In the 'postfeminist' age, body image concerns and bodily control issues are rampant amongst young girls and women. According to the National Eating Disorders Association, in the United States 20 million women suffer from a clinically significant eating disorder at some time in their life.[108] If a grown woman can want to keep the lights off, starve herself for a day and swear off chocolate yet again, after seeing cynically adulterated images of near-naked nubile pre-maternal females, one has to wonder how this is affecting our young girls in their view of their own bodies, and boys in their expectation of what women's bodies *actually* look like in the unadulterated flesh.

Young males are entering their sexual years distorted by extreme Internet pornography and girls are sinking in a sea of sexual suggestion and imagery. The pornography collections boasted by rapists and murderers are not benign, like a stamp collection. Don't say Dworkin didn't warn us.[109] Melissa Benn's question is on our lips: *"What Shall We Tell Our Daughters?"* There's more. What shall we tell our sons?

We live in a society where a woman's body, if not for the purpose of titillation (see Kim Kardashian's buttocks breaking the Internet), is viewed with disdain, distrust and disgust. Especially if the owner of the body is 'old'. The compulsion to 'lose the baby weight', criticisms of 'mummy jeans' and the feverish valorisation of youthful appearance replete with skinny and smooth body is a continuous onslaught against mothers and their relationship with and confidence in their bodies. We take it personally. We internalise hatred of the body, of 'droopy' breasts, of 'dimpled' thighs and of 'saggy' tummies.

The problem is, the political class has no interest in pursuing legislation which might be seen as curtailing the freedom of expression of men to physically and visually degrade women through pornography, or to curtail the media's use of outright lies with Photoshop. All the while, the fashion industry maintains an anorexic/androgynous paradigm (thigh gap, anyone?) of what a woman should look like: no childbearing hips, no body hair, no stretchmarks. Digital alteration of photographs of women elevate distorted body imagery to a new level. These are all feminist issues. Yet the political class consistently fails to address them. Why? Because they are deemed unimportant. Women's issues (small fry compared to, say, agricultural subsidies, defence or banking). These are feminist issues. They affect us as women; as mothers. They negate and erase the reality of maternal bodies. Our maternal bodies make patriarchy — not just feminism — uncomfortable: our blood, our milk and our wombs are to be controlled or suppressed. This is the heart of patriarchal control of our bodies.

When it comes to our bodies, the fact is, we are mammals. In truth, when it comes to pregnancy, birth and breastfeeding, the more we become in touch with our mammalian nature the better.[110] However, in an attempt to protect our daughters, Western culture seems to think that by ignoring their development, ostrich-style, we can pretend that they are not sexual beings (until they irritatingly get pregnant before they should). There are few occasions in our culture to celebrate a young girl's first bleeding, as a step towards womanhood. Instead, the rites of passage are to be found in elaborate proms, make-up and sexualised dress. We do not respect the girl and we do not respect the woman she will be, still less the mother she might one day become.

Ina May Gaskin nailed it when she observed that if men had something so absolutely amazing as a uterus they would brag about it, "and so should we". Yet, sex education has a charge to answer for: the way in which birth is depicted and shown to girls in their vulnerable years has every potential to shape how she will regard her birthing, in time, as a mother-to-be. For as long as schools have educated children about childbirth, so have generations of women been mis-educated on the birthing experience. Usually featuring screams, blood and gore, such videos of women giving birth are a disservice to each girl watching it. Even socially and within her own family, it is pretty rare for a young girl (or woman of any age, come to think of it) to hear any positive stories about birth at all (although this is changing, with grassroots movements such as Tell Me A Good Birth Story or the Positive Birth Movement). Popular culture either sanitises the experience or reduces it to a comical 'waters have broken and five minutes of blood curdling screams, begging a male doctor for pain relief, later, baby is born'. The message to her bellows: you must fear this experience, you are powerless, you are weak, and you will suffer. And we (the men and the patriarchal medical profession) are in charge and know better.

BLOOD AND BABIES

Menstruation, birth and menopause. Whilst they do not define us, they are part of most women's lived experience. To discuss and recognise these aspects of womanhood does not reduce us to our bodies. It does not *essentialise* us. The fear feminism has had of biological determinism is one thing — we cannot tolerate being reduced to our biological function — yet it is a mistake to put our fingers in our ears and ignore aspects of our being, our experience, and our bodies. We are human beings. We are mammals. Of the female kind. And a significant majority of us bear children.

And in order to be able to do that, many of us bleed. Blood. From our vaginas and wombs. Every twenty-eight days. Give or take.

Granted, not all women bleed, for a multitude of reasons — hysterectomies, low weight, continuous synthetic hormonal implants, polycystic ovary syndrome, menopause. We are not lesser women as a result. Some women get through each month without a *hint* of tearfulness or craving for carbohydrates or Ms Hyde coming by to lock our Ms Jekyll in the cupboard. But many, many women do not. We neglect part of our selves, a regular feature in our lives, when we ignore or try to suppress our cycles and the challenges we face when our bodies do the things our bodies do. Our "moontime"[111] is rather unique, to women individually and to the female of the species.

Menstruation features, monthly, in the lives of half the population of the world for, let's say, conservatively, thirty years. Despite this, menstruation has no pride of place. Instead it is relegated to the modern equivalent of the 'curse': 'the blob' or, worse, a destiny of skipping around in white jeans (if the adverts for towels are to be believed) to *Walking on Sunshine*. *vomit*.

Living with your garden-variety monthly ups and downs is hard. Some women endure pre-menstrual dysmorphic syndrome. Others experience endometriosis. This is a condition so misunderstood and so neglected within the medical profession that the gendered division of health care priorities means it rarely gets the attention it deserves. It is debilitating, yet women are practically compelled to suffer *in silence*, in an economic system which fails to accommodate their needs. When it comes, for example, to 'pre-menstrual syndrome', we can pathologise our experience (something is *wrong* with us) or we can name it as a womanly and female bodily and emotional (and extremely common) experience. I prefer the sound of the latter: it locates it precisely where it should be, namely, our experience.

The reality of women's lives in the modern age is relevant to our experiences of our monthly bleeding: the fact that we have significantly fewer babies, start having them later, and start our periods earlier, means that the red veil can cast a shadow over our lives. And we have to go to the bloody office when doubled over in pain. Yet, anyone who dares suggest the idea of *menstrual leave* is immediately shot down in flames.[112] It is a no-fly zone. It brings out the fear that any demands for sensitivity around women's cycles or bodily needs will be met with some git saying a woman cannot be Prime Minister because 'no woman should have her hand by the red button at the wrong time of the month'. That's what we get when we live in patriarchal misogynistic wastelands. No humanity allowed. Especially humanity of the female kind. The fact is that we deserve humane treatment *and* we are capable of leading free nations. The one does not preclude the other.

Women frequently suffer in their bodies. We live with and within our bodies. They affect our lives. Conditions such as endometriosis can affect our fertility. They can cause us agony: bodily and emotional pain. They can interfere with our quality of life. In feminism, we can keep going, we can keep on with the de-sexed, disembodied woman, or economic woman who is no different in presentation than man. But ultimately, we will fail women until we embrace our bodies. Yes, yes, we must not be *reduced* to our bodies; but we must *own* them, we must *live* them, we must *protect* them, we must *love* them. We have to acknowledge the place in our lives of our reproductive potential, power and experience. We have to demand that society accommodate and honour that — and that means being creative about how we can do that, rather than denying that it matters.

Pregnancy, birth, menopause — these women-only matters — raise the issue of equality. The 'sameness thing'. After all, the official line is equality. Not equity, fairness and justice — but e.q.u.a.l.i.t.y., as interpreted by sexists everywhere as "Fuck you, you wanted equality now you've got it. Struggle alone with that suitcase up the stairs", or "No you can't have maternity leave for a year, you want to be treated the same, don't you?", or "You're sacked — you've taken two days off a month with period pain. Grow a pair."

Biological essentialism, recognition and appropriate accommodation of difference is forbidden. Yet the different points in a woman's life in which she faces potentially significant transformative or at least deeply emotional experiences directly connected to her sex are invisible or downplayed, not least by women themselves, to our detriment. These are the five 'M's:

› Menarche

› Monthly menstruation

› Motherhood

› Mammalian milk-making

› Menopause

Each of these is an emotionally taxing event or process, but we must 'leave it at the door'. No wonder psychotherapist Rosjke Hasseldine describes "the problem with no name" as being women's unmet emotional needs.[113] They are shut down at regular intervals throughout our lives by a society which has no place for them. Although that is not to say these are the only reasons women have extra needs (of course not), but they are significant. They can carry extremely raw feelings. A woman's grief, confusion, disappointment, frustration (as well as pride, joy and relief) over these experiences are minimised. And we suffer for it. Those boobs, wombs, ovaries and vaginas — wouldn't life be so much *easier* if a woman could be like a man, eh, Henry?

THE FERTILITY INDUSTRY

In the twenty-first century the technology exists to bring pregnancy to women who would otherwise be unable, for a variety of reasons, to bear children. The templates are drawn for massive future strides in technological reproduction. Some academics and writers, such as Mariam

Irene Tazi-Preve are scathing in their view that scientists, out of patriarchal envy of the power of women to reproduce, are going all-out eventually to effectively to annihilate mothers. In *Motherhood in Patriarchy*, Tazi-Preve actually uses the phrase "final solution to the question of motherhood".[114] I winced when I read that one. However, if we see the patriarchal project in the context of oppression of mothers, then we must, at some point, ask: where will it *end*? If we are liberated from caring, from our children and from motherhood, including biological motherhood and physical bearing and birthing of children, what will this *do* for women, as a *class*? And what will it do for the human race? Do we want to be liberated from motherhood and care? Or is the act of creating, bearing and nurturing life of deep value to us as individuals and a species? What would a race of humans without deep bonds to family be like? Many might well say that close family ties (exemplified in the mother/child bond) make us more human, more caring and compassionate: skills that our whole species benefits from, not just our own children. These questions matter. We are entitled to ask them. We are entitled to answers. And if the answers are not the ones we want to hear, we are entitled to demand — and help to create — change.

When it comes to mothers, the fact that fertility treatment is a booming industry, the fact that many women spend *huge* sums of money to get pregnant, or to contract the commercial services of a surrogate, and the fact that many women grieve for a lack of fertility suggests that there is *something*, something *special*, about becoming a mother. Many women have evoked the yearning for children. The frustration of a desire to bear children is painful. That is not to say that everyone wants (or should want to have) children. But there are many women who grieve for not having a baby. The welcoming of a wanted child is joyful. And that's where I am at.

Yet (and this book would not be complete without reference to surrogacy and technological advances) it is crucial to recognise that there is a *need* for ethics and humanity in the way we surge ahead with the notions of surrogacy and other reproductive technologies. Commercial surrogacy is becoming a booming industry in countries such as India, where rich Westerners come with their money to rent women's wombs. When it comes to patriarchy, as Barbara Katz Rothman observes, "Like traditional fatherhood in any patriarchy, the point of baby-making is for people of power to use oppressed people to grow their seeds into their progeny, do the labor, the dirty work, the hard work, and create a child who will bear the name and carry on the life and work and values of the oppressor."[115]

Surrogacy is, perhaps, all this writ large. The reduction to host, under control and pimped for cash is something which the feminist movement *has* to start to address. Feminist Julie Bindel is preparing such a project.[116] As women, and as mothers, surely we must not tolerate the exploitation of other women in the name of motherhood. Liberating motherhood must not apply only to the privileged.

On the money question there is a curious anomaly. You would think it safe to assume that any government which expends funds to women to enable them to get pregnant (as the National Health Service in the UK does), sustain a pregnancy and have a baby, must, somewhere along the line, see that there is a value in reproduction and a recognition of a woman's biological drive to continue her genetic line. Wouldn't it be amazing if that very same government or political class recognised the need, want and drive to raise that child, to nurture that child and to be with that child once it is born and until the child is ready for independence? Yet what we get is the opposite: cut loose and on our own from the moment of cutting the umbilical cord.

The Embodiment of Creation

I begin to love this creature,
and to anticipate her birth
as a fresh twist to a knot,
which I do not wish to untie.

Mary Wollstonecraft

THE PREGNANT GAZE

The moment you share news of your impending motherhood, the advice starts. And it never stops. We are immediately under The Gaze of others, as Sara Ruddick discussed in *Maternal Thinking, Toward a Politics of Peace*. As mothers we will forever be under the scrutiny of others, the judgement of others, and the onslaught of 'expert' advice, 'well-meaning' advice, 'downright dangerous' advice, and, occasionally, warmth and guidance which we could never do without.

Becoming a mother, rather than being regarded as an act of maturity, seems to put us in a position of inferiority. It is regressive: we become patients, students, not mature independent beings. We are immediately placed under observation and control, forever reminded that we are not to be trusted with the job of growing, birthing, or raising *our own* children. We shift from the sexual male gaze to the mother gaze. We are treated to the lady in the shop warning us not to eat liquorice. The man at the bus stop reminding us not to drink alcohol. The colleague instructing us never to sleep on our back. As women, the policing of our behaviour can become stark when we are visibly pregnant: how far can we be a 'sexy mama' or 'massive frump' before we fail the 'right proportion' of sexiness and maternity?

When it comes to our new role as expectant mother, capitalism has a stake even in pregnancy. From the moment a woman believes, through every increasingly-sophisticated conception and pregnancy test, that she might have conceived, right through to the advent of the baby shower. We are charged money to have 3-D scans of our babies looking like trolls in utero. When it comes to bowing to the experts, magazines are devoted to the subject. Books abound with advice from self-appointed experts. From money to monitoring, the medical profession has a huge presence in our pregnancies. Women's bodies are seen as lemons, unfit for the task[117] and many doctors still focus on pathology rather than the miracle of uneventful — yet empowering — pregnancy and birth. Our bodies become public property. Or at least our baby bumps do.

PREGNANT FEMINISM

I will admit that I am something of a 'birth junkie'. I go weak at the sight of a beautiful pregnant body. I still find it amazing when you see a baby in the arms of a *mother* who, by the time of the birth, has transformed. She was a woman. Now she is a mother.

We recognise in our culture that pregnancy is a time of growth for the foetus, but overlook the emotional growth and massive, often permanent, physical changes experienced by the woman. It is not really very fashionable to say this, is it? We are supposed to aspire to *more* than this. More than the unremarkable yet miraculous process of gestation and birth. I have read enough feminist work to recognise the huge unease amongst feminists about whether and how far to recognise pregnancy and birth as something of importance for women. Nowadays, reproduction and mothering are practically invisible amongst those feminists (especially younger women) for whom it is not within their experience or their politics: Mothers are the Other in society and feminism alike. When it comes to business, careers, employment or simple courtesy, some women realise how appalling their behaviour had been towards pregnant colleagues or new mothers only after they themselves become mothers.[118] Given the arrival of motherhood at later and later ages, feminism and feminists have become less and less concerned with it: it is outside their reality. We plan for a decade or more to 'do it all differently', rather than be like *other* women or our own mothers.

Some feminists have shared horror at the state of pregnancy in such terms, "rather horrible that a parasitic body should proliferate within" your body or you might find this "monstrous swelling" frightening, to quote Simone de Beauvoir.[119] Some women reveal utter distaste for pregnancy and birth. With feminists like these, who needs misogynists?

A woman's right to control her body and reproductive freedom has been the cornerstone of the feminist movement, for good reason. For a woman, her ability to choose *when* she becomes a mother, *if at all*, is a fundamental part of her right to bodily autonomy and respect. The free availability of contraception and safe abortion is central to women's reproductive rights. It cannot be otherwise. Women have fought long and hard for the right not to be a mother, or not to have more children: to be liberated from the confines of their fertility. Not all women wish to become mothers. Others do not wish to have another child to add to their brood, for whatever reason. Some are not ready. Yet. Others have experienced trauma, or there might be a medical complication in woman and/or foetus. The choice must come down to the woman concerned. We have to secure this for all women, and resist pushback and restrictions. Reproductive rights are women's rights are human rights.

When we speak of motherhood, it must be one that is freely chosen, or accepted, not one that is imposed by external forces of law or morality. Yet, given that patriarchy is anxious to control women's reproductive freedom, it comes as no surprise that women continue to be forced to fight for the right to control their bodies. Florynce Kennedy is said to have remarked (and is immortalised in Internet memes as saying) that, "If men could get pregnant, abortion would be a sacrament". Amen to that. When we think about the reality of legislative priorities, the toleration of poverty, the denial of the reality of femicide and valorisation of war and guns, we know that reproductive freedom is rarely about life; it is about *control*.

If a pregnancy is to continue, it affects, singularly and exclusively, the woman carrying the embryo or foetus. Yet politicians and priests persist, even today, in seeking to control women's bodies by way of laws which seek to restrict access to safe abortion. It is the twenty-first century, but when it comes to the choice to end a pregnancy, women's bodies are still hostage to the religious sensitivities of others; to judgement by men in influence; and by women who forget their own privilege. Any time you hear a man talk about abortion in negative terms (an art perfected by Republican politicians in the United States) you have living, breathing proof that men want to control women's bodies. It's not about respecting or valuing life; not when it comes, as it does, from men who support the right to bear arms, who support air strikes which will lead to the destruction of life, or who resist adequate social security to ensure all citizens and children have a decent quality of life and access to basic means. It is about control. It is right there. The very act of comment. The very act of legislating against. The very act of criticising. The very promotion of 'punishment'.[120] Just shut up, man. It's got nothing to do with you.

THE TREATMENT OF PREGNANT WOMEN

For many women, her first pregnancy is arguably the first time that she has felt at one with her body: it is doing what it was designed to do. And it's marvellous.

I remember feeling awe-struck by my body, and at peace with the fact that it was doing what it needed to do in a repetition of a biological miracle performed millions upon millions of times through human history. It is a truly humbling experience. Fraught with anxiety at times, especially in the age of scans, testing and yet more scans. Full of our hopes and dreams. It is a truly sacred time for a woman.

Or it should be.

The treatment of a pregnant woman reveals a huge amount about how women are regarded and the value placed on our rights and bodily autonomy. We quickly find that our bodies and needs must submit to the system. Not the other way around.

Pregnancy initiates us into the fact that birth and death are far closer than we ever knew. When a pregnancy ends too soon, through miscarriage or stillbirth, it can be devastating for women and their families. However, the way in which many women are treated by the medical profession during and after loss can be inhumane, lacking in compassion, and downright cruel. Yes, medical staff deal with miscarriage on a daily basis. It is a common occurrence. But it is not common to the woman *experiencing* it. It can be heart-breaking. It can be scary. It can be traumatic. It is a major and defining life event for many women.

The fact is that there is a need for greater compassion and kindness in maternity services[121] — no more so than in the eventuality of loss. There is no title given to a mother who is without her child. Perhaps her predicament is too heart-breaking to name.

This is just one of the ways that medicalised/standard pregnancy care does not put the women it is serving at the forefront of their service. The medicalised path is the norm. Often a woman is forced early on to choose between two models of care ... if she chooses to deviate to one she feels supports her more as a human and woman, it is with strong warnings of danger.

Broadly, there are two models of care for pregnant women: the midwifery (read female) model; and the medical or technological (read male) model.[122] Of course, the importance of modern advances in medicine and technology must not be underestimated: they have saved lives. In the *appropriate* case, the involvement of medical professionals who are expert in pathology and complicated pregnancy and birth is extremely important. But as Naomi Wolf discusses in *Misconceptions, Truth, Lies and the Unexpected on the Journey to Motherhood,* "women deserve a birth culture that unites the best" of both models[123]: we need to respect that it is ultimately women who bring life and that our bodies are capable of giving birth, broadly unassisted by doctors. Our medical profession need only involve itself where the mother and child are in need, out of special circumstances, and it must involve itself with the *utmost* respect and veneration for that mother. Yes, skilled intervention saves lives. But skilled, hands off, low-stress maternal care is crucially important too.

Early Stages of Pregnancy

We become a mother in steps. Inching towards the day when a little one is in our arms, we try to visualize what it will mean, what the child will be like, how our lives might change. *But the truth is we have no idea what lies ahead.* We continue those baby steps in the hours, days, weeks and years after the birth — we live motherhood in stages. And it starts with *that* moment of discovery.

So we pee on a stick or ten. A blue line tells us what we hope to see or what we are afraid might be the case. Either way, bun is in oven. The conveyor-belt starts. In the UK your doctor refers you to midwife. Midwife books you in and makes your first date with the sonographer. These are the first of many medical appointments. V.O.M.I.T., a huge amount of peeing in cups, emergency visits to labour wards when you unexpectedly start bleeding. False alarm. This is before we even get onto extreme tiredness. Sorry, I meant debilitating fatigue. Actually, maybe that should be mind-shattering exhaustion. You see, in those twelve weeks a woman is building an entire new human being. All its organs. Everything. By twelve weeks, the foetus is fully formed. All done while pretty much nobody might know that you are pregnant. When you don't look pregnant. When you are expected to work, as usual, for your wage. It is quite astounding, really, that the female body is capable of performing all this, without, in the routine, healthy case, anybody doing anything at all. That's right. No doctors telling you "now relax and really focus — FOCUS — on building that foetus' brain". Your body is doing it. Your hormones are doing it. Your nutritional reserves are doing it. You, a woman, are creating and sustaining life inside your body. Whilst working, sleeping, out walking . . . No man will ever be able to perform such a feat of creation and of pure wonder. We must take pride in that. Your mother did it. So did hers. It is the reason we are all here. Take pride. Women create *life*. In and from our bodies.

But you might not immediately feel ready to march down the street proclaiming pride because you feel sick as a dog. If you escape all-day long sickness and have a nausea-free pregnancy I salute you. Sadly, many women do experience debilitating sickness, in some cases extreme (hyperemesis gravidarum has received more attention than ever thanks to a very high profile, royal sufferer, the Duchess of Cambridge). For women whose nausea and vomiting are not quite so debilitating that she ends up on a drip in hospital, the only thing I can recommend is to buy a bucket of ginger biscuits and then throw said bucket of biscuits at the head of anyone who suggests "have you tried ginger biscuits?"

Problem is, where there is an issue such as sickness, and the solution cannot be "allow this woman to rest, she needn't go business-as-usual at work, allow her to be waited on hand and foot, her older children cared for within her home by the village of women.who.have.been.there", the solution becomes "let the pharmaceuticals in". And then Thalidomide happens.

So, the first twelve weeks, woman, you have created life. And you will forever be told you have no right to claim that achievement, or be proud of doing something so every-day, or demand that this be rightfully accommodated and valued. It is your apprenticeship for motherhood under patriarchy. Welcome.

Middle stages of pregnancy

Blooming. If you're lucky.

Last trimester

Heartburn. Pre-eclampsia. Growth scans. Gestational diabetes. Sweeps and inductions. Pelvic pain, I hate you. Lots of foetal movement. Nobody giving up their seat on public transport. Despite your cute *Baby On Board* badge. Antenatal classes. Working all hours because we shouldn't expect 'special treatment'. How dare we?

Birth

D Day. B Day. The day that everything hinges on. Lights low, camera ready, and active labour — freaks out the patriarchy because it can't be scheduled in. *This* is where *all* the focus goes. Not the building and carrying the baby, not the caring of it thereafter. But this. One. Day. Where the patriarchal model has woman under control, strapped to the bed and in fear. Or it could be the day she is respected. She is worshipped. She is cared for and nurtured. She is calm. She is safe.

And then . . . she is a mother.

Fourth trimester

You thought there were only three trimesters? Well that's what they want you to think. A couple of days' lie in, if you're lucky. Then get on with it. Back to work with you. Don't be lazy. Share that baby, like a good girl.

In fact, many cultures have variations on the fourth trimester theme. The first three months after the birth when the mother is cared for, as she in turn cares for her helpless babe. Yup. We are born prematurely underdeveloped, in comparison with many mammals who are born to get up and go. Our babies are in need of direct physical contact and sensitive care. Dare I say maternal care? Dare I?

Despite my admittedly whingey description of some of the unhappy features of pregnancy, this is not an exhaustive list of the down-sides. And it doesn't even scratch the surface of the *good* bits. I can't really describe how I felt during my pregnancies: the connection and yearning; a sense of power and a sense of fragility, rolled into one; how, for the first time in my life, I felt beautiful. I struggle for the words to illustrate the timelessness of the experience and the spiritual bond with our ancestral mothers through the bringing of life in our wombs.

A writer without words is a bit of a problem really. But in the case of our individual, unique experiences of pregnancy and creating life in our bodies, you have your own story, don't you? You don't need mine.

CELEBRATING THE MOTHER-TO-BE

Where is the ceremonial marking of this momentous transition — social and biological — which happens in the journey from woman to mother? We celebrate marriage. We celebrate the birth of the baby. But nowhere is there an adequate celebration of the transformation of a woman in awaiting her baby. Why not? Can we dare to suggest that it is because pregnancy is seen at once as unremarkable and a nuisance to business interests? Because motherhood is not respected or valued? Because women themselves have forgotten that we are allowed to celebrate and support our sisters? Because to want, as a woman and a mother, is to want too much.

As Sheila Kitzinger noted in *Ourselves as Mothers*, pregnancy can be an emotional and spiritual time.[124] Given this significance, despite all appearances in our consumerist, work-driven culture, a beautiful way to embrace the mother-to-be is a blessingway or mother blessing ceremony. There is a lot of support. A bit of belly casting. A bit of reading of poetry (or whatever takes your fancy). Hair brushing or massaging the hands or feet. All a bit twee? Well what do you think happens at *weddings*? Hair styling. Dresses. Readings. Vows. Ceremony. Kissing. Lots of cake. Would it be too cynical to reflect on marriage as a patriarchal institution where women were considered as chattels — even today dowries are common in some cultures. So, sexual union or transfer of ownership from father to husband[125]: big party! But something involving a woman's body and her power; a woman who is growing and sustaining life inside her body? The nurturing of that woman? Nah, skip on. Not deserving of honour or pause or celebration. Get back to work!

So, wouldn't it be wonderful if there were to be a rite of passage for every woman — in a safe circle of women to hold her and reassure her, to bless her and to serve her, just for a day in the period before the birth? Wouldn't *you* have loved something like that? Wouldn't you feel *proud* to do something like that for your daughter, sister or friend? *No?* Is that because we are trained, as women, to be silent, accepting, not rocking the boat, not expecting a fuss? Why do men get to 'wet the baby's head', get drunk and get slapped on the back, yet the mother gets nothing but some stitches, stretchmarks and bags under her eyes? Yes, and the baby, too. But that's hardly the point. The time for the *mother* is in that prime month or so before birth. The bump all lovely and big and taut. The feeling of 'I've been pregnant forever' looming large. Shouldn't we owe her a bit of respect?

Yes, this is all too much to ask. Yes, it sounds like I'm a hippie. And you know why, don't you? Because we've swallowed the message that we don't matter; that we don't deserve to be cared for as ourselves and as mothers. We need to let go of that self-denial and demand better for our sisters and daughters.

It is probably obvious that I am *not* advocating a proliferation of baby showers. They are the *antithesis* of what I am talking about. Baby showers are a commercial event focusing on the baby and shopping. Cold hard cash and consumption. Money is to be given to companies for tat, female friends and family turn up, bring gifts for the baby and maybe mother (nipple cream anyone?) Granted, cake is eaten. But where is the celebration of womanhood there? Where is the celebration of the mother yet to be born? Because at present, really, what opportunities are there in pregnancy to feel nurtured? To feel heard? Not many. That said, many a spa will try to sell you a pregnancy pampering experience and toiletries companies will sell stretch mark cream which do.not.work.believe.me.i.tried.many (good old capitalism and optimism over genetic predisposition).

In terms of the central space occupied by women in pregnancy, there is plenty of time for the baby to come first. If women felt empowered and interested in pursuing a sisterhood which actually valued, nurtured, supported and loved each other with compassion and kindness, that would be a start, wouldn't it? Wouldn't that at least challenge the patriarchal system in which we operate to 'man down' a bit? Can we lead by example? We really do have the right. We have a lot to be proud of. By ignoring, with each woman, the needs of that mother even during pregnancy, we are setting the scene for the role of mother to be sidelined in society, economics, politics and media. Just look at how practically every Disney film has either a dead or absent mother. It's no fairy tale, women. But we can at least celebrate a mother's humanity and womanly power in creating life. Let's face it, we celebrate men who create films, iPods, bag-less vacuum cleaners, the atom bomb, and music. Wow. I kneel before you, masters of creation.*

---

* I didn't mean that last sentence.

BODY AND MIND

As Sheila Kitzinger stated in *The Politics of Birth,*[126] for human beings, birth is "to do with what is going on in our minds". There are increasing movements to raise the issue of how the mind and body work together in birth. Hypnobirthing advocates, experienced midwives and obstetrician-magician (okay, he's not really a magician, but he talks so much bleedin' sense) Michel Odent all point to the power of the brain, the mind and hormones in labour and birthing — for positive or ill-effect. It is a fundamental curiosity that a birthing woman needs to feel safe and respected during birth (more on this later in this chapter), and a woman's needs are just as great during pregnancy.

In a step which might horrify some women of sophistication, Odent maintains that we need to "de-humanise" birth.[127] Well, I'm sure plenty of maternity wards do that already, but that's not what Odent means. He talks about how "childbirth needs to be mammalianized". It is extremely important, for childbirth. So in some ways, it is our modern mind — our gender-neutral, educated, body-shamed, performance-anxiety-ridden neo-cortices — which can interfere with our ability to birth without artificial hormonal assistance. Sounds about right, to me. His fellow Frenchperson (see what I did there?), Simone de Beauvoir wrote that woman "is more enslaved to the species than is the male, her animality is more manifest".[128] No more so than when you find yourself *mooing* in transition.

How a woman feels in her pregnancy can have an impact on how she births and subsequently mothers her child. It is no coincidence that if a woman experiences low mood during pregnancy (we will look at mental health in **A Mother's Mind**) she is more likely to suffer from postnatal depression. Women deserve to feel nurtured, seen, heard and valued. There is not enough of this in everyday life, let alone during periods of greater, more intense need: pregnancy, birth, breastfeeding and mothering. Thing is, 'needs' and 'mother' often equates to 'mothers meeting needs' rather than 'others meeting *mothers*' needs'. It is somehow shameful to be seen as 'needy'. As modern women, we have been schooled in disavowing our needs as women — our bodily needs and emotional needs — just as much as our foremothers were expected to be all self-sacrificing and subservient.

Thing is, when political parties (even one set up by women, for women) neglect these issues, we have little hope that things will change for the better. After all, there is a tendency to be gender-neutral in all things, even birth, and no female politician wants to be *that* one going on about 'fringe' women's issues. Get back to the interesting stuff like nuclear arms.

BIRTH AND THE POWER OF WOMEN

Birth is significant. First, if it is not obvious, reproduction is central to the survival of our species. Second, women's health in pregnancy and safety during birth is a vital feature of the respect she should receive as a human being. Third, a woman is entitled to respect for the vital task (see number one) that she is performing in the interests of the continuation of our species.

What? You thought having children was the equivalent of buying a puppy? Well, some news for you, sunshine: children are not pets[129] and giving birth is qualitatively different from having a splinter removed. From a feminist perspective, the way we are conditioned to see nothing enormous and significant in the work of women in birthing their babies is just one of the many ways the strength of women is undermined. Just think back to the countless times you have heard the phrase "doctor delivers baby" or "father delivers baby" or "taxi-driver delivers baby". Erm, no. Mother delivers baby. Anybody else just *catches* baby. End of chat.

So the *work* of pregnancy, birth and motherhood are overlooked in our culture (by many feminists and patriarchs alike) but so too are the joys, beauty, power, majesty and spirit. It's actually a rather beautiful thing, the growing of a person in the body of a woman and the birthing of a baby in an empowered mother-respected environment. For some women, such as Michelle Quashie, we can feel that we are "Strong Since Birth".[130] It really can be one of the most powerful experiences in a woman's life.

But instead it is denied. Silenced. Ignored. Measured.

Not felt. Not spoken in its fullness.

Let's take some time in our lives to celebrate it.

As Sheila Kitzinger noted, birth takes place "at the intersection of time; in all cultures it links past, present and future. In traditional cultures birth unites the world of 'now' with the world of the ancestors, and is part of the great tree of life extending in time and eternity".[131] Childbirth is significant for women. It connects us to our maternal ancestors, our mothers and to nature. We bring life through our bodies, we open, we surrender, we birth our babies. We embrace skin to skin intimacy with our babies. We are strong. We *open* when we have our babies: our bodies literally open. Since having my children, the sentiment expressed by Leonard Cohen about the cracks being where the light gets in, became *moving* to me. We open. The light gets in. And we can shine. Look for that shining light* in a new mother. If you can't see it, help her find it.

I relate to Naomi Wolf's rallying cry in *Misconceptions*: "becoming a mother requires supreme focus, a profound discipline, and even a kind of warrior spirit. Yet our culture … suggests that motherhood is simple and effortless. It calls motherhood 'natural', as if the powerful attachment women have to their babies erases the agency they must show in carrying, giving birth to and caring for children".[132] In pregnancy, we are at once becoming strong and vulnerable. We take our steps towards a bodily, spiritual and emotional transformation: yet we still don't *know* what's about to happen to us, how *we* will be reborn. No one tells us that. Because all the focus is on the baby. What happens to us — positive and negative — is seen as incidental, not central.

Feminism must recognise the importance of the female birthing experience. It is not, of itself, a burden: we must celebrate and protect that experience. There is something so truly humbling about the birth of a mother (note 'mother' here, not 'baby') that it is a betrayal that this is a topic which fails often to receive the veneration which it deserves. As Barbara Katz Rothman notes, "birth is not only about making babies. Birth is about making mothers — strong, competent, capable mothers who trust themselves and know their inner strength."[133] Too right. A woman's birth experience is something which she keeps with her for the rest of her life. It is no small thing. Yet the treatment of women during labour and immediately afterwards can be shameful, and fails to respect the sacred period of birth and the fourth trimester.

The physiological and emotional experience of birth is something extremely precious and the strength and power of a woman's body and mind when she gives birth are wondrous. The vast majority of healthy women with healthy pregnancies are capable of something extremely physical and raw — and they *can* do it. We don't hear that enough. *We can do it.* What we must know is that the Biblical pronouncement that "in sorrow thou shalt bring forth children" is a not a life-sentence; it is not an oracle; it is a patriarchal mind virus, to quote Mary Daly.[134] We can give birth without

---

* I discovered shortly after my daughter's birth that her name means 'shining light'. For me, she is the embodiment of this process. My love, my light.

64

fear; in joy and with power. Just look at beautiful photographs shared by, for example, Birth Without Fear,[135] showing the moments of birth and freshness of life. Just *look* at the mothers' faces. That is what we need to see: potential, power and pride.

Where antenatal classes seek to prepare women for birth, there is no escaping the fact that the phrase "nobody told me ..." is often spilt from a new mother's lips. Nothing prepares you; and, paradoxically, we have just lived through an extremely physical process which may or may not have been traumatic, painful or complicated. I commented to a midwife that becoming a mother was like learning to drive the day after being run over by a bus. That said, at heart, it is less the external *appearance* of our births which matter, but the feelings we have *about* our births. Discussing this with Hypnobirthing practitioner Charlotte Tonkin, she is clear that, for many women the mode of delivery can be less important than the feeling she has of safety, respect and autonomy during birth: we can feel empowered despite intervention; we can feel violated despite an otherwise unremarkable textbook birth. There is more to a 'good birth' than the place, the orifice or the drugs.[136] The respect for the individual woman is, and must be, central to birth.

Aside from hearing about my mother's experiences of unmedicated childbirth, my own introduction to natural, informed childbirth was through the work of the late Sheila Kitzinger. I discovered many of her books when I was pregnant with my first child and I felt that this was a woman who was unashamed of celebrating the power of women to birth their babies, of championing the rights of women to give birth at home and of the calling of midwifery. Her confidence was contagious, her faith in women's bodies unshaken through years of working in the field of birth, writing about birth, and supporting women through Birth Crisis. To me, she was a true feminist. When it comes to the 'natural birth movement', I quote Nancy Rubin in *The Mother Mirror*, "this was motherhood without mystification, maternity 'without its make up on', a movement that has alternatively been praised and criticised by the medical community, feminists and politicians for its insistence upon the primacy of the mother figure in a child's life and of the child in the mother's life" ... it is "part and parcel of the feminist movement, and is based on the premise that if a woman is to be strong, she must take responsibility for her childbearing and child-rearing functions herself rather than remain dependent upon male authorities for guidance".[137] I would add that this also goes for those of us who would like a home birth but our partner 'thinks we should listen to the doctors' — double patriarchal bubble.

Kitzinger's American 'cousin', Ina May Gaskin, is similarly impressive: this is a woman who 'gets it'. Who sees birth as a normal, natural, womanly event. The accounts in her book *Ina May's Guide to Childbirth* of births at her community, The Farm, are awesome: a wealth of maternal heritage and history which is unusual to see and empowering to read.

Gaskin is clear that we *can* see the "true capacities of the female body".[138] What is so sad, frustrating and (ultimately) pernicious, is the way in which those true capacities have been hidden from us or even warped by 'entertainment'. Carefully edited hospital births, shown for maximum dramatic effect — perfected by the likes of *One Born Every Minute* — are a very different thing from sharing positive stories of birth or gentle, natural births. *One Born* is fear-based birth programming at its very worst.[139] If only every woman had the opportunity to hear the positivity of generations of women, empowered by their own bodies, confident in their bodies and attended to by sensitive women. What a revolution that would be. Thing is, the naysayers would be there going "but The Farm was a cult!" or "Kitzinger was a fanatic!" or "Grantley Dick-Reid (author of *Childbirth Without Fear*) wanted women to be tied to the kitchen".[140] Really? Pah! The proof is in the placenta: many women have had satisfying and empowering birth experiences as a result of their work. In Kitzinger and Gaskin's case, they have helped women discover and retain a female narrative which empowers women. Pretty feminist, that.

It comes back to the issue of our bodies: women must know the truth about their bodies. In the vast majority of cases, women's bodies do what they are supposed to do; in the vast majority of cases, women will be absolutely fine and capable of the physical act of birthing; in many, they will be more than fine. They can do it. Their bodies can do it. As Gaskin says, "It is important to keep in mind that our bodies must work pretty well, or there wouldn't be so many humans on the planet."[141]

Michel Odent is quite adamant about what childbirth should be. And it's not strapped, legs akimbo to a monitor under harsh lights. A birthing woman needs to feel unobserved and safe: the opposite of the patriarchal gaze. She is reliant on the optimal cocktail of natural hormones necessary for birth to take place: oxytocin, most importantly — *the hormone of love*. Our bodies make it when we are happy, cuddling, making love, experiencing orgasm, holding hands, breastfeeding . . . and giving birth. It is the very thing on which our bodies rely in order to experience vaginal birth — when not undermined by adrenaline or usurped by synthetic syntocinon. Love. It makes the world go round, your womb contract and your perineum burn, and encourages maternal bonding behaviour after the birth. But we are minded to discount his immense experience because he had the temerity to suggest that it might not always be wise to have the father at the birth.[142] Exclude a man from the birthing room? Respect the female nature of birth? Attest to the value of women supporting women during birth? How dare he? In fact, he is a little more nuanced than that. But that doesn't sell papers.

Odent talks too about the benefits of an experienced female attendant (midwife) who sits in the corner knitting (the craft being a physiological way to reduce adrenaline — oxytocin's nemesis in early labour). It makes sense. But my god, you would think he had suggested that all women should stay home with their kids, leave their jobs and wear petticoats.

Speaking of controversy, Mary Lou Singleton and Ina May, together with Woman Centered Midwifery and others wrote an open letter in 2015 to the Midwives Alliance of North America (MANA) in which they raised concerns about the recent erasure of the word "woman" in midwifery literature, to be replaced with "pregnant person" and "birthing individual". "Women are now all but missing from the language, as if we can separate woman from mother from baby. Woman is recognized now only in relation to her baby." I quote the following extract:

The root of female oppression is derived from biology. Patriarchal systems arise out of male attempts to control female sexuality and reproduction. Female liberation from patriarchal oppression, including brutal and demeaning birth practices, cannot be achieved if we are forbidden from mentioning female biology. Women have a right to bodily autonomy and to speak about their bodies and lives without the demand that we couch this self-expression in language which suits the agenda of others who were not born female. Gender, sex and sexuality should not be conflated. Sex and sexuality are based upon biology whereas gender is a socially constructed concept. We do not give birth with our gender identity but with our biology. The document refers to the midwife's need to be knowledgeable about the 'anatomy and physiology of the birthing parent,' as if the anatomy and physiology of birth were not distinctively female ... Birth transcends and goes deeper than the Western capitalistic concept of the individual. We live in the time where the dominant narrative is of the rights of the individual.

We must be careful to examine how individualism harms healthy human society. We must fight the forces destroying the living material world and telling us that cultural distractions are more real than life itself. There is life-giving power in female biology. As midwives we protect the lives of the life-givers: women, mothers, females, and their offspring. We must not become blinded to the biological material reality that connects us. If midwives lose sight of women's biological power, women as a class lose recognition of and connection to this power. We urge MANA to reconsider the erasure of women from the language of birth.[143]

Having birthed two people from my vagina and felt somehow more connected to my female body than I had ever felt in my life, I read this letter with interest. The tenacity and immense experience of the women who signed it is clear. The letter raises the questions whether we, as women, are losing our village of wisdom and womanly experience about birthing. *Are* we starting to lose our language of birth? Are we as women losing something: a right to name ourselves, our condition or our needs? For what? For whom? Why? What are the implications? How do we feel? Do these things matter?*

Either way, we must see birth as coming from the same place as *love*, rather than fear. We need to hear positive stories. We need to hear the positive experiences of our sisters and mothers. Birth is a legacy. We owe it to our daughters to instil (from a young age, and in reproductive education) faith in their bodies. We owe it to women to respect the birthing space, the birthing journey and to respect their wishes. Birth can be a self-fulfilling prophecy. We have to start respecting the prophecy.

POSITIVE BIRTH AND
HOW DARE A WOMAN BE SO SMUG

The birth of a child, and with it, the mother, is rightly a moment of huge emotional significance. I can hardly write about this without wanting to gush about the births of my children or stopping, and looking up at the photographs on the wall of my children as brand-new, puffy, slimy little babies and thinking back to the awesome power of my body in bringing them into this world. Feeling slightly teary at how they have grown so much,

---

* Of course they do. And we have the right to say so.

and how otherworldly the moments of their welcoming have become in my mind. Finally, I can put to one side all those birth stories people insisted on telling me when I was pregnant: now I have my own truth, my own legacy for my daughter to inherit, my own battle, my own journey.

Rare, is it not, to hear a woman speak in unbridled positivity about her birth experiences? Milli Hill is the founder of the Positive Birth Movement, an organisation with free antenatal groups across the UK and beyond, and powerful social media presence. Speaking at the Feminism in London Conference 2015, Hill said that the Positive Birth Movement was "built on a very old idea, that of women talking to women". She explained that women are "coming together and taking an active role, as opposed to a passive role, in their birth choices, and sharing stories, thoughts, hopes and fears about what birth is like". She discusses the versions of femaleness and childbirth which we see in mainstream culture: birthing women are "often disempowered, helpless, managed, controlled and passive. But via the sharing of images on social media, women are able to challenge this version, and take back their right — their human right — to a birth in which they are powerful, capable, real, in control and active". When it comes to whether it is currently considered safe for women to talk, unsupervised by the medical establishment, to each other about birth, she is clear: "the answer is no — it is not safe at all — because it threatens the status quo and raises women's awareness, not just of their right to dignity and autonomy in birth, but of their right to have the kind of birth that their culture would prefer to be kept secret". Under patriarchy, women's narratives, our stories, our power, have been suppressed; no more so than in our power to birth our babies without fear.

From a personal point of view, I am quite an expert in how one is supposed *not* to speak about birth in a positive way; and how one is supposed to play down the significance of the process to our psyche, our sense of womanhood, our sense of achievement. From some awkward post-natal groups, I am well aware of how one is expected to stay silent: it is the opposite of the age-old admonition that "if you can't say something nice, don't say anything at all". Rather, it is more like "unless it was horrific and traumatic you have no right to speak".

Let me be clear, I do not blame individual women for this unspoken code. As women, we have been socialized since childhood to silence ourselves. The code around birth-speak is also a result of failures in care itself; the unacceptable rate of poor treatment in labour and birth; and a result of failure to help women reconcile their birth experiences. Through all of this runs the thread of silencing of women, the fear of the power of women to empower and inform themselves about birthing and their birthing experience.

BIRTHING WAYS

Maternal guilt can rear its head for the first time in the birthing experience. Guilt for asking for pain relief. Guilt for needing forceps. Guilt for having a caesarean section. Guilt for pooing on the baby's head. Well, I'm not a fan of guilt, as I share later in **A Mother's Mind**. It's a toxic emotion borne out of self-criticism and internalised misogyny. We women are worthy of our own compassion. Things happen in labour that are unexpected, even under the most optimal and respectful care. Whilst I am committed to women's power in birth as a demonstration of women's power and strength generally, I *cannot* subscribe to the idea that a woman who gives birth assisted with pain relief or instruments or surgery is a *lesser* woman, a *lesser* mother or a failure. It is anti-feminist and anti-women. Not my cup of tea.

The National Institute for Clinical Excellence (NICE) has updated its guidelines to reflect the safety of birthing at home in women with straightforward pregnancies.[144] It tallies with the wisdom of many midwives that the outcomes of home births can be as safe as, and possibly safer than, hospital births. When it comes to giving birth in a woman's home environment, what is the one feature of birth which is present at home but not in hospital? Our haven. Our home is where the heart is. That is (usually) our safe place. Our home. Home tends to be a female-created space, our territory. When we birth in a hospital, that is the first and fundamental thing we lose. So it goes beyond simply the idea of a medical, technological model of childbirth. It extends beyond women being reduced to 'good patients'. For me, from a feminist perspective, it goes straight to the heart of it: where does a woman's power lie? Most likely in her own home. Certainly not strapped to a hospital bed under orders, in a hospital gown, and in bright light under a strained staffing schedule that says "it's Friday and I clock off at nine".

Something which is crucial to the debate about mothers generally is this idea of the home and private sphere: and it is relevant to birthing babies.

After all, it is the breeding ground of human beings, our bodies, ourselves, and, until recently, was our birthing and dying place too. Our home, our heart. It is not insignificant, yet our culture has deemed the 'private sphere' to be less important than the 'public sphere'. Indeed, with industrialisation came the split between public/private and male/female: therein lay a central division between male/female and power/oppression. We have to be able to speak the importance of home, from birthing through to living. Our movement cannot be restricted to an idea of liberation which demands that status and importance are only to be found in public places and in paid services: a fundamental way for us to do that is to push for something which dominant strands of feminism have failed to do. Reclaiming the respect and empowerment of the 'private sphere' is at the heart of the Purplestockings Movement.

MIDWIFERY AND DOULAS

The history of midwifery is also a history of women. Midwives and female birth attendants (doulas) have a long history of supporting the birthing woman. They have seen us, witnessed us, in our times of greatest need and exposure, throughout female history. They know a few things. It is no coincidence that in the domination of birthing practices by doctors and hospitals, midwifery was made illegal in many states in the US.

In terms of female support during birth, studies also suggest that the attendance of a doula, an experienced woman (often a mother herself) during labour, can reduce the need for pain relief and for medical intervention. In other words, the very act of having a woman caring for you in labour who is *detached enough not to bring her anxieties and adrenaline to the birthing environment* can improve your birthing experience and reduce the risks of unnecessary intervention.[145] Says much for the importance of female spaces, the beneficial effects of being nurtured by women, and the need to respect a woman's wishes in labour. Yet, if you read the right (wrong) book about birth, you would think that doulas are the product of reductive, essentialist and extreme birthing practices. Again, tell that to the huge number of women who can testify to the positive effects of warm, personal birthing support. Our stories, our narratives, don't matter. Objective analysis within the framework of, say, sociological and neoconservative frameworks, know better. This is just another example of the erasure of women's voices and experiences, particularly those of us on the ground, working the family landscape.

After welcoming my daughter into the world (accompanied by the same doula who had attended my son) I told myself that if she ever becomes a mother, one of the most precious things I can think to give her for her journey into motherhood is the service of a doula at her birthing. The absence of free provision of such support (in a society which neither prizes the female experience nor values women's needs in birth) demonstrates the lack of priority given to women in society. Wouldn't it be interesting to see how the reduction in the need for pain relief and C-sections alone would pay for this universal service? Wouldn't it? What's the betting no government ever takes that step: the empowerment of women is too frightening, and their continued suffering is key to the maintenance of patriarchy. Any benefit to her must be sacrificed for the benefit of, say, shareholders or business interests. Because money, not love, makes the world go round. Or else, the services of doulas should be unwaged, just like the massive amount of work women already do.

THE UNSPOKEN HEROISM OF CHILDBIRTH

As Ina May Gaskin says, "women's bodies are not lemons"[146]; yet, the reality is that there are women who die in childbirth. These are women who have been failed by their bodies; by unsanitary hospitals; by unnecessary interventions; by illness and by unchecked complications. *Women have died giving birth to life.* Throughout human history.

Whilst an extremely powerful act, the fact is that birth is also *consumed* with vulnerability. It is a process which is not without risk to baby or mother. That is part of what makes it so heroic. Women do this. Women survive this. Those who do not are our fallen sisters. According to the World Health Organization, about 830 women die from pregnancy or childbirth-related complications around the world *every day*. By the end of this year, over 300,000 women will have died during and following pregnancy and childbirth. Almost all of these deaths occur in low-resource settings, and most could have been prevented, including with the use of caesarean section.[147] We must remember them. In the UK each November we mark with a red poppy the deaths of those (almost exclusively) men who died in war. Perhaps we need to start a purple poppy movement, to mark those women who have died bringing forth life. They are our fallen sisters, whose memory is silenced and whitewashed. Hidden under statistics. They are mothers that didn't make it through whilst giving life. There are no statues to them. No days of remembrance. No medals of honour. Why not?

If we get through the birthing experience, whatever takes place, we deserve to *own* that. We did it. We deserve nurture, support, kindness, love, compassion and reverence. Time to grieve, to adjust, to reconcile, to be welcomed with pride and gratitude as the heroines we are.

It takes courage, you know, for a woman to carry a child and give birth. The closest thing men get to it is war and violence; dare I say that therein lies the appeal of destruction under patriarchal culture? To try to feel what it is like to face death? If we cannot create, we will destroy. Extreme sports through to murdering one's fellow man on the battlefield; a zero-sum contest in the experience of mortality.

Birth, for all its wonder, is an everyday occurrence for all but the woman and family experiencing it. Each act of birth is a heroic act on the part of a woman (remember Naomi Wolf's warrior spirit?). She will have put in the hardest work of her life, her body will have performed one of the most wonderful and awesome acts of which it is capable, and she will most likely bear scars of some type or another which will stay in her body or mind for the rest of her life.

How can it be that this ability of a woman to birth her baby has been consistently sidelined throughout history? How could be it be that minor heroics, sporting achievements, political and academic success on the part of men have attracted such adulation, envy and depictions in art, literature and the screen, yet the acts of countless women birthing their children into the world, at risk of death, injury or trauma, barely register? If we find this statement odd, perhaps this is a good time for us to examine our assumptions and ideas about worth and achievement, and heroics and courage. It's about time.

HUMAN RIGHTS IN CHILDBIRTH

Childbirth is one of the most powerful (yet vulnerable) acts a woman can perform in her life. She must have the right to receive adequate and supportive information during her pregnancy to help her to prepare for giving birth. She must have the right to birth her baby in her place of choice. She must have the right to attendants who will respect her, her body and her wishes. She must have the right to respect.

Reproductive rights. Sounds so simple. And at present they tend to be confined to access to contraception and abortion. But how about a woman being subjected to a C-section against her will? This is no horror story. Yes, I love my children. I grew them in my body and birthed them. Yet all the while they were in my body, despite my hopes for their lives after birth, I was under the illusion that my body was still my own and that I would have the say in what happened to it. Naturally, the growing foetuses in my womb were much wanted and I had stopped drinking alcohol, was eating well and talking to my bumps in excited prenatal mother-fashion.

But despite my personal affection for my bumps, I still take the view that a woman is entitled to bodily autonomy and full respect for her wishes about her body. Turns out, not everyone agrees. Not least 'foetal attorneys' and certain judges and doctors, the very ones with the power to bulldoze a pregnant woman's rights and invade her body, all for the greater claim of a foetus. It turns out that 'pro-life' and advocates of 'forced C-sections' are strange bedfellows indeed. Let us remember Angela Carder's fate thirty years ago. She had cancer; she required treatment; the US Court ordered a caesarean section against her will: her right to refuse surgical birth in order, effectively, to save her own life was deemed less important than the rights of her premature foetus. The baby died within two hours. Carder died two days later. The treatment of Alessandra Pacchieri in 2013 is the modern 'forced C-section' case, reported by *The Telegraph* and then nationally and in social media.[148] Pacchieri was an Italian woman who was said to have bipolar disorder. While on a trip to the UK for work, reports suggest that she had a psychotic episode, following which she was restrained and sectioned under the Mental Health Act. Her baby was forcibly removed by C-section and then put up for adoption. These cases raise important questions, ones we are still asking despite decades of feminism: are women deserving of basic human rights, dignity and respect? Are women's bodies (and our reproductive organs and potential) justification for our mistreatment or reduction to a powerless host?

When it comes to C-sections, faith in the power of women's bodies is one thing, and admiration for the process of physiological vaginal birth is another. Yet, as a good feminist, I could never subscribe to the idea that women should be denied a C-section on request: we have good reasons for asking for one, whether from an unspoken episode of sexual assault or abuse to a traumatic delivery with our first child. We have our reasons; we should have our rights. As Milli Hill writes, "Any woman who wishes to choose caesarean should have her concerns listened to and her choice respected . . . Arguably, she shouldn't have to explain her reasons — just asking her to do so introduces the idea that it's an outsider's place to pass judgement on their worthiness. Do we really think that a woman would request a caesarean for frivolous reasons? And if her reasons sound 'trivial', might there be others she is simply unable to voice?"[149] It's a curious anomaly that there are countless women who would love to be able to give birth uninterrupted, but face intervention against their wishes, yet there are others who beg for surgical help, but are refused. Women should, of course, be fully informed of the risks of such surgery to herself and baby. However, ultimately, the woman should have the right to make the call. Control of women's bodies: it finds its way into the birthing room *and* the operating room. The fact is that women and babies across the world have died owing to failure in maternity care, including the refusal to grant a C-section when requested or to provide treatment where it should have been indicated.[150] According to Rebecca Schiller, CEO of the human rights in childbirth charity, Birthrights, "True freedom of choice and bodily autonomy is an issue for almost all pregnant women, whether they want a free birth at home without midwives present or an elective caesarean."[151] Bodily autonomy: the right to a say in our bodies remains, under patriarchy, a battleground for women.

Birth is a feminist issue, whether surgical or vaginal; whether home or hospital. The woman at the *centre* makes it so. At heart, women's rights must include mothers' rights.[152] And human rights in childbirth are crucial.[153] We are women, gestating or birthing women, but no less human beings deserving of the respect of our basic human rights. No less deserving of care and dignity. We are human beings, not incubators. We are women. In *All That Matters*, Schiller asks the fundamental question about birth and human rights: "is all that matters a healthy baby?" If this means the trouncing of the dignity and the right to bodily autonomy of a mother, including a forced C-section against her will, is this respectful of women, let alone humane? If this means the failure to consult or obtain consent for intimate bodily interference during childbirth, does that fail women? Does it render us sub-human, merely an incubator for the delivery of a foetus? These are taxing questions; they are uncomfortable. Yet they matter. They matter to women who are in a vulnerable state, in which they have, most likely, surrendered themselves to care within a model which does not place the dignity and respect of the woman as central.[154]

When women are treated as less than, as incidental to, as incompetent in making decisions about their own bodies (particularly in the context of pregnancy and birth) it speaks to our very core of our values. We can start to see that our status as mother — our power to create and birth life — can be used against us: we can be held hostage, and our rights can be suspended at will. If feminism ignores the birthing room, focusing only on the boardroom, we fail women. We have to push for greater respect for women's bodies, our beings and our births. A feminism which ignores birth is a feminism which has forgotten its heritage: remember, we were all born of our mothers.

Mother's Milk

If a multinational company developed a product that was a nutritionally balanced and delicious food, a wonder drug that both prevented and treated disease, cost almost nothing to produce, and could be delivered in quantities controlled by consumers' needs, the announcement of this find would send its shares rocketing to the top of the stock market. The scientists who developed the product would win prizes and the wealth and influence of everyone involved would increase dramatically. Women have been producing such a miraculous substance, breastmilk, since the beginning of human existence, yet they form the least wealthy and the least powerful half of humanity.

Gabrielle Palmer,
The Politics of Breastfeeding

BREASTFEEDING IN WESTERN CULTURE

The problem with the topic of breastfeeding is that it is immediately *polarising*. It is immediately *personal*. Every one of us had to be fed as a child: we were all breastfed or formula-fed, to greater or lesser degrees. We may experience a strong subconscious reaction to a discussion about infant feeding. If we are mothers, the issue becomes even *closer* to home. It can be one of the most emotionally charged areas of our lives as mothers in those early days. We can carry it with us for the rest of our lives.

Yet, one biological feature that defines us as mammals is our mammary glands. They sustained our species for tens of thousands of years. Yet, the way Western culture reacts to our breasts, you'd think that they had been invented by the porn industry in 1970. Nowadays, breasts are everywhere, cleavage on show wherever you care to look. But get a woman and child sitting down together in a restaurant to nurse and you risk waiters offering napkins and expecting the baby to hide underneath or fellow diners muttering crude analogies about other natural bodily functions. When it comes to breastfeeding, any mother who strides in her own way, in responsive mothering at the breast, knows the storm she weathers. She faces The Gaze writ large.

Our breasts are part of who we are, they are part of our bodies — and I suspect it is at the moment, *that* moment, when we realise that our breasts are for public consumption and commentary, that we start to harbour feelings that they are unwanted guests. That we are *reduced* to sexuality. Objectified by, and for, men.

However, attitudes towards breastfeeding go beyond public perceptions of modesty and sexuality. When we look at the wider picture, we can see that the basis of hostility or discomfort surrounding breastfeeding in Western culture is *control*. The issue of control goes straight to the freedom of mothers to mother their babies, to the power of the female body to nurture a child, and to the free and environmentally-friendly act of nursing a baby from the breast. It goes to the freedom nursing mothers have from commercial exploitation of paying for an artificial substitute with which to feed their babies; and to a womanly act of intimacy between mother and child.

Within a progressive maternal feminism, we *have* to challenge the prevailing feminist notion that breastfeeding is a tie and a burden, and turn it on its head: patriarchal culture has convinced us that our breasts, our milk and our arms are not powerful, are not life-sustaining and are not important. The 'nursing in public' side of the debate is the thin end of the wedge: the freedom and support to breastfeed *at all* without sabotage is the central issue.

If we are overstretched, overwhelmed and under-supported, which many mothers today are, breastfeeding *can* present difficulties. But, contrary to dominant views in feminism, we are not oppressed by prolactin* and oxytocin or our breasts and our nipples, as though they represent some kind of biological Iron Maiden.[155] Germaine Greer, in *Sex and Destiny:*

* The milk-making hormone.

The Politics of Human Fertility, writes that "in modern consumer society the attack on mother-child eroticism took its total form; breastfeeding was proscribed and the breasts reserved for the husband's fetishistic delectation. At the same time babies were segregated, put into cold beds alone and not picked up if they cried".[156] Later, in *The Whole Woman*, Greer would say that the motivation for the interference with mothers' breastfeeding their young seems to have been "a combination of jealousy of the physical intimacy between mother and child and simple revulsion".[157] Well, you know Germaine, she's usually right. In other words: there's nothing so threatening to patriarchal structure and control than a pure expression of women's physical and bodily power. It is simultaneously envied and distrusted.[158] As the Internet meme says, "I make milk. What's your superpower?" Sadly, the answer in male-dominated comic imagery would be "I get angry, turn green and break stuff". Says it all, doesn't it? #PatriarchyValuesDestructionOverCreation

At the heart of it all, objection to or criticism of breastfeeding is misogyny in action, alive and well. It demonstrates a distrust of mothers, an envy of her life-sustaining power, and an unwarranted interference with the mother-child relationship. In human history we have regularly interfered with the giving of colostrum,[159] the first milk a mother produces — and which many mothers refer to as our 'liquid gold'. We have experienced persistent undermining of a mother's relationship with her baby and her bodily power to nourish her infant. In the culture of the law of the father, there is no room for the power of the mother. And birth and breastfeeding are powerful indeed: the process reveals a physical intimacy between mother and child. That said, far from an empowering, celebratory act of womanhood, breastfeeding is often seen as a demonstration of how women need to be liberated from the bonds to their children and their biology; and of how the 'milk police' are traitors against a woman's right to delegate feeding of her baby to another, using artificial baby milk, often derived from milk of another species. As always, those women, happily doing it all, are busy nursing with no time for writing about how wonderful it is. Ah, the struggle for airtime and for our voices to be heard! Perhaps we need to invest in some purple nursing bras, too.

At heart, the breastfeeding relationship, what is commonly respected as the *mother-infant dyad*, is unlike any relationship we might experience in our lives. It can be just wonderful.

Yet, for strands of feminism, the womanly and mothering hormones of oxytocin (the hormone of love) and prolactin (the hormonal ambassador of caretaking, according to Sarah Blaffer Hrdy in *Mother Nature*[160]) are risky things. After all, women's biology is something to be hushed up out of the fear of biological essentialism, reducing women to their bodies and drives; being 'exclusionary'; or something which interferes with the 'important' stuff of career and public status. Breastfeeding is 'oppressive', sisters.[161] Apparently. Funny that — I have found it, predominantly, to be liberating, powerful, intimate and spiritual. We all have our own take.

In cases where the breastfeeding experience has been negative, upsetting, challenging or frustrating, we have to respect the woman at the centre of it all. Our experiences are important. If we valued women, we could stop, try to understand what has happened, why a woman has felt let down or unsupported, examine the cultural constraints and context in which she sought to breastfeed, and consider why she may have felt uneasy with this physical act. But feminism *doesn't do* that. Instead, blame is left at the door of breastfeeding itself or 'pressure to breastfeed', not the inadequate training for health care professionals, insidious sabotage or undermining of breastfeeding by formula companies, or lack of skilled support.

Ultimately, we are assumed to be blinded by biological oppression.[162] In *The Second Sex*, Simone de Beauvoir wrote that "even nursing affords such a woman no pleasure; on the contrary, she is apprehensive of ruining her bosom; she resents feeling her nipples cracked, the glands painful; suckling the baby hurts; the infant seems to her to be sucking out her strength, her life, her happiness. It inflicts a harsh slavery upon her and it is no longer part of her: it seems a tyrant; she feels hostile to this little stranger, this individual who menaces her flesh, her freedom, her whole ego".[163] Welcome to feminist breastfeeding bingo. Pain? Check. Tyranny? Check. Slavery? Check. Misery? Check. Body woes? Check. Hostility? Check. Bondage? Check. Really, Simone, we loved your discussion of existentialism, your description of women as Other is now legendary, and your Frenchness was just so cool. But feminists really should stop with the breastfeeding myths, it's embarrassing.

In her book, *Shattered, Modern Motherhood and the Illusion of Equality*, Rebecca Asher recognises something about modern notions and practices of 'equality'. The moment baby comes, the scales fall from our eyes. Her work is an example of a privileged, educated woman who has suffered from what Andrea Buchanan calls *Mother Shock*; a baby during career and equal relationships — she didn't see reality, nor the truth of caring for babies, coming. When it comes to breastfeeding and the maternal bond, Asher frames the "biological bond" as tightening "to the point of constriction" and breastfeeding is a "hugely restrictive obligation" which women feel compelled to do out of fear.[164] Well, I'm not sure that many women would frame the beautiful and intimate nursing relationship in that way. But I suppose we could blame the men: they're the ones who got us pregnant.

In all, our culture isolates a mother, renders her an utter novice in all matters of baby-care and fails to invest in skilled breastfeeding support and education. Breastfeeding is natural but it does not, for many mothers, come naturally. It is a learned skill, after all. In traditional societies, women would be familiar with the normal course of breastfeeding and with any difficulties, from mastitis to engorgement, which can arise, and how to deal with them. But, in our culture, we simultaneously and contradictorily regard breastfeeding as 'easy' and 'difficult'; as 'hard work' and 'not real work'; and 'important' and 'neither here nor there'.[165] Perhaps the price to pay for the ascendancy of women into the world of the 'men' is that we know how to be fathers or workers; less so, mothers. Especially breastfeeding ones.

Ultimately, breastfeeding is either an embarrassment, a side-show, or a source of oppression from those who see liberation *from* lactation as an ultimate feminist victory. *Breastfeeding Older Children*[166] adds a whole other level to the debate. Yet, breastfeeding can be something many women hold dear for the rest of their lives. As breastfeeding mothers, it can be liberating to read and hear about women's relationships with their bodies, and, in particular, their breasts. An example of this can be found in Laura Dodsworth's work, *Bare Reality*, an important step in the move towards women's ownership of their bodies and their breasts, the refusal to be reduced to an object, and the beauty and diversity in human female bodies, emotions and lived reality. Because when it comes to the use of a woman's breasts for the primary purpose for which they exist, it is nothing short of radical to see breastfeeding as a feminist issue. More and more women take to social media to support others and find support for themselves in breastfeeding their children with pride, to blog about it, and to demand that our Western societies lose the lens of 'breasts as sexual objects'. We see proud mothers and their children, captured for posterity in a most womanly and nurturing act, in a visual and physical manifestation of a bond, a relationship of love and nourishment. We see love. Motherly love. Granted, not the *only* expression of maternal love, but a most glorious one nevertheless.

There are clearly many influences[167] on women in the decisions they make about feeding their babies. The problem is that, as women, we have little confidence and faith in our bodies: patriarchal history and culture have ensured it. Capitalism and artificial feeding contribute to the loss of confidence in our body's ability to breastfeed successfully. The economic structures which separate mothers and children for long periods of time from a young age also place significant barriers before women at the very commencement of their breastfeeding journeys. Whereas some feminists see breastfeeding itself as akin to a 'patriarchal conspiracy', the patriarchal impact works the *other* way. It has successfully divorced women from the power of their bodies, undermined women's faith in their bodies, and brought about a state of affairs in which women are at greater physical risk, for example, of cancer, by reason of not breastfeeding — while giving the appearance of liberation.

Our authority in breastfeeding has been undermined consistently under patriarchal culture. In his 1748 essay "Upon Nursing and the Management of Children from their Birth to Three Years of Age", Dr William Cadogan stated: "It is with great pleasure I see at last the preservation of children become the care of men of sense . . . in my opinion this business has been too fatally left to the management of women, who cannot be supposed to have a proper knowledge to fit them for the task."[168] That's us mothers for you! Feeble idiots with no clue how to care for our babies. Truby King, Gina Ford and countless 'baby experts' and 'baby trainers' have continued this expert supervision of mothers and their milk. We would do well to remember this maxim: *Every mother is some expert's failure.* Better to be our own woman, sisters.

DOUBLE-SPEAK AND SILENCE

The terms of the popular debate centre around what is *best*, rather than what is *normal.*[169] We talk *benefits of breastfeeding* rather than the *risks of* formula feeding. In our culture, bottle feeding is normal in that it is not only commonplace but the majority experience. However, bottle feeding is not biological or physiologically normal.

As a feminist, I am aware this is all highly charged stuff. We are in forbidden territory: we may not proclaim the joys of breastfeeding, of mothering and of nurturing. We may not question the 'victory' of freeing mothers from nursing their babies at the breast. We may not seek to reframe the issue as proclaiming breastfeeding as a feminist act: our bodies are amazing and we are immensely powerful in our ability to nourish and sustain life. If we are to make real progress we must be able to claim this power. We must be able to demand support and recognition for this work, for this motherly care.

But once again we are in a minefield: our bodies. As we know. We risk courting biological determinism and restrictions on our freedom if we point too far in the direction of our bodies actually having value, of our actions actually having positive effect, and of our mothering work as being important. We definitely can't look to the prolonged intimacy of breastfeeding as being "significant for the evolution of social relationships and eventually new parts of the brain, and new attributes (especially intelligence linked to empathy) that, because we possess them, are of special interest to human beings".[170] That would be, like, chaining mothers to their children, in the interests of the future of the human race.

But come on now, we're all adults. We can think about the meaning and implications of lactation and nursing. We cannot decide that we need to liberate mothers from lactation or time with their babies, in the name of emancipation and economic freedom. We have to at least provide the room, freedom and space to women to decide whether or not they wish to lactate and use that ability to nourish their babies. And if they opt to go down the "milky way",[171] that service, that nurturing, that work, should be valued and supported practically and economically. Not just given lip service in health service brochures.

When it comes to our bodies and their power, one of the tactics of patriarchy, one of the tools of misogyny, has been to silence women. If we are silenced in our informed debate about the risks of formula feeding, we fail women. If we are unable to inform women and provide objective evidence and materials to enable them to make their decision — an informed decision — within a culture which supports the decision to breastfeed, then we fail women. Feminism doesn't even confront, as a feminist issue, the health risks to women (including increased risk of cancers) in not breastfeeding. And that's before we even consider the children. Breastfeeding, and breastfeeding support and services are a fundamentally feminist issue. It's time we acknowledged that. Yet, its neglect within the mainstream indicates that problem: it is outside the experience of women who are not or are yet to be mothers, and may bring unhappy personal experiences of women who didn't enjoy it or struggled to breastfeed.

BREASTFEEDING AND ECONOMICS

Breastfeeding and economics? What next? Sex and politics? Love and Wall Street? Well, yes, they are connected. Bear with me. Gabrielle Palmer laid down the gauntlet to the artificial baby feeding industry in *The Politics of Breastfeeding*[172] and Marilyn Waring paid short attention to the issue of nursing in *Counting For Nothing, What Men Value and What Women Are Worth.*[173] Waring is critical throughout the book (not just in relation to breastfeeding) of the fact that the international economic system "makes no distinction between creative (or life-enhancing) and destructive production and consumption. It cannot identify what is good for us".[174] And this is the thing: breastfeeding is good for us and our children; yet our economic systems place absolutely no value on what we do or the process of breastfeeding itself.[175] Breastfeeding is the ultimate demonstration of how our society freeloads on women's labour and reproductive work. Our milk feeds human babies! It grows them! It nourishes them! It keeps them alive and keeps them growing on the most perfect, optimal, normal, natural substance. Yet, despite this, we are deemed to be *doing nothing.* When it comes to nutrition, our bodies do amazing work: it's just not regarded *as work.* Perhaps that's because it's *women's* work.

In the preface to the first edition of *Milk of Human Kindness, Defending Breastfeeding from the Global Market & the AIDS Industry*, Selma James and Phoebe Jones Schellenberg address the efforts of commerce to produce breast-milk substitutes, asking "what's wrong with ours — except we don't have to buy it?"[176] And therein lies the rub. When everything has a price, our milk is not priceless but worthless. This will not do, sisters. It absolutely illustrates the way in which our caring and nourishing work for our children is devalued by our culture.

Quite simply, the issue of breastfeeding work reveals the lack of value and prestige placed on work women do when it is work that *only a woman can do.* We are feeding our baby for them to grow and thrive. What can be more important than that?

And choice? What about *choice*? In *Milk, Money and Madness, The Culture and Politics of Breastfeeding*, Naomi Baumslag and Dia Michels address the fact that an "intimate and self-affirming life experience that is responsible for the survival of our species has been reduced to 'just one feeding option'"[177] at best and "a confining form of servitude" at worst.[178] Ah, the liberation of choice, key to the modern devaluation of women and the power of women's bodies. Yet, our milk is incomparable to powder and boiling water. It contains living cells, from our human bodies. We mothers must be able to have pride in this, yet our culture devalues it or insists that we feel awkward or ashamed about it. We do not see how it is life-affirming labour. It is intrinsically human and quintessentially female. Surely, we can take pride in that? Surely, we can demand recognition for that work?

So how about we think about the economics of breastfeeding *as work*? For starters, it doesn't exist. GDP *hates* breastfeeding. A bodily process, free to mother, free to infant, nourishing, requiring no paraphernalia and providing health protection for mother and baby, is a process which takes away from money for service; money for product; money for health treatment. We could say that breastfeeding undermines the notion of economics as a measurement of value. The sale of poison, of petrol or of toxins fuels GDP: the bodily, affectionate, maternal transmission of breastmilk doesn't even register. What does this tell us? In fact, a healthy *mother-infant breastfeeding dyad* is not counted in economic statistics of product and services (unlike black market drug dealing and prostitution, say[179]). A healthy GDP steals from the mother-infant dyad, maternal and infant health and the love of a breastfeeding relationship and valorises artificial commercial feeding of infants contrary to their and their mothers' physiological and biological needs.

So the invisible hand of economics (more on this later in **A Mother's Labour**) is the enemy of the invisible *breast*. By breastfeeding our babies we are sticking two fingers up to GDP. We are saying: keep your bottles, keep your processing of cow/soy/whatever products, keep your packaging, and keep your greed for profit at my and my baby's expense. Keep your over-priced probiotics and medicines. We are refusing to comply with your warped economic valuations of productivity in matters of infant feeding — for in GDP, money makes the world go round, not loving, milky, breasts.

A MOTHER'S PRESENCE OR PUMP AND DUMP?

There is a unique link between mothering and breastfeeding. To breastfeed requires mother's *presence*: to nurture one's child at the breast requires the responsive, bodily *presence* of a mother.[180] And it is our skin, our touch, our mammalian nature which in study after study has been proven to have almost miraculous effects on the health of both infant, and mother.[181] It has informed the practice of 'kangaroo care', the wearing of fabric slings and the keeping of the baby against our chest, skin to skin, for as much as possible: our bodies are nature's incubator. Our bodies are not oppressive: they bring life and keep our babies alive. This is amazing. We deserve to celebrate this.

But this is not fully communicated to mothers. In the 'breast is best' dialogue it is the *content of the milk*, not the *complete act* of breastfeeding which is stressed. In *Confronting Postmaternal Thinking, Feminism Memory and Care*, Julie Stephens addresses the age of economic participation and maternal separation from babies. She discusses how nowhere is the "materiality of embodied motherhood" more evident than in breastfeeding and how Western culture is "struggling with the issues of care and human vulnerability" and questions whether we have "moved into a new phase of commodification where mothers' breasts have become harnessed to industrial processes".[182] I would say that Stephens has hit the nail on the head. She refers to an article in *The New Yorker* by Jill Lepore, entitled "Baby Food", in which she illustrates how "professional women are increasingly referring to themselves as 'lactating mothers' not 'breastfeeding mothers'" and how the "motorized breast pump industry is booming, with the nation beginning to look like 'a giant human dairy farm'".[183] Plato would have approved. More on that in later chapters.*

Anne Manne recounts something interesting in *Motherhood: How Should We Care for Our Children?* about *touch*. She discusses how some women, particularly those with careers, fear that they might 'lose touch' with their clients or business. They pump their milk for feeding by a mother substitute. In doing so, they are physically and absolutely losing the touch between their babies and themselves; yet, there is a feeling, in our economic existence, that it is somehow *worse* to 'lose touch' with their business.[184] They are fulfilling their role as workers, despite having a young baby. Freed from nursing at the breast and freed to continue their worthwhile pursuits. These priorities are telling: they are part of the culture which does not just normalise but *expects* and *compels* separation between mothers and their babies. And nowhere is the reality of separation clearer than in the breastfeeding relationship. This is a feminist issue: we don't all want to sacrifice this part of maternal care.

Stephens is clear that the only way to address the failure to respect the

* Spoiler alert: the father of democracy was not a fan of the mother-child breastfeeding dyad. Votes for women, leave your prolactin at the door.

rights of nursing mothers would be "to reinvigorate the strands of feminism that are attuned to gender difference"[185] and on this, I would agree. Gender neutrality as a basis of policy neglects our bodies, our breasts and our milk. Women can believe themselves to be genderless, but this can come crashing down the moment that female bodily biology and lactation come knocking at the door.

Indeed, part of the reason why women do not breastfeed for long may not just relate to women's state of knowledge and understanding about the normal course of breastfeeding. We, actually, quite simply, are not accustomed in the West to seeing uninhibited, free, on demand and beautiful breastfeeding in all places of life. It is a learned, womanly art,[186] yet many new mothers are completely unfamiliar and, in some ways, uncomfortable with it. Many of us haven't even held a baby before we hold our own! No, in twenty-first century Western culture, women know that they must separate from their babies to 'get back to work'. Because mothering, as breastfeeding, is 'not work', is a tie and does not 'fit' in our modern existence. Better not to overinvest; better not to bond through breastfeeding beyond a nominal period of time, if at all.

In *Misconceptions*, Naomi Wolf calls it "unconscionable for our culture to insist that women 'choose' to leave their suckling babies abruptly at home in order simply to be available for paid work".[187] I agree: such a cultural demand is blind or hostile to the fact that breastfeeding *is* work. It neglects the emotional hardship on mother and baby of premature separation. The UK used to boast of twelve-months' maternity leave: twelve whole months, protected for the mother to care for her baby. It has now become parental leave: the mother may lose touch with her baby earlier than she would like. In the US, there is *no* maternal leave at all. Women are frequently compelled to leave their tiny babies, against their wishes, to 'get back to work'. Paid work looms large, despite the very real task and important work of breastfeeding our babies. Technology, as always under capitalism, has swooped in to replace the wet nurses of old with pumps, sterilisers and bottles. And the worst thing? It has been touted as *liberation*.

In her article, "The Work of Mothering",[188] Naomi Stadlen, author of beautiful unsentimental yet moving books about mothering, *What Mothers Do, Especially When It Looks Like Nothing* and *How Mothers Love and How Relationships Are Born*, discusses the popular view that a mother "will be wasting her intelligence and education, to say nothing of losing promotion opportunities while others overtake her up the career ladder. Doesn't it make sense, they conclude, for a mother to express her milk and then the task of feeding the baby can be shared?" She writes that:

> There is a good answer to this apparently reasonable question . . . [to quote La Leche League] 'Mothering through breastfeeding is the most natural and effective way of understanding and satisfying the needs of the baby.' In this single sentence, we are reminded that breastfeeding is not the whole of what a mother is doing. It's the more visible part. Less visible is the rest of mothering, which includes 'understanding . . . the needs of the baby'. Understanding requires sensitivity and intelligence. It's a responsible task and gives the mother an active role.

In her work and her books, Stadlen is one of the few writers who describes this activity, this responsive care, in discussions about mothers.[189] It is important that feminism regain an understanding of what breastfeeding entails and what responsive mothering of babies involves, instead of pushing for a commodified feeding industry under which women are 'freed' from their babies and their breasts.

This work of breastfeeding, this activity, this responsive care, is all but absent in feminist and political discussions about mothers and care, yet a mother is sustaining her baby from her *very body*. It is one of the most productive and human activities there is! Yet we fail to see it as work. The language we use, the standards to which we apply ourselves are predicated on non-lactating ideal workers[190] under patriarchal capitalism. No wonder so many of us experience a huge culture shock when we become mothers. We have become oddities.

What is particularly interesting is the emotional process of motherhood — the transformative effect of becoming a mother. How is this affected by economic policies? If a woman is compelled to return to work at twelve months, six months, twelve weeks, how does that affect her psychologically and emotionally in seeking to breastfeed her child? After all, she knows that the day will come soon enough when she will not be present for her child to nurse at the breast. She may feel uneasy about how to cope with breastfeeding on returning to work: it is often a worry which women express in seeking breastfeeding support. Despite laws on expressing milk at work, there are still barriers placed before women in seeking to access adequate facilities in which to pump.

So, women are encouraged to leave their babies. It's that simple. Gabrielle Palmer calls it the "culture of separation".[191] We are not expected to stay with them, to provide maternal care, to nurture them at the breast. Not in the twenty-first century neoliberal West. And the gift to these women? The breast pump. Millions are sold each year. The global breast pump market, which was valued at US$1.1bn in 2013, will rise to US$2.6bn by 2020.[192] Hey, there's money in human milk after all, so long as the mother isn't the one delivering it directly to her baby in the midst of human intimacy at the breast.

Let us be clear, pumps are not 'bad'. Many women rely on expressing in circumstances where they cannot be with their baby — perhaps the baby is in neonatal care or being tube fed, or bottle fed for whatever reason. It is valuable and important that women who have to be separated from their baby, or whose baby is unable to latch at the breast, are able to express milk and feed it to their baby. Pumps have a place for women who are seeking to re-lactate or build up their supply after, for example, supplementation with formula. This is no criticism of breast pumps.

What I am saying is that expressing milk to facilitate separation for "economic participation" is a modern phenomenon. Mother is reduced to a commodity-producing vessel.[193] Her product, measurable and contained. In bottles like that of her mammalian cousin. Now there is no *lactational* excuse for a mother to insist on being *close* or *present* with her baby: the pump is the key to her freedom, she is expected to exercise that freedom in *one* way. While some women talk of "pumping and dumping" milk after a night out, one might say we are expected to pump the breast and dump the child.

BREASTFEEDING IN THE AGE OF EQUALITY

When it comes to our buzz word — equality — nursing a child at the breast is a conundrum. It is a job only a mother can do. Breastfeeding is a reminder that females alone have the equipment for the natural nourishment of human babies. We are faced with the fact that we are mammals, and that babies, from an evolutionary perspective, expect to receive mother's milk. One might say that baby's need for mother is intense in the early years, as basic as the child's need for food.[194] And, my goodness, doesn't that make us all so very uncomfortable. It is almost verboten to say it.

Recent UK Shared Parental Leave (the uptake of which has been *extremely* low) rules have thrown up issues which directly affect the World Health

Organization's breastfeeding guidance that babies are exclusively breastfed for six months and then alongside complementary foods until the age of two. And beyond if mutually desired.[195]

Thing is, somebody missed the memo. Only the mother has the equipment to breastfeed, in routine circumstances.[196] Our ability to breastfeed is, simply, inconvenient in the age of equality. In countries such as the US, where paid maternity leave doesn't exist, let alone leave for the father, things are even *worse*. In *The Price of Motherhood, Why the Most Important Job is Still the Least Valued*, Ann Crittenden describes the health guidance on breastfeeding, a full year, at least, as a "sick joke in a country that entitles new mothers to no paid leave at all".[197]

Promotion of Shared Parental Leave before the baby is six months old manifestly undermines the UK's own NHS guidance — that babies should be nurtured exclusively at the breast during that time. It does so because it encourages mothers to go back to work from two weeks postpartum and leave the baby with the father or partner. It is a direct contradiction in message, let alone ignoring the fact that mothers need time to recover from childbirth and to bond with the baby that lived inside her for nine months. That is before you even consider the pervasive images of bottles on the Government website promoting the idea of the equality utopia, as though its own NHS guidance (and the compelling public health basis for it) does not exist. When it comes to breastfeeding, perhaps it is more appropriate to say that it doesn't know its nose from its nipple.

It all comes down to this: for formula companies to make a profit, and the state to reap the tax, mothers need to fail to breastfeed their babies or believe that there is no value in breastfeeding. Policymakers know it but do nothing to improve mothers' chances of success. I doubt we will find that printed on a tin of milk powder anytime soon.

In the age of equality, breastfeeding is at risk of being seen as a tie, rather than a bond, a hindrance rather than a womanly art of value for mother and child. That said, in our culture, the word 'womanly' sounds like an oddity nowadays. Only now heard in conjunction with 'hips' or 'demeanour'. Much in the same way that breasts are seen as sexual, rather than as for the nourishment of children, I suppose.

For many women, breastfeeding starts out as a way to feed their babies — and over time it becomes a way to respond to their needs for food, comfort, love, sleep, warmth, closeness and reassurance. This is one of the reasons I baulk at the idea that I am somehow replaceable in the early years (indeed at all), that I am substitutable by another relative or a stranger and that I am 'equal' only in terms of a capitalist game and economic agenda written by non-lactating males. Having breastfed my children is something I will cherish until the day I die. Not something I say very often, but, actually, as a human experience of bonding, nourishment and sensuality between two people who love each other, it is right up there with the best.

It might not contribute to GDP, as would the purchase of commercial substitutes and paraphernalia. It might be invisible economically and politically. Yet, the milk I provided for my children for over five years was precious, and the normal and natural food produced by my body to meet their changing needs. The warmth of my arms in its delivery was priceless.

There is *value* in that.

Part 2

A MOTHER'S MIND

Maternal Thinking,
Maternal Feeling

*Women's and mother's voices have been silenced,
their thinking distorted and sentimentalized.
Hence it will take sustained political and
intellectual effort before maternal thinking is
truly heard.*

**Sara Ruddick, *Maternal Thinking,
Toward a Politics of Peace***

THE GIFT AND GRAFT OF BEING A MOTHER

I am sick and tired of reading about the *burden* of motherhood. How mothers are tired, haggard and covered in sick; or how they are juggling it all; or how they resemble ghostly wraiths of their former self-fulfilled beings. Really. It's a sad, forlorn state, is Motherland. And the passport to happiness? Getting *away* from our babies. We have gone from the suburban happy housewife sublime to the ragged, miserable ridiculous. Yes, things can be extremely challenging sometimes. Ask any parent. There's a code, an unspoken knowing. We all know what it can be like, don't we? We *do* have to shed the "mask of motherhood"[198] which perpetuates the fiction that it is sparkly and joyous and easy and calm and collected and compliant and fun and more, at all times — we have to accept the fact that our experiences of motherhood are as diverse as us women ourselves, and that it has some fairly difficult moments, exhaustion and struggle. Feminism *had* to challenge the dominant stereotype that *all* women *should* and *do* find child-rearing fulfilling and fairy-light-fantastic. At all, or at all times.

Yet, it is important to see the positive side in motherhood as well as the strain — particularly where the pressure comes from circumstances outside our control and borne of the devaluation of mother-work, the isolation of mothers, class or race struggle, lack of support structures, and the financial pressures we are under. There are some mighty miserable memoirs out there which seem to be taken as gospel for all women by those eager to liberate women from motherhood. They are not seeing the bigger picture — they can see a grey canvas in the gallery, but they neglect to see the vibrant colour outside the windows.

In *Maternal Desire, On Children, Love and the Inner Life*, Daphne de Marneffe discusses how the desire of many women to mother their children has become taboo. Many women, including mothers who are committed to their work outside the home, still harbour deep attachment to their children. Yet, as de Marneffe observes,[199] what remains dogged with "contention and strangely unspeakable, is the territory of caring for children — of spending one's hours and days with them". I can relate to her feeling that "feminism has not always helped me. How many times I have encountered a feminist book filled with innovative ideas for changed gender relations, the acceptance of whose argument requires just one small price: that I relinquish my attachment to spending time caring for my children."[200] The price of caring for our children is, for many women, a high one. At some point, a woman, a mother, *has* to be entitled to write: "I am doing something I love" without guilt or fear. To say that what we are doing is valuable and important work. To demand change to reflect the importance of that work and to allow women to do it without penalty or oppression.

Earlier in the book, I referred to the fact that in *The Feminine Mystique*, Betty Friedan did not speak for all women: not all mothers were isolated in suburban homes. Many were — and are — grafting in jobs they hated and in which they were given no respect or status. Many women, at that time and now, would have leapt at the chance to have greater family time and to 'live the life' of a housewife. It would have beaten hard work in their jobs and hard work on the second shift, on top. Others were happy, actually, at home with their children — as millions are, right now (if only we could tackle the financial burdens, though, and the devaluation by society for what we do. We need a movement, or something. Something purple. Heard of anything like that, recently?) Many women had — and have — thriving communities and a feeling of sisterhood — whether relatives who live nearby or close friends, in which we can recreate the village that mothers need. We can choose to resist the pressure to become the agent of capitalist consumption and gleaming windows.

It was bell hooks who spoke about the home being a site of resistance in reference to working-class women of colour, and this is something I relate to when it comes to mothering. There is something subversive about refusing to play the game, although we are truly penalised for sticking to our guns. So on the one hand, we are penalised financially for caring — we are economically penalised — but I sense that, on the other hand, we are penalised for daring to proclaim something 'higher' than being a slave to the wage.[201] The only people, after all, who are permitted to *enjoy* their *lives* are those who enjoy their *jobs*. Or the super-rich. Not those who are busy nurturing their children. Because it's not a real job if we're doing it for our own. It only matters if we're being paid to do it for *other people's*. It demonstrates the "cultural contradictions of care".[202]

So, sisters, we have to be able to talk about care, nurture and *love* ... about the gift of mothering and about the way we feel about being a mother, caring for our children, and framing our lives in the way which is right for us. We can do this in conversation, in writing, and in campaigning. We don't need to be sentimental; we need to be realistic. But to be realistic does not mean we must reduce what we do to misery or oppression.

Because the problem is that in Western culture, you would think that being a mother was the equivalent of being a leper, and a miserable one at that, desperate to get away from the demanding brats and back into the *real* world where one can shed her skin and bathe in the light of *productive* human existence. Mothers-who-mother represent a curiosity, an anachronism and an embarrassment. Except on that one day of the year when the capitalist machine churns out pink flowery tat for people to buy on Mother's Day. *Then* we can bask in the light of sentimentality. But when it's over, it's back to a world where we don't even get to *mention* the word 'mother': it's *'parent'*, remember.

Well, this simply isn't good enough. We short-change and near-on *betray* our children if we give the impression that mothering is a drudge and that they are a burden or a hindrance to better things. Can we bear to ask how it might feel for someone to know that his mother couldn't stand being with him while he was a child? Aside from that, we undermine and devalue *ourselves* if we start to believe that we need to do something 'more productive' than sitting on the sofa nursing a baby, stroking her skin, while the housework waits; spending time with our preschoolers; walking our children home from school; reading with them before eating dinner that we have prepared, or just following our child's lead and sitting on the floor with them to play. The work of mothering, the invisible and practically indescribable work[203] is important and it is valuable. Somebody has to do it. Is it something which must, like everything else in the twenty-first century, be 'outsourced'? To other women? For low pay? The irony. The commercialisation of our lives; the commodification of experience. Just let us live. Just let us be. Just let us love.

Yes, I know that we used to send children up chimneys, out into the fields, and underneath the looms, back in the good old days when we had a dozen kids all of whom were assets who contributed to the income of the family. The concept of childhood, it could be argued, might well be a relatively new invention: as Alison Wolf puts it in *The XX Factor, How the Rise of Working Women Has Created a Far Less Equal World*,[204] children have become "both priceless and economically useless". But we are surely beyond the economic exploitation of our children nowadays, in the twenty-first century, when they are fewer per family and recognised for being immature people who need love and care just as much as food and water, to survive and thrive. If we, the human race, want to continue then it is *somebody's* job to reproduce and care for the children. After all they are not a lifestyle choice up there with cultivating bonsai trees. As Suzanne Braun Levine notes, "other people's children" will grow up to "be the ones writing our laws, curing our diseases, and making us laugh — or not".[205] Our children, other people's children, society's children, matter. If we don't believe all that, perhaps we should just say so and admit that children are an inconvenience, a distraction, a liability; and anyone who wants to care for them a lazy, worthless economic 'non-participant' breeder. But I don't suppose we will see many politicians coming out with *that* in the run up to elections. They talk about family-friendly politics all the while separating families from the cradle to the grave.

In my case, I cannot, and refuse, to see my children as a burden or a drain. I chose to bring them into this world. I take responsibility for raising them and instilling in them good values and healthy self-esteem. I suspect most parents feel the same way, whether in employment or not. Most of us *know* that a mother is an important person in a child's life. That is not to say that a loving father is not important — or a beloved grandparent, or a sibling, or a kindly neighbour, or a fabulous teacher or a best friend, or whoever.[206]

However, we have to ask why mothers need to bend over backwards to spare the feelings of others about the relative pecking order in our social relationships. Every family differs, of course. For some, the father is the primary carer, or a grandparent or step parent. In other families, the family is headed by a lone parent (predominantly the mother). We can, surely, respect the individual family and the individual woman and recognise that one size does not fit all; and that each parent can bring something of their own to their children.

In this context, it is an insult to women who have created life, sustained life, nurtured life and devoted loving time and energy to their children to suggest that they are undeserving of some kind of close bond with their children. It is a nonsense to say that they must surrender some kind of 'privilege' of motherhood.[207] Our relationships are varied, our emotional attachment to each person diverse, and our love for them different. Between people we love, we can feel differently for each; not less, but different.

Our children know this. They *know*. And so do we, deep down. Our mothers brought us life. It is important, it is special. We *have* to be able to *say* that. We cannot ignore it. Indeed, think about adult reunions with birth mothers you might have seen on television or read about. It forces us to reflect on what drives a grown man desperately to seek out the woman who carried him in her womb, yet was separated from him by adoption within minutes of his birth. Why does this woman matter to him? Is it just the 'myth' of the importance of mothers, our socialisation to place primacy on our mothers? Or genes? Actually, despite my love for intellectual debate, sometimes, who cares about the whys and wherefores in this situation? Sometimes it is what it is. Mothers *matter*.

Given this precious relationship, why then, is the literature so full of complaint about the intensity of our children's needs and the 'conflict' between our children's needs and our own? Why are women in the twenty-first century encouraged to disavow this most wonderful, primal and intense relationship as just *another* hurdle or hiccup in our economic or professional existence? Why is our love and attachment to our children deemed inconvenient? Dare we believe in maternal instinct?

Because 'maternal instinct' is legendary, isn't it? Some women are just 'natural mothers'. To some women, having a child comes 'naturally'. And because women are possessors of said instinct, it makes sense that they should be the ones to care for children, despite their possible individual preference not to. Even Darwin seemed to think that "woman seems to differ from man in her great tenderness and less selfishness. Woman owing to her maternal instincts, displays these qualities toward her infants in an eminent degree; therefore it is likely that she would often extend them toward her fellow-creatures".[208] Given that maternal instinct is so natural, women don't need to be supported socially and practically when they have children but they can just be left to get on with it in their nuclear bubbles. It's natural after all! Ducks to water.*

However, and this may surprise you, I resist the idea of an essential, inevitable, magical, maternal instinct. In its simplest message, it suggests that women simply *know* how to care for babies, *know* how to breastfeed, and *know* how to raise young children. For starters, it lets the men off the hook in terms of them putting in the effort to bond with and care for children. From a patriarchal perspective, notions of maternal instinct and essential feminine qualities have been used to oppress mothers into a corset-like gender role of nurture, home and exclusion from public life and education. Further, they deny the *supreme* amount of effort, patience, strength and courage which goes into caring for babies and young children, and the learning on the job, in small steps. Most fundamentally, it underestimates the degree to which we learn through example, culture and childhood experiences about *how to mother*. It also tends to neglect the hormonal input of oxytocin and prolactin, the love- and milk-making hormones, and the importance of touch. In a modern context, it forgets to mention that in a social construct which isolates women so that they are alone, unsupported and without maternal guidance of her own, a new mother is like a ship out at sea, with no lighthouse to guide her. No wonder many of us find ourselves on the rocks sometimes. We put in some serious graft, as mothers, don't we?

As Simone de Beauvoir said in *The Second Sex*, "One is not born, but rather, becomes, a woman".[209] We are female, we grow into adults. Into *women* (with a few stereotypes thrown in to measure up to). And so it is with mothers: we are not born as mothers. We learn, step by step, feed by feed, cry by cry, tantrum by tantrum, cuddle by cuddle, kiss by kiss, assisted by hormones, helped by our apprenticeships within our society, from seeing mothering happen and helping out to boot, and supported by a society which recognises the work which goes into mothering. We become *mothers* in a life-long process of care, bonding and affection.

---

* All of this is what is known in the industry as 'irony'. You might spot other examples throughout the book.

Yet, just as traditional pre-agricultural matriarchal societies might, if seeing some complicated technology of our time, assume it was seeing magic, so for generations women have shown effortless maternal instinct. But this 'magic' masks complicated genetic, psychological, social and biological processes which enable a mother to tune in, respond and grow to love her child. We can call it instinct. Perhaps we can remember that it is behaviour, it is effort, and it is the building of a relationship. It is love. So, perhaps we could agree that maternal 'instinct' can be cultivated; yet it can be *sabotaged* by cultural and social conditions which simply do not allow it to blossom. And our culture in the twenty-first century is hell-bent on separating mother and child, interrupting the early development of the mother-child bond, and ensuring that everything — from breast, to arms, to care — is substitutable and expected to be put out to tender in the market.

In her introduction to *Your Children Will Raise You, The Joys, Challenges and Life Lessons of Motherhood*, Eden Steinberg refers to the fact that motherhood is something beyond the "gauzy romantic ideals", but is, rather, a "profound opportunity for self-understanding, personal growth, and real wisdom".[210] Amen to that. In my case, my children have 'raised me'. They have taught me patience, shown unbending and fervent unconditional love, helped me to slow down and live in the moment, and guided me in acceptance and letting go. Many mothers have their own feelings of transformation and growth, don't they? We might be shy and not talk about it. Yet, perhaps, we *should* start to talk about it. We have the right. When asked about the transition to motherhood in an extensive survey by World Movement of Mothers Europe, the "overwhelming messages from mothers responding to this question are: 1. The birth of the first child constitutes a major and irreversible change in focus, priorities, and life-course. One never again sees life as one did before becoming a mother. 2. The responsibility of motherhood is supremely challenging, highly demanding, and worth everything it costs. 3. Because of this change, mothers develop a distinct perspective and should be allowed to speak for themselves. 4. Non-mothers should not presume to speak for mothers."[211] I would say that many of us can relate to these responses, can't we? They are certainly issues which crop up again and again in campaigning circles and on social media, and in conversation with friends and family. Our voices need not just to be heard, but to be respected. We need to push for this to happen, collectively and with real determination. No polite requests, no humble apologies.

When it comes to our Western culture and neoliberal patriarchal society, we are encouraged to think of 'self' and 'individualism' as representing the core aims of our existence — a happy, fulfilled 'self' and an independent 'individual' identity. Yet, as Anne Manne remarks, motherhood, "more than perhaps any other human project ... requires interdependence and reliance on others, the capacity to decentre from self and the surmounting of narcissism".[212] The problem is that our entire culture is based on the 'self': sufficiency; fulfilment; control; determination; identification; and, even, 'selfies'. It is rather counter-cultural to speak about 'putting others first'. Especially children (woman's ball and chain, if some schools of feminism, and discriminatory workplaces, are to be believed).

The fact is that we often must address and confront issues from our past and childhood, in order to be present, to be healthy and to be calm in raising our own children, and so the gift of a child in our life can also be a gift for emotional growth and improved emotional intelligence. Saying that, on return to the workplace, one might be forgiven for thinking that a mother becomes simply a blob of irrational, baby-obsessed snot: this is a rude awakening to a woman who thought she had experienced a form of enlightenment on becoming a mother. But instead is patronised: "get back in your box, silly woman, and leave your human development at the door". All that matters is *economic* development.

When it comes to our 'self', you might find the words of Toni Morrison, like I did, to be quite moving. I could relate to what she was conveying when she said: "There was something so valuable about what happened when one became a mother. For me it was the most liberating thing that ever happened to me ... Somehow all of the baggage that I had accumulated as a person about what was valuable just fell away. I could not only be me — whatever that was — but somebody actually needed me to be that."[213] I identified with this. The *transformation* of motherhood, the emerging of myself — one that I liked, one that my children love — is not something I will downplay. We have the right to share our experiences and to insist that our perspective is heard. After all, if we don't, the dominant narrative becomes "all mothers are miserable and in chains to their children".

In some ways, becoming a mother has been the making of me, yet it had to 'break' me, first. It required the breaking of a previous habit of control; the breaking of a selfishness which had always been able to run free; and the dismantling of a persona which had been built around me, but which never did quite fit. The transformation has been a form of freedom; the love of my children a gift and a thanks for me being who they have needed. For me, like Morrison and many mothers, becoming a mother has been *liberating*.

The reality is that we frequently change and are reborn. Throughout our lives. With each milestone, with each tragedy, with each loss and with each love. Becoming a mother is one of the most significant, life-changing events we will experience. Some view our past 'selves' as having died[214] after we become mothers — the lives we lead, the emotions, the experience taking us from *that* to *this*; from *her* to *me*. We might mourn the life we lived once, with the freedom, the irresponsibility, the equivalent experiences of ourselves and our partner, and the headspace free from the heartspace of our children. Yet, as mothers, we have been reborn and have been bestowed the gift of a child in our life. So I like the word '*mothermorphosis*' coined by Caroline Poser.[215] Because in becoming a mother, *we* emerge from the chrysalis, as our child emerges from our body; we are transformed from maiden to mother; we spread our wings as mothers during those early days, weeks, months and years. We *fly* into motherly love. And we can never go back.

MATERNAL THINKING

In *Maternal Thinking*, Sara Ruddick recognised that child-rearing requires consideration and commitment to peace-making, flexibility and patience. Far from becoming morons who don't use their brains, mothers can and do some serious intellectual work, often without realising it. More than this, our society rarely recognises this intellectual, emotional and personal work we do. I suppose that is because to do so would require us all actually having to *value* it. Peace and love are seen as hippie ideals, optional extras, not core ingredients of healthy, well-adjusted human beings.

When we stop to think about the mental work we do as mothers, we might relate to Ruddick's view that our societies, our family and our cultures require that we raise children with the following in mind: preservation, growth and social acceptability.[216] We need to keep our children safe and healthy; we need to ensure that they reach their potential in their growth and development; and we must instil the social rules for acceptability in our culture. Our mothering work requires *thinking*.[217] It is not brain-dead stuff; it is important work. Ha! I knew it! After all, my brain hasn't stopped whirring since the moment I saw two blue lines on a bit of plastic. The Internet is *not* awash with questions ranging from "how do I help my toddler with her tantrums?" or "how can I support my teenager in his anxieties about school?" That's a lie. It's *saturated* with them. And who is asking, pondering and fretting? Predominantly mothers.

As I see it, mothering is the work of nurture and care *when performed by a mother.* 'Parenting' might well be the fashionable term but it has a terrible habit of denying the *reality* that it is often mothers doing most of it, including the emotional work of family care. Something which leaps from the pages of Ruddick's work, though, is the 'maternal' as potentially owned and done by anyone, father included. The raising of children does require sensitivity and care; and I know that there are many fathers, my husband included, who are not only capable but excellent at that. But that, to my mind, is adequately described by 'nurturing' or 'child-rearing'*. 'Mothering' is something which should surely relate to the mother — are we allowed *nothing* to call our own? Virginia wanted a room — I'd settle for the right for my work as a mother to be recognised and respected *as* mothering in the meantime.

One of the feminist objections to the term 'mothering' has been, I suppose, the inherently gendered nature of the term and its suggestion that care and nurture can only be performed by mothers — *and* that it comes naturally to them. Neither of which are true. It's the old 'essentialism' chestnut. I prefer to see it from the other side: to erase the term 'mothering' and the work of care when done by a mother — mothering — we let women down. It is a form of care. It is a shade of nurture. It is a flavour of love.

So, I mother my children. I do not parent them. I am their mother, I show them love — mother love. When I care for and nurture them, I am *mothering* them. When my husband shows them love, cares for them and nurtures them, it is his own brand of nurture. It is *not* mothering.[218] To describe my work and that of other mothers as 'mothering' is not oppressive to men or others: we are respecting and valuing mothers. Perhaps therein lies the attempt to remove the very word.

In her article "The Work of Mothering", Naomi Stadlen reflects on how the word 'mothering' has become less popular[219]:

---

* The alternative, 'fathering', is rather awkward as it does rather suggest the act of copulation and fertilisation, doesn't it?

Most literature today is about 'parenting'. Many partners love being parents and are willing to take part in the care of their babies. 'Parenting' describes the equality to which many couples aspire. New mothers are often asked: 'So when are you going back to work?' People expect baby-care to be shared and that mothers will get back to their paid work promptly. Does this mean that mothering isn't as special as people used to think? Is the word obsolete?

Well, not in my book. However, I would answer that it is in danger of becoming so. Not only the word 'mothering' but 'mother' and 'woman' to boot. Yet, we have to ask, what are we *afraid* of? Why are some of us concerned to toe a line which puts women and mothers *behind* it? Why are we becoming hesitant to speak the name 'mother' or to use the phrase 'mothering'? I suppose it has its roots in the fact that we have been oppressed because we are mothers; that we fear causing offence in our identity culture; that we have been disadvantaged in the workplace because we are mothers; and that we are seen as worthless (in places) because we are mothers. This will not do, sisters. We must be able to speak our name; we must be able to celebrate our work and demand that it be valued.

Stadlen points to the way in which mothers are "persuaded to see their babies as impediments to their careers. The interests of mothers and babies appear to conflict." But she is clear that "instead of a battle of conflicting needs, the two together can achieve shared satisfaction and harmony".[220] Our relationships with our babies and our children need not be a source of tension. We can be proud of mothering our children and we can be proud of our transformation as mothers, through mothering our children.

Perhaps this is one of the reasons why many mothers feel slighted when faced with the suggestion that what we do is not only not valuable but inconsequential. We are expected to shrug off the permanent rewiring of our souls, our hearts, our brains and our capacity for deep love and 'get back to normal' and 'get back to work'. It took me a number of years to understand why I felt these messages to be painful: the dismissing of my experience; the diminishing of the significance of the changes I had undergone; the trivialising of the importance of what I was doing as a nurturing, present, responsive mother. The idea that a mother who has had time out of the workforce to care for her children has something to bring back — new skills, honed skills or new assets in experience, outlook and success — has been patently crushed in our culture. Psychologist Aric Sigman calls this negativity 'motherism'.[221] As mothers, we must insist on our 'human capital' retaining our actual humanity.

And our brain? It's not mush, actually.

Whether it is intense preoccupation in those early years or tiredness, or susceptibility to continual interruption[222] by little ones with intense, immediate needs, I don't know. But the prevailing view is most certainly that having a baby renders a mother a befuddled mess of suspect intelligence and sense. The dreaded 'baby brain'. If we are not dumb, we are Betty Friedan's depressed housewife heroines.[223] Apparently. I suppose that line is part of the patriarchal script which requires disdain for mothers. We can face flippant remarks from partners, family, public and colleagues alike. Strands of feminism have barely concealed their view that becoming a mother is a risky strategy for our mental capabilities, risking the withering of our brains in the pot of our progeny. The fact is that despite the line that women's human capital and brainpower wilts when she cares for her young children, "the only things that atrophy when a woman has children are her income and her leisure".[224]

The fact is that there are positive impacts of childbearing on a woman's mental faculties but we are socialised to think our brains have turned to Play Doh. In *The Mommy Brain, How Motherhood Makes Us Smarter*, Katherine Ellison braved the issue and decided that it was time that the condescending and insulting stereotype of the mother with the baby brain is demolished. In many ways, it makes sense that motherhood should either be neutral in its effects on mothers' mental agility or a force for improvement: if we became half-wits, our children would have died and the human race would never have survived.[225] If we had no sense of our children's needs or how to improve our conditions to ensure their survival, we would have remained in the Stone Age. The work of women, after all has been a driving force in the advancement of the human race: creation and preservation of life, creativity and initiative, and the drive for quality over quantity.

Problem is, we risk being accused of suggesting that women without children are intellectually moribund. "You're making out being a mother is the height of achievement for a woman" (I'm not) or "you're suggesting that you're better than me because you're a mother" (I'm not). I'm just sick of the outright lie or subtle implication that my brain has disappeared along with my wedding-day waistline.

Ellison addresses five attributes of a baby-boosted brain — the "nearly uncharted wilderness" of mothers' brains — namely enhanced: perception, efficiency, resilience, motivation, and emotional intelligence.[226] No "vomit on hair" or "I put washing up liquid on my cornflakes" in sight. What an exquisite relief. No need for guilt, sisters: parade your grey matter with pride. While we may temporarily experience a fog, through rewiring of the brain and fluctuating hormones, the fact is that, honey, the kids didn't shrink your brain. To echo Ellison: you have a transformed and even improved Maternal Brain.[227] Indeed, in 2015, research by neuroscientist Craig Kinsley and research scientist Kelly Lambert, of the University of Richmond in Virginia, concluded that having a baby expands the brain; and improves strategic thinking, judgement and empathy; and that pregnancy, far from being some minor event, represents a "developmental period every bit as important as sexual differentiation or puberty".[228] What is astounding is how mothers in Western culture today are effectively told that they should continue as 'normal' and 'get back to work'. Then, when we realise how differently we feel and how 'out of place' we are, we risk thinking there is something wrong with us. And we don't even allow ourselves to own the transformation.

So, becoming a mother does not a pathetic, befuddled incompetent make: something the workplace has to face up to and stop penalising mothers or refusing to hire them. Society should honour and value the skills that mothers can bring. It is something we, as mothers, should take some pride in. We are allowed to, you know.

UPS AND DOWNS

Mothering our children can be a real joy. Seeing their faces, hearing their belly laughs, touching their skin, feeling their love. I cannot compare it with anything else. I feel the responsibility, yes. I experience worry and frustration, frequently. The popular phrase "this too shall pass" has helped on many an occasion. Because mothering is not easy. It is not valued by wider society. However, being with my young children beats, hands-down, anything else I have ever done. My relationships with my children have grown over time and have blossomed through our shared journey and experience. We have a close relationship. I love their company. I know this time will be up all too soon. I am *allowed* to feel that way. And by vocalising it I am not criticising anyone else who has chosen a different path. Or whose experience of motherhood has been markedly different.

To acknowledge the joys of motherhood is not to deny that women face discrimination and oppression by reason of the fact that they are mothers, whether in the workplace or within society. Or that it can be hard sometimes. Frequently, even. Absolutely overwhelming at times — particularly if isolated within nuclear families, with little support. Or that we *all* need to 'refill our cup' — including getting enough rest so that we can care for our children and not burn out. Some women find this in the form of other work outside of mothering, and that is their right for which they are entitled to respect and support. This might well come during the baby and toddler stage or later — every mother has her own path, her own journey and her own personal *calibration* for care. In my case, my aptitude for cuddles and reading with my children, say, is way higher than my inclination for mopping the floor, cleaning the dishes or working outside the home. When it comes to housework, it is my humble view that, actually, the early months of child-rearing should require the mother do very little housekeeping *at all*. After all, she's already got a day and night job of caring for a baby. #BadHousewife

Yet, announcing that the 'housework can wait' can also gain us a gleaming badge of 'bad mother' — so we often get on with it and exhaust ourselves or feel guilty about living in a 'pigsty' or for our partner picking up the domestic slack after his leisurely, respectable, back-to-normal, sojourn at the office for eight hours. We feel guilty and incompetent. Despite the fact we've done a twenty-four hour day since the birth of our beloved baby, requiring care, nurture, milk, responsiveness and love. We need to rest and fill that cup: not fill our spare half hour with filling the washing machine. But that's too much to ask, even within feminism. It seems that mothering, rather than housework or gender norms which still insist on sexual division of domestic responsibility, gets the blame. Time we demanded that the conditions of our work as mothers reflect our and our children's needs, rather than the work being delegated in the name of equality or liberation.

However, the reality is that some women really do find being a mother to be an unhappy experience and for care-work to be overwhelming and burdensome. They are elated at the idea of a fulfilling career, rather than spending their time with their babies/toddlers/preschoolers. That is their right. I do not adhere to gender rules that stipulate that all women should find caring for children worthwhile, easy or enjoyable. Combine different personalities with our culture which sees many mothers coming to motherhood after enjoying a feeling of limitless autonomy and, oh, how that can clash with the limitless needs and vulnerability of babies. The unforgiving social and financial structures in which we mother can be the icing on the cake. Adrienne Rich nailed it in her sentiment that motherhood as an *institution under patriarchy* is very different from mothering in the *experience*.[229] It can be difficult, as things stand. When I discuss in later chapters about care, something which we must bear in mind is that *mothers* need to be cared for too and we need the capacity to care for *ourselves*.

What? You thought mothering was always, in my estimation, all roses and tweeting doves and "the hills are alive with the sound of music?". Sadly not. In many ways, it is because of my experience (enjoying mothering, loving my children and *wanting* to be with them; but also struggling at times; and simultaneously seeing society's contempt for what mothers do, "especially when it looks like nothing"[230]) that I feel so strongly that Western culture has got it wrong. There is such little investment and support in society and the *work* of child-rearing that it is no wonder some women can't wait to get back to the office, where they get to receive respect, have some peace, and supportive adult company. The common phrase "getting back to normal" forgets that each new child, each new stage of our lives, brings a *new* normal.

Our emotional needs *as mothers* can often be deemed unimportant. Despite the need to be available to our children, we can be at the mercy of the level of nurture *we* receive ourselves while mothering our own children. This relates just as much to women who are compelled to 'go back to work'. The burdens can be intolerable. Yet, liberal feminism places mothers' emotional health at the bottom of the pile: economic participation is the cure-all; childcare the red herring; liberation from housewifery the aim. What differences could be made in the lives of millions of mother-women if we reprioritised care, supported mothers, valued family life and structured public services around our lives, not just around employment? But as always, this is probably too much to ask. After all, the stakes are only the emotional health of women, the needs of children and the happiness of a significant proportion of our population.

Mothers are expected (and it is pressure we place on ourselves just as much as that from the outside) to be calm, collected and loving at all times. There is no room, in the myths of motherhood,[231] for human fallibility. We feel guilty for wanting some time to ourselves; and we find that even when we get it, depending on the age of the child, all we can do is think about them, anyway. The bonds of love, eh?[232] We have to remember that, as with anything in life, there are ups and downs; there are many moods of motherhood.[233]

The problem is that these very natural feelings have been taken in some quarters to herald a departure from the oh-so-antiquated idea of motherly love. From motherly love, which necessarily includes tenderness, joy, patience, sacrifice (in one way or another) and responsiveness, to the idea of maternal *ambivalence*.[234] I was interested to read more about this psychoanalytic-bastardised idea of what love feels like for mothers. Because I accept, of course, that there are many women who find mothering difficult, challenging and unfulfilling — out of emotional difficulties connected to their own childhood and experience of care and nurture, their mental and physical health, their current situation or relationship or financial pressures. I also recognise that as mothers, we are people too. Many of us surely have needs for something outside of give-give-give. We all need respite and support. If we don't get it, of course we get frustrated and resent the situation we are in. We can burn out. Especially if we are doing this alone, isolated and without help, practical assistance and encouragement.

But it seems that there should surely be a section in the library entitled "Knackered, Miserable and Happier at the Office", filled with books such as *A Life's Work* by Rachel Cusk and *Why Have Kids?* by Jessica Valenti. Some of the books I have read, quite frankly, almost hit the bin the moment I finished them. Often, the word 'mother' is only really used in conjunction with 'burden', 'loathe' and 'tired'. Indeed, Joan K. Peters, in *When Mothers Work, Loving Our Children Without Sacrificing Ourselves*, goes so far as to claim that "ambivalence — not serenity — is the fundamental maternal experience" — the "truth in mothering".[235] Strange, I would have said it was 'fallible humanity': it includes negativity, it embraces our flaws, yet it does not pit us against our children in such a crude way as this 'ambivalence theory' tends to do.

Such books, written by women who have from all appearances take little pleasure in mothering (after all, it isn't for everyone), and who yearned, like Betty Friedan's educated, middle-class, privileged, white, Happy Housewife Heroines, for 'something more' have been published, read and celebrated as though they represent the truth for *all* women and *all* mothers. This discourse has informed the debate, the political priorities and feminist discussion. Thing is, those of us who really enjoy mothering are just getting on with it. Mostly happily, but increasingly penalised and marginalised for it.

In our culture, we are celebrated as mothers if we announce that we couldn't possibly bear to be stuck in with the kids all day, need to be a 'good role model' and want to get back to the workplace to 'lean in'.[236] We are encouraged to delegate the care to some other, low-paid, woman, probably (just 'outsource'; how hard can it be? Ignore the women we are outsourcing *to*). We are told it is normal *and expected* to hate one's children as part of our love. But the thing is, if we lean in *too* much, we may well topple. And nobody will be there to catch us. We have gone through the mothermorphosis and we need some support: is the answer to down tools and 'get back to work', wherein lies our salvation and our wings?

ANTENATAL AND POSTNATAL DEPRESSION

It's huge, folks. If it hasn't happened to you, it's happening around you. It might have happened to your mother, your sister, your neighbour or friends. And chances are, you didn't — or don't — have a clue. According to the Maternal Mental Health Alliance, more than one in ten women develop a mental illness during pregnancy or within the first year after having a baby. In the UK, mental illness in pregnant and postnatal women often goes unrecognised, undiagnosed and untreated.[237]

In the light of the prevalence of emotional upset in postpartum mothers, feminism has to say that women's rights have to include our *wellbeing*. And that *has* to include the wellbeing of mothers. It has to start to discuss the *social* conditions in which we mother, and the lack of support we receive for that work. Because mental illness, depression and anxiety do not simply happen in a vacuum. We must look to the human being at the centre of it all, listen to her, support her, and care for her. Yet, this is often missed.

What happens instead is that politics and feminism talk about employment rights, parental leave, media representation, and boardroom participation; all the while our sisters are depressed and we don't mention it (whether they are at 'home' or in employment) and we fail to push for a more humane society which values mothers, care, children and emotional needs.

One thing that leaps out in the research about depression in postpartum mothers is that women are often 'pathologised'. A perfectly understandable and human reaction to a significant life-changing event, hormonal fluctuation, exhaustion and lack of support can be reduced to an illness. Something *wrong* with us. 'Postnatal depression' might be convenient shorthand, but it potentially disguises the reality of what new mothers are experiencing. The phrase 'mental health' neglects 'emotional health' or 'emotional wellbeing', tending to stigmatise or bring a clinical element to a woman's emotional experience. This is not to say that some women do not experience significant chemical imbalances and postpartum psychosis, or that some women do not benefit from medication. Lives have been saved and women helped greatly by appropriate medical intervention.

However, the biomedical understanding of the causes of depression is only a partial representation of a much bigger picture.[238] Indeed, psychologist Richard Bentall wrote in 2016 about how television programming about mental health often reduces mental health to a purely physical "something wrong with you" rather than a human "what has happened to you?" approach.[239] We can risk neglecting the social and environmental factors at play in mental health; and nowhere is this more apparent than in the case of antenatal and postnatal depression. Add to this the socio-economic conditions in which we may well be struggling. Stir in the politics which dictate the amount of food on our table, the resources our family has access to, the heating of our homes. Sprinkle in the social isolation or lack of practical support and we may be facing immense — and entirely understandable — strain.[240] But instead hormones take the blame. The fact that we are depleted, deprived and devalued doesn't feature very high on the list of political priorities.[241]

We discuss a mother's hormones, personal inadequacies, appetite and physical state; yet we could serve women *better* by acknowledging what is *actually* involved in the task of being a new mother.[242] We need to acknowledge the reality, accommodate the mother's needs and *support* her. What a difference this would make. The social causes of depression are rarely mentioned, yet we could play the game of postpartum depression bingo. We can call out experiences from isolation to lack of support. The fact is that, in this game, mothers rarely win. Really, if we didn't string mothers up, we wouldn't then have to try to find ways to cut them down. As Mia Scotland, author of *Why Perinatal Depression Matters*, notes, we effectively torture new mothers and then wonder why they get mentally ill.[243] Motherhood is extremely important work; yet we are left to get on with it without being cared for ourselves.

At times, I have referred to the 'split' between private/public domains. This marginalises women and minimises the importance of the home and the value of the work done in raising our families. The reality of this work and these experiences, including the energy we put into them, are practically denied. The result? When we struggle, or are exhausted, or in desperate need of help *in that work*, we are branded 'ill' or we berate ourselves for 'failing'. Nowhere is this public/private domain more oppressive than when society devalues the work of postpartum mothers, isolates them in nuclear families without a support structure, impoverishes them in time, money and status, and (in the US) expects them to get on with business as usual from as early as two weeks postpartum. They are expected to be *leaning* in,[244] not *lying* in. This is no victory for women. How on earth has this happened?

If we valued mothers and their work, we could insist that women are adequately supported in their own home while they are caring for their baby. What radical stuff!

We could explore basic or carer's incomes so that a mother could choose to buy in mothers' help to fill the gap that post-industrialisation and neoliberal social structures have left in the lives of our communities, or her family could afford for her partner to take part-time work to support her practically. We could invest in social centres in every neighbourhood with comfortable furniture and kitchens to encourage and support communal cooking of meals — from breakfast through to dinner. We would stock our centres with toys, books and music. This was probably the rationale for 'children's centres' in the UK under the Labour governments, until the Conservatives took aim at the 'soft stuff' and cut funding. We could encourage women (ourselves included) — to live more 'communally'.

It is this communal living issue which has often been raised by feminism but under a different banner, namely, let's all raise each other's kids and let mothers be free of bonds to their children. That is *not* what I am talking about. I'm not talking about children being divested of a close relationship with their own parents — or having a harem of mothers to choose from. I'm invoking the communal, sisterly, supportive, accepting, kind and loving circles of a group of like-minded mothers. How that is a *haven*. One of the features of the twice-monthly breastfeeding support groups which I facilitate and which I believe is extremely precious is the fact that they take place in mothers' *homes*. We bring food. We make tea. We help each other, in more ways than one. We feel, for two hours, that we have a village. And we *thrive* in it.

When it comes to care of children, we could encourage mothers to find 'alloparents' or 'allomothers' to support them *in their mothering*. This would ideally mean seeing to a toddler while mum is nursing the baby; this could involve playing with the children while mum prepares the dinner;

this might mean gentle arms to hold a sleeping baby, while mum has a shower, or a nap, or has a haircut. This practice has a long history in human 'childcare'. Allomothers are usually women, often related or otherwise known intimately, trusted to care lovingly and responsively for the child, with whom the child has had ample time to bond and grow familiar.[245] They tended to be picked from sisters, aunts, grandmothers, close friends and neighbours. Many of whom are, inconveniently, now at 'work'. I am talking about fundamental change to socio-economic structures so that fathers are not effectively 'absent', as the breadwinner/dependant or dual-income nuclear family often requires. We, as mothers, can be cared for during our postpartum experience. We can demand that this is honoured by our society and workplaces. Problem is, our culture takes the view that family is 'important'; just not when *women* need it.

In *Love's Labor*, Eva Feder Kittay is clear that "just as we have required care to survive and thrive, so we need to provide conditions that allow others — including those who do the work of caring — to receive the care *they* need to survive and thrive".[246] Bingo, sisters! All this time. All this time, we forgot that mothers need to be cared for too. Wouldn't that make a difference to mothers? Wouldn't that simple, humane step alleviate many of the strains that many new mothers face in their new, often alien, role as nurturer of fragile, defenceless, needy human babies? The mother-shock we met in **Mother's Milk** needs to be absorbed by more than the mother herself. If the impact isn't shared, is it any wonder many women feel shattered?

As things are, something always has to give. The problem is not motherhood; it is isolation — or, to quote Adrienne Rich, "the solitary confinement of full-time motherhood",[247] devaluation and economic marginalisation. The problem is not parental leave; it is the lack of *family* leave. The issue is not childcare (although it has its place), it is lack of *support* and lack of any financial alternative. The question is not full female employment, it is the lack of recognition that mothers are already working when they are caring for their children. The solution is not compelled employment to justify a wage, but the fact that care-work is unremunerated so that mothers face *financial strain* through receiving *no income* when they care for their children.

Where there *is* support and recognition of the needs of women and mothers, the *rates* of postnatal depression are far lower.[248] Where the fourth trimester is respected, women are nurtured so that *they* can nurture their baby. We can criticise social assumptions that it should be women who do care-work. I would agree with that; the more men we get caring, perhaps the more it would be raised in esteem (the ultimate stamp of approval under patriarchy). However, this does not detract from the place that *mothers* have in the lives and development, security and health, of their infants who, until birth, lived inside them and who regard their mothers as their whole world.

The postpartum period is not, either, simply a matter of baby-care: dry, clinical, notions of practical tasks without any recognition of the fact that we are building a relationship, teaching a child about life, love, interaction and trust. Mothers may well breastfeed given the opportunity and support. Biology isn't a cruel master. Rather, it's the social conditions in which we live our biological bodies with our lactating breasts, which tend to go against us. The postpartum period is important for a woman's physical and emotional recovery from birth and for getting to know this brand new human being. It is extremely important. Our bodies have performed an amazing task and we have been through the mill. We are entitled to *rest*. As much as a father has had to deal with the transition to the idea of parenting, he has not delivered a human being through his vagina or abdomen or experienced the significant emotional and hormonal upheaval which comes with giving birth.

As a feminist, I view this issue through the lens of 'what matters to women?' What is important for women? What can we do to make the lives of women better? What can we do to make the lives of *mothers* better? How can we shape our Western selfish, isolated, capitalist, exploitative, neoliberal, uncaring, unsupportive, anti-social culture into one which values care, carers, mothers, families and children and communities? Because if we answer that question, we will, most likely, reach a conclusion which will make *everyone's* lives better. Under patriarchy, we have come to segregate our women from wider society, unless they play by the rules and leave the mother role at the door. The public sphere is still the world of men; and it will remain so unless we (feminists included) think more creatively about how we can support mothers on the ground. And if one more person says 'childcare' I will scream.

LOVE'S LABOUR

So are we, at some point, going to accept that motherly love is important to our children and to ourselves? And are we going to accept that some children need that love's *expression* in *person* and in *action* more frequently and intensely than others? Babies, young children and those with special needs, particularly. Because the squeamishness about the importance of loving care and nurture seems to run so deep through feminist thought and equality politics that we are in danger of worshipping individualism as though it is a virtue.

Love is a feeling, but it is also a verb. If we are separated from our children except for, say, thirty hours waking time a week (consisting of twenty-four hours at a weekend and a smattering of time in the working week) we have a manifestly restricted window in which to shower our children with responsive care and love-in-action. We can be forced into long-distance relationships with the people with whom we are not just developing relationships but who are immature, growing, vulnerable and dependent. Young people. People who are in great need of love, support and guidance.

In *Why Love Matters*, Sue Gerhardt, a psychoanalyst, is adamant that a baby's earliest relationship is incredibly important. It can shape our nervous systems. The development of the brain can affect future emotional wellbeing. There are many respected studies and theories about attachment and the importance of responsive care, from Bowlby through to Sears. However, because of their implications for the basis of neoliberal patriarchy, they are deemed controversial and subjected to deconstruction to see if we can dissect mother care and love and find a heart still beating. However, there are many of us who would say that the receipt of responsive care should be a child's birth-right. If we believe it doesn't matter, what does it say about our view of humanity?

Many parents, and I am one of them, prefer to see our children as being worthy of love, care and responsive nurture. They are fragile at birth, they are immature in their brain development, and they are physically dependent for many months in comparison with other mammals. They need to be cared for. We were all babies. We all *needed* that care. We have a duty to care for our young. That fact is not a patriarchal conspiracy: it is a necessary part of our humanity.

The gatekeepers don't want to hear the hard truth: children have needs for responsive care and are wired to desire it from their parents. Yet, in our economic system's keenness to separate mother and child, particularly in the US where maternity leave is beyond abysmal, we forget these needs. The question is, are we neglecting the emotional needs of many mothers and all children for the provision and receipt of loving care? Do we really want to say that it doesn't matter? Are we willing to take that risk?

Germaine Greer commented in *The Whole Woman* that "the experience of falling desperately in love with one's baby is by no means universal but it is an occupational hazard for any woman giving birth".[249] We are rendered, in some ways, hostage to our love for our children. The pull to mothering, for those of us who have experienced it, can be less a decision we make consciously, but something which consumes us, guides us and surprises us. We had no conception of the attachment we would feel. Who knew? Who knew we would love our children the way we do. We become like workers without the right to withdraw our labour: at the mercy of a society that freeloads on that love, that labour and that mother-work. But it's the system that has to change; not our love. To quote Naomi Wolf in *Misconceptions*, "Women's willingness to sacrifice themselves for the good of their children is something that our society — from individuals to institutions — relies upon. It is useful leverage in pressuring women of all classes into giving in, in different ways, to unequal deals, negotiated hesitantly from the place of weakness that is one's concern for one's child."[250]

It is this unfairness, this inequality in bargaining power and respect, to gain fair recognition and value of our work as mothers which lies at the heart of the struggles of women under patriarchal culture. We love our children. We care. We have a weak spot which is undeniably exploited by a society which fails to fulfil its duty to the reproducers of the human race.

Janna Malamud Smith's *A Potent Spell* (echoing Euripides' description of motherhood as "possessing a potent spell") explores this vulnerability of a primal drive to protect and care for her child with whom she has built an attachment.[251] We work, and are expected to work, for love, not money. This is one of the reasons mother-women who have taken time out of the workforce to raise their families are at risk of poverty in old age and lower wages on return to the workforce. But it needn't be this way. We needn't penalise a mother (or any carer) for doing care-work. But we *do*. Why do we think that *is*?

Could it be time to invest in love and start making demands? We need to channel John Lennon and talk about love and peace. *Imagine* it. Can we, as Western nations, step back and see what is rotten in our ways of life, in our refusal to value family time and family life and our neglect and penalising of one of the most basic of human needs? Love.

THE SILENT FEMALE SCREAM

In *The Feminine Mystique*, Betty Friedan described the plight of those desperate housewives as the "problem with no name".[252] American women of a certain class were being told that their role was to seek fulfilment as wives and mothers, that they could "desire no greater destiny than to glory in their own femininity", and were subjected to 'expert' instruction on everything from breastfeeding (mostly sabotaging) to "making marriage more exciting".[253] They lived within a culture in which women were told what to do. They were hostage to society's expectation and decree that they enjoy housewifery and servitude to husband, children and the kitchen sink.[254]

However, the fact is that women now live in the capitalist mystique — no happier, more exhausted and with just as little choice as our foremothers to order their working lives as they wish. And a large part of that is due to the fact that, to echo Katrine Marçal in *Who Cooked Adam Smith's Dinner?*, we simply added mother and stirred. There was little structural change; no economic revaluation; and workplace rules still predicated on breadwinner/ dependant models. Our emotional needs remain neglected.

Rosjke Hasseldine, a psychotherapist and writer in the US, is clear that women's emotional needs are not being met and that women in the US are "not doing very well". Like me, Rosjke takes the view that there should be no societal *expectation* that a woman *must* be responsible for childcare, or that women must conform to what *society* expects of them. In conversations, we discussed the need for women to be respected in what they want to do. In all, she is clear that women's needs are not being met. Rosjke advocates that women feel compassion for themselves and their mothers, but, crucially, recognises that the women's movement must recognise that sexism, inequality and invisibility impact how women feel about themselves. The housewives of Friedan were screaming a silent scream. Who can blame them? But women are still screaming.[255] Rosjke is clear that women must "learn how to believe that as a woman you have the right to be heard, valued and respected, and to know that anything less is just not okay".[256]

When it comes to mothers, Rosjke makes it plain that "no one is taking care of mum" and that women are frantically treading water. Too true. What she repeatedly hears is "that we want to feel loved, cherished, valued and known".[257] These needs are crucial; yet Western culture sees them as surplus to requirements. An added 'extra' or 'buy one get one free' in 'dog eat dog' capitalism. For all the talk nowadays of equality, of boardroom participation, closing of the pay gap, and of parental leave, the needs of mothers are still neglected. We may want those things but it is not all. We need to have the space and freedom to actually live our lives, for our needs to be met, and to be valued. We must be able to arrange our lives in the way which suits us, sharing care, apportioning care at different stages, re-entering careers, prioritising care. Our inner world and our emotional needs are neglected in our modern Western culture. And it is harming women's wellbeing. Feminism has to be able to identify that.

It is the fat-free, zero calorie, cardboard tasting existence which we are led to believe will 'do', within a patriarchal, capitalist, neoliberal society that is a real problem. We face the *exploitation* of our desire to mother combined with the simultaneous and contradictory *denial* of many women's desire *to* mother. We end up financially at risk. Disadvantaged in the workplace. No public support for the *work* of mothering. No value placed on the care we perform for our families when we mother our children. There's something of a pattern going on here. Something's got to give. The least we can do, socially, is to invest in mothers and children. Support the work of mothering, reduce workplace penalties for mothers who do want to re-enter the workplace at a time of their choice, and cut them some flaming slack.

In the age of professional mobility, we move to the city. We move to where the money is and where the jobs are. My mother lives some distance away; a source of regret when I had children of my own. When patriarchal nuclear family structure isolates women away from female family, away from community and into forced employment away from their children and their loved ones, we have to stop at some point and ask, 'where's the love?' We risk swallowing the message that a woman needs to be an island — just like no man is. As bell hooks writes in *All About Love*, "Capitalism and patriarchy together, as structures of domination, have worked overtime to undermine and destroy this larger unit of extended kin … Globally, enlightened, healthy parenting is best realised within the context of community and extended family networks."[258] This is not to say that partnership, intimacy and privacy are not desirable or possessed of positive points. I'm not engaging in a critique of the family as some 'bourgeois' construct. I'm criticising the economic and workplace structures which isolate women from wider community, family and their partners.

When everything we do is geared around paid employment, our worth is placed in the number of chips we bring home, and our self-esteem is predicated on measured assessment of performance, what happens to our sense of community, society, family and love? When we are geographically and socially isolated, cloaked in individualism, what happens to our community, our village? Arlie Hochschild talks about how home can become work and work can become home,[259] and doesn't it feel like that sometimes? This disconnection must surely affect our mental health, our sense of belonging and society — to feel cared for and to care for others, to have time for care and time to rest. To live.

A CIRCLE OF MOTHERS

Growing up, I remember the derogatory phrase 'mothers' meetings', to signify trivial conversations over the garden fence or over cups of tea between mothers of young children. These meetings would have been seen as less important than the Union Meetings or the Boardroom Meetings or the Parliamentary Committee Meetings. This view still persists today. Yet, it is important for a woman to maintain a sense of support and sisterhood with her fellow mothers. This is something which helps to make the experience of mothering fulfilling and enriching; not simply our development as a mother, but growing socially and in friendship with other women who, like us, are growing into motherhood. However, this is something which the compulsion to engage in employment outside the home interrupts. Particularly early on.

In her book *What Mothers Do, Especially When It Looks Like Nothing*, Naomi Stadlen talks about circles of mothers and how the support and information exchanged within them, without division or rivalry, is incredibly important for mothers. She is clear that mothers who come to meetings have a need to be *heard*. We don't need *advice*, though we may seek information. But mostly, we need a hearing and we need compassion.[260] And that boils down to allowing a mother to speak. To use her voice to vocalise the difficulties she might be having, to bemoan the lack of sleep, or whatever it might be. Or simply to share her pride in what she is doing or her surprise at a new development. Mothers need to be heard.

In the supportive company of women, we receive a boost in our oxytocin, the love hormone, which studies show can be a protective factor for people under stress. We *need* the company of women. We *benefit* from the company of women. That is why we retreat to the company of trusted friends and have a cry. Sadly, often the thing we let go of when under stress, and under patriarchal social norms, is the very thing which would help us: the nurturing company of other women.

What is striking about new motherhood in Western culture is that we are suddenly thrown into the practical world — not to say the emotional world — of baby-care. As I mentioned earlier in the book, we have no real apprenticeship for mothering; we do not have the language to describe the acts of mothers in comforting, the ability to be interruptible at.any.time,[261] or the state of being a mother doing the mothering. We lack the village — we lack the circle — unless we seek out a substitute village for ourselves. Many women talk of the moment when they realise they have found their 'tribe' — and although at times this might reflect a common outlook or practice in mothering, it goes deeper than that. It reflects the absence of something we need as women and as mothers: a supportive and loving circle of mothers in which we can take our place. Okay, some women raised in traditional societies may well comment that overbearing matriarchs or unsolicited involvement or counsel can be undermining or a cause of tension. We are human beings, after all, not perfect. However, arguably, the more we mother in community, the better for us.

When it comes to our feelings about our new place as mothers, in my case, the notion that what I was doing was not seen as valuable or important gnawed at my self-esteem, and it is within that context that I came to value Naomi Stadlen's books. They helped me to realise the work I was doing as a mother, in each little step, each dance, each interaction, each kiss and nurse and cuddle *was something*. And something of value, at that. We need to *hear* that, as mothers in the twenty-first century. Because we live in an echo chamber where care is not valued and mothering is seen as an indulgence or torment, depending on one's point of view. It's deafening.

And so, in the right setting, with like minds, we can enjoy the music of mothering, together. We can be reminded about that, we can support each other and we can hear each other. The company of women and the company of mothers is a vital and necessary resistance to the onslaught of the market, the economic and the impersonal.

That's right: we need the company of women. For solidarity, for activism, for social justice (as well as coffee and cake). Perhaps this is another reason why patriarchy has distrusted and belittled mothers' meetings, women's groups, and safe spaces for women: they hold massive potential for empowerment and collective strength. And we can't have that, can we?

The fact is that motherhood can bring out the protector, the fighter and the agitator, and working with groups of women who campaign for mothers can be enriching and energising.[262] It is a great opportunity to hear from other mothers about their experiences in feeling politically neglected, or socially looked down upon, or criticised for 'not going back to work' when they feel — they *know* — that what they are doing as mothers is important and valuable work. We must not be afraid of using our voices, of speaking up and demanding change. The moment we label it politics we might think we have no place: but think of it as real life. You have the right to stand up for your life and the quality of life of your family. *Your personal is political.* The powers that be just don't want you to remember this.

A Mother's Place is in the Wrong

Gentlemen, mom is a jerk.

Philip 'Misogyny Incarnate' Wylie,
Generation of Vipers

MOTHER-BLAME

Before we examine the "mother-blame game",[263] it should be said that there are children who have been mistreated by their mothers. Most people would agree that functioning ovaries, a womb and a vagina do not guarantee that a woman is going to be able to raise well-adjusted, healthy children: just as the begetters in the male class boast a considerable number of its own undesirables.

But that's not what I'm talking about. I am talking about our culture's readiness to label a woman a 'bad mother'. Quick as a flash. *Bad mother.* The ultimate mark of shame.

And one with powerful currency. The way in which mothers are viewed in psychoanalysis, psychology, self-help, media and social and economic policy is poor indeed. When it comes to the bookshelves, just take a read of *My Mother/My Self* by Nancy Friday or *When You and Your Mother Can't Be Friends* by Victoria Secunda and try to greet your mother without hissing "bitch!" or crying yourself to sleep for having the misfortune of having a witch/smothering idiot/detached moron (delete as appropriate) for a mother.* You see, mothers are to blame for everything. *Everything.* And if you're really lucky, you might become one!

Single mother? Bad mother. Old mother? Bad mother. Young mother?

---

* Don't worry Mum, I'm not talking about you.

Bad mother. 'Stay at home mum'? Bad mother. Disabled mother? Bad mother. Career woman? Bad Mother. In prison? Bad mother. Addiction problems? Bad mother. Depressed? Bad mother. Vibrant social life away from the children? Bad mother. And the children? Hoodlum? Mother was depressed. Autism? Mother consumed a glass of wine in pregnancy. Addiction? Mother was detached in infancy. Married to a violent man? Mother failed to protect you from a violent father. Fear of commitment? Mother didn't love you enough. Desperate for love, and clingy? Mother loved you too much. Angry? Mother didn't attend to your every emotional need. Got a problem? Blame mother, show your wounds, and collect your patriarchal misogynistic matraphobic prize.[264] As Paula Caplan discusses, the frequent, informal assessment by both "real and armchair psychologists" is "if you really want to know why this child is a mess, just look at its mother!"[265]

So, the fundamental issue that women face when they become mothers is how to navigate this minefield and how to diffuse the bomb of blame. One of the advantages of women being 'in the workplace' means that the old objections of miserable, frustrated housewives is less potent; however, this is usurped by a mother being blamed for being absent. No matter what a mother does, she is at fault. Our culture is littered with examples of the bad mother. We find her in books, television and movies (*Psycho* Norman Bates' mum was a prime example), we refer to her in our language and metaphors ("he needs to cut those apron strings") and we experience it for real in our relationships with our own mothers (a relationship with the potential for the most "painful estrangement", to quote Adrienne Rich[266]). So, when it comes to work which is supportive of women and eager to find ways to accommodate women's reality, Caplan's *Don't Blame Mother* beats some professed 'feminist' work hands-down.

That said, it is a fallacy to believe that a mother does *not* have an influence in health and emotional development of her children. There were good reasons for Bowlby's attachment research and conclusions; neglect and maternal separation are not the founts of healthy emotional development in young children, yet just how far his research is accepted to be transferable to children in 'good enough' care is controversial and by no means universally accepted. Whatever the case, in Caplan's book the image is conjured of Mother's place as Murphy in *One Flew over the Cuckoo's Nest*: sit too close to your child and you are smothering and intrusive; sit too far away and you are cold, narcissistic and distant.[267] The asylum which is Western culture will never believe mothers are not to blame, and will continue to keep her imprisoned in guilt despite her attempts to show she is 'good enough'. The fear is, at what point will we have to surrender to the lobotomy at the hands of the patriarchy? And who is wielding the scalpel?

It is one of the inherent contradictions[268] though, that although a mother is to blame, she is *also* to be idealized and revered as "The Angel in the House",[269] or the natural, warm, caring, nurturing, perfect mother of sentimentalised mythology. In Shari L. Thurer's *The Myths of Motherhood, How Culture Reinvents the Good Mother*, she shares how "our cultural idealization of mothers" means that we will inevitably criticise them for having faults.[270] Yup, my children will be shocked to find out I'm a mean cow sometimes and not just the source of milk. Mothers, as important as they are, do not have a magic wand, nor does the fact of their having had a whole human being pass through their vagina make them into a pinnacle of virtue. It hardly needs to be said.

However, the contradiction between "women's inferior status and their special power as mothers"[271] is a fundamentally feminist issue which rarely receives attention: why should we tolerate our children witnessing the most important person in their world, receive such little respect, value and support in society? How does that make a mother, and her children, feel?[272] How many adults hang onto the 'idealized mother image'[273] and feel sadness that mother cannot love and protect them or be everything they need her to be? When we, too, become mothers, we turn that idealized image on to ourselves. And we never measure up, either. It needn't be so hard[274]: we can push for social, cultural, economic and political change to finally value and accommodate the real work mothers do and accept mothers themselves as the multifaceted human beings they are. Remember that old lament: mothers are people too. We must not tolerate being society's paradoxical scapegoat sat on a pedestal.

Mothers, the majority of whom are decent people, must be forgiven their weaknesses, must receive compassion for their failings and foibles, and seen as human beings who have their own lives, their own emotional needs and their own fears and dreams; and as women who have, ultimately, had to survive in a patriarchal society. Crucially, it is important to recognise that daughters who harbour resentments against their mothers[275] would benefit from seeing the mother-blame culture for what it is, and see how far it permeates personal relationships, social relationships, popular discussion and debate, social policy, media and entertainment and feminist works.

After all, every feminist is a daughter and carries her own axe to grind. Perhaps one of the fundamental weak spots in feminism is our keenness to 'do it differently' to our mothers — we don't wear their flares or their aprons, and we won't wear their feminism, either.[276] Moreover, our view of older generations must inevitably be clouded by our resentments or pride in our mothers, depending on where on the spectrum we fall. Matraphobia relates to the fear of "becoming one's mother": a sentiment nobody puts on a Mothers' Day card but must have spilt from the lips of many women in private.

However, when it comes to mother-blame, surely we can look to *other* factors in our lives and in the lives of our mothers which have influenced our misery, worries, fears, and flaws? Patriarchy and its socio-economic structures run through our experiences like a river. As Rosjke Hasseldine advocates, women would benefit from mapping their mother's story, to humanise her and to understand her. Does it always have to be mother? Or could it be the pressures she was under; the poverty she was kept in; the abuse she suffered as a child which damaged her and put limitations on her ability to mother with presence and warmth? In *Maternal Thinking*, Sara Ruddick addressed the "socially caused and politically remedial" problems, such as, war, poverty and racism, which "twist a mother's best efforts".[277] The social conditions for women in which to raise their children should surely be one of the biggest issues for feminism — we cannot expect mothers to do their work in conditions which frustrate their efforts and impoverish their family of safety, money, love and security. Yet, we do. We expect her to mother as though the world were a blank slate. As though her love and work could and should whitewash all of her culture's ills. We expect her to delegate mothering, else she is just not 'feminist'.

At heart, whether it is out of society's gender role expectations that we *look to mother* for love and for support, or whether it is something *about* the woman who gave us life, it is a tough one to pick apart. We are all born of mothers; we either had one growing up or we didn't; and we may or may not have had a satisfying relationship with her. We have our own mother-story to cloud our response to this issue, and to the issues of mothers generally.

A tenet of liberal feminism appears to be an unwavering need for disavowing of motherhood — or for it to be relegated to a pastime, or matter of strict proportional sharing with a partner and the relinquishing of the 'privilege of motherhood'. Or else we are patronised as making a 'choice' and this should be respected, even though it would be better if we got out there and 'contributed'. There is much talk in liberal feminism and by many modern feminists about the need to be a 'good role model' for one's daughters by getting out to work. Well, it depends on what the values are, I suppose. In capitalist neoliberal individualist patriarchal society, a woman is often driven to prove her market worth, no matter her preference for being with her family and working from the home. Profit over people.[278] Especially female ones. Market over mothers. Good role models come in many forms: surely it is more important that a mother have autonomy, self-determination, be authentic, fulfilled and financially secure, *however this is achieved* for her.

If we can see the myths of motherhood (many of which are in fundamental and direct conflict) for what they are, we can see that a mother is not just in a double bind but trussed like a Christmas turkey. And don't mothers get a good roasting. Mother-blame is a culture within media, psychology and society generally, which forms the backdrop for mothers to get on with ordering their lives as they see fit, including prioritising mothering their children at a particular point in their lives.

As Shari L. Thurer states, "never before have the stakes of motherhood been so high — the very mental health of the children. Yet never before has the task been so difficult, so labour intensive, subtle and unclear"[279] — and, I would add, undervalued and unsupported. This must form a foundation of feminism: how to support mothers, rather than simply displace them.

THE "MOMMY WARS"

The mother-blame culture is one of the key reasons I reject the idea of mommy wars *between* mothers alone: it is society generally which judges mothers and finds us wanting, whether we breast or bottle feed, whether we 'stay home' or 'go out to work'.

When it comes to 'mommy wars' whole books have been written on this subject, such as *The Truth Behind the Mommy Wars, Who Decides What Makes a Good Mother?* by Miriam Peskowitz; *Mommy Wars, Stay-at-Home and Career Moms Face off on Their Choices, Their Lives, Their Families*, edited by Leslie Morgan Steiner, and *The Mommy Myth* by Susan J. Douglas. The Internet is weighed down by this mythical warfare, including those cynical DIY adverts for formula companies.

It is said that mothers are divided into hostile camps that resent and judge each other, and will, given the chance, tear each other down. Sounds a lot like patriarchal Empire-style colonial superiority and domination to me, rather than the lived reality of most decent mothers' lives.

In truth, most parents are not engaged in mommy wars. There might be the odd 'nasty' out there who will gladly take a swipe at another, but this is far from the regular, decent parent simply trying to do their best. Peskowitz argues that most parents simply want more options: there are no convenient polar opposites of 'out of the home' and 'at home' mothers. After all, there is the family life cycle to bear in mind; there is the battle to get greater flexibility and workplace acceptance of parents' (mothers *and* fathers) caring responsibilities; and there are mothers who work part-time, from home, or for themselves. I agree with her when she comments that "the parent problem is a serious, structural problem" and her acknowledgement that individualism is poorly suited to caring for our children.[280] We can't be islands when we have children: they need to make it to the mainland, the family bed, a mother's arms and a mother's heart.

When we are mothers or mothers-to-be, the fact is that we will be judged. And we need to keep this in mind. To quote Vanessa Reimer and Sarah Sahagian in *The Mother-Blame Game*, we have to "internalise and mitigate" maternal failure.[281] This extra element of our work means that we anticipate and prevent "a child's potential failures" and accept "responsibility for the child's life outcomes". And we do this all the while "deeply embedded patriarchal ideologies and systemic inequalities continue to operate unnoticed".[282] In other words, we mother in the midst of misogyny and the market. This is the stuff of feminist importance; to steal an oft-made feminist complaint, it is not a 'fringe issue'.

As mothers on the ground, we can stand that ground and refuse to engage in judgement of other mothers where those mothers are doing their best with their children's interests at heart. Otherwise we are submitting to patriarchal misdirection; attacking each other, when we should be challenging the structures which effectively penalise us for reproducing the human race.

TOXIC GUILT

The joke goes something like this: "How do you spell 'mother'?" Answer: "G.U.I.L.T." Okay, Adrienne Rich put it more poetically when she wrote "the invisible violence of the institution of motherhood, the guilt, the powerless responsibility for human lives, the judgments and condemnations, the fear of her own power, the guilt, the guilt, the guilt".[283] Mothers and guilt go together, it seems, like peas and carrots, duck and orange, and mac and cheese. We can do no right; we are to blame; we fail our children. With that, I go to bed safe in the knowledge that my children will reach adulthood to learn that their mother invested time, energy and love in them, all the while aware that everything I was doing for them was going to screw them up, somehow. So I might as well be happy and just go with it, and apologise if I've overstepped the mark, tell them daily that I love them, ensure that I have something in my life which I can call my own which does not hinge on or involve them, feel relatively content, and give them eye contact when they are speaking to me. It's the least I can do.

There are those feelings of guilt that we may well feel for the multitude of ways in which we fear we are failing our children or their futures and the injustice of a culture which fosters the feeling of forever being consigned to roles from Eve's daughters burdened with sin; to Freudian smotherers; cold callous absent spectres; or Friedan's pathetic housewife heroines. Yet, we must bear some responsibility for the raising of our children, their behaviour, their manners and their emotional security now and in the future, and their education. We are their mothers: adults in position of power and influence over young children, despite the absence of power in society generally. Granted, it is not our *sole* responsibility, nor a responsibility that is solely *ours*, as mothers. It takes a village, after all. But that does not take away the importance of the place of mother: it is not 'maternal gatekeeping', it is honouring our status and respecting our work. We cannot allow ourselves to be shy of doing this: patriarchal culture has buried the power of women and mothers enough. It is time for a resurrection.

And so, we have to recognise that, as mothers, we do have an impact on our children; they are not evergreen plants with low needs for light and water. Adrienne Rich nailed our more dramatic fears when revealing that "for years I believed that I should never have been anyone's mother, that because I felt my own needs acutely and often expressed them violently, I was Kali, Medea, the sow that devours her farrow, the unwomanly woman in flight from womanhood, a Nietzschean monster".[284] Our children do have needs. They are developing, immature people, and we are the adults with a duty to care for them. They are not blank slates; though they have much to learn about human relationships and responsible behaviour. We can have our needs. They do not cancel out those of our children. We need not fear becoming the sow with the farrow: we can settle for being fallible human beings.

Rosjke Hasseldine talks about the toxic guilt which is at epidemic proportions among women.[285] Mothers string themselves up, mentally climb up on the stake and burn, or emotionally subject themselves to the stocks. Why? Because they feel guilty that they are not good enough. Not beautiful enough; not patient or enthusiastic enough, not earning enough, not smooth enough, not happy enough, not liked enough, not skinny enough, not fashionable enough, not earth mother enough, not career mother enough, not talented enough, not skilful in the kitchen enough, not adventurous in the bedroom enough, not sporty enough, not hairless enough, not organic enough, not energetic enough. Not enough. Women are not enough. We do not feel guilty because we are not good enough women or good enough mothers. We feel guilty because we are women. Patriarchal society has made it so, in a process of death by a thousand cuts, over thousands of years. We have forgotten that we are worthy, powerful and important. We are something, not nothing. We are enough. We are worthwhile human beings.

Remember, the message women receive about Eve is that a woman was responsible for sin. Our lesson from Greek mythology is that women are grotesque and apt to turning people to stone. Our legacy from the witch hunts is that women were responsible in society's eyes for ills of weather, crop failure, illness and more, such that they deserved to be tortured and burned at the stake. We learn that most heads of state have been men; except a few such as a Virgin Queen and a Bloody Mary; and that a King's many wives were treated to a lottery of death, divorce or beheading for their cares. As girls, we grow up in a patriarchal society with a history replete with tales of men, or fallen, wicked or incompetent girls and women, and with a popular culture's stories of absent mothers, cruel stepmothers, dead mothers, mean mothers, or inadequate mothers. We paint our story and that of our own mothers on the canvas of patriarchal woman-hatred. It is the backdrop. It is the narrative. And it is a destructive one bent on undermining us, disempowering our very beliefs about ourselves, and warping our awareness of our place in the world and in history. This narrative informs us and our outlook. Our village of support is barren, and the equivalent of WANTED posters exposing the sins and frailties of mothers are flapping in the wind. When we add to this the fact that woman-hating is not the exclusive preserve of men (internalised misogyny is alive and well) mothers have an uphill struggle against others and ourselves.

So. Guilt. It is no understatement to say that as mothers we feel it deeply. And it is borne in part from hatred which we have somehow turned against ourselves. It is fed by standards and expectations, conflicting messages about good and bad mothers, and patriarchal consumerist capitalism. Happy days.

Just as there are the wicked stepmothers, the all-nurturing perfect, groomed, smiling, coiffed mothers, and the emotionally distant, fragile mothers in popular film, our culture has its 'mother myths'.[286] We are judged for our failings *and* for our successes. And we feel guilt when we don't measure up. What we need, as mothers, is to bring it all back down to earth. To admit the negatives, celebrate the positives, expose the betrayals and demand change to allow us to be mothers, not Others.

Paula Caplan and Rosjke Hasseldine urge us to uncover our mothers' stories and the stories of our female lines. We are encouraged to see the liberation within this. They are clear that mother-blame as a culture is insidious and all pervasive. We face simultaneously conflicting messages about our role and authority. We are expected, and expect ourselves to:

› be all nurturing at all times, but with a 'full' life of our own;

› be caring and loving, but with a calm and detached professional persona;

› be attentive to children and self-sacrificial whilst simultaneously pursuing capitalist individualist marketplace goals;

› be natural and instinctively motherly and warm and know what to do in all matters child-related, whilst obeying experts in matters of birth, breastfeeding and child-rearing;

› have warm, honest and loving relationships with our children, without conflict; while maintaining healthy distance from our mothers/children in a society which distrusts overly-involved mothers or overly-dependent daughters/sons;

› be in charge of children who behave perfectly and compliantly, in a culture which does not trust the mother to raise her children according to her own values;

> be involved in the education of one's child, while being forced to work so many hours away from the family that it is practically impossible;

> share care of the children with others, despite the unavailability of extended family, or the presence of abuse or incompetence in the father, or lack of public investment in community projects which would enable decent substitute care to be found.

I haven't listed them all. We all have ones to add, don't we? And you might not agree with anything I've said; yet it is one of the most interesting yet neglected areas of feminist theory: how we treat society's mothers and how we mothers treat ourselves.

The inner voice, after all, is quick to chide us: "you're a terrible mother". Our inner worries are quick to threaten us: "if you don't get your son to stop hitting his sister he will become an axe murderer when he is seventeen". Our inner fears torment us: "my child hates me". Our inner courtroom judges us: "you are failing your children". We can end up mirroring society's judgement against us. This won't do, sisters, this won't do.

Most decent people then would agree, I am sure, that a parent should do right by their children, so far as they are able with the information and emotional resources available to them. I'm not talking about 'intensive parenting' or 'helicopter parenting'[287] here. We all know what our children most need: food, warmth, love, responsive care, and time.

It is also important to recognise that how we behave towards our children has consequences: the way we raise our children is important for their future emotional and physical health. We can't take our hands off and declare "nothing to do with me, Guv". However, the payoff has to be greater respect for mothers for the work they do in raising their children; greater acceptance of the role that fathers could and should play in the family, where they are present and decent; and economic and social change to enable parents to do the work of raising their families without strain, with support and with means.

Laurie Penny illuminates the guilt thing as a form of misdirection: "The engine of capitalist patriarchy runs on the dirty fuel of women's shame, so whatever we choose, the important thing is that we blame ourselves. That way, we don't blame the system."[288] Well, sisters, let's set our sights on that system. It has the words patriarchy, misogyny, capitalism, neoliberalism and sexism written all over it. Let's cause that earthquake. Let's stamp our feet and march our purple stockings right up to the gate of power. Let's lose the guilt. Or at least stick it on the rubble we leave behind.

SACRIFICING 'OURSELVES'

How often have you read an article which tells you how to get your life back after having a baby, or how to reclaim time for 'yourself'. How to 'put yourself first'. As though you, now, as the mother of children, are somehow separate from, threatened by the 'real you', the pre-kids you, that must be brought back to life. Motherhood is often identified with self-sacrifice (both chosen and unchosen) which is at odds with our culture of individualism.[289] When a woman becomes a mother, our culture believes, she must fight to remain 'herself'. That she must not allow her life to "grind to a halt".[290] The feminist script has forgotten (or perhaps wilfully overlooked) the truth that many women, in becoming mothers, have found a *new* self. We have become, as Sheila Kitzinger said, "ourselves as mothers".[291] This is not the "Mummy Mystique" or to say that becoming a mother is somehow our "full stop"[292]: we all, surely, need something for ourselves, whatever that may be and however small and unique, which does not depend on or relate to our children (for our benefit and our children's). To quote Sarah Ditum: "As a feminist, I would never advise any woman to declare that her capabilities had topped out with reproduction".[293] That observation reminds me of Anne Roiphe's remark that "it is better not to have the sum of one's worth in the bank of motherhood".[294] I'm all for self-fulfilment (in whatever form that comes) and for women nurturing their interests and their talents. We are human beings with our own needs and our own spark: we need not be the gofer, the life support system, the servant to others, with no time or space for our own basic or wider needs. The question is, must we pretend that our priorities, as mothers, often don't change after we have children, for a short time at least? How can we ensure that our lives respect the transformations we undergo and our new priorities? It needn't be a zero-sum game of "who can have the shortest postpartum recovery before getting back on the Blackberry". Most radically, how can we insist that our needs are met, that others care for us, to enable us to care for our babies and children? How can we ensure that we can resume a career, pursue a career, change career, or otherwise engage in pursuits which bring us satisfaction and use our skills without discrimination?

Instead, the main focus of much of feminism is the praise of mothers' retention of 'self' and authenticity as represented by — you guessed it — working and earning a wage: work is absolutely understood as that which takes place *out* of the home; and worth is directly related to the receipt of pay. Apparently, we must make sure we 'work' so that we do not sacrifice ourselves to motherhood. We just have to hope no one notices that capitalist neoliberalism expects everyone to be a wage slave and women to be the wife and mother on the second shift. That just because we are told to identify with our pre-child-bearing self, someone, usually us, will be doing the life changing work of raising our babies. It forgets that for many mothers, we want to be with our children. We are not "living through another's reflection"[295]: we bask in our children's love and they bask in ours. We become *their* mirror: to know they are seen, loved and known.

My copy of Joan K. Peters' book *When Mothers Work* has the words "*All* Mothers Work" scribbled all over it, to echo the UK maternal feminism organisation All Mothers Work.[296] Language: it speaks volumes. Self-sacrificial motherhood is a byword for martyrdom, it seems; and nobody wants a martyr for a mother. And yet, there has to be some room, in the early years particularly, for a degree of putting the child first. Do we *want* to be awake at 3am seeing to a screaming baby? No. Do we sacrifice sleep to tend to her? Yes.* Do we *want* to have days of exhaustion tending to a poorly child? No. Do we absolutely anchor him to our body, enveloped in arms, with tender touch and soothing words, regardless of the social events or office meeting we miss? Yes. Having children *involves* sacrifice. But then, sacrifice doesn't sit well with capitalist individualism, does it? Unless we are sacrificing our time for the benefit of capital. *That's* okay.

When some writers talk about self-sacrifice, they are almost always defining 'ourselves' by reference to 'pre-motherhood' or 'extra-motherhood' identity and activity. Yet, for many women, we undergo a fundamental shift in our outlook. If we no longer feel enraptured by the 8.30am breakfast business meeting and 8.30pm client drinks then that is our prerogative as parents. The system should change, not us. If we feel that service to our family, love for our children, and support of our communities are valuable and important, then that should be respected. We might simply care less, for a time, about the things we once enjoyed. That is not to say that we don't undergo a huge adjustment or that the changes we undergo compared

---

* Although this may well be contentious: so called "sleep training" for babies and young children is big business.

to that of our partner are not significant — or a cause of resentment in the 'who's more tired than who' stakes. Before this book went to press, I attended a lecture by Germaine Greer in Conway Hall in London. Conway Hall is slap bang in the middle of my old, professional world. But those days are long gone. Instead, just walking along Holborn, without my children, without the suit, without the stress, without the leather handbag and heels, and without a salary in the bank, I felt like an alien. A foreigner. A tourist. A misfit. A ghost. After all, my entire twenties were spent living in London. Working in London. Living London. Living 'equality'. I now live a life, my forties looming, broadly centred around my children — they take up my daytime hours. My evenings are my own, although they are rarely spent outside the home. I'm not complaining about this: I gladly and enthusiastically left my career to be with my children. I'm rocking the 'private sphere'. I don't have to wear a bleedin' suit anymore. It's great.

In reality, I occupy an extremely small geographic area nowadays. So when I found myself back on the old turf, it hit me that my physical world has literally and absolutely shrunk. It reminded me that, while my and my husband's lives have both changed since having our two children, it is I — not he — who has faced the most significant and fundamental *day-to-day* transformation in my routine, my geography, my patch, my clothes, my outward status and my income. Almost everything has changed. Yet, when my husband walks that walk, gets that bus, grabs that coffee, wears that suit, hails that cab and works that career, he remains outwardly and functionally the person that he always was, in the place he was always in, out there, in the 'public sphere'.

Jean Bethke Elshtain wrote about *Public Man, Private Woman*. Her writing begs the question of why it is that 'public' success or participation is regarded as the sole marker of status, of worth and of citizenship. It is no stretch to the imagination to see how this bias affects mothers who want to take time out of the workforce to care for their children at home, and how this can affect our sense of self-worth. Of suddenly finding ourselves in a completely different world. Outside of the Internet, my public presence during the week of Monday to Friday has consisted, consistently, of walking to and from places with my children: activities, school, playgroups, swimming, volunteering and play within a two-mile radius of our home. I am well and truly going about my business as a mother in the 'private sphere' and operating in the 'shadow economy': the one of care, connection and children.

However, despite my temporary constriction in location, I have almost certainly, since becoming a mother and looking after my children on a day-to-day basis, experienced an expanded emotional range and traversed an extended intellectual terrain. It forced me to write. It forced me to find ways to connect with other people totally unrelated to professional concerns. And so it was that I listened carefully to Germaine Greer's lecture at Conway Hall, in which she raised the issue of invisibility and powerlessness. In short, she encouraged us to make a noise. To make a noise is just what I have intended to do with *Liberating Motherhood*. We are still here. We are still 'ourselves'.

The degree to which we can devote more of ourselves to our 'self' beyond motherhood will inevitably change throughout our lives and throughout the lives of our children. After all, I can't imagine my son wanting me to wipe his bottom when he is fifteen, or my daughter sharing my bed, attached to the breast at the same age. For me, I have no doubt that the early years will not hold the same attraction for me for years on end: it is the cycle, the changes, the seasons, which have always appealed to me the most. I suspect I am not alone in this: our children grow; it is the long-game of family life.

At heart, however, I agree with Sheila Kitzinger that "intellectualizing about parenthood may make it all rather more difficult".[297] Rather, "becoming a mother ... is also a social transformation, and one of the most dramatic and far-reaching that a woman may ever experience in her life".[298] Why, sisters, is this not recognised? Given that children are "treated as a private indulgence", I would tend to agree with Kitzinger that one of the consequences of that "social attitude is that increasingly women approach birth and the initial tasks of motherhood in a business-like spirit, determined to do it well, but concerned to get back to the situation, in both their working and their private and their social lives, that existed before the baby was born".[299]

We are so used to appraisals, measurement, performance, goals and achievement orientated social and work lives that having a baby can clash with those elements of our existence and create one almighty confused, immeasurable fleshy culture shock for modern mothers. To quote Melissa Benn, "motherhood will almost certainly come as an enormous shock to a future generation of girls educated to succeed not breed".[300] The temptation to bring 'control' to the situation — verging on control of the little human being herself, from feeding, to bowel movements, to crying, to sleep — can be strong indeed, for some mothers. After all, we can't feel 'out of control': not where control is prized more highly than connection. Not where the dominion of self speaks our culture's language of success.

Kitzinger appreciated the challenges a mother in Western culture in the twenty-first century might well face in her social isolation, expert-supervised, commercially-targeted, performance-driven society. Investment in public services and social structures is being squeezed. We lack practical apprenticeship for the task of mothering and feel pressure to prove ourselves, and "perform perfectly as a mother"[301] in an "Anti-Mother Culture".[302] It is time to stop pitting mothers against their children. It is time to stop expecting mothers to hang on to some idea of a concrete pre-child self which rejects or denies their new connections, feelings and responsibilities that are born along with her children. Each mother inhabits a new reality.

When we strip everything away, we can see that our culture's worship of the separate self, is in truth, a fantasy [303]: the mother experiences first-hand the sense of an expanded self, one which includes her children. But this important, powerful and intimate reality is something to be denied. No wonder we can feel a conflict[304]; no wonder we become rebels in the house of individualism.

With all this in mind, I often come back to my mother. She always said that with each child, we gain more heart and more space for love. So perhaps it is less that we *lose* ourselves, and more that we *gain* a greater capacity for letting others *in*.

HOW OTHERS CAN DO IT BETTER THAN MOTHERS

We have already touched upon Sarah Ruddick's theory about The Gaze: how mothers are under scrutiny of others, especially *experts*. Now *they* really know how to raise the kids. The fact that few of them agree amongst themselves is neither here nor there. Despite the contradictions, the intensity of advice from experts, health visitors, teachers and others, can affect our confidence in our ability to do the job. Ruddick observes that "advice from experts, widely varying moral perspectives of other mothers, teachers' disapproval, and the complexity of her children's responses conspire to undermine the confidence she may have developed".[305] Too true. This is no more so than in the case of delegated care: how others can do it better; how we owe it to our children to hand them over for stimulation that we 'cannot' provide. Add capitalism to the stew and you get 'superior' professional childcare within a market-driven industry.

After all, when the emotionality, connection, need for attachment to family members and the sense of expanded self are put to one side as irrelevant or unimportant, and mothering is seen as 'not work' the next logical step is to make it more efficient and economical. This is what we are seeing now. Mothering and care are being removed from mothers and added to 'the market' in commercial childcare. The work of raising children is being moved from mothers to others. Joan Williams calls this the "full commodification" model.[306]

In the UK and nations such as Sweden, there is a firm agenda that state provided and inspected childcare is superior to the care that a mother, or father, can provide. *Twenty-four hour* universal childcare may have been the feminist utopia, but it is probably a dystopia for the children, away from their parents and the familiarity of home during the night while parents are compelled to work shifts in the market, and for the families forced by circumstance to use them. Because it is not privileged families who will be using night nurseries. It never is. Those who have shown up to 'lead' and 'succeed' will most likely have *live-in* help: it is not about widening access to top jobs, it is about ensuring a steady stream of insecure workers in unsociable hours. So when we use night nurseries we can suspect that, far from a feminist success, it is a capitalist victory: it is not for our benefit; it is to facilitate our exploitation. Liberation indeed.

Then there are the touted 'benefits' of childcare, even for babies and toddlers. The assumption is that a parent with a child at home is not providing 'enrichment' or 'education', 'socialisation' or 'peer exposure', or professional, detached expert care. Maternal care and love, it seems, doesn't make a child's world go round.

Mothers just can't be trusted to raise their own children, you see. We get it wrong, you know. The socialisation a mother provides one-to-one in loving responsive care is nothing compared to the synchronised wailing of babies in the 'baby room', or the Lord of the Flies grabbing of toys between toddlers in the 'toddler room'. If we really took in the message we receive from daycare providers, political statements and popular commentary, the situation is thus: the socialisation she provides by going to playgroups with her child is inadequate; the exposure to varied geographies and age groups in day-to-day life is irrelevant; the familiarity with life outside lurid coloured walls and plastic toys is age-inappropriate; the mother's guidance in learning, speaking, emotions, walking and all things is nothing compared to preparing a child for school within approved infrastructure. Because success in school is vital for success in the workplace. And so the wheel turns. The best childcare is that which acclimatises humans as young as possible to the demands of the workplace and institutional compliance. In the chapter on **Care-work in a Postmaternal Culture** I will discuss the work that mothers do when what they do is mothering. For now, it is enough to say that mothers have been distrusted to provide care to their children as long ago as the birth of democracy.

Yes, matraphobia has been around that long. Plato, one of the founding fathers of Western democracy, was no fan of mothers. In his utopian tract, *The Republic*, he wrote that women should be divested of their children at birth and those babies sent to nurseries out of town to be cared for by women who know better — professional nurses, no less. Mothers were not to be trusted. In *Motherhood in Patriarchy*, Mariam Irene Tazi-Preve discusses the concept of motherhood and how Plato advocated the severance of the mother-child relationship:

> *When the children are born, they will be taken into custody by the proper officers, whether male or female or both, for offices are to be held by women as well as by men. Yes. The good offspring will be taken to the nurseries, to nurses who live in a separate quarter of the city. But the inferior offspring if one chance to be deformed, will be hidden in some unreachable, unknown place.*
>
> *Yes, he said, that must be done to keep the breed of the guardians pure. They will provide nourishment. Mothers who are full of milk will be brought to the nursery. But taking every precaution to prevent the mother from recognising her own child, and if more are required, other wet-nurses will be hired. Care should also be taken that the mothers only nurse for an appropriate amount of time, the night shifts and other tedious care should be left to nurses and attendants.*[307]

Horrific, no? The 'guardian and philosopher state': the blueprint for the patriarchal republic writ large. No place for mothers. The birth of democracy was founded on the death of maternity. And the reason Plato recognises the need to separate mothers and children? Power. The need to crush the power of mothers underfoot, to be replaced with the mind. Of men. Utopia is a place free of mothers it seems. And Plato wasn't alone in this. B.F. Skinner's 1930's Behaviourist utopia *Walden Two* also proposed the rearing of children apart from their mothers, and Huxley's *Brave New World* had babies bred in hatcheries. The kibbutzim in Israel in the 1960s-70s, and many cults have insisted on children being raised separate from their mothers. It is the easiest way to indoctrinate the young with the mind of the master, without the inoculation of the love of the mother. Feminism too has loved the idea of communal child-rearing and diluted mother bonds — all in the name of liberation, eh?

According to Tazi-Preve, the patriarchal project is not simply an issue of dominance of men over women; it is relevant to how it deals with the issue of motherhood. She discusses matricide in its forms through history, from the murder of Mother-Goddess and witch hunts in Europe, and is clear that patriarchy seeks the erasure of mothers and even the act of giving birth through women's bodies and wombs, through our social set ups and technological advances — mechanical uteruses might be some feminists' idea of liberation, but to many mothers it is dystopian in the extreme. It is thought-provoking stuff; it is unflinching, thorough and fearless. I am inclined to agree with her. And you might well reach the same conclusion when you take it all in.

So, where are we? Well, it's clear. 'Mother' is a misfit in the machine. For starters, radical feminism wants to see the abolition of gender. Yet, identity politics say "long live gender" but down with 'the body'. Then factor in the truth that utopian patriarchy insists on the disempowered reproductive class. Then sprinkle with the fact that our economic system's ideal worker is basically a robot. The result? We are expected to be an unfeeling, grafting, unfettered automaton. And this applies to mothers *and* children. Our children must be raised to be the compliant institutional cog, not the free-range, free-thinking, secure, happy, human being. Adult workers have to be unencumbered and free from caring responsibilities. The assumption that women are not free from these responsibilities provides huge tension between the rules of patriarchy and capitalism. But in essence, it is the long-game of compliance and exploitation. I recognise that these are big issues. For feminism. For politics. For economics. But, arguably, this process of dehumanisation starts with the deposing and 'neutering' of mothers.[308]

So when I speak of mothers I am clear that it is women, mother-parents, not a de-sexed parent that I am talking about. We have to question the fashion for speaking about parenting, about parents and 'sharenting' as though a mother and father are absolutely and entirely interchangeable at all or in all cases. As though equality means 'exactly the same'; as though equality means removal of a mother's bodily and emotional reality.

If we speak of parental leave, we can erase mention of postpartum *recovery*, perineal tears, breastfeeding and mother love. If we talk about pressures on parents, it conveniently leaves out the *de facto* gendered distribution of family work; it conveniently leaves out the discrimination experienced by mothers in economic policy or in employment; it conveniently conceals the feminist nature of the mother issue. If we talk about single parents, as some organisations do, it neglects the gendered fact that, say, 90% of those parents are women. Mothers. Many of whom may have experienced mistreatment by their partners or other hardship. Others are lone mothers by design. Government policies which remove money from the family disguise, by their careful use of genderless language, the fact that in many cases the state is removing money from *women*. Domestic violence* services increasingly use language which, so as not to appear sexist, subconsciously suggests that women are 50:50 perpetrators of rape, murder and assault on domestic partners; hey, that's equality for you. We talk about people, not women. Parents, not mothers. The rest is just a coincidence. It conveniently masks the gendered nature of much rape and murder, and the desperation of women across Western culture to find ways to bring themselves and their children out of abusive relationships. Economic policies which penalise mothers do not differentiate explicitly between men or women, those with children and those without. So any financial hardship which befalls mothers is just something that happens to a *person*. Nothing to do with being a mother, or being a woman. She's human capital, the maternal — not female — eunuch,[309] disembodied and without a name.

So, in some ways, a mother's place is not only in the wrong; her place is nowhere to be seen, unless it is for criticism or for the good bits to be claimed by others. This fails women. It conceals hardship, misogyny, unfairness, discrimination, marginalisation and mistreatment. Suddenly, women are pregnant people, or chestfeeding people, principal carers, homemakers, employees, parents or people with uteruses. And before you know it, with the assistance of mother-blame culture, 'mother' becomes a dirty word.

---

* Domestic abuse often starts during the woman's pregnancy. What does this tell you?

GOOD MOTHER, GOOD FATHER

In all, we can appreciate the modern expectations on and of women when they become mothers: the social expectations, the cultural standards, the bodily expectations and the sense of family obligation. We've been there, haven't we?

We can reflect on what is 'best': best for children, best for women, best for mothers, best for fathers, and best for society. And we can bet that at least two of those will clash abominably. We can accept that our assessments of good or bad mothers are inherently biased, flavoured by the culture we live in, the family we were raised in, the privileges we enjoy or the oppression we suffer, the class of our family, our disabilities, the colour of our skin, the wealth of our nation or the dominion of our souls to whichever religion is the dominant one of our creed. Yes, there are those mothers who make mistakes (some grave) or who commit atrocities. Yet, the vast majority of mothers do our best, we want to be good enough, and we *are* good enough. Our history can tell us something: we have continued to reproduce, no matter how we supposedly regarded or treated our young through the ages.[310] And our humanity tells us something else: that we have the capacity for love. And mother love is one of the sweetest there is.

However, when it comes to the popular discussions about how to solve the 'mother problem' and how to liberate mothers from motherhood, the fact remains that a sizeable majority of women actually love their children and many of them want to be with them. We have had generations of dispute about women, reproduction, children, childcare and heteronormativity. We have had successive debates about the place of mothers, the economic imperative, and the oppression of women through their reproductive role. Who *knew* that we had been ignorant, unwitting players in the carousel which has gone round and round the garden, destined never to halt and let mothers off for a breather?

Ultimately, we have to be able to stop and insist on our right to view our mothering, parenting, working, struggling and living through the lens of connection, humanity and love.

We must respect and value mothers in all our diversity. We cannot neglect those who are particularly vulnerable. No amount of misery memoirs from professional or literary women who loathed their maternity leave is going to reflect the richness of many women's lives or the love they feel for their children. And no amount of political or social policy which is predicated on breadwinner/marginalised-dependant is going to do justice to families; just as no amount of shared parenting or equality utopia is going to allow for those families for whom mother-care is important, at least in the early years or where the father is not present or simply not up to the job.

Indeed, one of the striking issues about shared parenting, and the serious amount of support it seems to receive from some liberal feminists, is the unwavering assumption that *all* fathers are present, decent, willing and as capable *on an individual basis* of nurturing and developing a bond with the child or providing the care a baby, toddler or older child needs. The early years of babyhood and toddlerhood are markedly different (say, in breastfeeding and greater attachment needs) from the older, verbal, more emotionally continent school years.

We talk about *mothers'* failures; we haven't even stopped to think about pitfalls of unsuitable men being at home with babies, toddlers and young children. I am not saying that more women are necessarily more capable of being competent hands-on parents than men: I am referring to male pattern violence, aggression and sexual abuse which objectively points to the existence of men who are manifestly unsuitable to caring for children. Those men have no place stepping in to 'share care'. We also have to countenance the possibility that some men will gladly sit at home doing nothing while mum works to the bone in a job *and* on the second shift. #NotAllMen

These are feminist issues; sharing care may be wonderful when the care provided is decent and when it is suitable for the unique family, but we have, at least, to accept that this is not a universal experience or potential framework for a sizeable number of women and children. Not all fathers are present; not all women co-parent. With whom, in this situation, is such a mother to share care? The invisible man? If policies are restricted to helping only those who can safely share care, as the modern answer to the breadwinner/dependant model, what are we to do for mothers who do not fit that mould? #NotAllFathers

The fact is that care of children is pretty much seen as the wooden spoon, and shared care is touted as the answer to spreading the burden. We continue to see imbalance in care even in our own families and in the woeful uptake of shared parental leave in the UK. The link between masculinity and success at work still holds huge sway for many men; and many a decent father might simply not *want* to be spending serious amounts of time with the kids instead of being the big man in the office.

The breadwinner/dependant model can lead many men to feel pressure 'to provide' and to 'succeed at work': to fulfil what they see as 'their part of the bargain'. The entrenchment of 'gender roles' has been the focus of feminism for decades. The 'pressure to provide' and 'work as worth' are examples of why gender stereotypes, gender rules and constrictive notions of femininity and masculinity are damaging to society. We also need to bear in mind those women who have bought wholesale into the belief that 'career is worth' — *they* don't want time away from the office either. They are too busy leaning in. The price for us women having *become* the men we want to marry, is that no one wants to be the mother at home — not those who 'aim higher' anyway.[311] The fact is that unless we change our social, economic and political cultures, no amount of tinkering with parenting will achieve anything. I will discuss **Going Dutch** in the next chapter. For now: for families where it works, at the right stage in the family life cycle *for them*, where combined with a restructuring of market-work to reduce its burdens on all our lives, then shared care would have much going for it.

So my assessment must not be taken as saying that many individual fathers are not going to be decent, or that the vast majority of men, and society generally, will not benefit from greater expectations that men do their fair share of care, build their nurturing skills, nor that children would not benefit from seeing more of their fathers, when those fathers are loving and good enough. If we had social policies which limited the hours we could spend in paid work each week, then that would be a start. If we valued care more with a carer's income, you'd also bet more men would do it — it's the *carrot*, you see. Ultimately, if a liberal feminist wants equality, we must accept that there are at least as many men who are as unsuitable for caring for children as some women are. That said, there are many men who are well suited to caring for the children and who do as good a job as the legion of mothers who have done it throughout time. But I refuse to hand out the medals to the men and sit back while women are handed the *stick* of mother-blame.

So, when we can stop and say with confidence: *as a human, mother, woman, I am worthy, I am important, I have a place and it's where I want to be*, then feminism has actually achieved something.

Whereas, at the moment, we can summarise all the different ways in which women, and mothers, are penalised in our Western culture. We are penalised for staying home (we are rendered dependent, vulnerable and devalued). We are penalised when we go out to our jobs (we feel guilty, we feel stressed, we feel anxious and we are penalised with lower incomes through the 'mother penalty'). If we stay home, we do not have an income. If we go out to work, we may well spend a large proportion of the family income on childcare. And then there is misogyny in action against women generally.

And the upshot? Mothers are penalised for existing. Misogyny's got nothing on the oppression of mothers. Doesn't matter which shade you put on it, which slant you take, which solution you come up with of day and night universal childcare, shared parenting, removal of children to Plato's nurseries, artificial wombs or enforced domesticity. Society has no place for mothers aside from in the wrong and paying the price.

It is time for us mothers to be respected, in all our diversity. Career, shared care, exclusive homemaking, 'sequencing' and more. And with this, it is time for society to reflect the value of service, of love, of commitment and connection. Love and family: it need not be a feminist felony. A woman's place can be wherever her heart is, if we finally allow it. And that requires fundamental change to the way we live, work, share, invest and distribute society's wealth, assets and services. Feminism has been busy fiddling with the fray, while mothers burn; it's not just the lack of will within patriarchal establishment to push for radical reordering of society, it's a lack of imagination.

CAREERS, WORK AND LIVELIHOOD

I have explored various aspects of motherhood and will, in later chapters, talk about 'work' and about 'care'. However, what I must discuss (briefly, for the issue is a book in itself [312]) is the issue of work outside the home when that work is enjoyed, fulfilling or a much-loved career. When work outside the home is enjoyable and fulfilling, it can be a source of pleasure and satisfaction. There is no denying that. It is important for many women — for themselves and for their families. After all, many mothers remark that, for them, their career or their work away from the children makes *them* better, more patient, mothers. They personally feel less resentment to their children for the incessant demands; they may well feel able to offer more to their children, in one way or another. Of course, this applies just as much to hobbies, volunteer work or creative enterprises: we all deserve *something* for ourselves.

However, when it comes to work outside the home, let's not forget, too, that ambition to succeed in something, to make a mark, to excel, to leave a legacy, to create or to reach one's potential in whatever field, is not the preserve of men or women who are not mothers: we are all unique in our talents, skills and inclinations. Our participation in the public sphere should be open to us, no questions asked. It's 'feminism for dummies'. As much as I discuss the frustration of many mothers who are compelled to get a job or return to paid work in order to survive financially when they would prefer to be with their children, there are also mothers who are frustrated in either being unable, after motherhood, to continue their career or much-loved jobs or are penalised in some way when they do. A mother's place is not in the home. It is where *she* wants to be. After all, if she doesn't want to be with her children full-time or part-time, she will hardly be capable of providing the responsive care they need and the resentment would no doubt leave a negative legacy. Her duty — with the father or partner, if present and/or decent — is to ensure the children receive the care they deserve, albeit not from her.

So, we agree, that just as there are many women who want to dedicate a period of time to their home life, there are equally many women who either want to engage in work or career full-time or continue their career or jobs part-time. Yet, mothers can find themselves kettled* by a capitalist patriarchal frontline into unwanted 'housewifery' (not everyone's cup of tea, as we know) or unhappy workplace conditions (full-time with no allowance for family life but penalties for presumed care responsibilities, or part-time with sacrificed income, standing or promotional prospects). It seems that motherhood is the misfit in the machine — whether the washing or the capitalist variety.

The reality is that many women face significant barriers at work or in prospects for promotion, or salary or working conditions. They face resistance to more flexible arrangements or working from home. They may face difficulties in finding affordable childcare — although many now benefit from significant subsidies in the UK on joint incomes up to £300,000.[313] Many women experience discrimination in the workplace by

---

* Kettling is a police tactic for controlling large crowds during demonstrations or protests, by which large cordons of police officers contain a crowd within a limited area. Protesters are left only one choice of exit controlled by the police — or are completely prevented from leaving, in order to deny them access to food, water or toilet facilities.

virtue of being a mother — whether by losing their job while on maternity leave or being displaced on return. These are all feminist issues. They go to the *heart* of this movement: how to support mothers to frame their lives and their work (whether that work is market-work or care-work) in the way which is right for them and which does not sacrifice financial self-sufficiency and autonomy. Because, as things stand, a mother does not have this fundamental right. It forms the blind-spot of feminism — seeing only the childcare side of the coin. As much as we need to find ways to liberate motherhood, we must also liberate our livelihoods from 'ideal-worker automaton' expectations.

Many mothers, for example educated women who have pursued fulfilling careers before becoming mothers, wish to continue their work outside the home. Some may want to take time out while their children are young, yet face the 'maternal wall' when they try to get back to their career. Others continue in their career but find the cost of childcare to be extremely high (although the complete loss of salary if she had instead cared for her children full-time would be financially devastating) or the conditions under which they are expected to work are unforgiving of family life. Many of these issues could be addressed by the shared-care approach which I discuss later in **Going Dutch**, and a reconstructive feminism of the kind argued by Joan Williams in *Unbending Gender*. Change the *workplace*. Change those expectations. Challenge those assumptions about productivity and 'presenteeism'. Fundamentally, we need to ask why our career or jobs intrude into our personal lives in the way that they do — for everyone, not just mothers. It would go some way to reducing the resentment of some colleagues of women's maternity leave — or 'holiday' as some may scathingly mislabel it[314] — if everyone could benefit from a greater work/life balance. We could consider what we could do about it, for example: reducing the working week for all; reducing the working day for all; promoting universal 'part-time' work; or ensuring that flexible working does not penalise someone in their career in financial or professional terms.

We need to ask why a woman's career should take a hit by virtue of the fact that she does not want to sacrifice time with her children to the tune of full-time delegated care. Women who find satisfaction in their work — whatever that may be — are surely *entitled* to balance this in the way which suits them. However, until we address the overwhelmingly masculine workplace structures which expect full-time devotion to the workplace, lest we wallow in the purgatory of penalised or 'feminised' part-time work, little is going to change. The expectation that it is the *mother* that takes a 'step back' or goes onto the 'mommy track' is one of the barriers facing women in their career: we need to push for fundamental change so that both partners are free to reduce their working hours, to enable a greater balance for family life. I will expand on how this could be achieved in the chapter on economics and basic income, but for now, just as I argue that women who want to care for their families should be supported to do so, we must also push to liberate mothers from negativity and penalty arising from their decision or desire to engage in work outside the home.

Part 3

A MOTHER'S LABOUR

Care-work in a Postmaternal Culture

*So much of our early gladness vanishes utterly from our memory: we can never recall the joy with which we laid our heads on our mother's bosom ... Doubtless that joy is wrought up into our nature, as the sunlight of long-past mornings is wrought up in the soft mellowness of the apricot, but it is gone for ever from our imagination, and we can only **believe** in the joy of childhood.*

George Eliot, *Adam Bede*

POSTMATERNAL CULTURE

Forget postmodern postfeminist this and that. We live in a *postmaternal* [315] culture: we are encouraged to use 'parent' and 'parenting', to 'share care' and to 'delegate care'. But it goes beyond language; it goes to the way in which we order our lives and how our infrastructure jealously divides love and home from work and status; and care and nurture from worth and productivity. As women under liberal feminism, we "give birth to *ourselves*", not *babies*. [316] As explored by Alice Rossi, our existence is now dominated by *eros* (sex, passion and infatuation) rather than *caritas* (loving-kindness, the ethic of care). [317] The mother, and motherlove, seem to belong to a bygone era.

In some quarters, care and love of children are deemed effectively to be a social 'fad' (children weren't precious before 1872 or something) or a source of oppression of women (you're just breeders, Offred).[318] This shows just how far our views of worth and purpose have deviated from our humanity. The fact is that, for many women, breastfeeding and nurturing their babies is something they treasure. These experiences can surprise us: they can feel "entirely gendered"[319]: in other words, we might finally relate to Shania Twain's lyric, "Man, I feel like a woman". If we cannot name this or claim it, then what on earth is feminism about? Professions and appearance? The right to be just as emotionally stunted as the father who lives in the office and 'doesn't do the soft stuff'? The right to a hyper-sexualised image? We must aim higher, sisters. We must dispense of postmaternal feminism and embrace a maternal feminism and activism which does not treat maternity as an embarrassment.[320] We were supposed to *change* the system, not walk blithely in, welcoming our exploitation and ever-increasing hours working away from home.

In truth, Western culture seems to hate its mom and want to act all grown up and, like, independent. There is no place for nurture, care, dependency or the maternal. I can relate to this: since writing about women and mothers, I am frequently reminded that the word 'maternal' is practically taboo and 'exclusionary', or a sign of some kind of feminine weakness. Strands of feminism seem to give the impression that emotions and care are — like lunch — for wimps.

Julie Stephens describes how the "maternal and the values associated with maternal forms of care have been largely rejected in the public sphere and marginalised or conflicted in the private domain" and how this has "taken a toll on the personal lives of women".[321] I think many of us would agree. We can sense that there is something amiss. We sometimes can't put our finger on it.

We have been encouraged to see value outside the home and fulfilment in the workplace away from our babies, toddlers and young children. When we reject that, we are left with the clear impression that we have failed, that we have no status and that we are throwbacks. I know I did. We can feel that way every single time we hear about political drives to get more women 'into work'.[322] As though a woman's wishes or the needs of her children were irrelevant. We have no political support for our care-work as mothers and our citizenship is practically dependent on our being 'economically active adults' (read: working for pay). There are many obstacles in front of us if we want to care for our families without financial risk or a pounding in public standing. They have been laid down for generations by patriarchal culture, and capitalism has now managed to cement the deal. Feminism has simply failed to recognise that workplace participation will never free all women. We can tinker with the edges, but the patriarchal capitalist machine will continue to whirr. With that in mind, to echo Audre Lorde, we should remember that the master's tools will never dismantle the master's *machine*.[323]

In all, for our pretensions to something 'more' and for all our society's pressure to engage in anything *other* than mothering our young children or growing our families, there is something undeniably precious about the mother-child bond, something unique about what a mother can bring to her children emotionally and for the rest of their lives, and something extremely fulfilling about enjoying a loving relationship with one's children. We *know* this as mothers. We needn't apologise for it.

As Naomi Ruth Lowinsky notes in *The Motherline*, "Mother is the first world we know."[324] It is the "essential human relationship".[325] Is that not worthy of recognition and celebration? For us as mothers, for society and our children? How can we be expected to sever the umbilical cord and be off with us (practically or emotionally) without effect on our children or ourselves? Most crucially, do we stop to realise that separation and devaluing of mothers is a culturally cynical step in the subordination of women? The end game being the erasure of mother, the life creator. The process has been long and crafty: the place of mother is denied, stripped of importance, status and respect. And all that is left is the continued march towards the further disempowerment of women, reduced to their use-value in the neoliberal patriarchal project.

Don't believe me?

Just stop to reflect on the minimising of the bond between mothers and their children; the prevailing suggestions that mothers are substitutable; the increased pressure on mothers to separate from their babies and young children so they can resume their rightful place as human capital in the capitalist machine; the lack of recognition of the value of care and motherly socialisation; and the drive to substitute mothers from gestation through to practical care through to the exercise of authority. These factors affect the ability of mothers and allies to campaign for the proper recognition of mother-work, the value of love and care and the necessity of bringing humanity into our social structures and political policy. If every single cultural norm dismisses it as: 1. non-existent; 2. worthless; 3. an individual indulgence; 4. a waste of time, human capital or productivity; or 5. an anachronism, we can end up feeling like we are Cassandra's daughters.* We battle to bring people to their senses and for politics to take note before we are relegated to the 'wrong side of history', just as feminism and patriarchy alike seem to think women were born on the wrong side of *biology*.

Feminism has rightly had a problem with the cultural stereotypes of femininity given how notions of women as weak snowflakes without the ability to engage in the world on a level with men have been used to keep women down. However, we can risk losing connection and maternal pride if we do not stop to talk about our bodily and maternal experience and mammalian female mother behaviour. I, for one, reached saturation point in terms of masculine popular culture and narrative when I realised I couldn't really bear to feign interest in yet another male-hero-saves-girl-saves-world yarn. Through training and supporting mothers as a breastfeeding counsellor, I turned my attention to the creation of life and the sustaining of life by mothers. I prefer to hear the stories of women around me, just as I resist the idea of worshipping a Father in Heaven, preferring to keep my feet on the ground, embraced by Mother Earth.

As it is, when not worshipping male Gods, we worship the dollar, the celebrity and ruthless individualism. The Goddess is dead; the mother exiled. Long live capitalist patriarchy.

Because when we view the totality of patriarchy, capitalism, technology and feminism we can see the postmaternal culture flourishing.[326] And this postmaternal culture is toxic for mothers and children, for the environment and, ultimately, for humanity. That might well sound radical; but what kind of wellbeing, health, happiness and security are we really getting out of capitalist individualist consumerism? Why is it radical to insist that we can do things better? That we can place humanity and care at the centre of policy? In his 1909 short story *The Machine Stops*, E.M. Forster predicted the road we're on, the technologies that encourage disconnection and our estrangement from the natural world and humanity. Long live the Internet, right? Forster's book was supposed to be a dystopia, not a prediction.[327] We must find a way to recover and prioritise connection and to honour relationships of nurture and care.

When it comes to gender, as much as feminism and equality are linked in our language and association, the reality is that gender *neutrality* is not the same as gender *equity* or fairness. It neglects the bodily, social and

* Cassandra was a Greek mythological prophet. Problem was, nobody believed her predictions. They had no trouble believing her brother, though.

relational reality of many women. The fact remains that mothers are often the whole *world* to their children, just as children can be the whole world to their mothers.

With all that in mind, we mothers must be able to demand a place for the *maternal* in our culture. Our society must start to value mothers and children, must start to recognise the care-work that mothers do and the importance of that work now and in the future lives of our children. Because as it stands, we tolerate worldwide governmental expenditure which invests significant sums in our death: trillions of dollars on nuclear weapons, or enough to kill us many times over.[328] Yet our politicians deny we have means to support our citizens, invest in care and invest in *lives*. The value of death, it seems, is higher than the value of life. We need to declare that state of affairs to be inhumane, destructive and *pathological*. We need to support mothers properly and reconfigure society to move beyond the market experiment to one which supports and invests in care and life, not destruction and isolation. Our culture has to start to recognise the rich fabric of our lives.

THE FABRIC OF THE FAMILY: A STITCH IN TIME

While writing this book I took up knitting. Yes, the heresy of it. A former professional, a feminist, erstwhile wearer of black denim has been knitting. And, frankly, I don't think I could have finished this book without something where I could switch off, do something creative which does not include words, writing or reading. And I have realised just how challenging something like this is to our modern perception of what constitutes worthwhile activity for a woman. It is pretty much on par with confessing that one uses doilies for a plate of biscuits, warms one's husband's slippers before he arrives home from the office, and flounces around in a housecoat with a feather duster all day.

When I shared my new hobby I was met not with horror, but "me too!" When I spoke at the Feminism in London conferences, two sisters sat in the front row knitting and crocheting (I think one of the projects was a vulva). So, a few scarves down the line, a couple of booties, a few baby hats and two beautifully hotchpotch blankets for my children which I hope they will treasure in Peanut-like affection, I am something of a convert. And I have found it to be one of the most provocative and controversial things I have done for some time. Why is this? You're getting warm.

Why is it strange for a woman in her late thirties to decide that she wants to knit some stuff for her family rather than get a tattoo, smoke an e-cigarette, or lift weights? Why is it more curious for a woman to admit to enjoying knitting — really, really, really — more than watching reality TV or prosecuting a felon? Why is it considered throwback and retrograde for a woman to embrace doing something really quite simple, meditative, creative and generous?

Well, because it's a throwback image, isn't it? The image of a woman sitting in a comfy chair, knitting, while her kids play around her, occasionally hop on her and twiddle the yarn. And doing this while others are working at jobs for money, doing 'important stuff', doing 'productive stuff', 'contributing to the economy', 'doing the right thing' and 'discharging their responsibilities to society'.

Yes. Knitting has turned out to be one of the most rebellious things I have done for a long time. Forget falling down drunk on too many occasions. Conveniently forget that tongue piercing. It is a reminder to myself and others that I am outside the grind. You can't be tense, angry, stressed or rat-racing when you're knitting: it's impossible, folks. You are outside of GDP the moment you toil hours to create something, then gift it in love to someone to treasure. For free. You are not counted. You are deemed to be doing something 'crafty': a mere hobby. Not something productive and valuable in its own right.

And it is much like raising children. Every day since my children were born we have stitched our lives and experience together. Those repetitive movements of love, nursing, cuddles; those occasional dropped stitches of yells and tantrums and parental fails; the days where the pattern is so vibrant you wish that time could stand still.

So, to answer your question you must have been mulling: what the purl has knitting got to do with a book on mothering? What has yarn got to do with it all? Well, it's in the fabric. It takes hundreds of moments, hundreds of deliberate motions, hundreds of not-so-deliberate actions, along with much presence and dedication, to raise a family at home.

Yet, for all our society cares, we may as well grab a £5 acrylic jumper from Primark and take up that nursery place. We can outsource the work, after all, can't we? The work and love that goes into raising our children full-time, the dedication and skill, and the presence and creativity are completely ignored. They are increasingly diminished. They are almost universally devalued. Mothers can't be trusted, you see, to get on and bring up their kids: we cannot trust them to knit their own children. To choose their own yarn and select their own needles. Uniform, official-rated, professional staffed, primary-coloured, plasticised, institutionalised Early Years Childcare is the much-admired Walmart jumper of child-rearing.

Ah, but there are those small studies which show benefits to children who have been in childcare. Well, there are those children from extremely deprived and dysfunctional homes, who, through said childcare, receive respite from pretty poor conditions in terms of parenting and responsive care. Is it ethical for commentators and politicians and childcare providers to extrapolate a benefit to *those* children as applying to *every* child, as though every child from a loving and (that old phrase) good enough environment and parenting will benefit similarly? Is it ethical that studies which show the opposite for children from good enough environments to be suppressed, ignored and misrepresented?[329]

There are billboards outside many a nursery saying "THE PLACE TO GROW AND LEARN. Taking children from two months until five years; professional staff; stimulating environment; Good Official Rating." We simply don't hear the opposite perspective: "Being with a parent is wonderful for children. Home, Shops, Parks and More! The place to grow, to be loved, to be kissed, to be cuddled, to be known. The place is home!" plastered on our windows or repeated by politicians and media in soundbites. During election season, the letters I and others in campaign circles received from politicians all trotted out the same line about how childcare is good for children, without any finer examination of which age, stage, which personality, temperament or ability of child, what childcare setting, which carer etc. There was no recognition of the unique child and their unique needs. There was certainly no accompanying recognition that children are served well by maternal or parental care. Mothers, after all, have an increasingly apparent duty to be out there working for pay, not being with their babies and toddlers. What was once something calculated to lead to the liberation of women — paid work and participation in the 'public sphere' — is now well and truly *constricting* in its own right for those who would prefer to be with their young children. We face not only economic pressure to be doing something 'productive', but experience an insidious gaslighting* which convinces us, or tries to, that we are inadequate in what

---

* Derived from Patrick Hamilton's 1938 play *Gas Light* and subsequent film adaptations about a woman whose husband gradually manipulates her into believing that she is going insane.

we can offer our children compared with what a 'professional' can.

It is reaching the stage where mothers will have to prove that they are the right people for the job of caring for their own children. Just like we have no place knitting a hat for our children when we can toe the 'commodity line' and pick up a mass produced beany from Gap.

CONNECTION AND DISCONNECTION

It is within this context that we have to talk about *connection*, not *commodification*. Many of us know, as mothers, that the process and bond of mother/child connection can manifest itself as the "anti-commodity"[330] in our culture. It is certainly seen as 'anti-*feminist*' in some circles. Yet, it isn't feeble or weak to acknowledge this: rather, it is one of the strongest bonds we will ever know. We are connected to our children in body, spirit and love.

The problem is, our modern existence and working structures *rely* on *disconnection*: 'work' from family; parent from child; the personal from political; reason from emotion; charity from kindness; love from sex; mind from body; life-creation from destruction; consumption from need. This brings to mind the poetry and writings of Robin Morgan, who so neatly tackles the genius of the patriarchal project: it skilfully institutionalises the disconnection and compartmentalising of aspects of our lives.[331] As she said, "Sisterhood is Powerful". Well, so is *motherhood*, sisters. We have to *claim* that. We could say that to live a life which prioritises connection is an act of rebellion. And purple stockings suit rebellion just fine.

If we stop to look, our language can reveal the extent of our culture's disconnection. Take the phrase 'work-life' that presumes that life is what is happening when you are *not* engaged in market-work. Shame then that we spend the vast majority of our waking hours in our jobs, particularly in the US, which boasts extremely long working hours and pitiful rates of holiday entitlement. Remember the 'ideal worker'? But how can we '*connect*' when we are apart — parents, children, partners — for so many of our waking hours? We might consider this: the number one regret of the dying is never "I wish I had spent more time at the office".

Our experiences under a stunted feminism can have another impact. When we are schooled in aiming for the stars and pushed to 'succeed', we can risk seeing our vulnerabilities and needs as *failures*: no more so than when we become mothers of helpless dependent little babies. Because mothers? We too are vulnerable in those early days, weeks and months, and *we* need to be cared for, as *we* are caring for our babies. Vulnerability is not a failing: it is a necessity for connection, according to Brené Brown.[332] I would tend to agree with her. It has been when I have shifted the 'mask' that I have been able to connect with others meaningfully. My children have seen me warts and all, emotionally laid bare, and I too have seen *them*. Love can grow from the opportunity and authenticity to connect. We *know* this, don't we?

But somehow, it is shifted aside. When it comes to feminism and women, the disconnection and 'duality' of body (women) and mind (men); of work (market) and love (family); and public (man) and private (woman) affects our socio-economic policies, our social values and the continued debate about *equality*. We are misdirected from seeing that women perform the vast majority of the world's work (much of it unpaid, much of the rest underpaid) and from seeing the inherently masculine structures which have flourished under capitalist patriarchy.

So, connection. We have to start to demand that politicians and economists, and feminists at the very least, widen the intellectual debate to include "connection-based equality".[333]

DEPENDENCE AND EQUALITY

After all, when it comes to connection and dependence, '*equality*' is a quandary: we might well hear the word 'dependence' and immediately think 'drugs', 'co-dependency in addiction' or 'welfare'.[334] And the reason? The neoliberal hand has been busy turning a necessary and inevitable part of the human condition into a frailty, a flaw or a felony.[335] Dependence is something which renders us somehow *lacking* as a citizen: *unequal*. Those of us at the coalface of care know that superficial ideas of equality marginalise carers because if we are busy seeing to the *needy*, the powers that be can ignore *our* needs and rights. They can pathologise us into 'dependants' in a language which usually reserves such labels for miscreants, addicts or otherwise 'pathetic people' our society can 'do without'. Dependency has been thoroughly stigmatised.

It's been decades since the birth of neoliberalism and it's becoming *second nature* to neglect the importance of dependence, this fundamental part of our *human nature*. And what a conflict this can cause for us mothers. Yet, the fact is that dependency is not only *part* of the human condition in terms of relationships, it is an intrinsic feature of human society.[336] As Martha Fineman says, it is *inevitable*.[337] Our babies, for example, are absolutely vulnerable and dependent infants. As mothers, we know this all too keenly. That said, dependence goes deeper. For starters, a logical chain of dependency flows through our existence: we are all *interdependent*. Even this very fact is frequently downplayed, ignored or even denied: each of us depends on others, to greater or lesser degrees, from the food transported to the shop to be bought, to the clothes made to be purchased and worn, from the workers who collect our rubbish, to the doctors who diagnose and treat our diseases. None of us is an island, however much we pride ourselves on self-sufficiency and independence.

Think about this: what *decent* person would *deny* that we are as valuable and worthwhile human beings as anyone else even when we are not capable of meeting our own basic needs, through, for example, infancy or infirmity? Citizens are not composed *only* of able-bodied, healthy, adult, mentally fit, ideal workers. We all have different care needs at different points in our lives. At some moments we will all, every single one of us, be reliant on someone else meeting our needs, helping us, feeding us, caring for us. You would think that rational self-interest would require our awareness of our *own* liability and risk of becoming dependent as well as memories of being a dependent child: we need to put some humanity and compassion in the bank for a rainy day. Because it *will* rain on all of us someday. Many cultures recognise this 'reciprocity' of familial care: the wheel turns. It doesn't just speed off to a 'better' road of capitalist individualism. Western culture increasingly sees dependency as a burden; however, such an attitude does no one any favours in the long run. Not the 99%, anyway.

We have to start to speak the fact that it is not indecent or deviant[338] to be dependent on others to meet our needs at times, frequently, or permanently, depending on our circumstances. It is not a frailty: it is *humanity*. And the existence of those who are unavoidably dependent requires a sufficient body of people who are prepared *to look after them*. And the consequence of this? Those who care *for* dependents are, too, dependent on others financially, whether within paid employment, by state support or within private domestic arrangements. Putting aside the 'money issue' for the moment, this state of secondary dependence is, *of itself*, no bad thing. It is what it is. This is hardly an outrageous observation, yet our culture reels at the idea.

After all, recognising and accepting dependency goes against some pretty deeply held (but warped) values of *individualism*. It raises an extremely uncomfortable issue: must we provide a suitable infrastructure for supporting dependants (both the cared for and the carer)? Do we consign dependence to the 'private realm' and render carers of, say, children (overwhelmingly women) at the financial mercy of a partner? Capitalism and strands of feminism — both — have preferred the latter, and proceeded to exploit or pity women for financial dependence on men. Or do we see it as a matter of social justice and responsibility? Must our societies formulate welfare states or economic policies which honour our debt to those who care for the unavoidably dependent? Yes, sisters. Yes, they must. We have to start to challenge the dominant ideology at the heart of capitalist neoliberalism (and the feminism which has bought into it) of *individualism*. As Anne-Marie Slaughter says in *Unfinished Business*, "We value people of either gender who invest in themselves more than we value people who invest in others."[339]

These are *crucial* questions which we need to ask and for which we need to demand answers; and they go beyond the issue of mothers. They also encompass, for example, fathers who stay at home to care for their children; husbands or wives who care for their spouses; grandparents or kinship carers; parents who care for disabled or sick adult children or relatives; and adults who care for their elderly parents. What do we say to them? Do we pit them against those who earn a wage? Do we pit them against each other, in vying for state support, requiring them to prove their worth and their right to dignity? When it comes to *women*, how far do patriarchal and exploitative capitalist values *rely* on women providing *unwaged* care, on which our society can freeload and from which it can wash its hands of financial responsibility? The idea of breadwinner/dependant is the antithesis of the modern equality model, yet there is a simple answer to the question of how to balance the books: value care and support dependency workers and financially compensate dependency work.

Because, as mothers, we know what dependence looks like. It has a human face. It can have tiny hands. When we care for our children, we deserve more than being dismissed, in turn, as 'dependent' (when effectively used as a slur). We deserve not to be marginalised and exploited; or insulted and criticised as 'not contributing' or not providing 'equally for the upkeep of the family'.[340] Only in a society which prizes working for pay and gaining *extrinsic* economic gratification could the *intrinsically* human dependency work be so cruelly derided.

We need to ask not, as Simone de Beauvoir did "how can independence be recovered in the state of dependency?" but how can we deal fairly with the *fact* of dependence?[341] In our culture, caring for people is costly to care-workers — whether waged or unwaged — and we "are unable to be equals in a society of equals".[342]

The reason? Our socio-economic policies have consistently failed to honour our society's duty to those who care for the dependent. Why? Well, in part, to *reduce state liability* and responsibility to citizens who *are* dependent and those who *care* for the dependent; and in part to ensure *commodification* of basic human needs, from childcare centres to care homes for the elderly. The market has invaded the realm of dependency and ensured that those left outside the market are branded as outliers who deserve to remain out in the cold. And so it is that in failing to tackle these issues (and even contributing to the insult) mainstream liberal feminism has failed mothers and provided support to the neoliberal project instead.

If we are to truly address women's vulnerabilities and the exploitation of women and their labour, then the reality is that we have to start to value care. We have to *really think about what we mean* when we talk about equality: for whom, in relation to what and in what context?[343] What is clear is that we must start to talk about the realities of human existence, including the dependency of the vulnerable and the needs of those who care for them, without marginalising either of them. We have to challenge the idea that equality is reliant on economic opportunities within the market. Eva Feder Kittay says "any idea of equality that is located in the autonomous, free, and self-sufficient individual, who joins only with similarly situated others does not easily recognise the dependency that has so occupied women's lives. By failing to recognise this dependency, such conceptions of equality effectively *exclude* women".[344] Amen to that, sister. It is time we challenged these individualist neoliberal expectations as pathologically anti-family, anti-child, anti-women and inhumane. They literally deny our human needs: and nowhere is this clearer than in the case of our children.

CHILDREN'S NEEDS

While I am well aware that I have framed this book from a feminist perspective, I have done so with one eye on the kids (metaphorically and literally). Those little whatsits who dare to come into our lives and turn everything upside down, or those precious people who have lit our souls aflame, depending on who you talk to. Yes, there are plenty in between and it depends on the mood of the mother when you ask the question. But it's time to put the kids first, in this chapter at least. Because, just as breastfeeding is often absent in mainstream feminist discussion, so too are our offspring, save within the context of abortion, childcare, ambivalence and imagery of a very cute millstone around our necks. So, before considering the 'socio-political implications' of women caring for children, or the 'neoliberal conservative hegemony' which simultaneously and contradictorily decrees that women must earn a crust *and* stay home to bake the bread for free, I am going to talk about the kids. As Anne Manne says, "Deeper even than the 'social construction of motherhood' or patriarchy, are children's faces, full of hope and expectation that you will treat them well."[345]

But when it comes to children's needs, where on earth do we *start*? Do we look at childcare only? Do we look to 'shared care'? Do we take in breast/bottle, crib/bedsharing, pram/sling, wood/plastic and day-to-day choices parents make? Or do we discuss the historical development of childhood: where children have gone from fully integrated human beings within our tribes and societies, to economically productive units in post-industrialisation, to precious jewels in the 'nuclear-family-shaped' Western culture?

Do we restrict ourselves to believing that if a child's needs for food, dry bum and warmth are met then we can be off, forgetting those times *we* had all those things but still needed a hug, reassurance, loving arms, attention or a kiss and that tick-box responses would have seemed cruel, detached and inhumane? Do we believe children are born as a blank slates where everything depends on us (cue toxic guilt and full-on sacrificial 'overparenting'),[346] or do we see them as fully-formed human beings who will grow up despite us, not because of us (cue hands-off, wrap-around care for longer than an average adult's working day, minimalistic parenting then boarding school and intimacy relegated to 'optional')?

Or do we see the combination of factors, the nurture, the innate personalities, freedom from bullying, protection from abuse, emotional support, enrichment, education, silliness, the home environment, the wider society, the responsive care, the protection from harm, and love, as all featuring high on the list of what matters when we care for a child? We can bear in mind that children need responsive care, and that if provided by ourselves or by a good 'alloparent' we have chosen, then we are doing alright by our kids.

As human beings who are fallible, we can only offer our necessarily imperfect, but loving and responsible, care. However, this is not to be taken that children are 'resilient' and can survive mistreatment, neglect or whatever. It is about decent, loving, humane, good enough care. And how that is the best anyone will ever receive.

As my mother has always said, school-aged and adolescent children have emotional needs which are just as great as infants and toddlers. We can see it around us and we can remember it ourselves. After all, we were young once, weren't we? However, our culture seems to believe that children over three months old should be, or are, pretty much self-sufficient or, at least, should not show any stubborn attachment to one particular caregiver. Especially mummy. We talk about 'separation anxiety' without stopping to consider the very real emotions a child experiences when they are apart from their preferred carer*: "it is an emotion closest to grief".[347] Children are praised for being settled, when this might well be interpreted to mean *quiet*, with no thought as to their actual feelings or long-term emotional impact.[348] Discussions about the needs of the under-threes for secure attachment and responsive care from primary carers are *evidence based*.[349] Yet, talk of the needs of babies and young children rarely get top billing: they are demoted below full female employment and affordable childcare headlines in political briefing papers. And teens? Invisible. After all, parents of school-aged children are encouraged to go *out* to work, without thought to the needs of older children after school and during school holidays. They are left in the no-mans-land of childhood: too old apparently for family care; too vulnerable for self-sufficiency. Well, there are plenty of us who want to be there for our teens before and after school and during the school holidays. They have their needs. Why do our socio-economic policies treat them as though they don't exist?

When it comes to our children's health and wellbeing, we read it, we see it and we know it.[350] Childhood obesity is at crisis point. The time children

---

* You know, mother, usually.

spend in front of screens, whether tablets, smartphones or television, is increasing. Many children spend huge amounts of time in non-family care. Too many children arrive at school tired and hungry. Eating disorders amongst young children are on the rise. The frequency with which children are assessed within the school system has increased massively and is inflicted on younger and younger children. In respect of child and adolescent mental health, anxiety and medication are on the rise, but services are woefully underfunded. Sexual assaults *by* children are on the increase. Tolerance for children in public seems to have disappeared (count the tuts in public when you have a toddler experiencing high emotion on the floor of the supermarket). Provision for childhood activities in public are low on the list of priorities: just marvel at the lack of free and safe places for children to play outside, closure of libraries, and lack of investment in community projects for children compared with investment in nuclear weapons. The crowning glory? Child poverty exists in twenty-first century Britain (one of the richest nations in the world, the home of Oliver Twist) and in the United States (the land of the free and innovator of the soup kitchen). Our 'Constitutions' should surely be renamed 'Contradictions'.

We could bear in mind that we have two ways of measuring success in a country: GDP and happiness. Despite the fact that wellbeing is arguably one of the most important issues facing our children, it seems our kids are not doing particularly well on the happiness front. Aside from cases of abuse and neglect where parental failures have not been adequately addressed, there are many children from otherwise good enough homes who are being worked too hard at school, having too little family time and are miserable. Yes, I know, so are the adults. So is that cat who broke the Internet. But, come on. News about our children's welfare does not make happy reading. Perhaps all this is a product of the absence of 'affective rights' featuring highly in public priority: we focus on the socio-cultural, political and economic systems[351] forgetting the human beings at the centre of it all. No room for the affection, the love, the care or the humanity of our lives.

We must speak loud and clear that (as emphasised by World Movement of Mothers Europe) "parents desire to invest in their children. They have a natural sense of responsibility and a concern to act effectively. Ultimately, they are held responsible by society for negative outcomes. These motivations, concerns, and responsibilities should be acknowledged and considered seriously in any discussion or implementation of state policy. Many tensions experienced by mothers derive from the impact of employment and taxation policy on the range of child rearing and family choices parents believe they have. Information and awareness of the consequences of state policies on parent and child wellbeing are necessary for wise decision making. Parental engagement and effectiveness in rearing the rising generation will impact the long-term sustainability of European society more surely than many other matters presently considered important."[352] When are policymakers going to listen? Children want more family time and parents want to give it to them — if only we could.

Sue Palmer talks about *Toxic Childhood,* and her work is well worth a read. Oliver James talks about the importance of our early experiences in shaping our mental health[353] and tells us *How Not To F**k Them Up.* In *Raising Babies,* Steve Biddulph asks "Should Under 3s Go to Nursery?"[354] And in *Motherhood, How Should We Care for Our Children?* Anne Manne speaks about the care of children and our children's wellbeing. It is a challenge to read some of these books' lengthy, detailed and fearless discussions on children, appraising studies and narratives about the effect of substandard, inappropriate group daycare, for example. Discussions of childhood emotional wellbeing can bring out a feeling of defensiveness, guilt or regret about our own choices or behaviour as parents (whether using childcare or caring ourselves) and invite reflection about our own childhoods.

Perhaps this is why the subject of our children's wellbeing is taboo. It hurts too much. Combine this with a fear that accepting children's needs means women are lumbered with the job of meeting them, and it seems that childhood, like care, simply isn't valued: it is verboten.

However, as difficult as it is, we *have* to face our responsibility and our duties to our young. And we have to face often painful issues from our own upbringing. At some point we have to ask ourselves: does the care of young children have an impact on the adults they will become? Dare we look at the origins of love and hate,[355] psychopathy and neurosis, anxiety and depression? What factors are at play? What can we do better? Because if we are indeed overseeing an epidemic of toxic childhood, we have to recognise that our poisoned children might well become contaminated adults. Many of us prefer not to look, and our governments restrict their concern for our children only insofar as they might become compliant and institutionalised economic units. The UK Government is stuffed to the brim with a boarding school elite who (arguably) actively distrust love, connection and warmth and close emotional bonds, particularly with one's mother. No wonder the neoliberal project is so feted and the stuff of human lives ignored as though it is merely incidental to economic growth.

However, whatever our discomfort, we have to speak it. How can we justify the 'childcare' debate focusing almost exclusively on the rights or obligations of parents to engage in paid work, rather than the needs of children to responsive, loving care? How can we justify a significant *class* of people (children) being marginalised in political and economic debate with their needs, their interests and their emotional wellbeing relegated below the bottom line? Because that is what is happening: with every corporate step staking a claim to greater and greater commodification of care; with every politician appointed to 'Secretary of State for *Childcare* and Education' and with every economic policy which forces families to put babies into group daycare against their wishes. It is becoming old-fashioned, even taboo, to 'advocate for the baby' or 'speak for the children'. However, we must start pushing policymakers to address family and community life as a priority instead of regarding the welfare of families, children and the vulnerable as an inconvenient hurdle or, at times, a human shield propped before economic and business interests. As mothers, we are uniquely placed here. We have been agitators for social change and social justice in the past. We need to continue that tradition for ourselves, our children, and generations to come. We needn't fear causing guilt or offending anyone else. After all, we all feel guilty anyway, don't we, no matter what.

We can push for recognition of the importance of a child having time with his or her family, especially in the early years and in *adolescence*, two periods of significant emotional and development upheaval. When politicians talk of the family, they are often talking about sexual union and conservative marriage within 'heteronormative' conditions: what they seem not to do is to recognise the needs of children and parents for time together as a unit. Yet, children of the 'stay at home parent' are frequently pitied, for having the misfortune of having an overbearing, lazy mother who doesn't have a life of her own (for an exemplary example of this, see Joan K. Peters' *When Mothers Work, Loving Our Children Without Sacrificing Ourselves*). Even I wondered, by the end of her book, whether my children were going to be stifled, disadvantaged, insular adults because I had dared to look after them myself. Yet, I remember the words of Elaine Heffner: "the art of mothering is to teach the art of living to children".[356] What we do is important, yet our confidence can very easily be knocked — and isn't this just what the powers that be are engineering?

There are many aspects of our work as parents which we could, and should, do better. Others are controversial and nobody wants to agree whether x is a good thing or y is going to breed a maniacal serial killer. However, at heart, can we accept that it is a central part of our work to ensure that our children feel held by loving arms, are physically and emotionally safe in a loving home and are seen through the eyes of parents who love them? As Carlos Gonzales says in *Kiss Me!*, we can raise our children with *love*.[357] It's the least that we can do and it is the least that they deserve.

After all, if *we* don't love, listen to, play with, engage with and guide our children to give them a secure base[358] from which to explore the jungle out there, no one else is going to do it for us. Although we can hire someone to do the practical care, our *relationship* of parent and child cannot be outsourced along with the laundry or the changing of the baby's nappy. As Anne Manne discusses in *Motherhood*, "we do not expect an adult to easily replace a beloved person with another. It violates our sense of the preciousness of individual people, and even our sense of what love is. Yet we expect this of a baby."[359]

WHO CARES ABOUT CARE-WORK?

With all that in mind, I have no doubt that this chapter wades into choppy waters. It might raise high tides of emotion and could trigger waves of guilt. It is loaded. It is personal. Yet, we *have* to begin, as a society, to talk about the importance of *care*. What is it? Why does it matter? Who does it? Why? What happens if we don't? Do we want to think about it? Who needs care? Who cares?

Well for starters, in the context of *care-work*, 'care' is about service to others. It is not a feeling; it is an action. Care is not owned. It is *given*. Yes, we can certainly care *about* someone: to care about another involves emotion, affection and thought, and it is a significant part of what we do and experience as parents. It is the emotional labour of parenthood. However, when it comes to the work of care, it is a verb and it is a gift. When we care *for* someone, it is a peculiar and intrinsically human endeavour. So when I write about 'care', it is the physical, attentive, affectionate *work* of care I am talking about. It requires bodily and emotional presence and sensitivity to another's needs.

So what of the *recipients* of care? The fact is that those in society who are most in need of care are undoubtedly babies, toddlers, young children and adolescents; postpartum mothers, the sick or disabled; the elderly; and the dying. We will have fallen into most of those categories at some point. Indeed, all of us need care, in greater or lesser degrees, *throughout* our lives. We all get sick sometimes, or bereaved, or troubled: and we depend on someone to help us in our dark hours. We need human *connection*. Although we might stretch to accept that we were all babies once, we don't like to admit our inevitable mortality and fragility. However, we must begin to recognise that the *need* for care is the *common denominator* of our humanity. As Anne-Marie Slaughter was clear in *Unfinished Business*, care is an inevitable and important part of our lives.[360] Remember our discussion about dependency? Well, dependency and care are facts of life and a fundamental part of the human condition. One could say they are the two feet upon which humanity stands.

And the children? The unavoidable truth is that our young are in need of care. And while we might be able to delegate some of this work, they still need their parents: they need to build a relationship, connection and love within their family.[361] It is a crucial aspect of our humanity: the growing of people does not end at birth; it is a process of development which takes time, presence and commitment.

When we are away from our young children, we might be thinking *about* them; we might be doing tasks which *concern* them; we might be feeling *affection* for them. However, whilst we can care *about* our children, a key part of the growing of relationships is the extent to which we care *for* them.[362] In this context, the cold hard reality is that when we are not *with* our children (babies and toddlers particularly) we are not caring *for* them. It is not to say that we are not doing something for them in their absence: earning a wage to provide food or clothing, or making arrangements for something, or organising their dentist appointment, for example. However, the fact is that we have *delegated care*, whether to a relative, a friend or a commercial provider. Unlike many things in our consumerist, technological culture, we cannot perform *virtual* care for our children. There is no care remote control. Whilst it has been thoroughly commodified, care has not, as yet, been automated.[363] Indeed, despite neoliberal pretence that the market is best placed to provide services from care to education, our intimate relationships (in which tenderness, care and love play a central part) *cannot* be put out to tender. There are limits to the 'commodification' of our care-work and the outsourcing of our relationships.[364] It's that *other* inconvenient truth nobody's making a film about.

Children know when they are being fobbed off; they know when their parents have not come to their school play; they know when they have adequate substitute care but that their mother or father are busy, as always. They know that 'quality time', when the rest of the time is 'no time', is a poor substitute for showing up in their day-to-day lives. We could say that children need "child time".[365] They deserve to be raised in a society in which their right to parental involvement in their daily care is valued, not discouraged or frustrated by socio-economic policy which deems the parent's duty to be the ideal worker rather than the present and engaged parent. Or we can be honest and say "damn those pesky kids" as though we are some baddie from Scooby Doo, and get on with fashioning a society in which the young know they are the wrong side of adulthood. Our children are treated nowadays as tiresome, needy, sapping interlopers in our individualistic world. Our culture tells us that we are 'equal' and that mothering, and children, should be dispersed[366] as though they are handfuls of pretty confetti.

The thing is our children are *not* confetti. They are living, growing, fragile human beings. They need to be fed, watered and loved. They need their security and their emotional needs to be met. We needn't go 'full pelt' into attachment parenting to acknowledge the need of children for secure attachments to primary caregivers. A child needs a sense of belonging, a sense of being valued, especially by their parents. Academic Kathleen Lynch, in a 2015 speech asks, "Why is there silence about the emotional labour required to reproduce humanity? . . . What we now have in effect is a care-less model of citizenship."[367] This rings true, doesn't it? Our culture suffers from 'who cares syndrome'. And the answer is, increasingly, nobody cares. And those who do are *nobodies*. As Martha Fineman notes, "taking care of someone such as a child while they are young, until they 'become their own person', is work, represents a major contribution to the society, and should be explicitly recognized as such".[368]

We can debate whether women and mothers naturally possess or exhibit a 'feminine ethic of care' or whether that is one of the sources and tools of our oppression as women; but we have to recognise that *someone* has to care about our children. Surely we have to acknowledge that we — men and women alike — have, at some point, to nurture those we love. That our children are vulnerable and dependent. That, with that, comes a *degree of* sacrifice. It is a basic factor of human life. It is non-negotiable. Our children are not Aztecs who are calling on an unfathomable blood sacrifice; they are mammals who want our milk; they are human beings who want our love.

It's plain to see: in our culture, neither care, nor carers matter and dependence is viewed as deviant. We have to be 'self-sufficient'. We should be 'independent'. We should be our very own personal stock-market. However, these values simply do not work when we have families. As Lynch and others discuss, we have to recognise the importance of '*affective* equality' and 'affective *labour*'. The 'affective' (as opposed to 'political', 'economic', or 'socio-cultural') is "concerned with providing and sustaining relationships of love, care and solidarity".[369] But instead, this seems invisible or inconsequential for major political parties. What does that tell us? That it doesn't matter, that it is not valued. That the only equality often discussed is *financial* or *workplace*. However, it is clear that the *affective* is the important stuff of humanity which other fields seem to leave to the footnotes. It is what politicians talk about when they talk of the impact of relationship breakdown and family values on our society, whilst pursuing policies which undermine them.

When it comes to family care, there is a distinctive spectre of market competition under capitalism looming over our every decision. Parental care is effectively a thorn in neoliberalism's side. I will be talking about economics in the next chapter but for now, it is becoming increasingly apparent that the commodification of care is not going away and it is not going to ease up. The market has its grip, after all. And it wants care-work to submit, and families to be squeezed out of the business of caring for their own children. Just think about it: when we talk about care by a parent, we are often faced with the fact that society views maternal care as having a very strict timeframe of acceptability: you have twelve months if you're lucky in the UK. And the US? No paid maternity leave at all. So how long can we realistically allow mothers to recuperate, bond with their babies and care for their families? Well, if two weeks are good enough for Marissa Mayer.[370] After that? Nurseries and nannies will gladly step up to the plate. Anyone left insisting that they want to care for their children has to live off the scraps. As with breastfeeding, capitalism and GDP have no place for loving maternal care: it is free, it is powerful, it operates outside the framework of client/consumer, money/services and measurement/ competition in a system which demands profit in the free market. Money and capitalist infiltration into one of the most intimate and fundamental aspects of our lives. What could go wrong?

Care-work (even when commodified) is seen as low status and low worth. It remains 'gendered', in that it remains *women* who care for babies and young children in nurseries. We might well pay our cleaners more per hour than we pay our nannies. We certainly pay our plumber a significantly higher sum. And bankers, even higher. Care is devalued then, whether it is commercialised or unpaid. We have to stop and ask *why* this is, and what on *earth* this is going to do for our humanity and our future.[371] Will the devaluation of care lead to poor care? Care cannot be reduced to the short straw, yet our culture's treatment of care-work is to calculate its commodification, and count the cost. Yet, not everyone wants to delegate care: some of us want to do it, if only finances would allow.

ALLOPARENTS AND DELEGATED CARE

We mother in the context of contradiction[372]: we are expected to care for our children well; but others can do it better. The problem is, there are many women who are distressed at having to leave their children in the care of others. This is a *feminist* issue: it is the flipside of the affordable childcare coin. Yet, we are told that substitutes — 'alloparents', 'allomothers'* (something discussed by Sarah Blaffer Hrdy in *Mother Nature*), 'othermothers' or daycare-workers — should be brought in to care for our children. They are necessary: they are liberation. But only to free us to market-work. We are offered substitute care, rather than support in our care-work. We receive the message, loud and clear, that we mothers should get away from the kids and get to work for better things.[373]

The set-up goes like this. The solution to our tiredness is for us to get back to the workplace so the alloparent or assortment of alloparents can do the childcare.

› 'Displacement' not respite: the solution is to delegate the care of the children for significant periods of time, not for mother to have an afternoon off here and there while a trusted grandparent or the father looks after the children.

› 'Work' not family: the solution to being exhausted with two small children is for us to 'find ourselves' (at work) while the goody bag of

* Remember them, from earlier in the book? They are usually women, often related or otherwise known intimately, trusted to care lovingly and responsively for the child, with whom the child has had ample time to bond and grow familiar.

alloparents do the childcare; not to have the alloparent help with older children while we see to the baby or have a nap.

› 'Work' not leisure: the solution to feeling depleted and having no time to oneself or *'something of one's own'* (closely related to that *room* Virginia Woolf advocated) is to 'find a job' (and give that time and energy to an employer to exploit), rather than insisting that the father step up, or family rally round, and ensure the mother has some time for her own pursuits — whether an afternoon for sport, reading, studying or time with other women. Or whatever does it for her.

In short the prescription for tired mothers is more work. 'Proper' work. We forget that mothers need support for their work *as* mothers. In her essay, "'But She Has a Nanny' ... With Accompanying Eye Roll", Rebecca Jaremiko Bromwich honestly tells how the "demands of paid work were manageable: it was the unpaid work of bearing children that I couldn't manage on my own ... I needed support in my work".[374] *This* is the neglected terrain of feminism. We may want to care for our children, but this does not dispense with our needs to be cared for ourselves so that we can look after our children without unacceptable strain and isolation.

Yet this issue of isolation and lack of support is neglected in favour of workplace participation. Our culture views 'work' as the solution and 'exclusive mothering' as the problem. For mother *and* child. Despite the fact that working-class women and women of colour (who have often borne the brunt of double shifts of market-work *and* domestic work) may well see employment as yet another burden, rather than liberation. But, as usual, those women are not heard or heeded. It is the disaffected middle-class isolated housewife striving for satisfaction out of the home that has been canonised as the saint of self-fulfilment through paid work. Under this rule, support of the mother in her work gives way to disconnection through displacement of the mother as the provider of care. In patriarchal neoliberalism? Surely not! In the age of the individual, there is no room for a mother/child dyad. It's too much like a two-headed freak, out of place in the circus of self-interest and 'independent', lonely, big-heads. The ringmaster? Patriarchy. The lions? Capitalism. The clowns? Think about that one.

I should say that this is not a criticism of the *notion* of allomothers. Or, for that matter, the deployment of them. Nor is it a challenge to the importance of community or of children having a place in a wide network of people who love them, or the ability of mothers to rely on others to do their job of mothering or to engage in something outside the home (including paid work or career) for the length of time of their choosing. In case it has escaped you, this is exactly what I *am* arguing for, especially in the context of mothers who want to care for their children. For mothers who willingly look after their children themselves, support is important for helping them *in* their work; not to divest them of that work or that place. It is important to give respite to those mothers *from* their care-work; not to encourage them to get a second job on top as though they're not *already working*. Because a mother's work is not nine to five. Imagine Dolly Parton's take: "Working 24/7 what a way to make no money". Nobody else is expected to work that long, unsupported, unpaid, undervalued and without sufficient rest.

Alloparents have a place: of service *to the mother*. In a society which doesn't care, and in a society in which other women are not *around* to help, the only allomother we can rely on is a low-paid stranger. Usually women. Nothing like the reliance on women to do the work of caring, so long as it's not us *important* women doing it; so long as it's for a (low) wage; so long as it's not within the family or community structure; so long as it's for other people's children and not our own. Welcome to the wonderful modern world of commodification: take-away pizza, outsourced ironing and bought-in mother-care.

What I *am* challenging is the misapplication of the notion of the value of alloparents to the rules of neoliberal, intensive workplace participation, by which a mother is separated from her young children for regular and/or long periods of time and at a distance.

I am challenging the notion that it is better for a young child to be placed in a carousel of care than the care of a willing mother. The fact is that alloparents and a 'village' *have* traditionally supported mothers and the work *mothers* do in mothering. Yet, the practice in traditional societies where an allomother takes the child for a short time while the mother does some other work nearby (translated in modern Western culture to the grocery shopping, or doing the laundry, or cooking the family's meal) is a very different thing from a ten-hour childcare a day or night-nurseries in the hands of someone not sufficiently invested in the child, far away from the mother while she works in the market economy.

After all, advocates of alloparents are not *advocating* for allomothers to help with the children while the mother does the *housework*, or cooks the *meal*, or washes the *clothes*; that would be far too helpful, too practical, and far too radical.[375] That would demand recognition of that as the work a mother does when she raises a family, especially with young children. No. We need the housework to be done by the *fairies*, and the childcare to be offed, so that the real job of the mother — the valuable one — is that done within the market for a wage in our genderless equality capitalist utopia of self-actualisation through market labour participation. In other words: a mother's place is in the office; a child's place is in childcare.

Factors to keep in mind in respect of the alloparent issue include: the *age* of the child; the number of carers; the location; and the level of affection and responsive care shown by the substitute. These all matter. Yet, they rarely feature in the discussion. Blanket statements are made by politicians, with little flexibility for the child, the family or their preferences. The unique child has unique needs and characteristics. Some children are breastfed on demand, or would be if given the opportunity. Some are shy or highly sensitive in group settings and with strange adults. The younger the child, the more intense their needs; the younger the child, the fewer people she may tolerate being cared for beyond her primary carer.

We have to have respect for children's needs for secure attachment and for consistency in their early years. We have the right to question whether the responsive care of our babies and young children and the building of relationships and love with our children can be adequately achieved in group daycare or substandard substitute care. It is important and relevant to consider the adequacy of frequently changing, low-paid, overworked staff with too many babies to do justice by in a group daycare setting. But, I suspect, the mothers forced to use such care are not those who are busy taking over the boardroom. The privileged women, and their feminist politician sisters, will most likely use a nanny but advocate group daycare for the plebs.[376] It's *Animal Farm* all over again, with a moo moo here and an oink oink there.

The argument about alloparents also neglects the fact that many families with a primary carer at home nevertheless use playschool, kindergarten or preschool for young children from about three years of age for a number of hours a week. Here, you will find: *de facto* alloparents. Substitute care! It's a miracle! It's fabulous! Bitesize chunks of play away from mum and dad. You couldn't make it up! When the placement is right for the child; when the hours are the right balance; when the activities are appropriate; and where the substitute carer is warm and responsive, you've got a *great* example of the benefits of alloparents, right there.

These alloparents are other adults (predominantly women) caring for children in age-appropriate settings in place of the parent. In legal speak we say the alloparent is *in loco parentis;* and such care is extremely widespread. When older, they go to other alloparents in the form of teachers, and beloved dinner ladies, for a significant number of their waking hours. So we already *do* have a society in which children are out of the custody and supervision of mothers for over six hours per day, five days per week for a large proportion of their childhood. And it doesn't stop there, if the child is lucky, and if they have 'affective equality', older children often happily skip off to the grandparents' house for the weekend, to get away from mum and dad and eat chocolate until they feel sick, and go to bed late, and have Coco Pops for breakfast instead of porridge. Children go to play at their friends' houses or the neighbour's house down the road; they might well go to clubs and sports teams where they will love their supervisor as a role model who is, like, so much *cooler* than mum and dad. It's their *job* to find their own place in the world eventually, and to seek a place for themselves as they grow, outside of the potting soil of home. If lucky, they have a community and an extended family to call on as a tribe, to fill their sense of belonging. We all have a need for belonging to *wider community*.[377]

So, we can see that what politicians and many liberal feminists are *really* talking about is the care of *babies* and *toddlers*. Just a few short years of each child's life. Nobody seems to want to believe that there are women who want to do it; let alone value them or what they do, when they do it. They do not accept the importance of this work. How it is *hard* work: hence why so many women have said "get me out of here" rather than "support me in my work and pay my partner to have three months' leave in the immediate postpartum period at the *same time*". Or, "pay me a subsistence wage to prevent my marginalisation and vulnerability, enable me to get respite and enjoy leisure, to enjoy my children, and value me and my children as though we matter as much as the industrial machine". Then, "welcome me back to the workplace without discrimination or penalty, honouring the skills I have developed", and "organise the workplace for the benefit of human beings". After all, even the most demanding feminists have never felt able to demand all *that*. It's too, you know, *demanding*. It's too unrealistic, when our reality is patriarchal neoliberal capitalism. It's a dog eat dog world. Everyone should be fighting for the scraps.

What the current childcare and alloparent discussion is *not* about is ensuring that mothers have a society which values them and which is vibrant with a community of parents and adults who care, within safe and loving villages, which supports her work as mother, and allows her respite and time to 'fill her cup'. It is *not* about providing care for the carer, to ensure that the carer's needs are met so that *they* can "survive and thrive".[378]

It *is*, rather, about the means to offer escape from *affective* labour and to escape to *market* labour. It is a convenient way to convince a mother that she is failing her children by remaining at home in the early years; and must find something more productive to do than mother her children. Talk of shared care by, say, the Women's Equality Party, is compliantly restricted to the *postpartum first year* 'parental leave' rather than based on *long-term* options and socio-economic reform to enable families to enjoy more family time *together as they grow*. Policies remain predicated on women remaining *in* the workforce, with limited time out. Even the term 'maternity leave' is now firmly out of favour. Remember what we talked about in **Postmaternal Culture**?

I say that each mother must go with her personal conscience and must be supported in the decision she makes when it comes to childcare. If she has a partner, it is a team decision: childcare, after all, is a joint responsibility of both parents. However, we cannot talk of 'choice' when the choice is a 'rock or a hard place' in which the rock is economic marginalisation and social isolation and the hard place is workplace participation with no room or forgiveness of care responsibilities. It neglects the diverse set-ups — from lone motherhood through to mothers with disabilities — and assumes we are all ready and waiting ideal workers with a wife at home. We must push for greater reform of our socio-economic policies so that we are not constrained to make 'choices' which are, in effect, compelled sufferance. After all, this is not the *Sufferance* Movement, some hopeless capitalist sister of the Suffragette Movement. It is the *Purplestockings Movement*. And it's got legs.

With this in mind, we have to push for change. Our public policies and employment regulations must recognise this central fact: family, where there are two involved and decent parents, is a team sport. If a mother does not want to provide the care, and neither does the father, they have to find that alloparent who will, and they should be empowered to find a decent one. That involves adequately funded services. Yes, you heard right: I have no issue with state funding to prevent childcare being physically dangerous or emotionally neglectful, understaffed or staffed by those who have no place looking after vulnerable dependent children. It is the least we can do socially, if we are to hold true that mothers should not be tied by their reproductive biology to the work of raising children at the expense of work or career outside the home. See, I'm a good feminist, really.

All that said: *others* should not be more valuable than *mothers* when it comes to care of our children, in terms of investment or reward. If we want equality, sisters, we should at least start *there*.

The money should be paid to the family: a parent should have the right whether to pay an alloparent, or use the money to support the family while one of them does the care.* The money should follow the child; whereas, at present, the only people *not* worth financial investment in childcare are those who care for their *own* families. How is this right?

There is also the significant issue of special needs or illness in parent or child. From autism to physical disabilities in children to autoimmune diseases in adult women, what happens when the needs of mother or child are greater still? Working outside the home may be out of reach, even if the mother would like to. Do we continue to fail carers and children by failing to support or financially support families in this situation? Do we continue to isolate such families? Do we recognise that carers of those with disabilities or intense needs have their *own* needs for respite or real opportunities to share care and be cared for themselves? I have heard some moving accounts of mothers seeking to gain greater respect and support to mother their children in circumstances where the mother's disability has drawn suspicion and condescension, unacceptable delays in finding suitable housing, and criticism for her predicament. Where is our compassion? Why do we see a collection of human beings, each with their own needs, and condemn them for failing to be self-sufficient or for 'being a drain' on resources? Where a child has extra needs, do we recognise the needs of the mother for greater support? After all, her decisions may well be even less based on her choice than a mother whose journey has had fewer challenges. Alloparents, in this context, are especially valuable.

So, if we have survived this minefield, we can agree, (if you take a humane, progressive, maternal feminist stance to the issue of childhood) that all children require loving responsive care. At some point, we have to be able to advocate for the children, the most voiceless, marginalised, yet dependent, in our societies. As mothers, perhaps it's the least we can do. It's not always about us. It's not always about the paycheck or the kudos.

* I will explore such systems of 'homecare allowance' as seen in, for example, Finland in the chapter, **The Politics of Mothering**.

Children have intense needs for care.

Yes, our feminist concerns prick up when we reflect on what this means. We can de-genderise mothering and talk parenting the whole day through. But if it is still the vast majority of mothers as opposed to fathers who take leave to care for the child, or who sacrifice an income to continue to provide care, or who are penalised by a society which doesn't value the care she provides or recognise even her *desire* to look after her children and the value of that care, nor the barriers she faces when she attempts to re-enter the workforce or do so under the conditions that she feels are right for her family, then we are engaging in doublespeak and partying like it's 1984**. And that leads to policies and debate which fail once to mention the word 'mother' in true postmaternal style. Now *that's* an insult. *That's* oppressive.

THE 'OPPRESSION' OF MOTHERING

Talking of insults, something which crops up time and time again is that the work of mothering — the task, activities, and emotional work of being a mother and raising our children — is dismissed as 'oppressive'.

It seems that to do mothering is to be a victim, especially in the eyes of certain quarters of feminism. Is mothering devalued and the mothers seen as worthless? Often. Do isolation and economic impoverishment of mothers make the work of mothering harder? At times. But is mothering actually oppressive of itself? No. As Shari L. Thurer remarks in *The Myths of Motherhood*, "to suggest that mothers are made miserable by mothering is egregiously inaccurate ... in a cold and ruthless world, the relations between mother and child may be the most genuine, natural, spontaneous and exquisite love there is".[379] Too true, as many a mother will attest.

Indeed, it is one of the most liberating, human, loving, spiritual and rich experiences I have ever had. It is something I am grateful for every day. Ask many a mother, grandmother and great-grandmother. And don't just ask those who resented or resisted it. Sara Ruddick was equally keen to resist the prevalent view that mothers are, "by virtue of their *mothering*" [my emphasis] principally victims. She describes the characterisation of mothering as victimhood as an "egregiously inaccurate account of many women's experience and is itself oppressive to mothers".[380]

**It's that George Orwell again.

For all of the difficulties, for all of the tiredness, I would not relinquish this work, this time, this loving guidance, presence and care of my children. And, after spending two years researching and writing this book, surrounded by the narrative of mothers, and being a mother in the thick of it, I know that I am not alone in that feeling. Yet, a common feature of being a mother of young children who is not also in the workplace is how we are continually told we must be "going out of our minds with boredom" or "sitting around all day" or "feel bad for relying on your husband while he works really hard to support you". Yeah, I feel so guilty about that. Because I'm doing *nothing* important. *cries*

The notion that we are all "stuck indoors" is one aspect of the assumption of the oppressive nature of mothering: you will have noticed that I have rarely, if at all, described mothers who care full-time as 'stay at home mothers'. The reason? Because we are rarely just at home. Mother-work is private *and* public[381]; it is in society, in our towns, our schools, the shops, the doctors, the clinics, the playgroups, the friend's house, the café, the library, the bus station, the swimming pool. Our *office* is the world. Yet, often, we are derided as being "at home all day"; or we are patronised as "we must help them out of this oppressive private sphere". The echo-chamber of derision or pity against mothers is becoming deafening. It's not feminism: it's misogyny.

What is oppressive is not the mothering of our children; it is not the love, the cuddles, the nurture, the feeding, the little things and *everything* that mothers do. Rather, it is the social conditions that devalue us, that ignore us, that impoverish us, that render us at the mercy financially of a partner, or fail to invest in public services which *enrich* our office. So when I discuss, as I have in the course of this book, the difficulties faced by mothers in organising their lives or in the periods when they might have emotional needs that are unmet by a society which doesn't care, none of that — none — diminishes the fact that mothering our children can be one of the most precious and fulfilling things we do.

This is not to say that the experience and work of mothering is for everyone, nor every woman suited to it. Some women, I hear, quite enjoy a bit of shopping for clothes. I can't bear it. Others enjoy triathlons. Not my cup of tea. Yet, mothers are frequently universally derided or pitied for the work they do, the mothering they do, and the lives they lead, without any recognition that *mothering* is not oppressive for many mothers. That it does not make us victims. Of patriarchy, of men, or of ourselves. To recall Adrienne Rich's distinction between the *institution* of motherhood and the *experience* of mothering, we could well say that motherhood under patriarchal capitalism might well be a pain in the GDP but that doesn't mean the relational stuff, the love, the humanity of raising our children isn't precious indeed.

HOUSEWORK AMIDST THE HEARTWORK

The Feminine Mystique released us (well, privileged white women, anyway) from a miserable housewifery and launched us into a capitalist mystique, but as Betty Friedan subsequently recognised in *The Second Stage*, Honey, we forgot the kids. She scrambled to put the genie back in the bottle, proclaiming that the family is the next feminist frontier. In that spirit, Purplestockings, we have some trekking to do. Welcome to the politics of housework.[382] Let's just say that, for women who do not have the domestic help (the metaphorical wife-at-home), they are having to *do* it all. For them, the equality-project is not working: it is exhausting. For those women who are at home, the equality-project insists that they are unequal dependent parasites and an embarrassment. Sisterhood isn't just dead, it's mortified.

When it comes to institutions, one of the lingering stereotypes of mothers who forego market-work for care-work is that they are nothing more than deferential, brain-dead, desperate prisoners of the institution of housewifery. The domestic sphere is seen as thoroughly old-fashioned for us modern women, taught to go for the corner office, not the kitchen. So what a shock it is when we have our babies — consumed with the heartwork but not doing much of the housework in those earlier days, weeks and months — and defining ourselves as 'mothers', yet still finding ourselves referred to as 'a housewife'. It knocked *me* for six.

Yes, blow me down, I have used the word 'housework'. Well, who do you think does it? Those fairies? I suppose for privileged women with buy-in help, it might as well be. But for the rest of us, we still do a disproportionate amount of it whether in employment or caring for our children at home. It's the second shift, remember? What's that saying? "A woman's work is never done." It certainly isn't when what we do, from childcare to cleaning, is rarely regarded *as* work. For mothers, it should surely be "A mother's work is never recognised".

Yes, the work of home is often conveniently forgotten *as work*. But it is important work: if it is not done and children live in squalor the mother invariably gets it, health suffers and all the ill-effects of poverty, including social exclusion, ensue. If we fail to run our errands or do the shopping, we have nothing to eat; if we fail to cook for our family, we starve or we live on takeaways with all the ill-health which follows. Anyone who has done housework knows it is tiring — the fatigue and never-ending cycle of housework has been well documented, if we have not experienced it for ourselves.

It is worthwhile reflecting on the fact that, feminism or no, ten-hour shifts or no, lone-parent or not, housework — cleaning, ironing, cooking, shopping and laundry — has to be done by *somebody*. Whilst I don't want my worth to be tied to how shiny the taps were this morning[383] (none of us do, surely) the problem is that the work of home and care is still *there*. It is simply not on for women to be expected to do it all: and to be doing it all for *free*. Because we *are* still *doing* most of it ... or responsible for outsourcing it. Yes, men *are improving* their performance of housework ... by an incredible one minute per day per year.[384] My goodness, talk about the slow turn of the screw.*

The truth is that housework has been subtly integrated into the role of mother or status of woman. The history of domesticity is quite interesting, if you are so inclined to read further.[385] However, it is the twenty-first century and we live in the age of equality: housework is part of living, not a necessary feature of womanhood. And it should be shared as a fundamentally unisex activity. Men: get thee to the washing machine, mum's been working hard enough, whether keeping the baby alive and fed or working in the market, just like you did all day too.

All this said, there *are* those of us who see homemaking as satisfying. In *Radical Homemakers*, Shannon Hayes is clear that "homemaking is not something that stands in the way of our deeper fulfilment; it becomes the fertile ground that feeds it".[386] And what's wrong with that? To each, their own. Perhaps the rise of the term of homemaker is a nod to the work that goes into making and tending a home. No doubt it is more popular than 'housewife', given its subtext of 'oppressed bore'. But just as there are those people who, for some reason, enjoy skiing or eleven-hour slogs in the

---

* Ok, I owe my husband a nod here to acknowledge that he has never been shy of the washing machine, the dishwasher or the cleaning. For this, and much more, you are a credit to your mother and yourself.

office, there are also those oddities, men and women who choose to "make family, community, social justice and the health of the planet the governing principle of their lives" and challenge the prevailing economic systems which ensure that "he who holds the gold makes the rules".[387] Don't they know they should be out there serving the neoliberal machine? That said, the question should be: Why should their 'social capital' take a hit, just because they see themselves as more than 'human capital'?

My own 'road to Damascus' moment came when I was on a mountain top, alone, with a book and a realisation that this was the first holiday I had had in years, that I was miserable in my profession, and that I wanted 'out'. Mind you, this was fully seven years before my son was even born: it wasn't a pull to children, it was a pull to 'getting a life'. According to Emily Matchar in *Homeward Bound*, 'parenting' seems to form but one part of a series of complex and intertwined facts which create a "pull to domesticity in an era of anxiety".[388] These include rising distrust towards government, corporations and the food industry; concern for our environment; economic anxiety; discontent with our dominant work culture; the appeal of 'hands-on' work in a world dominated by technology; and an "increasingly intensive standard of parenting".[389] Whatever the motivations, there are many who relate to this movement.

Hayes delves into pre-industrial history to demystify the origins of our modern notions of 'housewife' and 'public and private spheres' and concludes that, as the industrial revolution turned, men and women eventually "stopped working together to provide for their household sustenance" so that, for economic purposes, the Western home was "no longer a unit of production. It was a unit of consumption".[390]

Of course in reality, the home is very much a unit of production: most crucially the reproduction of the *entire human race*, as well as the productive work performed silently and unwaged by, usually, women at home. It brings to mind Simone De Beauvoir's view which betrayed a most misogynistic attitude when she wrote that women's work in the home is "not directly useful to society and produces nothing" and that the housewife is "subordinate, secondary, parasitic".[391] She may as well have said housewives are *Other*, and revealed herself to be a hypocrite too. Indeed, not simply a hypocrite but a dictator, revealed by her discussion with Betty Friedan: "we don't believe that any woman should have this choice. No woman should be authorised to stay home to raise her children. Society should be totally different. Women should not have that choice, precisely because if there is such a choice, too many women will make that one".[392] We could be "giving up too much" and living "half a life", according to Leslie Bennetts in *The Feminine Mistake*.[393] According to some, "policies that reward families for having housewives, or encourage women to assume the housewife role do more harm to women, and should be avoided".[394] Writer Elizabeth Wurtzel spits, "women were losing their minds pushing mops and strollers all day without a room or a salary of their own ... Let's please be serious grown-ups: real feminists don't depend on men. Real feminists earn a living, have money and means of their own".[395] In other words, we are prostituted/feeble* women because we step up to the inevitable care-work for our children.[396]

With feminists like these, who needs patriarchal neoliberal capitalist accumulation?** It is right there: we deserve no support, lest we *actually* make the choice to care for our children or benefit financially. We will let the whole side down, sisters, in the capitalist patriarchal game. We are unfeminist if we demand support from partners; we are unfeminist if we demand state support. We mothers basically risk being excluded from the club unless we put on work-clothes and flash our own cash at the doormen.

The message is loud and clear: mothers can't be trusted to make the right and sanctioned choice about how to frame their lives.[397] To be a mother at home is a stultifying vocation apparently.[398] We cannot trust silly women to make their own decisions, you see. They're dependent, not fully adult or equal. 'Stay at home mothers' get it wrong and suckered in by mother-love, not knowing what's best for them. *Diddums*. We are, indeed, those women who Maureen Freely describes as forgotten by feminism,[399] although perhaps forgotten is the wrong word. We are, actually, targets to be sniped at. And by women who aimed for, and got, 'better'. Condescension from other women. Less a sisterhood, more mean girls in business suits talking down to the 'little woman' at home. Just like men have done for generations.

The fact is that I and many maternal feminists are well aware of the downsides to caring for our children and keeping the home: we know we risk being 'put out of a job' on divorce and being significantly worse off for the rest of our lives; we know that we are up against the 'maternal clock'

* Take your pick.

** My publisher worries that my use of these phrases might be intimidating. I intend no intimidation — just imagine me writing such sentences in my purple fluffy dressing gown on a sofa. If really necessary, imagine my estuary English working-class tones wrapping themselves around these ugly words for ugly concepts.

which penalises our every second out of the workforce; we know that we risk financial inequality and vulnerability as a result of being out of the workplace. With that, comes increased personal vulnerability. We need more flexibility to enable parents to share care, at the right time for them if it works (by no means attractive to everyone at each stage of a child's life). However, the focus on workplace economic participation and equality loses something rather important: our humanity, how we want to live our lives, and that inconvenient truth: that many mothers want to spend time with their children, many of them exclusively for at least the first few years of life. The traitors that we are. We are punished financially as a result because of the stark truth that what we do is not recognised as worthy, worthwhile, or as *work*.

There has to be a recognition somewhere that seeing to our children and home is valuable work and that there are plenty of people who want to do it, at least for a few years. And surely this should be their right? Do we have to penalise a woman for taking a short time out of the labour market? For decades after? *Why?* Well, like, patriarchy. Bear in mind that older women who are beyond family responsibilities of young children still face discrimination: this is not to do with time out of the workforce. Family responsibility should not get the blame. It is misogyny, sexism and ageism. And there's nothing worse than an old woman. Unless you are young woman of 'childbearing age'. Really, it's just because you're a *woman*.

If we valued care and home, economically and socially, much of the 'Feminine Mistake' argument goes 'poof'. But that's the problem with patriarchal feminism. They want us to play by the rules or get beat. They want us beguiled by the Patriarchal Capitalist Mystique. Well, we need to change the rules, sister. Think bigger. We do not need to play the game of 'submissive little lady at home, dependent and deferential to her husband': we can insist on self-determination and autonomy, the right to frame our lives as we see fit depending on our family circumstances and desires, and, most importantly, the right to an income of one's own even when engaging in care-work.

WHAT IS WORK, ANYWAY?

All this said, many women are understandably suspicious of reducing their relationship with their children and everything they do for them and within the home to 'work'. It throws up the dilemma: what is work, anyway?[400] As the popular meme goes, we needn't dread the question "what do you do for a living?" We need to turn it around to "what do you live to do?" You can probably gather by now that I agree with bell hook's argument that "rethinking the meaning of work is an important task for future feminist movement".[401]

The issue of 'work' *must* be central to a progressive feminist movement. For mothers, if we do not describe our love labour *as* work, then how can we ensure, in a system which forces us to justify ourselves, that it is recognised and that we are financially supported? We are required, effectively, to prove our worth and to justify what we do to avoid being impoverished or financially dependent within private relationships. It tends to demonstrate, does it not, a paradox at the heart of what we regard as 'work'. It is so valuable, it is not work! It is so intimate, it is not work! It is so important, we must do it for free! Mothers end up wondering, justifiably, that when everything is 'for sale', 'commodifiable' and 'has a price', "Why so much of the work they do goes unrewarded."[402] For women who do the work of home and children, unwaged, our culture's refusal to remunerate or value it is nothing short of a vagina tax.

In all, the issue of work goes beyond housework and heartwork. It goes to our day-to-day lives and activities within our societies and communities which simply do not seem, under patriarchal capitalist rules, to qualify as 'work' and are thereby denied monetary compensation. For example:

› Running one's own *business* might *look* like work — but it gets muddy if there is no, or little, turnover or profit. *Then*, it might just be regarded as a 'hobby'.

› *Serving* someone a cup of tea at a parent and toddler group looks like work — until you see it is all voluntary, done by retired women, and no money changes hands.

› *Supporting* fellow mothers in breastfeeding looks like work — until you see the motivation being altruistic compassion and the reward heartfelt gratitude, so that the training and time spent in doing it are seen as leisure.

› *Educating children* is work — until you are deemed to be a 'home educator' because you are educating your own kids, in which case you are 'not working'.

There are a great many activities which are all crucial to our society and our families. Yet, they are not often classed as 'work'. Often the common denominator is that the work has traditionally been done by women. What are the chances! Such a coincidence![403]

Women — mothers — have *always* worked (whether on the land, educating their children, in a job or in the home). Whether it has been deemed to *constitute* 'work' is another thing; whether it has been deemed under patriarchy to be *worthy* of 'pay' is yet another. As World Movement of Mothers Europe observes, "Mothers have always worked, but what has changed is the world around them and the devaluation of the work of caring which they have always done. In the Survey of Mothers in Europe, through their messages to policymakers, mothers are clearly claiming that their devoted unpaid work should be recognised and valued as a vital and irreplaceable investment in the future of society."[404] The fact that many families wish to provide education to their children themselves is also a factor which must be borne in mind: the assumption of the State to provide education to our children was a recent historical move, and families retain the right (in the UK and US at least) to educate their children themselves.[405] Yet in sacrificing a salary to do so, they are cut loose, unsupported and at times even criticised for it.

So we do not recognise work when we see it or even when we *do* it. It isn't a question of *idleness*, as explored by Bertrand Russell in *In Praise of Idleness*, or the fact that, "The idea that the poor should have leisure has always been shocking to the rich." For women it comes down to this: the idea that a mother should have leisure is even *more* shocking than the poor having it; being 'jobless' is equated to being 'workless', and, lo, we immediately devalue or discount the *actual* work, albeit unwaged, that a mother does, when she does it.

It's not like footballers, tennis players, musicians, and apparently vacuous celebrities who are rewarded handsomely for their 'work' of kicking a ball around a field, hitting a ball with a racket, playing a guitar in front of a bunch of people, or posing for naked selfies. *That's* real work. That deserves elevation to riches or, at least, an income of sorts. For some reason. Yes, yes, there is *industry* built around their work. Unlike mothers at home: all they do is reproduce the human race, keep little people alive and growing, teaching, loving and investing in the future of humanity. Human beings: *every* industry is built around them. Nothing important there.

We remain forced to prove our worth, to protest that we are somehow 'deserving'. It brings to mind the way in which Victorians used to speak of the deserving and undeserving poor, attitudes which continue to prevail in individualist neoliberalism. Work hard and you'll be a success! Struggle? It's your fault. Get paid a lot? You must be the pinnacle of virtue and talent. Doing well? You're a cut above the underclass. Conveniently forget about inherited wealth, expensive educations and nepotism. Funny how we never really speak with the same venom about the deserving and undeserving rich, aristocracy and slave-trade heirs. Politicians talk about productivity in terms of 'hours worked', money exchanged, and the graft put in, no matter the nature of the work we are doing, what we are sacrificing to do it, or the fact that we could probably do it more productively in a shorter time, with more flexible working conditions and greater life satisfaction.

As bell hooks remarks in *All About Love*, some people embraced a "Protestant work ethic, convinced that a successful life would be measured by how much money one made and the goods one could buy with this money ... in keeping with this shift in values from a people-orientated to a thing-orientated society, the rich and famous, particularly movie stars and singers, began to be seen as the only relevant cultural icons. Gone were the visionary political leaders and activists."[406] This observation interested me — the theme of money, work and prestige runs counter, it seems, to subsistence, love and value. The terrifying political rise in the US of a very rich and famous white man, when seen in this context, seems to have some explanation. Money *trumps* decency and intellectual (and socially responsible) political vision, eh? Celebrity culture throws up an anomaly: we worship celebrities' 'cribs' but we are discouraged from sitting next to our babies' ones.

It's fascinating to stop and think about work. What is it? Why do we do it? For whom? How? Where? For what? In many ways, our views of work and our puritan 'work ethic' and worth all fall apart, particularly when automation and technology eliminate more and more tasks from the pool of human labour.[407] We see the division of market workers on the one hand and 'Others' on the other, whether volunteers, carers, mothers, the 'unemployed' and the 'deviant'. The reality is that, nowadays, we no longer talk about redistribution of wealth, let alone labour. Yet, when we stop to consider 'what work is' and the value of 'work', we are confronted with the fact that not all paid work is valuable, not all valuable work is paid, and not all work is *valued*. Nowhere is this clearer than when we talk about care or when we talk about mothering.

In many ways, we cannot begin to answer the dilemma of what we do about women, mothers and unwaged work until we also grasp issues of social justice, labour distribution, wealth distribution and fair leisure. When it comes to work then, we have to be creative about what we *regard* as 'work' but also how we approach 'work' as a structure, a tie and an obligation. Many jobs could allow for very great flexibility in terms of hours and place of work. The very fact that capitalist accumulation relies on our presence, labour and productivity being owned and exploited is one almighty resistance to such greater flexibility. I won't even *start* on the 'feminisation' of part-time work and low-wage, low-security nature of such work. After all, it is only low-wage and low-status because the powers that be refuse to reward it adequately, particularly given the 'gendered' nature of the work. It is a well-known phenomenon that work traditionally done by women becomes higher status and better paid when more men take it on; but that work traditionally done by men sees a lowering in status and a dip in financial reward when more women do it.

The fact is, there are so many grades between the 'stay at home mother' and the 'working mother'. For starters, both are working, just in different spheres. There is also the fact that many mothers who do provide exclusive care of their children work outside the home in evening shifts and weekends. They literally have two or more jobs and no leisure time. Other mothers care for their families and combine it with volunteer work, charity work, community projects or help at their children's school. Some mothers take the first three years out of the workplace and then return to it during the child's time in preschool. Others return when the children are older. There are many women who run 'virtual offices' alongside the crayons and Lego. There are others like me who volunteer alongside the children for a few hours a week, spend their days with their young children then write books in the evenings.

With all this in mind, we have to start to challenge the idea that work is only work when it is: paid; done outside the home; for forty-plus hours a week; nothing to do with raising children and running the home; and nine-to-five. Otherwise it ain't real work, *is it*? We need to create an economic and welfare system that recognises the flexibility in what constitutes work, and what 'contributing' to society *actually* entails. Because as things stand, we've got it all wrong.

The editor of *The Social Artist*, Dr Frances Hutchinson, discussed the observations of Rudolf Steiner: "money and work are two different kinds of value which cannot be exchanged. All that can be exchanged is money and the product of work. If, therefore, I give money for work, I do something false. I create an illusory process." Hutchinson expands on this: "here we are brought to confront the very foundational assumptions of the institutional framework of the corporate world economy. Presently, the money tail is wagging the socio-economic dog: it is necessary to work for money in order to gain the legal right to an income. Calls for a national dividend, universal, basic or citizen's income, raise the key question of money. What is money? Where does it come from? How can it be turned from master to useful tool?"[408]

The question is, when are we going to see our socio-economic policies, and mainstream feminism and politics, tackle 'the mother issue' in more creative ways than compelling women to get back to the workplace? There has to be a creative approach to all these issues, which takes on board the diversity in women and their lives, their skills and their inclinations. Whilst Adrienne Rich reflected on the way in which the potential of women has been massacred on the site of motherhood,[409] it is time to contemplate just how far we should now be expected to massacre motherhood, love and care at the site of workplace patriarchal capitalism.

LEANING IN TO CORPORATE PATRIARCHY

Speaking of capitalism, I have mentioned *Lean In* already. Perhaps it's time to stop and look more closely. In 2013, Sheryl Sandberg, COO of Facebook and former bigwig at Google, released a book called *Lean In: Women, Work and the Ambition to Lead*. In it, she skilfully demonstrated just how far feminism has come to be understood as a way for women to lead (forgetting that to lead, you have to be leading somebody), to gain ambition (forgetting that many women's ambitions undergo significant ebbs and flows and changes in character throughout their lives), and to succeed in the workplace.

I wonder whether Sandberg had got the corporate memo containing Nancy Fraser's observation that, in order to 'lean in' we have to 'lean on' someone else.[410] Usually low-paid women. Forget social solidarity or class struggle; conveniently downplay capitalist neoliberalism's destructive effect on our society's wellbeing; and show absolutely no understanding whatsoever of the origins of the women's movement, our oppression based on our reproductive capability, and our exploitation in unwaged or low-paid work with no opportunities to push for promotion or pay increases. Just bang on enough about power, influence, ambition and 'hard work', and it'll all be okay. The rest of you? Lean *over*.

In May 2016, shortly before this book went into production, I was interested to see Sandberg's social media Mother's Day posts about single parents, particularly the *mothers* who were raising children on their own. She confessed that she did not "really get how hard it is to succeed at work when you are overwhelmed at home" and that for many single mothers, "Each and every day they make sacrifices, push through barriers, and nurture beautiful families despite the demands on their time and energy. I realize how extremely fortunate I am not to face the financial burdens so many single mothers and widows face." Sandberg had been widowed a year before. She has clearly undergone a shift in outlook since *Lean In*: "We need to rethink our public and corporate workforce policies and broaden our understanding of what a family is and looks like." I would agree with her.

However, notwithstanding Sandberg's recent epiphany, it is clear that the Lean In philosophy continues to hold sway. The central problem is that the philosophy effectively seals Sisterhood's coffin. We are to compete. We are to preserve the elite (into which we can, if we are lucky and work really *really* hard, make it). As Nancy Fraser observes, "Where feminists once criticised a society that promoted careerism, they now advise women to 'lean in'. A movement that once prioritised social solidarity now celebrates female entrepreneurs. A perspective that once valorised 'care' and interdependence now encourages individual advancement and meritocracy."[411] These values clash in vibrant colour. Education, service and worthwhile labour are all valuable and necessary. Ambition and ruthless capitalism, not so. A corporate feminism which fails to apply any analysis or social justice to the wider picture has no vision beyond the vistas of the boardroom. As mothers, we have to bring our perspective to this debate, to add our purple to the colour clash of capitalism.

As Silvia Federici notes "the radical core of feminism [has been] buried under years of institutional co-optation and postmodern denial of any ground of commonality among women".[412] Well, sisters, if you are reading this and you are a mother, and if you feel unhappy with the way in which care is treated then let's *find* some common ground. We have the capability and the nous to dictate our own rules, our own standards and our own priorities. We need to insist that workplace and socio-economic structures reflect these priorities, rather than crush them. We don't need to *Lean* in. We need a movement. Purple stockings ready? *Legs* in.

In her work *Lean Out*, Dawn Foster is critical of Sandberg's approach, reminding us of the question that "if 1% are leaning in, what are the other 99% supposed to do?" Melissa Benn asks whether we should "lean in — or lose out?"[413] I would add that, in capitalist 'choice' feminism, the freedom to make decisions about one's fate requires the freedom and resources to *make* choices. It assumes an independence and self-sufficiency which we know to be unrealistic and, rather, inhumane. Many women have few choices, and little autonomy to fulfil our actual wishes. How many times have we heard mothers say "I wish I could be at home, but I can't afford it"? A significant number of women want to be with their children: our culture is refusing to allow them. *Why?*

We have to ask: How can feminism pursue a hard-nosed capitalist self-sufficiency but neglect the issue of dependency work which, in reality, many women do unwaged? It fails to 'look beyond the corporate machine', to accept diversity in men and women's lives, including their inclination to put family life over market-work. In effect, Sandberg is the heroine of "trickledown feminism" under which more women with power should mean better conditions for all women, right?[414] Well, this is manifestly not the case. Trickledown *economics* didn't work: the 1% is getting richer and the rest of us are getting poorer. Why on earth do we think it will work with women's rights?

Sandberg's experience is so detached from the reality of most women's lives, particularly working-class women, that it is hardly accurate to call *Lean In* a *feminist* work. Rather, it is a corporate propaganda ensuring that the message is swallowed thus: if you work hard (read: in your job) and neglect everything else, you too might make it to the corner office and 'be somebody'. As the Suffragettes didn't say, "*Gloats For Women!*"

Just think of the implication of a system which demands that women who show 'ambition' are equal, but those who care are losers. Because that's where we are. And this is no feminism. Something to consider, though: if we are continually exhorted not to 'lose ourselves' in mothering or to put too much of ourselves into our families and children, why, oh why, has Sandberg's case that we should lean in to the workplace and put in our all been celebrated? It's simple, isn't it? We can be expected to sacrifice ourselves for the corporate machine; but we are to be discouraged from making sacrifices for our families. We have to show up and put in the time 'at work' but have little time for our children. Why is that, do you think? Might it be something to do with patriarchal neoliberal capitalist free-market individualism? Roll on up, Purplestockings — it's time to talk 'economics'.

The Invisible Hand that Rocks the Cradle

Are the cares and duties of the mother, her travail and her love, commodities to be exchanged for bread?

Charlotte Perkins Gilman,
Women and Economics

ECONOMICS 101

My husband's main complaint when I talk about economics is that he "doesn't know what neoliberalism is". Awww, bless him. He loves me so much he doesn't even try to mansplain.[415] To be fair, many people don't go much for economics in their spare hours, and I don't plan to go too academic in this chapter, so stay with me. But, over time, my love did get the joke, "what's the opposite of feminist economics?" Answer: "economics". Boom, Boom. He would often joke back that feminist economics never took off because women are rubbish with numbers. Ah, the humour in the Olorenshaw household. It's a blast. So, a pause before we go on for a quick tour of economics, capitalism and neoliberalism, just for context.

Economics

It's smoke and mirrors. So I recommend you put on your feminist gasmask before we delve into the realms of *The Wealth of Nations* (the economics 'bible'), the invisible hand, self-interest, competition, individualism, capitalism, productive activity, GDP, game theory, efficient market hypothesis, Milton Friedman, human capital, John Maynard Keynes, privatisation, free trade, small government ... If your feminist filter is working well, some words might well keep coming to you. Power. Sexism. Inequality. Injustice. Devaluation. Capital. Money. Control. Inhumanity. And we are conditioned to think there is nothing we can do about it; that women simply have to 'fit' into a system which is shaped liked a male. One might be inclined to call that system *economicus phalluseam simpliciter*.

Our first stop on our journey is *The Wealth of Nations*, the foundational tome of modern Western economics, written by Scottish economist and moral philosopher, Adam Smith, in 1776. It assumes that 'economic man' (and it *is* the male it is talking to and about) is a rational individual acting out of self-interest. Some 'invisible hand' works behind everything within economics. The fantasy desert island is the utopian stage for the exercise of economic man's will. Robinson Crusoe is to economics as Tiger Woods is to golf. Economics has traditionally only counted things which matter: isn't it funny how *that* has almost consistently been taken as things that *men* have done? It's strange how *that* happens. Whereas things *women* have traditionally done (and many continue to do) such as mothering, breastfeeding for six months and beyond, changing nappies, building bodies, hearts and minds, educating, teaching manners, nursing sick children, getting feet measured, comforting fears and wiping tears, baking bread, making clothes, knitting hats, keeping chickens, cleaning, laundry, chauffeuring, counselling, cooking, negotiating, mediating, soothing, working in the community, serving neighbours, helping at school, running the PTA, homework, building her child's self-confidence and self-esteem and generally sustaining, nourishing, and preparing children for their productive futures for the benefit of society? Come on, now. Economics is only supposed to measure things that *matter*. And mothers and children don't. Women just do the things that men rely on so that *they* can be the ideal worker and get on with the things that *do* matter, out there, in the public sphere. Where real life is. Ironically, the very genesis of the word economics, *oikonomia*, is the Greek word for 'household management', yet under masculine-dominated economics, the household and those in it (read: women and children) are invisible. Turns out the invisible hand is reliant on an invisible *wife*.

Capitalism

The subject of one of the Marx Brothers*, Karl, who wrote about it in *Das Kapital*, is a social, political and economic system in which those who

* Come on now, I'm allowed a little fun, right? It's my book and I reserve the

control the means of production (say, the factory and materials) thereby exploit the producers (the workers) of the product and get bloody rich off the back of resulting capital, leading to increased power and influence, *ad infinitum*. So one's shareholders are basically pimps with increasing amounts of bling.

Feminism used to have a lot to say about capitalism; although more recent liberal feminists have been well and truly seduced by it and don't talk about redistribution or alienation any more — not when they farm their shirts out to be ironed by immigrant women, send their children to nurseries to be cared for by low-paid women, and have their house cleaned by women on a pittance so that they can get on with achieving equality or leaning in. Social justice is too inconvenient and socialism is *so* old hat. Like some communist's beret — what was his name again?** When individuals are reduced to 'human capital' and 'human resources', there is no room for humanity. There is just the 'ideal worker' who obeys the "no uterus rule"[416]: the ideal worker is someone who used to be a man with a wife at home but no need for allowances for family,[417] but now includes a woman who must pretend that she too has a wife to support her and look after the offspring. The problem is that the woman is penalised for the fact she doesn't have that wife. She is still assumed to have care responsibilities for her family, given our resistance to reformulating our workplace structures to encourage parents of *both* sexes to take time out to care for their families.[418] So: the ideal worker is basically a machine, but come the automation revolution, we'll all be made redundant and a robot will have our job. Then it will just be 'capital' and we will be, what, dead? Many of us don't buy the idea that full technologizing of services and production of goods will be liberation, especially not for women, particularly if it occurs within the existing neoliberal capitalist structures. Rather than free up time and leisure — as envisioned by many over the years, including Marx himself, it will simply widen inequality in wealth and resources between the 1% (what would once have been termed the 'bourgeoisie') and the rest of us (hands up who knows what 'proletariat' means?).

---

right to insert wisecracks conjuring the image of comedy duos critiquing socio-economic constructs, destructive hegemonies and androcentric political-economic theory. With feminism and writing, if I didn't laugh, sometimes I would cry.
** Che Guevara. #PowerToThePeople #OrWasThatRobertLindsay? #CitizenSmith

Neoliberalism

Capitalism has always worked against the working classes and women (the reproducers of the next generation of workers). But its hardcore heir, 'neoliberalism' has taken the economic to a new level: not only is there no community or society, there is no humanity, no love, no social conscience and absolutely no hope for women and children. If Marx thought alienation — a worker's loss of the capacity to determine their own lives or believe in their right as an autonomous human being — was rife under capitalism, it ain't got nothing on neoliberalism. We are not so much alienated as dehumanised and detached from each other and ourselves.

Neoliberalism is the prevailing Western capitalist ideology in which the markets are allowed to run riot, policy is framed to serve the market, and everything and everyone is reducible to commodity. Privatisation and individualism are central values of this system. Self-sufficiency and self-interest are elevated to virtue, rather than seen as the enemy of community, society, solidarity and compassion. If you don't have a job, or a home, or food on the table it's because you're not working hard enough or are undeserving. The perfect conditions for banking crises. One might say that Margaret Thatcher is the mother (the irony) of this heartless, ruthless and uber-competitive system and Milton Friedman the daddy. Workers are no longer even people, you know, just human capital. Practically automatons — until *actual* robots take over our jobs. We are economic units or future economic units. Don't believe me? Just reflect on the day your office relabelled 'personnel' as 'human resources'. It should have caused riots in the street. 'Economic man' is now psychopathic 'neoliberal man' with no empathy, no remorse, no humanity and no responsibility. We have sleep-walked into this ideology without people on the ground really grasping what it is and what it means.[419] We have to stop and ask, how did we get to this? We are like those frogs in warming water. We've got to jump out.

Neoliberalism loves *austerity* for the masses but privatisation and wealth for the few. After all, austerity politics is one example of how we can talk about balancing the books off the backs of people, without decent folk realising the inhumanity of the measures involved; how we can talk about deficits, without remembering the deficit of care[420]; and how we can talk about debt, without recognising that we are impoverished in time, if not in money too. We are, to quote the title of Madeleine Bunting's book, *Willing Slaves*.

Under neoliberalism, we can have the cheek to talk about the 'feminisation of poverty' — a significant proportion of the world's poor are women[421] — without stopping to think about what this *means* and why this is the case: because our culture wilfully and obstinately pursues economic policies which put women at significant financial risk. Turns out, having a functional uterus is justification enough for rendering a person poor and keeping her poor. The increase of 'female headed households', the impact of neoliberal individualism, and unforgiving workplace structures ensure that the spectre of poverty is very real, for very many women. We talk about this impoverishment of women and the financial struggle a lone mother will face. And we give her the neoliberal gift of compelled workplace participation, as though the work she is already doing in caring for her baby is not important. Neoliberalism expects nothing more than unwavering commitment to the market: something many mothers are simply unable or unwilling to do and something which is actively toxic to aspects of our lives which do not fit neatly into commodification and wages for services.[422] To quote Beatrix Campbell, we live in "neopatriarchal neoliberalism".[423] And it's not friendly to women; far less to those who are mothers.

GDP

GDP stands for 'Gross Domestic Product'.[424] Forget the old maxim about marrying one's housekeeper*: basically, GDP goes down the moment you take your child out of nursery and care for her yourself. Those of us in campaigning often speak of the huge value of unwaged care-work: if we had to pay someone to do it, or if we lose an income to do it, we are talking billions. We all know that without the labour and care of millions of women across the world, the economic system and society as a whole would fall to its knees: the 'public sphere' only operates because there is a 'private economy' underpinning everything. There might well be Adam Smith's invisible hand, the mysterious force within economics. But one has to wonder: what about the hand that rocks the cradle? Because that hand *is* invisible in economics.[425] And it certainly *isn't* ruling the world.

The System

Rather, our political, economic and social systems ensure that the invisible hand of the mother at home is bound and empty. Bound to the 'private

---

* When a man marries his housekeeper, GDP goes down. The work's still done, but it is done for free. By a woman. So it doesn't count. Yup, that's economics for you. #Patriarchy'sAuditors sphere'. Empty of the means of independence and freedom, and ignored by mainstream politics in a system which denies her existence and denies her means. She is isolated in a social environment which frustrates her from clasping the hands of her sisters, the other mothers, and the community of women of our now tumbleweed-ridden village. Our village has become the desert island (remember that?) of many an economist's wet dream. Yes, a mother's heart may well be full of love. But many an invisible heart is breaking.[426] It feels the weight of pressure to be 'out there doing something important or worthwhile'; it is in peril to financial penalties for daring to choose love and not money, for the mother's choice is exploited, her work taken for granted.

To sacrifice economic 'independence' is perilous for women. On that liberal feminists and I agree. Yet, unlike those feminists who see employment during her child's early years as the route to salvation, there are many within feminism who have campaigned for alternative routes of protection, fulfilment and autonomy for women who are mothers. Because not all women, not all mothers, want to be freed from their children, freed from care-work and freed from what they believe is the important stuff in their own lives. We are just sick of being penalised and forced 'out to work' when our work at home with a baby, a toddler and a school-age child is work enough, thanks.

Those mothers whose hands are tied to the *workforce* by psychopathic neoliberal man despite their preference to be with their children (even for a short time) have faced a hard time under patriarchal capitalism, and neoliberalism has swooped in to seal the deal. They do not *have* it all — they are *doing* it all and they are missing out on what they actually want. Family time. Even if only for a year, two years, five years, ten years. Respect for the family life cycle does not mean that a mother will be forever 'out' of the labour market. She simply wants to lean in to her *family*, to give her children a loving mother to lean on. And there's nowt wrong with that.

The question is this: is modern liberal feminism only concerned with woman when she bears striking resemblance to economic man? When unencumbered? When 'independent'? When 'economically productive'? How is this *feminist*? How does this even begin to support mothers when they do or want to care for their families at home?

FEMINIST ECONOMICS AND WOMEN'S UNWAGED LABOUR

So I have talked about care-work: the unpaid and undervalued labour of women. It is a feminist issue. A *fundamentally* feminist issue. Yet it remains very low on the priorities of mainstream feminism. As bell hooks said in *Feminism is For Everybody*:

> *From its earliest inception feminist movement was polarized. Reformist thinkers chose to emphasise gender equality. Revolutionary thinkers did not want simply to alter the existing system so that women would have more rights. We wanted to transform the system to bring an end to patriarchy and sexism ... Most women, especially privileged white women, ceased even to consider revolutionary feminist visions, once they began to gain economic power within the social structure ... they could maximise their freedom within the existing system. And they could count on there being a lower class of exploited subordinated women to do the dirty work they were refusing to do.*[427]

And therein lies one of our biggest problems: the unwillingness of a privileged class of women to challenge the system that had given them power, wealth and influence. That glass door is shut, and it's soundproof. We can see this in the women of our acquaintance, or ourselves, or in the public eye, who have tasted 'success' and 'economic comfort' and just how far they have removed themselves from the Others. And before it is firmly sealed, that glass door swings back in our faces: a greater issue facing women on the ground than any glass ceiling. The fact is that in the Second Wave of feminism, there was a split between a branch of feminism which got on the economic gravy train and that which pushed for the system to value the gravy boat on the dinner table.[428] Let's just say the train is viewed as more lucrative and more self-fulfilling than the dinner table.

So, let's look at feminist economics. There is some fantastic work out there. I have put lots into the footnotes in this chapter, so that we don't get too bogged down. I'm considerate like that.

So let's start with *Feminist Economics Today, Beyond Economic Man*. The Feminist Economics Manifesto. Not as well-known as the Communist one, mind. But one to challenge your assumptions. Basically, Marianne Ferber and Julie Nelson show how contemporary mainstream economics are dominated by masculine priorities, in which the "market" is worshipped and "heroic individualism" emphasised, interdependence is ignored and family and social relations are bottom of the heap.[429] Really, sisters, we have to start to see this: at the core of our socio-economic debates and corporate feminist priorities, the stuff of human lives is ignored — or at least that of the female ones. But that's okay — it's patriarchy after all.

The fact is that, as noted by the UN Women's Progress of the World's Women Report, "Domestic work makes all other work possible."[430] It acknowledges that, "if the economy worked for women ... the paid and unpaid work that women do would be respected and valued" and "they would have an equal say in economic decision-making: from having a voice in how time and money are spent in their households; to the ways in which resources are raised and allocated in their national economies; to the broader economic policies set by global institutions". As Anne-Marie Slaughter notes, the fact that domestic work underpins everything is "true regardless of whether that work comes from domestic workers or unpaid family caregivers. The labor of domestic workers is critical to the function and growth of national and global economies".[431] The challenge is for us to push for economics to reflect and value unwaged work, women and care.

Katrine Marçal's *Who Cooked Adam Smith's Dinner? A Story about Women and Economics* challenges the notion of economics as some kind of inevitable, benevolent force rooted in human nature and examines the issue from a firm, critical, feminist perspective. If we can't ask about 'economic man' without questioning why the female is nowhere to be seen unless she apes the male, then we will hardly get far in pushing for change in what is valued in our society. Marçal is clear that economic man — male — is the one and only sex, echoing De Beauvoir's *The Second Sex* and her critique of the treatment of women as Other: "Our standard economic theories are based on a fictional character whose foremost characteristic is that he isn't a woman."[432] Indeed, there is not just a second sex, there is a "second economy", the work a man doesn't traditionally do but on which he is dependent to enable him to "do what he does".[433]

And that second economy? Full to the brim with women, caring, mothering and nurturing. Not so much a core[434] or shadow economy as an invisible, devalued, neglected and punished one. In 2016, the Office of National Statistics UK (ONS) published *Household Satellite Accounts: 2005 to 2014*,[435] the value of "home production in the UK, including adult and childcare, household housing services, nutrition, private transport, clothing and laundry and volunteering". It states that:

Measures of the value of home production, although not captured within National Accounts, are important to gain a deeper understanding of the substitution of activities between the household and the market. The proportion of total home production to GDP has grown by 3.9 percentage points, from 52.2% to 56.1% between 2005 and 2014. The total gross value added (GVA) of home production was £1,018.9bn in 2014 ... GVA of informal childcare was £320.6bn in 2014 making it the largest component of home production, accounting for 31% of the total. The value of informal childcare grew by an average of 6.0% per year between 2005 and 2014 despite increasing substitutions from home to paid childcare for children under 5.

Did you catch that? Unpaid work was valued at over £1 trillion.* This is equivalent to approximately 56.1% of UK GDP. When we say that the core economy and army of unwaged workers underpins everything done in the market, and that the market economy simply would not *function* without the significant contribution of unwaged carers and domestic workers, this is what we are talking about. It is a massive, core, economy. The foundations on which we stand. The figures are huge and the work is extensive. We rely on it. And our society ultimately exploits it.

#EndSociety'sFreeloadingOnWomen'sUnpaidWork

According to Shirley Burggraf, "the family is actually the primary engine of economic growth, and yet it has never been recognised as such".[436] She points to the fact that "getting 'women's work' done when women are no longer volunteering their unpaid or underpaid labour is what much of the public discussion of family values is really about".[437] The fact is that when women are working outside the home, it leaves a huge gap in the necessary pool of willing carers. Conservative agendas which promote 'traditional family values' in which home is private, finances between spouses sacred and untouchable, and care naturally provided by the mother, seek to fill the gap in the traditional way, by encouraging women to, effectively, 'know their place' (the kitchen). However, what social conservatives do not argue for is for unwaged care to be financially compensated. We women work for love, not money, you see. Because gentleness, loving care and nurturing is innate in the birds, innit? And no one wants to give women money to go feathering their nests, for doing 'nothing'.

---

* I have to restrain myself from putting my little finger to my lips at this point, *à la* Austin Powers, to emphasise the magnitude of these figures. Just say it: One *trillion* pounds.

Marçal suggests that feminism has to take the step beyond simply adding women and stirring: "the next step is to realize what a massive shift this has been, and to actually change our societies, economics and policies to fit the new world we have created".[438] Refreshing to read. Fearless in her assertions. Compelling are her arguments. Thing is, what she is saying is not new: the powers that be and the feminists that get the mic are just not listening. Their interests in maintaining the status quo (which now includes the interests of elite women) are too great.[439] Nancy Folbre, Ailsa McKay, Selma James, Silvia Federici, Maria Mies, Marilyn Waring and Martha Fineman, among others, have all criticised economic policies which fail to take into account adequately the contribution of half the population and the work they do when *what* they do is not, say, exchanging corn for cash or other traditional transactional worthwhile enterprises.

It's an unsettling moment, when you think back over experiences you have had which bear this out; when you realise that the failure to acknowledge, let alone compensate, women for the massive amount of unpaid labour they perform (on which society, their partners and their children, absolutely and irrefutably depend) is rooted in a system which effectively proclaims: "work traditionally done by women does not matter just as *women* do not matter".

The problem is that, at heart, patriarchal neoliberalism will not *tolerate* equity and justice for women. It might try to sell '*equality*' (hey, it's nearly spelt the same as 'equity'): but it will be within its rules, on its terms and will be disembodied, de-sexed and de-humanised. It will certainly not apply to everyone: some women will be more equal than mothers. Work will always be 'out there'. Well, we must start to insist that what we are doing is important work. It's not a new idea — we may have simply forgotten it or not realised that generations of women have been trying to shift this oppressive view of our labour.[440]

How about we take a look at the landscape of labour? There is currently significant *unemployment* in the UK and the US. Simply put, there are more people than jobs available for pay, leading to a mismatch between the numbers of women compelled to 'get a job' and the *availability* of paid work. And patriarchal capitalism doesn't want it any other way: it enables employers to exploit insecure workers, heighten competition for jobs, and get away with paying the least possible to willing or desperate employees. Add to this the fact that, when it comes to female employment rates, the increase of female employment sits within *existing* inequalities,[441] in terms of gender segregation in the market-work performed and the wage gap, and more.

Then we have our working conditions and 'work-life balance' if we *do* take paid work: the labour market remains unfriendly to families and the non-ideal worker. Despite the movement of women — mothers of young children — into the workplace, there has been no positive transformation of it. Yes, there are greater flexible working conditions and part-time roles available than thirty years ago: however, this is the economic equivalent of the bargain bucket in terms of job security, pay and status of occupation. The price to pay for reduced working hours and recognition of care responsibilities is, it seems, hefty. Rather than a wholesale revaluation of the world of work for all citizens, including maximum working hours per day, a shorter working week, basic incomes, greater encouragement of working from home where possible during windows of time suitable for the employee, and more, we have remained in an 'ideal worker-shaped' economy. And those children, the sick, the elderly, our lives, have no place in it save as a *burden*. I often wonder why we retain the idea of 'Monday to Friday' and 'nine-to-five' when we have the wealth, labour and technical opportunities to organise our workforces in a far more balanced way: four to six-hour working days; three- to four-day weeks. Why *not*? Why should our 'weekends' be significantly shorter than our 'working weeks'? Why? We know why. We are stuck in a feudal mindset, with a capitalist twist. We have fallen for 'work' as 'worth'. We attribute status to the work we do and the things we can buy. But at heart, it's capitalist exploitation, financial priorities framed for the benefit of the privileged, and control. Because, despite our pretentions to something more, we are human capital, the pool of human labour, rather than human beings worthy of living our own lives with autonomy, self-determination and respect.

In terms of policy, we could be forgiven for thinking we were the invisible woman. Policy reform as carried out in Western states creates, according to Mary Daly and Katherine Rake, "an obligation to be in the labour market and regards participation in paid work as being equivalent to social inclusion".[442] This is a real problem for mothers. In effect, we are rendered non-citizens and unproductive, confined to the private sphere and disregarded from public life. When social inclusion and empowerment is necessarily tied to employment outside the home, mothers and homemakers are clearly going to be marginalised.

Neoliberal politics and economics want and rely on this; liberal feminists point to that as the basis for encouraging maternal employment; and patriarchy has us in chains either way. The implications of the split between public/private, from industrialisation onwards, has yet to be addressed in more creative ways than simply to continue to laud the 'public sphere' of men, trying to get more women into it and more men out of it, and to continue to ignore those left languishing in the private, second economy. Time for a revaluation of the contributions made by men and women in the home and the community: without it, wealth, sex and class inequality will continue to widen.

The fact is, ultimately, if we stop and think about where we are now economically, the women's movement has become "you too can be a slave to the wage". In mainstream politics and economics, mothers' and women's unwaged work, continues to be seen as 'incidental' and so exploited, as 'privilege and choice' rather than crucial to our societies and within the rights of every mother to do — supported rather than cut loose. A non-exploitative society should surely be the start of our feminism: as it is, modern feminism is resembling 'how do I feel and what shall I wear?' individualism, not realising that, economically, many women are wearing chains.

With all this in mind, we need to transform our idea of what economics is all about and who and what it is supposed to serve, namely, the basic needs of all in the household — of all in society.[443] It should fundamentally *not* be about the accumulation of more and more wealth and power at the expense of others and through the oppression of women. We need to regain a feminism which has critical awareness and analysis of issues outside the pop cultural and one which is predicated on human wellbeing, justice and freedom from exploitation. Tinkering with gender pay gaps and boardroom quotas is about a useful as deciding what colour to make the nuclear weapon with women's names on it.

At the root of it is the way in which elements of feminism have elevated 'economic participation' and decried 'economic inactivity', having almost uncritically bought the lie that is 'economic man' and got into bed with that neoliberal brother, psychopathic man. Get thee to market, mother, from your child's cradle to your own grave.

Ultimately, we have to focus not on equality but *humanity*.[444] The importance of care in our societies, the willingness of people to do it, and the desire of many mothers to care for their own children (without risking poverty to do so) are sidelined in discussions about, for example, equal opportunities in the workplace and about the pay gap. The shadow economy, the female economy, the care economy — the neglected economy — it props up everything, yet you would think it was a fringe issue. The dominant culture fails even to question employment-as-equality policies as completely skewed *against* women. Forget the female eunuch, we are the maternal eunuch.

But how I love when feminists talk of how it is so unfair that, because of the infamous pay gap, women in the UK workplace work for free from September until December. As I said to some of them: try working for free from *January* and see how you feel *then*. The injustice of unwaged work, it seems, is only grasped by women today when they realise it is happening to them too. It is a symptom of the way in which feminism has crept into neoliberalism's pocket, I suppose.

So too in late 2015, there was a proliferation of articles in which feminists suddenly realised what 'emotional labour' meant and how they were doing all this work when men weren't doing any of it![445] The gender imbalance of work, indeed. Mothers of children at home are unpaid for 100% of the work that they do, emotional, physical and nurturing, and all. The fact is, as Melissa Benn notes in *Madonna and Child, Towards a New Politics of Motherhood*, "one of the ironies of women's new status as workers is that the other side of the traditional woman's lot, her domestic life, the thousand physical, emotional tasks of the everyday, has disappeared from public view".[446] Perhaps the only way to get it back into public feminist view is to encourage them to think of when *they* are the ones organising the birthday cards at work. Or something.

The reality is that talk of the pay gap is predicated on wages: it neglects the work done *outside* the wage structure. If we were to talk of the *income* gap, and actually stop to think what that actually means (namely, that we still penalise women financially and socially for having babies — and even more so if they want to be the ones to care for them) then we can start to see why women are more likely to be in poverty in their old age and why they still have less in their pocket than men. Including the one in her bed. The answer? Because we still refuse to put money in *hers*. She risks alienation, inequality and vulnerability within relationships and society. Capitalism could have it no other way.[447]

FACING UP TO CAPITALISM'S HANDMAIDENS

This all begs the question: where do we go now? In *Fortunes of Feminism, From State Managed Capitalism to Neoliberal Crisis,* Nancy Fraser describes the Three Acts of Second Wave feminism. It is Act Three which we need to push for, sisters. The stages are as follows. Act One: the personal is political. Act Two: identity politics. Act Three: a "reinvigorated feminism" joining other "emancipatory forces" to bring democratic control to "runaway markets". This movement will "retrieve its insurrectionary spirit" including its "critique of capitalism's androcentrism, its systemic analysis of male domination, and its gender-sensitive revisions of democracy and justice".[448] In essence, we have to start to recognise how male interests have dominated economics and start to consider the effects of policies on women, with social justice firmly in mind. Purplestockings, roll on up. Perhaps this need lies behind the frustration of those of us who see the efforts of, say, the UK Women's Equality Party as lacking in depth, flavour and boldness to push for fundamental structural change. I share Fraser's concern that despite assuming, as feminists, that women were fighting for a more "egalitarian, just and free" world, the ideals which have been pioneered by those women who are influential in the women's movement and in politics, are serving "quite different ends".[449]

Fraser criticises the "dangerous liaison" between women's liberation and neoliberal free-market philosophy. We used to have a "radical worldview", yet we now speak in "individualist terms".[450] This is it, isn't it? We're all islands, just like men aren't. We have to start to recognise that individualism and isolation are not good for women: we need social solidarity and the recognition of interdependence. Dominant quarters and players in feminism have to stop to think and see just how far boardrooms have overtaken grassroots-priorities, how waged work and equality in the workplace have dominated politics and feminist debate, and how, as Fraser says, feminism has become "capitalism's handmaiden".[451] Even the agendas of the United Nations and European Union are arguably firmly neoliberal capitalist: most of their female empowerment rhetoric is predicated on 'economic participation'. The problem of the undervaluing of unwaged care-work persists within feminism and dominant economic organisations worldwide. And the result? Women are kept poor because care-work prevents them from 'working' and enjoying full human rights and economic security. If the focus is on employment, rather than other ways to support women, then the financial implications of care-work will continue to work against us.[452]

So, the reality is that there has been a capitalist infiltration into the feminist movement: it is un-feminist to stay at home with your children; women should get out into the workplace and aim for the corporate stars. We women can also be good and successful capitalists! What liberation. Let's just let *those* women, the unimportant ones, do the "shit work"[453]: the childcare, the ironing, the cleaning and the sex with our husbands. Feminism in all its 'choice' glory and all its trappings of women-at-the-*top* has forgotten that there will always, under this brand of feminism and this neoliberal market existence, be women at the *bottom*. But that's okay. You're doing alright, you're putting in the hard work and you're a success. Your soundtrack is *Girls Just Wanna Have Hedgefunds*.

Yet, on the ground, it takes a 'dual income' nowadays to afford a decent standard of living — a significant departure from the breadwinner/ dependant norm of the pre-1980s era. We have witnessed improved access for women to the professions, the military, politics (though still pitiful), and the acceptance that a woman can do anything a man can do. Feminism may have gone after "welfare state paternalism",[454] however, it did so without forethought about their economic dependency on the charity of individual men when women are without a social financial safety net. Or it was part of a calculated drive to compel women to engage in the workplace in order to avoid that very fate.

In effect, feminism promoted a capitalism which exploits low-waged women (whether mothers of young children or not) in insecure employment. The result is that the new norm is the dual-income family that lives in the shadow of declining living standards, increasing poverty, increased working hours, decreased job security, and multiple shifts of jobs and home. Alongside this, it promoted the vulnerability and economic isolation of a mother who dares to want to care for her children, through resistance to social payments to reflect the work a mother does when she cares for her family. What a victory.

MONEY IN MOTHERS' POCKETS

You won't find claims that "marriage is the foundation of a stable society" here, sisters. What we need to push for is *progressive*, not conservative. Truly feminist, not capitalist. And it is this: we need to put money into the hands of women to prevent economic isolation; to recognise the work of care and home; to free mothers from obligation and potential oppression at the hands of a partner; to enable women to live without struggle as a sole parent, if that is their choice or need; to enable women to have greater decision-making powers within the home; and to enable mothers to avoid impoverishment as a result of caring. Put money into the hands of women in more ways than one: by ensuring a fair wage in the market when in employment; by ensuring a basic or carer's income when doing care-work; and by reviewing family property laws within marriage and upon divorce when in relationships. All these things are at the heart of objections to giving women money: financial security gives women freedom. And we can't have *that* under capitalist patriarchy. Nor feminism, it seems.

In short: if we care for our young children, we require resources to feed and house them and ourselves, at the very least. What an outrageous demand: the demand not to be impoverished or rendered economically vulnerable by virtue of our seeing to the needs of someone who is in need. This very issue, and the reduction of it, even by feminist politicians, to issues of personal choice within the private sphere, is one of the fundamental issues which has faced women since the industrial revolution and within domesticity. It hasn't gone away. All that has happened is that the work is still there, but is increasingly commodified; the work is still there but women are encouraged not to do it, unless it is for low pay, for a third party. It is pure misdirection, and shields a continuing and core injustice against carers, particularly women.

If we take a moment to read a little about the Wages for Housework petition we might — just might — be able to get past glib objections that "those Wages for Housework people want women to be paid for cooking, cleaning and children when they should be doing it for free/it prevents their self-fulfilment/it tempts them back to domesticity*." What objections tend to boil down to is that work is framed as 'out there'; value is seen as 'out of the home'; and mothers who care for their children are not, even

* Take your pick depending on your appetite for exploitation, marginalisation or careerism.

by many feminists, deemed worthy of a financial payment to ensure that they have what all feminists wanted, once, namely economic *autonomy*. On care-work and economics, we could echo Chimamanda Ngozi Adichie's reflection about women's humanity and culture[455]: if it is true that the worth of women to a wage for care-work is not our economics, then we can and must *make* it our economics.

But self-fulfilment? A few years in our long lifetime is a blip, and many mothers enjoy their time with their children. Self-fulfilment comes in many forms, not simply packaged in a career-looking box labelled "feminist approved self-actualisation". In any event, money in a woman's pocket couldn't possibly help her resume her studies when she is ready . . . could it? It couldn't possibly encourage her to pursue her own artistic talents or fund a start-up business? All things which could, down the line, lead to greater economic autonomy after the immediate demands of family have subsided. In a way which suits her family and herself. Money in a mother's pocket is money invested now and in the future — for herself and her children.[456] Yet, this issue still remains on the fringes. We have to bring it back to centre with a bang.

As mothers, perhaps we worry about making demands. It's just not becoming, right? However, we have to send the message to our politicians that if they want to capture the imagination of millions of people in employment with young families who are currently trapped in feeling that 'something's got to give', they should start thinking bigger. So. An income for care. Ain't it radical? After all, Virginia Woolf didn't just advocate a room of one's own — she talked of £500 too. A carer's or universal basic income satisfies at least *one* of those.

However, like everything else, talking of money can seem a little grubby. Just how much are we devaluing care — of others, of ourselves and of our ability to do it? Everything can be commodified, after all — sex, care, ironing, cleaning, dog-walking, cooking — and our reduction to client/consumer and service provider is a fundamental part of the neoliberal project. It is perhaps one of the reasons why so many women who actually support mothers and carers are hesitant about payment in the form of 'wages' or 'carer's incomes': are we to reduce *everything* to the pound sign? How do we value it? Is it 'opportunity cost' (the loss of income the carer would otherwise be earning); the 'replacement cost' (how much to pay someone else to do it?) or what? Who is the employer? What do they get back for their dollar in terms of bureaucracy: official inspections of parenting?

Annual reports from the household to account for time, cost and activity? If the state paid us for it, would they then set limits — could they say how tidy our house should be, how we are to care for our children? Could it lead to further state intrusion into our private lives, setting standards for us all and removing autonomy? In times of austerity, will this money be found? All understandable concerns. Especially within patriarchal capitalism or patriarchal socialism. Money can, however, always be found for war. When priorities are set by a male elite, or women who have elevated themselves to power, surely we can ask *why* these priorities rarely include women and children on the ground. And women have always, under patriarchy anyway, been oppressed and controlled. It's *that* which we need to resist — our misplaced priorities and the control of women — not a payment to mothers to reflect their unwaged work.

Are these issues (the conflict between humanity and money) a convenient get-out clause for a patriarchal neoliberal culture which allows mothers and carers to see their work as 'above money'? We work for 'love'. And we pay the price in a system which exploits that altruism and marginalises the carer. It was a line I used with the children: "Daddy works for money; I work for love". Perhaps more accurate would be: "Daddy is deemed worthy of a wage; I am devalued and economically marginalised because I care", but then, it was in response to a throwaway question from a five-year-old on the school run, I didn't want to get political at 8.30am while pushing a pushchair uphill.

However, as Selma James and Global Women's Strike have said for decades: *all women count.* The collection of James' written work in *Sex, Race and Class, The Perspective of Winning* is important, and contains her pamphlet *A Woman's Place*, written in 1952. In it, there is a very clear resistance not just to the obligation (and fatigue) of doing the work of home, but the obligation to do it for *free.* We know this feeling, don't we? It's Friday evening and we are exhausted. We are also unrewarded with no pay check to call our own.

A Woman's Place was written over fifteen years before Betty Friedan wrote about *The Feminine Mystique.* James recognised that when a woman has money to call her own, she has a "feeling of independence not only about the money that is spent, but about the decisions that are made in the house". Power. Within relationships and within society, can be affected by a dollar in woman's pocket today, just as it was in 1952. She foreshadowed Arlie Hochschild's observations about the "second shift"[457]: the women with whom James worked in the factories had neither cleaner nor willing husband to dust the furniture and wash the clothes. And there are many of us who remain in this situation. Our partners may well help with some tasks, but they might well be the glory jobs of reading bedtime stories and carving the roast.[458] In the decades since James' 1972 pamphlet, *The Power of Women and the Subversion of the Community*, written with Mariarosa Dalla Costa, she was clear that it was not a case for wages for house*wives*[459]: it was as much a demand and a *perspective* about the work done, and a recognition that once valued more, then more men would be prepared to do it. Doesn't feminism want this, after all?

Yet, demands for payment have been consistently refused worldwide; and resisted by capitalists and feminists alike. At some point, we have to ask, are mothers simply not entitled to money in their pockets? Are mothers not entitled to have their important work valued? Are we to continue to be marginalised and penalised for caring for our families, as though this work is valueless? As though *we* are valueless? As though other women in the workplace, who also chose to have children, are doing work deemed more important?

When I discovered James' work, I began to understand why I had felt so vulnerable in my new role as a mother: unwaged, caring for my family, rather than besuited, professional and paid handsomely for my trouble. It went beyond a decimation of status. I had a history of trade union activism professionally and within my family; I knew all about strike action, withdrawal of one's labour, exploitation and negotiation, and bargaining power. However, a mother who cares for her family — doing something valuable and important — is rendered vulnerable to a partner (her decision making: her bargaining power in terms of acceptable behaviour and treatment within the personal relationship); she is exploited by society (in terms of its freeloading on her unwaged work which would otherwise cost significantly more to the state to provide); she is unable to withdraw her labour (out of the safety and interests of her children); and is invisible (politically and socially deemed to be 'in the private sphere'). So far as withdrawing her labour, a mother is without a picket line, even if she does have a picket fence. Indeed, Ann Crittenden concluded as much in *The Price of Motherhood*, thus: "in economics, a 'free rider' is someone who benefits from a good without contributing to its provision: in other words, someone who gets something for nothing. By that definition, both the family and the global economy are classic examples of free riding. Both are dependent on female caregivers who offer their labor in return for little or no compensation."[460] This issue consistently goes over the feminist head, too busy peeking out from the parapet to see the women still labouring on the ground.

We have to start to scrutinise the new social contract and the political and economic issues which are raised by unwaged care. Yet feminism has largely washed its hands of this; presenting the shiny cup with the words 'Get a Job — Be Equal!' on it. When feminism rightly fought for women to be freed from economic and financial dependence on men, they missed a trick. They didn't read the back of the note which said 'money': for there it said "reward women's work and empower mothers". When they saw 'money' all they could see were 'jobs'. It is half the picture. The pursuit of women's economic autonomy purely by paid work under capitalism has neglected a significant proportion of women — mothers — who were compelled to add poorly-paid, low-status, exploitative work to the unwaged work of care and home upon which society continued to freeload. We have to remember that as much as many women want to get a job, we also want to 'get a life'.

Which brings me back to the *illusion* of work. I have been clear that when a mother cares for her children and runs her home, she is working. Perhaps this has been out of necessity: to employ the familiar language, the language of currency, under neoliberal capitalism. The value of work. The evil of idleness. In order to justify the fact that we are worthwhile human beings, we are reduced to pointing to the work we do, the value of it and society's need for our labour. It goes to the fundamental need to demonstrate that we are 'deserving' of an income to enable us and our family not to starve to death, or live on a bench out of carrier bags, or live in a warm home free of damp and vermin. And perhaps, in reality, this is where the debate and the socio-economic system all shield a *wider* inhumanity. The value of work versus the value of money versus the value of human beings.

Contributions to society are greater than that which is currently contracted for pay: just stop to think of the volunteer work undertaken by countless citizens; think of the unwaged care; think of the artistic and musical creations which enrich our culture. 'Contribution' and 'citizenship' need not, if we stop to think about it, be contingent only on what we do to make *money* under capitalism.

FAMILY ALLOWANCE

The UK welfare state was created in 1946. But where, pray tell, did the impetus for that massive social change come from? Where did the idea for Child Benefit,* enshrined in 1946 as Family Allowance, originate, for example? Where did the process for the provision for something humane, responsible and ethical, to bury the Poor Law and Workhouses start? Well, the women's movement and Suffragettes were a significant driving force in the creation of the welfare state.[461] The Suffragette movement was not just about votes for women. Except that, well, obviously it was.

The Suffragette and women's movement was about the involvement of women in the story of their own lives; the ability to participate in the public arena as human beings; the development of financial independence for women; and the greater influence in public policy, particularly in matters affecting women, predominantly mothers, and children. So why is the Suffragette movement commonly reduced to the bare bones of participation in democratic election, some woman being run over by a horse at some derby, and the mum in Mary Poppins singing about 'Votes for Women'?

Well, it quite conveniently obscures the fundamental importance of the women's movement of the late nineteenth and early twentieth centuries (and the efforts made after the victory for votes for women and election of women to Parliament) in the development of policies, driven by women themselves, to improve the lives of women, their financial security, their health and that of their children. And a key figure in all that? No, she is not a Pankhurst.

Eleanor Rathbone is, quite simply, one of the most important, influential, tenacious and dedicated campaigners, activists and politicians never to have been celebrated by popular and mainstream political understanding and discourse. Not only was she a Suffragette and campaigner, she became an independent MP in 1929 and campaigned tirelessly for the rights of women. She was particularly moved by the needs and rights of mothers, compelling her to become the mother of Family Allowances — the original mother's payment. She was the author of *The Disinherited Family* and ultimately, a parliamentary advocate for the rights of women.[462]

She was alive to the injustice for women in being at the mercy of a

* A direct payment to families in respect of each child, per week. Originally a universal payment (irrespective of means) and originally paid directly to *mothers*.

partner who is in receipt of the wage, for he who earns it owns it, and he who has it in his pocket controls it. The vulnerability which befalls a woman, a mother, in this situation was deemed unacceptable, then. And it is still just as unacceptable, *now*. The oft-forgotten fact is that women had pressed for Family Allowance to be paid to *mothers* to enable them to have some state recognition of their work and a payment to ease her vulnerability, irrespective of the family income, to a man. This knowledge has been lost in gender-neutral language of recent times and in the fashion for the word 'parenting'. People have forgotten that women fought for the payment to be made to women, not to the man of the house. Rathbone resisted the proposal of the House of Commons to pay it into the man's pay packet — threatening to vote against her own measure. Such a method of payment would have undermined the entire *rationale* of the payment as going directly into the mother's hands (the family wage into the man's pocket is something to be treated with caution, given that the man receiving it gets the say in how it is spent). She won.

At the very heart of Family Allowance was the support of *mothers*: to remove or at least temper the indignity and precariousness of financial dependence on the whim of a man; to acknowledge the state's duty to mothers. It was money directly into the hands of women. One of the most feminist successes of the twentieth century. Under the universal scheme, whatever the man's income was quite simply neither here nor there: it was the woman's right to receive a state endowment in recognition and recompense for her work as a mother. It reflected the truth that a man's income is no measure of his generosity to his family.

Yet, in the twenty-first century, there are, yet again, women who have not a *penny* coming into their homes in their names as a safety net. The payment (renamed in the 1970s to Child Benefit and subsequently disassociated from the original feminist justification) was removed after 2011 from families where one member was a 'higher rate tax payer'. Even in families where the mother was a 'non earner'. The family is a unit, when it suits the state, after all. And so, there are women who have been rendered entirely financially dependent on a partner, vulnerable, and invisible.

Many women in 2011, driven by a politics of envy, cared little for the removal of Child Benefit for 'other' 'better-off women'. Despite the fact she has no money of her own. Despite the fact that two earners earning the same, pre-tax, as the single 'higher rate tax payer' pay less tax and are significantly better off as a result. But, hey, that's individualism for you.

This mother is rendered at the mercy of the goodwill of her partner (read: in most cases, a man). Remember feminism? It seems to have *forgotten this*. A financially abusive partner does not *cease* to be so on earning a higher than average wage. The bills of the family are the same for that family as for the dual-earner bringing home the same pre-tax sum, but a greater total post-tax wage. Who, then, is better off, here? There is interesting work about the poverty of women within families — the discrepancy between the standard of living of the man and the woman *within* the household.[463] A man who reduces his partner to beg for money for personal necessities is not rendered generous by virtue of a higher rate tax code. A woman is rendered vulnerable, whatever the financial status of her partner. All for her decision to sacrifice an income to care for her children herself.

The alliance that was once cross-class women, forging the Suffragette movement and the strides in improving state provision and support for citizens, has been broken. We have to resurrect some kind of sisterhood — a motherhood — to fight for the rights of all women not to be financially marginalised by reason of caring for their children. The fact is that now the universality has gone, the rationale is forgotten, and neoliberalism reigns, it is only a matter of time before it disappears altogether. Consider this, too. The genderless language used by politicians when discussing the family is not, contrary to the belief of women perpetuating it, serving women well. It is not capable of even acknowledging the existence of 'mother' as an entity, let alone allow her the right to speak, be heard, and supported. And, in a whisper, the right to a mother's stipend — the Family Allowance — can be taken away.

The US hasn't even got to first base on this (or maternity leave, for that matter). When you combine that with the restrictions we are facing in the UK, women remain where we started over one hundred years ago: still seeking recognition for our work and still seeking state acceptance of a degree of financial responsibility for it. By removing a hard-won payment from the hands of a mother, the UK government performed the most sexist and retrograde economic step of recent times. Our rights are moving backwards, not forwards: we have to form a movement to get things going in the *right* direction.

In Western culture, in otherwise apparently wealthy nations, there are women who, by virtue of their choice to mother, are cut loose, and on their own, at the mercy of their partner. For politicians to have failed to raise or prioritise this as unconscionable demonstrates the poor regard in which mothers at home are held. We must remind the powers that be that, as Ann Crittenden remarks, "A society which beggars its mothers beggars its own future."[464]

BASIC INCOME

If we accept that mothers should be respected in their mothering work, rather than being forced to 'earn a living'[465] what other financial measures could be on the table to prevent their economic marginalisation? Capitalists and feminists alike have continually resisted the demands of the Wages for Housework Campaign, dismissing the idea of a living wage for carers, and deflecting calls for a universal basic income. Could it be because those at the top don't want to *share*? We can't have people on the ground having greater autonomy, can we? We need a steady stream of people desperate for pay, to do jobs nobody wants to do, for a pittance. Objections run deep. When it comes to women, the system relies on mothers 'having to justify our right to exist'.

So, basic income has been relatively low on the public consciousness. Until now. The time for a basic income is coming, and the movement is gaining support around the world from academics, activists and economists alike — including two Nobel Prize laureates in economics.[466] Other countries are piloting the scheme, including regions in the Netherlands, Finland and Canada. It is gaining momentum. And rightly so. One bonus for the maternal feminist camp of a citizen or basic income is that — *poof!* — the demand for *justification* for the payment of money to a *woman* for her *domestic and care labour* is removed. The universality removes the argument that 'wages for care' or 'wages for housework' will somehow entrench women in gender roles, ghettoising mothers in the home. As though many women aren't ghettoised in low-income, low-security, and low-status *workplaces and industries*.

During the writing of the book, I corresponded with Basic Income UK about the increasing momentum behind the movement internationally. They define 'basic income' as a "payment from society which is unconditional, universal, made to each individual and high enough to maintain human material existence. It can include other collectively provided universal and unconditional services such as healthcare and education; and perhaps in the future transport, housing, energy. The availability of these or lack of them will have an impact on how high the payment needs to be". The payment would be:

› Unconditional: without any requirement to do work, to look for work, to participate in other government programmes or services. It will also come without outside controls over how people might spend it.

› Universal: available to all.

› Individual: available to each individual, regardless of household status.

› High enough for material existence: basic income, possibly in combination with collectively provided universal services, will be enough to live on and participate fully in society.[467]

Unlike some other global groups pressing for a global income, the UK branch presses for the income to be *high enough to live on*. Others only demand that it be unconditional, universal and individual. There have been many forms of basic income explored by diverse organisations over the years, including social credit.[468] However, the principal feature of a universal basic income is that it is not means tested or based on household income and it is not a negative income tax or guaranteed minimum income (which is conditional on acceptance of any job offered and is withdrawn on the basis of earned income).

The issue of the *individual* award of a basic income is directly targeted to the need to tackle inequities inherent *within* households. One of the limitations of the current feminist approach to equality is that it is predicated on labour-force participation, wages and opportunities in the workplace. What these policies completely fail to do is to look within the household — within the family — at the inequalities of income between its members. Whether out of embarrassment that some women still insist on getting married and pregnant, despite our aspirations to 'better' things. Or out of a misguided view that earning one's own wage will always be sufficient to ensure parity between partners and in society, the family remains the private domain (even for feminists who criticised the very issue of public/private dichotomy and all the dangers and vulnerabilities it brings for women).

"Show me the money!" you say. Always. Where is it coming from? Who pays? How is it delivered and calculated? There are many ways if we can find the will . . . Tax on the 1%. Financial services tax. Savings on bureaucracy of means testing and enforcement. Ensuring global corporations actually pay tax morally owed. The measure also has the ability to pay for itself: through savings in health spending; savings in criminal justice; increased spending by the public in the service industries and commodities. For starters.

Oh my, the commies are coming. Well, for starters, it's not communism. It's just a timely antidote to psychopathic neoliberal capitalism which has overseen the widening of wealth inequality in the West, the worsening of poverty even within rich nations (including child poverty) and financial crises which demonstrate that our financial systems and elements in our banking infrastructure are not overseen by some benign 'laugh ourselves to death' character from *Mary Poppins* but, rather, amount to a gamble, a racket and a cartel. And the 1% wants to keep as much of its wealth to itself as possible: the richest 1% now has as much wealth as the rest of the world combined, according to Oxfam. They will never cope on less, bless them.[469]

Most importantly, it is the human implications of a basic income, which appeal. People are crying out for a more humane system than austerity for the masses and increased wealth for the few. Basic Income UK explains that:

A basic income separates human subsistence from working for a wage. It recognises that society depends on a lot of work which isn't paid for — especially the daily care for children and others, but also voluntary efforts to improve the environment, increase social and democratic engagement, pass on skills. Basic income takes away the danger of impoverishment if someone devotes him/herself to the care of others.

Bingo. You see, I didn't just include basic income to throw a curve ball: it fundamentally addresses the problem of what to do about the provision of care; the feminisation of poverty; recognises unpaid work, including the education of our children if we choose to provide it ourselves; the gendered nature of care; the vulnerabilities of unwaged workers; and the inequalities within households. Most importantly, it starts to address the unfairness of society continuing to freeload on the labour of millions of women.

In *Inventing the Future*, Nick Srnicek and Alex Williams observe that a basic income would go some way:

towards recognising the unpaid labour of most care work. In the same way as the demand for wages for housework recognised and politicised the generalised way in which we are all responsible for reproducing society: from informal to formal work, from domestic to public work, from individual to collective work . . . basic income is a fundamentally feminist proposal. Its disregard for the gendered division of labour overcomes some of the biases of the traditional welfare state predicated upon a male breadwinner model. Equally, it recognises the contributions of unwaged domestic labourers to the reproduction of society and provides them with an income accordingly. The financial independence that comes with a basic income is also crucial to developing the synthetic freedom of women.[470]

A universal basic income is indeed one of the most feminist proposals of recent times. As Malcom Torry argues in *101 Reasons for a Citizen's Income*, a citizen's income would "contribute to both equality and independence for women"[471] and would:

value unpaid work ... the old hierarchy of esteem would be replaced by a new one in which work was valued for its quality and for what it achieved. Unpaid education and caring work, unpaid organisation of leisure activities, unpaid political and campaigning activity: all of this can be of enormous value to our society, our community and ourselves.[472]

A basic income could ensure girls and women have an income while they continue or resume their studies. It could enable them to leave abusive relationships, and avoid potentially harmful or exploitative work.

The failure of, say, the Women's Equality Party to champion this measure is, in this context, surprising, as well as disappointing. It goes to show how far the 'lean in' philosophy has warped the view of equality, I suppose. Rather, we must press the fact that it is *economic autonomy and self-sufficiency* which is liberating,[473] not *work per se*. It is freedom to care, invest in education or engage in fulfilling work, which must surely be the point for women's liberation, not the freedom to be exploited in a job we loathe and in conditions which are oppressive. And as we saw in **What is Work, Anyway?**, not all work is liberating. Especially not for working-class women, or indeed those who enjoy their career but find that the ideal worker infrastructure interferes with the quality of their home life. It is the sister of the Purplestockings Movement: *liberating livelihood*.

You may or may not have been familiar with the concept of a basic income before now.[474] Campaigners internationally point to experiments and pilots which have taken place throughout the world. Basic Income UK explains that it will:

› provide a more secure and substantial safety net for all people;

› help reduce inequality and end extreme financial poverty;

> ›   downsize bureaucracy and make benefit fraud obsolete;

> ›   contribute to fewer working hours and better distribution of jobs;

> ›   reward unpaid contributions such as caring and volunteering;

> ›   help us rethink how and why we work.

These arguments will either appeal to you or not, depending I suppose on your outlook on humanity. There is no accounting for selfishness, as Thatcher expertly showed us, but neoliberalism has audited it to perfection.

When it comes to the feminist case for equality for women, economic emancipation of women, liberation of women from oppression within relationships, and the freedom of women to autonomy and self-determination, basic income is an important issue. Women with money in their hands provides: a means of escape; 'independence'; safety; improved prospects for and investment in her children[475]; security; food; warmth; clothing; access to education; and the removal of stigma for 'not working'. At least. Within the leveller of a basic income is inbuilt the valuing of unwaged work and care; and the valuing of human wellbeing.[476]

The late Ailsa McKay's exploration of a citizen's basic income is important and truly feminist.[477] She explored how poverty and social exclusion remain significant problems worldwide and how there are significant gender-based inequalities which are particularly related to modern labour markets. She was clear that the work, life and family experiences of women had been largely ignored. This would make sense, I suppose, given that any advocates of a basic income would probably have been shot if they had come clean, at the outset, and made the feminist nature of the policy clear. McKay recognised (as many feminists have) that one of the fundamental problems with economics is that to "add women and stir" fails to account for the "very different social experiences of men and women in market-based economies"[478] or for "differential impacts on men and women".[479]

As mothers, we know what our experiences are. If we have sacrificed an income to provide care, we have taken capitalist alienation to another level. McKay's work is, in this context, worth a read. What stands out from it is the recognition that what matters is equality in *citizenship* for women. That is a very different thing from equality in the workplace or in pay: and this is where the issue of a basic income comes into its own. It removes the fundamentally skewed cultural and social assumption that a woman's worth is only connected to her work outside the home and that, in order to be a free citizen, she must enter the workplace irrespective of family circumstances and the preferences of many to provide care, at least in the early years.

We have to start to engage in debate about economics and politics. Economic policy has to lose its gender-blindness and see that there are men *and* women in our societies, not just economic man. That there are mothers, not just ideal workers; and that there are human beings, not just human capital. What is striking about this approach is that it goes against everything we are supposed to know and stand for as feminists: we are the same as men; we can do everything a man can do; we should have the same opportunities as anyone else in the job market. The problem is that the life experiences of many women (most notably, mothers) demonstrate that there are flaws in this economic approach. And a basic income is one of the most important aspects of reform in what is commonly known as 'welfare reform', 'social security' or 'state handouts' depending on your political view.

So, social justice and a philosophy to enhance social freedom, alleviate poverty and redistribute wealth. Perhaps, given that the basic income campaign would have to face down free market neoliberalism as well as patriarchy, it has got its work cut out: we struggle even to "articulate policy change" in the light of the discourse of "capitalist hegemony".[480] That is to say: we require a feminist and humanist translator to turn policy and economics into humane versions of their ruthless selves. This is a challenge. It even goes to our notions of rational choice, the role and influence of the market in our lives and our desire for profit and consumption. It opens up debate beyond our restricted ideas of economic and political structures, social policies and 'gender equality'. After all, 'equality' when it boils down to "you too must be a good little capitalist", is not justice, fairness or equity. It is economic bondage: where, once, women were the female eunuch, we are now the economic eunuch, too.

In her 1984 piece *Putting Feminism Back on its Feet*, Silvia Federici wrote that not all women would want to work outside the home: if compelled, they would do it for the money, not because they considered it a "liberating experience".[481] Indeed, as bell hooks writes, women of colour and working-class women have said for generations that they want to have more time with their families and to "leave the world of alienated work".[482] Yet, our voices have been dismissed, for generations. A basic income would redress, in part, the compulsion to find paid work in order to provide our families with the necessities and to value the work of care and home.

Kathi Weeks argues that one possible basis for a basic income is a payment for our production of that of value above and beyond "what wages can measure and reward".[483] What if there was an alternative way of doing things, and one which runs through the issues I have raised, namely, what if a basic income were to be considered as an income not for the "common production of value, but for the common reproduction of life"?[484] This is not to say that people would be paid for having children, or incentivised to having children (although in some countries, low birth-rate is becoming a concern in terms of the replacement level).[485] It is also not to say that people without children don't get it: it simply values living over producing or consuming things and 'life' over 'stuff'. A challenging take — one which I am sympathetic to, from a humanist perspective, from a feminist perspective and from a mother's eye: life as a "counterpoint to work".[486] Basic income and reduced binds to workplace are central to the Purplestockings Movement. Hey, nobody said I couldn't be radical, right?

WHY SWEDEN DOESN'T HOLD THE SOLUTION

Scandinavia always comes up at this point in any discussion about progressive approaches to work, welfare and childcare. In short, Sweden, for all the lore of equality utopia, basically engaged in massive social engineering and imposed an ideology which is being taken up by neoliberals throughout the West. It brought in universal childcare, and with it the brutal *expectation* that all women engage in the workforce and place their babies in childcare. Behold the female employment figures: women are no longer being penalised for having uteruses! This is the panacea for gender inequality, we are told.

Yet, behind the scenes, the gendered division of labour persists in Sweden: it has just moved from the 'private sector' to the 'public sector': from home to public. Women are no longer mothers at home; they are mothers to other women's children in nurseries. Women are no longer mothers at home; they are teachers to other women's children in schools. Women are no longer carers at home; they are nurses to other people in hospitals. Women are no longer homemakers; they clean other people's houses. And pay? Gender equality in terms of income is not achieved: women still earn less than men. Women boast extremely high levels of anxiety. Men still dominate the 'top' professions. Dare I mention worrying rates of anxiety in Swedish children, the children of the universal childcare project? Perhaps this is why Sweden is looking into a six-hour working day. Something's got to give.[487]

GOING DUTCH — EXPLORING A SHARED APPROACH

How about 'splitting the bill'? We could explore more progressive and fairer ways to order our societies. Forget Sweden, much more productive would be to look to the Netherlands where shared care is popular and the rates of part-time work are high so that each family effectively has one-and-a-half jobs. Adult and children's wellbeing is pretty high.[488] A Dutch city is also looking into basic income.[489]

We have to start to find ways to ensure greater flexibility and allowance for career breaks in the early days, up to the age of three to five; to respect the importance of family work and to recognise that parents want to spend time with their children in those crucial early years. Studies, surveys, conversations and our own experience tell us that people often desperately wish to prioritise their families over the workplace. Feminism and politics should respect and reflect this, rather than acquiesce to the "family's subordination to the workplace".[490] Politicians talk about family values. They talk about strong families. Yet they oversee economic and social conditions which require family members to spend very little time together. This issue — family time — is at the centre of the Purplestockings Movement.

What of the UK/US systems? While I see real value in a shared care approach — including the message that fathers need to step up in their physical and emotional care of their children — I have reservations whether this should become the *universal* model within the *existing* socio-economic structures (we have discussed the US/UK hardcore neoliberal model already). It is usually predicated only on that crucial first postpartum year: maternity leave has become 'parental leave'. Many mothers feel uneasy about whether mother and child should necessarily be compelled to be separated on the altar of equality, during the first year of a baby's life — particularly if we are to have any hope of sustained breastfeeding. Some are concerned that vulnerable women will be pressurised to return to their jobs against their wishes. This reflects the reality that some women live in unequal or abusive personal relationships. Yet these concerns are rarely acknowledged. As women, I suppose we are used to that.

Some issues to consider about shared care within neoliberal economic and workplace structures:

1. It assumes a present and/or *competent* co-parent.

2. It does not take account of the different life stages of the child and the diversity of families. For example, in many families the mother is irreplaceable in the early years, particularly in the light of breastfeeding. However, as those children get older, there is greater potential for sole or shared care by their father.

3. As things stand, economic and workplace structures effectively prohibit deviation from ideal worker performance — care doesn't sit well with devotion to the office.

4. Part-time work under neoliberal capitalism is often underpaid and insecure (directly because of the fact that it is *women* who tend to work part-time, so that their work continues to be devalued whether it is home or flexible market-work).

5. It does not take account of the wishes and inclination of many mothers to care for their children *themselves*, nor the mother/child bond and children's developmental needs for *consistent* responsive care (arguably greater achieved by a primary carer).

6. It potentially downplays the importance of the workplace accommodating and welcoming *re-entry* into the workplace by mothers who have taken periods of time out of the workforce to raise their families (ten years out of market-work in a long lifetime is a very short time) during which time they *have* been busy working, just not valued or paid.

7. It neglects to address the very fundamental issue of workplace status and performance as a sign, for many men, of *masculinity* within patriarchal culture. This is something of a chicken and egg issue ... the more men work part-time and care for children, the more childcare will be seen as acceptable for men, the less hold the masculine work culture could have.

8. There is potential for pressure on women — particularly during the postpartum period, to 'return to work', thereby losing out on recovery and building relationships with the baby.

9. It does not address the need for valuing care in terms of basic/ carer's incomes.

10. It sidelines the idea of *family* care — both parents having leave at the *same* time in the immediate postnatal period, in which the father's entitlement to simultaneous leave is not taken from the mother, but rather reflects the family as a unit — and neglects more radical long-term work/life balance issues.

11. It has the potential to deflect from the very fact that unwaged family care and housework is *already* work — such that a second job on top is not necessarily going to appeal to *all* women at each stage of the family life cycle.

12. It fails to take account of disparity in earnings between partners, such that shared care would significantly damage the family purse depending on their occupations, if there were no carer's or basic income to bridge the gap.

13. Ultimately, imposing a shared care system on *all* is to bring yet another rigid social contract: "share the care whether you want to or not, despite the individual child's needs, whatever the age of the child, whatever the inclinations and wishes of the parents".

Yet, if placed as *one* aspect of a system which had wider flexibility for parents to choose how to set up their own families, it would be an important and valuable asset in the movement to arrange our lives in a more humane — and family-friendly — way. It would require fundamental changes to workplace regulation (for example maximum working hours and days, to reduce the impact of market work on our home lives), distribution of wealth and labour (universal basic income, and redistribution of jobs to counter a high unemployment economy and increasing loss of jobs to automation), and ideas about masculinity as 'provider' or 'performer'. It would enable each family to have a financial cushion — state payment — for caring work or as a basic income, which would lessen the impact of lost earnings. It would challenge ideas about masculinity being inextricably linked with the size of a man's, *aherm*, office.

At heart, we must start to change our ideas about the optimal way of living and working, including allowing for full-time care or shared care, or a combination of both over the time the children are dependent, and valuing the work that care entails. One aspect of shared care which might well work is the fact that the more men do it, the more they see that it is work, the more they will see it is deserving of financial recompense. After all, can you imagine substantial numbers of *men* working for free? The unions would go nuts.

So, there is certainly a *place* for accommodating the sharing of care where desired and possible, reducing working hours per day and introducing maximum working days per week within a system which ensures a subsistence income. Bertrand Russell put it this way: "many people escape even this minimum amount of work, namely all those who inherit money and all those who marry money. I do not think the fact that these people are allowed to be idle is nearly so harmful as the fact that wage-earners are expected to overwork or starve. If the ordinary wage-earner worked four hours a day, there would be enough for everybody and no unemployment — assuming a certain very moderate amount of sensible organization. This idea shocks the well-to-do, because they are convinced that the poor would not know how to use so much leisure." For women, objections come down, at heart, to a class system, a patriarchal system, and an unwillingness to distribute income to the female of the species in recognition of her work, let alone her humanity. Most women would, I am sure, settle for seeking recognition of her unwaged work rather than going the whole hog for greater leisure time. Leisure might well have been something open to men in Russell's view, but no woman could surely get away with demanding financial investment for *leisure*. How dare we demand the right not to work? Even if only during the spare three hours we might have on a Monday morning.

We could also start to look at the overhaul of workplace structures and basic incomes as having a place not just in sharing *care* but in allowing for *joint* care and sharing *leisure*. It is this which has to form Nancy Fraser's Third Act: a creative, bold feminism with social justice firmly in mind.

You will remember that back in the early chapters, I spoke frequently about the need of mothers for support and to be cared for while they are caring for their babies. I addressed some of the feminist concerns about mothers being isolated and unsupported while they care for their families. Well, doesn't that all rather point to the need for a system of simultaneous leave or workplace structures which enable time for both parents to be *together*? To do some care, *together*. *This* should be the focus of shared care. Such an approach would enable the family to benefit from joint care and mutual care. *Interdependence*. The carer to be cared for. Radical, right? Yet what is feminism if it can't think big? I often think of the (with hindsight, short-sighted) prediction of Alexander Bell that "I truly believe that one day, there will be a telephone in every town in America."

Current feminist discussion of shared care is the telephone in every town.

We could think bigger. In the discussions about shared care predicated on baby-as-baton, we are not taking the logical *next* step. Namely: human wellbeing, reduced imposition of workplace exploitation for all, and greater investment in family time. More joint care. Respite for carers which does not involve another job on top. Fathers having time with their whole family — partner included. After all, as willing slaves we spend such little time together as a unit: should this too not be a priority in policy? Would this not bring greater social benefits? Would this not challenge the masculine culture of workaholism? Would this not reduce pressures on relationships? Would this not dismantle the maternal wall of penalties faced by mothers in the workplace that they are assumed to have sole caring responsibilities? Would this not permit mothers to re-enter the workplace, or retrain, at the right time for them? Without penalty?

It might just be the solution we are all needing. Employees are working ridiculous hours, burnout is epidemic, costing our economy a fortune in sick pay and health care. With some imagination and tenacity, we could see a culture of healthy work/life balance. Humane workplace terms and conditions, including lower working hours. And an important part of this would be *joint* care: not sequential 'passing the baby buck', but significantly more care at the *same* time, as a *team*. This type of shared parenting holds real attraction: and a universal basic income allows for greater family time as a *unit*, rather than splintered into shifts or ships that pass in the night. It would enable the sharing of the joys of family time. It would enable greater time with relatives from extended family, who would similarly face fewer constraints from overwhelming workplace burdens.

It is *this* which should be the focus of a feminism which talks about shared care — not a shared care predicated on drawing the short straw and sharing the 'burden' of care or, conversely, divesting mothers of their 'mother privilege'. As though the mother/child bond was unfair on the men. Well, this is patriarchy, I suppose. Combine this with the nature of neoliberal capitalism: that the market wants your time, your presence and your blood. It wants your insecurity and it wants you hostage. It's the power imbalance which keeps the rich getting richer and the rest of us getting poorer in money, time and energy. The knock-on effect on wages would be significant; and therein lies another objection. If there is enough work to go around, we are not so easily exploited; we can demand pay in line with the *demand* for the service, rather than what the guvnor feels he can get away with. I know, I know. I'm a right anti-authoritarian. But then, respect for authority, when that authority is one which exploits you, is never one I felt happy to respect.

Yet, Adam Smith would be turning in his grave at the thought of self-interest giving way to mutuality, and human-interest taking centre stage. It comes down to the ethic of work, doesn't it? The need to be seen to be doing something of economic value in order not to starve and for your children to be safe and fed; the overestimation of the value of paid employment. We buy the line that employers can't possibly stretch to more employees, with more liabilities for pensions or workers' rights, in redistribution of labour. But the work is there. There are people queuing up for work. A basic income and flexible shared care approach is radical because it frees up so many of these issues: the time we spend in our jobs; the value of unwaged work; the interdependence of human beings; mutual care; and the capacity to live our lives and enjoy some leisure. Life is for living. Let's remember to share the meal not just the bill.

FUTURENOMICS

So, I'm no fan of capitalist exploitation. I must be a socialist then, right? But hark, what about the fact that communism and socialism haven't always fared well for women and children? Well, you will notice that I haven't really talked about socialism as a proposal or for critique. And for good reason. To my mind, labels don't always work: we might immediately start discussing Marx and reducing my argument to a rehash of Marxist feminism; or link my words to socialist feminism and start to dissect that; or start to refer to socialist countries where children are almost exclusively in childcare. No. I would prefer to think about the fact that "the repossession by women of our bodies will bring far more essential change to human society than the seizing of the means of production by workers".[491] Socialism hasn't always addressed unwaged labour or been entirely friendly for women or mothers.[492] A socialism rooted in patriarchy is patriarchy nevertheless. So, no. While socialism of old has much to recommend it (most notably the ethos of social justice as opposed to accumulation and exploitation) I have avoided plucking socialism from the dualist left/right patriarchal buffet table.

Rather, we need to start being braver about our future and the vision we have for our lives and our labour. We have talked about 'work' and 'economics'. We have talked about basic incomes and family allowances. Well, what we need to talk about, to explore, and to promote are realistic and humane ways to redistribute wealth *and* labour, keeping automation and technology in check for the good of humans rather than the 1%, and the exploration of basic incomes and greater leisure time for our citizens. A partnership approach, not patriarchal hierarchy. Social responsibility, not capitalist individualism. To enable life to be lived; to enable family to be enjoyed and children to be nurtured. We need a renewed social justice and economic models to serve humanity, not the market, to value care, not competition, and to allow for creativity and wellbeing rather than destruction and anxiety.

As a mother, I want to raise my children with hope for them to have a safe, healthy and happy future in which they are responsible citizens and decent people, in service and care of others, and in respect for others and themselves. I suspect I share those hopes with many mothers across the world. Yet our political and legal systems ignore these very basic issues. Economic and social policies effectively suggest that our intentions for our children are to divest ourselves of these burdens as quickly as possible, to live in a future of fetterless trade, self-interest, global-market and polluted air, sea and land while people work to death. That's not our dream though, is it? I want to see a society in which the work of our citizens is valued: including the currently unwaged work of family and home.

As feminists, we must start to demand that our political and economic systems live up to our dreams, for ourselves and our children. The fact that we don't is a telling demonstration of that old chestnut: we are silenced out of fear or shame, of not wanting to want too much, not wanting to demand or expect, lest we overstep our mark. Thing is, if we don't speak up, if we don't demand the political system *reflect* rather than *dictate*, nothing is going to improve.

We need to see new alliances, internationally, within a true women's liberation movement, rather than tinkering with the edges of economic capitalism in which the female, the mother, her work, her power and her worth isn't valued. That was the feeling in the room at the Feminism in London panel on women's unpaid labour. The panel was chaired by Mel Tibbs of Mothers at Home Matter, featuring yours truly under my Politics of Mothering and agitator of the Women's Equality Party hats, Esther Parry, of maternal feminist organisation All Mothers Work and academic Dr Karem Roitman. It was clear from conversations with attendees of the panel discussion afterwards that we must capture the political mood, face-down economic issues which continue, as always, to penalise women and work traditionally done by women, and to challenge the march of neoliberal austerity which fails women and children first and foremost. Parry was absolutely clear: "Achieving equality without getting rid of the system that enforces and normalises inequality is pointless and impossible. But mainstream feminism took on more of a 'if you can't beat them, join them', attitude. For the first time, women were being allowed to experience small tastes of what patriarchy said held value." And therein lies our mission: not just to challenge patriarchal capitalism, but to defy dominant feminist thinking which is masquerading as women's rights.

The Politics of Mothering

It may be the cock that crows,
but it is the hen that lays the eggs.

Margaret Thatcher

TO MARKET, TO MARKET

Talking 'politics' is a little like playing Battleships. We all have our perspectives, not immediately obvious to others. If we are doing well, mate, thanks, then we can pretend we are not just one bad day from Shit Street. If we are struggling, we face shame and the benevolence of food banks for our trouble or, at the very least, sleepless nights about our ability to put food on the table or keep our home and bodies warm. The basics, you know: food, water and warmth.

Yes, politic-talk is immediately divisive; it is immediately exclusive. It's not so much a lack of consciousness as a resignation and learned helplessness of the majority of people to feel able to *do* anything about how we live, how we relate, how we earn, how we spend our time and money, or our ability to tell the boss to stick it. We switch off from engaging in politics, from critiquing economics and from involvement in movements which 'aren't for us'. We hold back from speaking our minds, out of fear of rocking the apple iCart. And we buy what we are sold in the Western neoliberal marketplace. Nobody wants to be that ludicrous 'shrill woman' banging on about rights, redistribution or social democracy — it's the twenty-first century, after all. Marx is dead, long live the Market. Because you're worth it, you minion.

We deem 'women's issues' to be peripheral, 'fringe' or 'special interest' as though they don't affect at least 50% of the country directly. A significant majority of cuts under 'austerity' have affected women disproportionately. Women continue to do the world's work, much of it unpaid, unvalued and unsupported; and the rest, underpaid and insecure. The grassroots,

233

for women, is more patchy turf, neglected, underfed and worn underfoot. Yet, feminism is gaining headlines, mostly for 'equality' shindigs, periods and men claiming to be one (a feminist) despite all appearances that he is something quite to the contrary (a capitalist) and we have a campaign asking nicely for our legislature to have some semblance of a gender balance. The 50:50 Parliament campaign, gaining momentum in the year of the Suffragette movie, calls out the 'something rotten in the House': the unbalanced, privileged, white, male and establishment bias of those in the hallowed halls of political power of Westminster.

While we're talking of women, it has been over thirty-six years since Margaret Thatcher became the first female Prime Minister in the UK. It is over twenty years since she left office having done little for women either in general in this country or for fellow female politicians; having birthed into being a neoliberal state which has no place for a *welfare* state. Indeed, the dismantling of our welfare state has been a slow process, beginning with the indoctrination of generations to the view that 'independence' and 'self-sufficiency' are not only possible but desirable and ending with 'sink or swim' economic and social policies in which we scramble for the scraps from the masters' plates. 'Dependence' has become a dirty word; 'welfare' has also become grubby, a result in part of the discovery by television producers of the drawing power of 'poverty porn' and 'welfare-scroungers'. We are human capital. And, with this as context, where are we? Where are we going? To market, to market, my friend. Everything is to serve it: war, banking, healthcare, education, childcare, food, you, me, him and her. Sent to market so the market can feed itself — the fat pig at the farmer's table. And the rest of us? Swill in the trough.

Social media has a vocal contingent of political debaters and activists. But it's not enough. When a huge majority of people feel frustrated and impotent about their ability to do anything about the way in which family life and market-work are set up, yet do not take to the streets, we know that those in the corridors of power can sup their Bordeaux in full knowledge and contentment that they can wring us just a little bit more, turn that screw a full circle, and watch while we argue amongst ourselves about our 'hard paid taxes'. We have accumulated fear, resentment and isolation; they have accumulated capital off our backs. And nowhere is this more manifest than in the case of women's unwaged labour.

MATERNAL POLITICS

In terms of politics, feeling a little bit like someone with a message, in 2015 I published my pamphlet, *The Politics of Mothering*. I wrote that as a mother of two young children at home, enjoying and seeing real value in what I and others are doing by caring for our families, I felt insulted and neglected by political, economic and social policy in the year of the General Election.

Setting my sights on politicians, the pamphlet demanded:

True democratic engagement of the many politicians and policymakers who seek to justify: (i) increasing separation (often compelled through financial hardship and penalty) of parents and children, and at earlier and earlier ages, despite the family's wishes; (ii) restrictions on available support to those who seek to prioritise family care often at considerable financial hardship; and (iii) a blinkered economic lens and ideological encouragement of all mothers to engage in paid employment without any consideration of the desire of many to remain home with their family and the benefits to individuals and society at large of those mothers doing so. It reminds them that they have a democratic duty to listen to what many mothers want and invites them to stop the ceaseless discrimination against mothers at home and to start valuing family care.

So this seems a good opportunity to explore and expand more on those issues and to announce loud and clear that the attempts by the political class to push for full female employment is manifestly undemocratic. It goes against *everything* that we know mothers actually want. It fails to recognise the diversity in women's preferences or the unpaid labour upon which the market economy relies. Ideological attempts to incentivise women back into the workplace and to penalise those who wish to care for their children amount to social engineering with no mandate. To quote Anne Manne: "if the trajectory of public policy pushes families towards institutional childcare and punishes parental care, it is in clear violation of the principles of a democratic state".[493]

Lies, Damned Lies and Childcare

A recent UK survey found that a significant number of mothers want to care for their children themselves; yet the headline message of the survey fails even to mention it, emphasising childcare and maternal employment instead. Here are the relevant figures, based on a survey of 6,198 parents in England with children under fifteen who were interviewed for the study between October 2014 and July 2015.

› Over a *third* (36%) of the mothers in employment (66% of the mothers) would prefer to stay at home and look after their children if they could afford it.

› Over *half* (54%) of the mothers in employment (66% of the mothers) said that if they could afford it, they would work fewer hours to spend more time looking after their children.

› Around a *half* (47%) of those not in employment (34% of the mothers) do not wish to gain employment.

That is quite staggering, is it not? If you combine those figures of **36%** of the 66% in employment and **47%** of the remaining 34% not in employment, you get almost **40%** of all mothers asked want to stay at home with their children.

If you then factor in the 54% of employed women who said they would work *fewer* hours and you have a large proportion of an entire generation of women who are desperately calling out for a solution to their financial worries which does not compel them into longer and longer hours away from their children.

These should be headline figures in a study which finds them, surely? The headline figure could well have been: "Around 40% of mothers would prefer to stay home and look after their children if they could afford it. " *But no.* This is The Department for Education's *Childcare and Early Years Survey of Parents 2014 to 2015*, published in March 2016.[494] It tells us everything we need to know about the agenda and priorities of our governments when it comes to mothers and children: childcare and employment. Not social justice, wealth redistribution, basic incomes or valuing care. Rather, it's about the bottom line and an increasing drive towards 'full female employment'. Despite the wishes of a great many mothers, it turns out.

Take a read of the survey and reflect, too, on the language used, for it betrays a wholesale devaluation of care-work when performed by a parent: "workless" and "non-working mothers". Hey: we *work*, we just don't get *paid*. There is a massive difference.

This is not a questionnaire where people were asked about childcare but a hefty proportion weren't even parents. No. This focuses on the use of childcare and the motivations of parents, specifically mothers, to use it.

Unlike *The Family Test*, which I will come to shortly, this study actually names mothers and focuses on women's decision to 'go back to work'. The reason? To push the ideology that all women need to get 'back to work' and, more, that most women want to. It just goes to show: gender-neutral language goes out the window when the agenda is 'set sights on mum and get her down the Jobcentre'.

The way this study has been presented demonstrates that it is not a study to find ways to reflect family preferences or choice. It is a document predicated on the ideological agenda to get 'women into work'. It is a document to justify ever expanding commodification of childcare provision. As such, significant and important findings are effectively suppressed.

Just take a look at the Executive Summary at the beginning — which most people read and assume covers the salient points. Wrong. In this study, the "Executive Summary" is a bastardised, photoshopped version of the actual findings of the study. Here's how. The Executive Summary's section on Mothers, Work and Childcare on page 13 talks about:

› The proportion of mothers in employment (66%).

› How many of the 'non-working' mothers would prefer to go out to work if they had the childcare (53%). [Which, by implication, should mean that fully 47% of mothers who are caring for their children are happy to stay at home, thank you very much. But that would skew the focus, rather, wouldn't it?]

› Common reasons for women to go back to work, including combining work and childcare, job opportunity or 'their financial situation'. [Read: desperation in 28% for an income.]

› 'Working mothers' found childcare helped them to go out to work.

That's all there is to see folks. Childcare, childcare, childcare. One would be forgiven for thinking that's all there is to it. Nothing more, nothing less. Mothers want to work, childcare is the pill.

But soft, what light through yonder window breaks, on page 26? A bit more, actually. Like some of these glaring omissions from the section on Methodology.

› A quarter of couple families (26%) consisted of one parent working full-time and one 'non-working parent'. [Wow, just look at that: 28% full-time, 28% full-time and part-time, 26% single-income. Yet, the way it is set out suggests that there is a significant difference; that single-income families are somehow a tiny minority.]

› Employed mothers were also asked what other factors influenced their decision to work. Two in three (66%) said they needed the money, almost half (46%) said having their own money was important. [This is unsurprising, considering that a mother who cares for her children becomes unwaged, and thus financially penalised for choosing care-work over market work.]

› Of the non-financial reasons, enjoying work was the most frequently mentioned reason (64%), followed by a desire to get out of the house (26%), and feeling useless without a job (25%). [On this last point, it seems that the way in which society devalues what mothers do, and the resulting feelings of low worth, is now used as a stick to beat us back into work outside the home.]

› 'Working mothers' were asked for their views on different working arrangements. Over half (54%) said that if they could afford it, they would work fewer hours to spend more time looking after their children, and over a third (36%) said that if they could afford to give up their job altogether, they would prefer to stay at home and look after their children.

Quite astounding, eh? A survey about childcare and mothers. A survey to help formulate policy on childcare. And the only findings put on the billboard in the Executive Summary are those which support the ideology of maternal employment and commodified childcare. These are the figures and statistics trotted out by politicians keen to emphasise the demand for childcare. When we do finally reach significant figures which show that mothers in employment overwhelmingly would prefer to reduce their hours and significantly would want to give up work outside the home, they are tucked in at the end in the hope that nobody will notice. After all, it's well boring having to read through pages and pages of statistics and shit.

We have to start to ask the question: when, oh when, are these figures going to be acknowledged by the mainstream parties? When are the actual wishes of mothers, overwhelmingly for greater financial support to care and freedom to make choices which honour their wishes going to be respected? Many mothers want to look after their children themselves. Don't just take my word for it. None of this is new! It has been a consistent message, despite ideological drives to 'get women into work' and despite decades of brands of feminism trying to convince us all to 'want something more'.[495]

FAMILY POLICY

The fact is, there are now just under two million mothers at home in the UK: these women are branded 'economically inactive' by the Office for National Statistics (ONS).[496] The value of informal childcare is calculated by the ONS as a jaw-dropping £343 billion per year: 23% of GDP (remember that?). Tellingly, and infuriatingly, the ONS fails to mention the word 'mother' once. Yes, really.[497] For other statistics, remember the figure of one trillion pounds reached by the ONS in 2016? Informal childcare formed the largest proportion of that figure. Family life is not a fringe issue: it is the *central* issue, for economics, for politics and for feminism. We simply need to catch up to that view.

What about UK governmental policy? I take you to *The Family Test*,[498] the UK government's 2014 guidance to its own departments about how a "wide range of government activity has a direct or indirect impact on families". It warns that "as a whole we do not always think systematically about how policy can support strong and stable family relationships or how we might inadvertently impact on families". What is staggering is how this objective (to introduce an explicit family perspective to policy development) *neglects* the existence of 'mother'. It, like the ONS, denies the very *word*. She is nowhere to be found. The policy nobly asserts that: "Families have a major impact on the life chances of individuals and strong family relationships are recognised as an important component of individual, community and national wellbeing". Yet, despite mentioning the role that 'fathers' play in raising their children and considerations of, say, 'grandparents' and 'siblings', among others, not once does *The Family Test* mention 'mothers' or 'maternal care', not even in the context of pregnancy and birth (this brings to mind the erasure of the word 'women' in maternity care literature which we discussed earlier). Perhaps the high point of the hypocrisy is that this 'family test', from a right wing government which promotes neoliberal capitalist individualism, would surely be failed by every.single.policy. it.announced. But hey, perhaps they hoped we wouldn't notice *that*.

Now, these omissions were either by design, which should surely ring some major alarm bells for mothers and those who support women's rights, or it was a subconscious expression of mothers being simply taken for granted, missing from policy, missing from consideration and hung out to dry. Given everything I have discussed in this book, which would *you* say it is?

Politically, there is a 'mother problem'. Women can, ostensibly, take advantage of equality of opportunity; women are free to engage in paid labour; and they are increasingly economically autonomous. But when that woman becomes a mother, all bets are off. From policymakers, politicians and those who subscribe to the perceived universal dissatisfaction of mothers, the message is that all mothers feel chained, oppressed and miserable raising their families; and that they are our saviours with the promise of full female employment and universal childcare. Even the EU and the UN are in on that act, with targets for increased female employment: the question is never asked, "At what stage, despite whose wishes, into what industries or for what pay?". And certainly not, "Despite what alternatives, such as a basic universal income, a carer's income, fairer tax arrangements, income splitting, or family-recognition fiscal policies?". The EU seems to think too many 'stay at home mothers' is a problem of itself — a "social challenge" that needs addressing by the UK.[499]

Politically, there seems to be very little higher level examination into mother-work, the institution of motherhood versus the experience of mothering, the value of care, and the constraints of neoliberal economics. Policymakers in the US, UK and Europe are ignoring a large population of the voting public. It doesn't really make sense: don't they *want* our votes?

Decision makers are simply not listening to the experience of mothers themselves. One could argue that domestic, European and international political establishments (including the UN) are channelling a neoliberal market philosophy and its bedfellow, liberal feminism, to pursue an agenda in which labour participation between men and women are equivalent, for everyone to take up their rightful place as a cog in the machine.

The average age of first-time motherhood in the UK is now thirty.[500] A woman is likely to have had significant economic participation in the workforce before becoming a mother; she is likely to bear significantly *fewer* children than her predecessors (having benefited from greater contraceptive and economic freedom); she is likely to retire from the workforce at a significantly *older* age than women face today; and her life expectancy is long indeed. Accordingly, her childbearing and child-rearing experience will form but a very short chapter in her life. So the political obsession with *continuous* workforce participation and work, work, work, till you drop risks denying her potentially the one period in her life when she might actually enjoy a rich, important, worthwhile occupation of being a mother at home.

There is a significant element of compulsion, too. Economic factors are compelling many mothers into employment despite the desire of many to raise and support their family. The question is: why do the mainstream political parties deem a mother to be unworthy of assistance when she makes the decision to sacrifice an income to care for her children? By this point in the book, you might well have your answer.

So, mothers in the West today are in an impossible situation. Our very title is being erased from government policy on families and general political discussion in a pernicious Orwellian language trend in which the words 'mother' and 'women' will be deemed 'damaging' or 'anti-feminist' or even 'phobic'. This erasure affects our ability to campaign, to demand our rights be honoured and to label the issues. It's the right of 'naming', to recall Mary Daly.[501] When it comes to women, it's not being a parent; it's being a *mother*. It's not the cost of childcare; it's the cost of *living*. It's not feminisation of poverty; it is mothers being *oppressed, unsupported, unvalued* and *sacrificed* in political systems which recognise them only in their capacity as employees and impoverish them as a result. Indeed, the 'feminisation of poverty' has been tolerated and encouraged by our economic and political systems, yet it is blamed on motherhood.[502] But there is an extremely easy way out of it. A carer's income. A universal basic income. Acceptance of social and state responsibility to those women who are caring for families. But the powers-that-be won't touch that: it does away with a huge source of coercion against women. We have to demand change: we cannot tolerate this any longer.

WHY HAVE KIDS?

Most of us will have come across this remark at some point: "Why have kids?" Consider, for fun, some commonly uttered 'truths' in the Internet's comments sections.

'Don't have children unless you can afford them.'

The cost of living means, quite frankly, that many a family cannot afford to have children without help or, in many cases, being forced to be separated from their children despite the family's wishes. Are we really suggesting that only the rich should have children? Are we fans of *eugenics*, now? Do we *really* lack the humanity to see past the dollar? It is utterly disingenuous to suggest that having children is simply a personal venture of no wider societal benefit.

'Why have children if you are going to work?'

Didn't I tell you: women cannot win.

'Why should we pay women to do something they have chosen to do?'

Don't you remember the discussion about children not being poodles? 'Other people's children' will grow up to be your doctor, your lawyer, your grandchildren's teacher, your nurse in the care-home, the spouse of your child, the father of your grandchildren. We would not be paying women to have children; we should be recognising the value in reproducing the human race, caring for children and preparing them for future citizenship. We would be refusing to perpetuate manifest and deep-rooted patriarchal and capitalist injustice against women: the idea that their work doesn't count; that they should do it for free; and that *they* should pay a price of social and economic marginalisation. Or do we only pay people for *jobs* they choose to do?

'Why work so hard at work when you want to have kids, anyway?'

The flipside. The decreasing fertility of women with careers is a phenomenon which has been well documented. There is the very real issue of the desire of women for children if only their career would enable flexibility to do so, and before it's too late. How can we push for promotion, only to step back when baby comes along? How far are women punished in the workplace for having children? These are feminist issues. For some women, they simply find that they are unable to have children after decades of professional success and 'doing it like a man', and they feel a deep loss of the opportunity to have had a family. These are very real emotions for women, and very real dilemmas. We have to be able to address the fact that our workplace structures and ideal-worker-shaped economy present women with the 'either/or' dilemma of 'succeed at work' or 'breed at home'.[503]

Having children and seeking to care for that child yourself is deemed by the mainstream political parties to be a 'lifestyle choice',[504] either a privilege for the wealthy or a frolic for the 'feckless'. Such parents are deemed lazy, unambitious and unproductive, rather than performing a public service, undertaken at considerable financial cost in the loss of income by women across the social, educational and economic spectrum. The work of mothering is valuable, albeit unfashionable, and, as such, mothering is ignored by policy, deemed worthless and inconvenient. Why have kids? Let's see what happens when we don't. #AdiosHumankind

FAMILY AND FISCAL POLICY

When it comes to families then, what does the state see? It's rosy, so long as it's a man, a woman, two children, within a married, nuclear, suburban family with minimal demands and with sufficient privacy thresholds to ignore the risks to the mother inside the house at the mercy of the breadwinner and labelled 'desperate housewife'. It's deviant, when it looks like one woman, three kids, inadequate housing and needs for extra social support. Family values: the quieter the better.

There is a significant and often devastating extra tax liability for a family where children are cared for by one parent and the other earns a very modest wage, compared with a dual-income family earning the same total family income (itself a family who will also cost money to the state in subsidised paid-for childcare). The UK Conservative new 'Universal Credit' system will force low-income families to forego loving parental care by one parent, including lone-parent families. When it comes to mothers and children, there really are no 'broad shoulders'. Austerity? A euphemism for financial and political violence against the vulnerable: let them eat shit. Budget cuts? A byword for hitting *women* where it hurts: in their pockets.[505]

The reality is that there is a cost inherent in raising children: the cost of *living*. The fact that this cost applies just as much to a family who requires paid childcare as those who have *sacrificed an income* to provide the care themselves is suppressed in debate about families and the care of children, yet it is significant. It renders many single-income families significantly worse off than dual-income families, yet successive governments have chosen to prioritise the dual-income family, raising it on a pedestal and deeming it greatly more deserving of state support. In short, many families are struggling financially — single-income families with children *especially* so. Lone parents face an even greater burden. Of course when I say 'parents' I mean 'mothers' in the vast majority of cases. But when policies discriminate against lone parents, it has nothing to do with the fact that they are women, mothers, does it? No, not at all.*

---

* It's that irony again.

Yet even in the case of the 'rosy' family, let's call it something super academic, like the *political progeny paradigm*, there is a manifest unfairness in the state treating a family as a *unit* where payments are made (minimising state exposure), yet treating it as a household of mere *individuals* where tax is removed with no adjustment for family care responsibilities (maximising tax income). This policy of differential treatment depending on the state's interests demonstrates a contempt for families with children and an eagerness to exploit those families. Simple as that.

Just think about this double standard for a moment. When it suits the government, to reduce its costs, it employs a 'family unit' approach: a global assessment of the resources of the family, the income of the family and the outgoings of the family. However, to apply a similar principle to income tax is avoided. Instead, an individual approach is employed, thereby rendering a parent who chooses to care for the children economically invisible and worthless (with a tax code which serves nobody), and maximises tax revenue at the expense of a significant number of families on very modest incomes indeed. I can appreciate one benefit of taxing people as individuals: it removes the barrier to women from seeking an income, which might be taxed immediately because of the loss of a personal allowance; but the current system is too far the other way. The personal tax allowance of the mother or father providing the care is dormant, an insult, a taunt: "You're worthless and your family deserves to be taxed to the hilt." Really, the need for a transferable tax allowance to reflect the worth, the value and economic contribution of the unwaged work and care that a mother (or father) provides, *must* be recognised.

What other fiscal or social policies could be introduced to support families where one parent cares for children? We have already discussed the wages for housework demand and basic income. Although caring time out of the workforce is now recognised to some degree within pension entitlements, there are other measures which require consideration too[506]:

› Transferable tax allowances to balance the family tax liability and abolish the family care penalty currently in place.

› Optional income-splitting tax system, as seen in Germany, for couples whereby a parent caring for children is legally deemed to own half the income of the waged parent, and is taxed on that income.

› Homecare allowance, as seen in Finland, Norway and France. "Child home care allowance can be claimed by families with a child under 3 years of age who is not in municipal day care. The child can be looked after by one of the parents or another person or a private day care provider. Child home care allowance includes a care allowance and a care supplement, which depends on the family's income. The family's income has no effect on the care allowance. To qualify for the allowance, the child must not be in municipal day care and the family must have at least one child under 3 years of age."[507] Unlike the way in which Child Benefit is now seen in the UK, homecare allowance is not to cover extra costs of children. It is a salary paid to the parent (usually the mother) who stays at home full-time to care for their young. It is extremely popular.[508] It also fits with the concern of many parents and child development psychologists, that the period of birth to three years is a crucial period in their development. It gives the freedom to the parent to make the appropriate choice in their family's case.

What is striking about these proposals is the degree to which they respect the diversity in families and the way in which parents wish to balance family and market work. They achieve a significant feminist aim: enable women who care for their children to be recognised for their work and protected from economic and social marginalisation by virtue of that work. They do not give preference, as we see in the UK and the US, to dual-income families or to families in which women seek to work full-time, but are, rather, neutral.

But at the moment? Families where one parent provides the care are exploited, penalised and discriminated against in fiscal policy. Consider a family of four, the Jones',[509] where a sole earner earns £20,000 while the mother performs the childcare within the family. They are liable to pay £3,445 in tax. So far, so what? Right? Well, compare their significant financial burden with a dual-income family of four, the Smiths, who bring in £20,000, but split between them in varying proportions. Their total income tax bill is just £490 *and* they receive entitlement to financial help towards commercial childcare providers. *Look* at those figures. The Jones' are penalised by £2,955 in extra tax, all for the privilege of a mother wishing to remain at home to care for her children herself. Family-friendly politics, eh? An extra tax burden of £2,955 is a huge amount of money. It is the difference for countless families between living comfortably and living on the *edge*. Who is keeping up with these Jones', exactly? The figure of an extra £2,955 tax liability applies right up to incomes of £30,000 (the majority of working families, potentially). It is a disgrace. I use that example because it tells you everything you need to know: the values behind an individual tax system* which cares nothing for family life and which perpetuates the invisibility and worthless status ascribed to mothers and children.

When the state giveth: you are a unit.

When the state taketh away: you are on your own.

If any political party values fairness, perhaps this direct contradiction in how the state calculates entitlement versus penalty should be addressed. Surely it should work both ways. If you calculate your own duty to your citizens by assessing them as household units, you should perform the same calculation method to assess them for liability for tax. The political jargon of 'hardworking families' and 'families who do the right thing' is, in this context, a singular insult. Tell Mrs Jones she does not work hard to support her family. Tell her on the doorstep while you canvas for votes. I dare you.

SHIRKED STATE RESPONSIBILITIES

Let's take a look at the United Nations Universal Declaration on Human Rights.[510] There you will find, in Article 25: "(1) Everyone has the right to a standard of living adequate for the health and well-being of himself and of his family, including food, clothing, housing and medical care and necessary social services, and the right to security in the event of unemployment, sickness, disability, widowhood, old age or other lack of livelihood in circumstances beyond his control. (2) Motherhood and childhood are entitled to special care and assistance. All children, whether born in or out of wedlock, shall enjoy the same social protection". Did you see that? *Motherhood* and children. Looks like our politicians didn't turn to page two.

How's this for double standards: a mother is liable to prosecution and civil sanction should she fail to care for her child; yet the state, politicians, and commentators feel at liberty to suggest that a mother at home, dutifully caring for her family, performs no valuable role, is not worthy of recognition and is a burden. Every child needs caring for: the question, always, is who is going to do it? Having children is not a private, personal matter. Reproduction and the decent care of necessarily dependent children are, quite simply, necessary for society. Women reproduce the entire human

---

* Perhaps, for fun, compare Amazon's UK tax figures. Or Starbucks. (Hint: they don't pay very much). What does it tell you? That families are seen as plankton for the public purse.

race — the future human capital for your machine. However, we are witnessing social and economic policy which does not live up to the state's responsibility to mothers; rather, it treats them as invisible and worthless.

By way of hypothetical example, if a mother were to leave a child at home, alone, for significant periods of time every day, she would be prosecuted for child abandonment or child neglect. The state imposes a duty of care onto the parent; and we all recognise the moral duty of care. If a mother fails in that duty by leaving a child unsupervised or by not arranging suitable substitute care, she would be criminalised. Yet, despite these criminal and civil duties on parents, there is no accompanying responsibility of the state *to* a mother, no recognition of a mother's work and performance of her duty, no reward for the work she does, and no respect for work or status of mother. We regard her work as entirely altruistic, her children as a hobby, and her actions as a matter of private choice. This line runs so deep that it is trotted out by politicians, friends, family, economists and people on the street without any pause to reflect on the utter absurdity of what it is they are saying, namely: women's work is worthless; mothers are expendable; and children are Chihuahuas.

Just stop for a moment and think about what that means: it means that the state recognises that a child must be cared for. It is prepared to sanction any mother or father who fails in that duty. Yet, we are living in a society in which a mother who performs that duty, performs it well, willingly and lovingly, is treated by the state as a burden, acting out of personal choice, and regarded by politicians of every colour as a waste of space.

Picture too, if you will, the social situation many mothers now find themselves in. Libraries are closing. Children's centres are closing. Cutting, say, the availability of something as simple as 'Bounce and Rhyme', 'Story Time' and 'Messy Play' can be a real blow to families with young children at home, fuelling isolation. All of these are lifelines for carers and children, yet no doubt regarded as utterly petty by many professional people and politicians. Playgroups can be few and far between, often relying on volunteers (many of whom were, in their day, housewives). For a government to cut funding to services, groups and activities which support parents in raising their children at home only for policymakers and commentators then to say to parents: 'you are failing your children by not providing access to enrichment' (and nudging them along to use childcare to fill the purported gap) is cruel and rich indeed.

The answer is not increased investment in institutionalised childcare and more hostile attempts to force mothers into workforce participation. Rather, it is proper consideration of the needs of a society which actually values young children and their parents; and investment in public services and the community. Not increasing separation of children from parental or maternal care against the wishes of the individual family.

I have already discussed the invisible hand that rocks the cradle and how it really isn't ruling the world; the economic man has roped in feminist sister and left mother out in the cold. The work is here, the debate is happening, the campaigns are continuing, the voices are rising — but women and allies need to listen up, think about what is happening and demand that the invisible hand of mother has some bleedin' money put in it. The time is now.

MATERNAL ACTIVISM

Understanding the issues involved is the first step. Taking this knowledge out in the world is the next. This is maternal activism. There are many women who have been campaigning for years. What is long overdue is for the rest of us to join them, in solidarity, and for the gatekeepers of policy to listen up. We have to regain a sense of vision. You will find a list of organisations at the back of the book — reach out beyond these pages, join them, join us and put on those purple stockings*.

Throughout Western society there are organisations, groups and academics who are trying (against immense and coordinated resistance which reaches across patriarchal, capitalist and liberal feminist lines) to get the issue of care onto the table. We are trying to get the issue of 'equality' to be examined critically, rather than restrict it to issues of 'pay' and 'market-work'. Our concerns are truly feminist: how to ensure the full humanity, citizenship and economic empowerment of women? The difference lies in our answers. Where motherhood is currently deemed to be a burden, we encourage people to see it as intimately concerned with our humanity. Where the workplace is seen as the site of empowerment, we question whether wage-slavery is empowering to those outside of the privileged elite. Where we are encouraged to talk about women's potential, we prefer to

---

* You know you don't *actually* have to wear purple stockings. Just get involved. Nothing will change without enough of us *agitating* for change. Doc Martens are a good look, though.

discuss individual women's interests and preferences and how one size does *not* fit all.

The UK organisation Mothers at Home Matter works tirelessly to represent those families who would like to prioritise family care. To quote from its discussion paper, "Who Cares About the Family?", it exists "to represent families where children are cared for at home by a parent, as well as families who would like to choose to care for their children themselves but find the barriers too great". The organisation has three core aims, namely:

1. To promote understanding of children's developmental needs, focusing on maternal care, the importance of family time and a loving home environment.

2. To campaign for changes in the tax and benefits system to allow mothers and fathers to allocate more time to family-based care at key stages of the family life cycle . . . especially penalties faced by families who dedicate time to caring.

3. To enhance the status and self-esteem of mothers at home by encouraging and celebrating motherhood.

You will notice that nowhere does the organisation say that it is campaigning for *all* women to stay at home; or all women to become *mothers*; or no *fathers* to be carers (indeed, there are many who support the organisation). But it does something extremely important, some might say feminist: it seeks to promote policy and systemic change so that women are not penalised, rendered vulnerable, devalued or isolated by virtue of motherhood. It is not prescriptive and is a 'broad church' of political views ranging from radical feminist to socially conservative. What it does is advocate for the family and to advocate for fairness in policy. Chair Marie Peacock is clear that:

A family life cycle approach is essential and a sequential pattern of care and work is as acceptable as any other choice. Mothers and fathers need time to care and time to work, but not necessarily both at the same time when raising a family. Children's developmental needs must be prioritised and this takes doses of time and love. If we truly believe that parenting is a shared project, then parents need at least the option to be assessed jointly and treated as a household when they have care responsibilities for children — and also for other family members. It makes little sense to treat people as separate individuals when they've embarked on the journey of family life. Mutual support and partnership working is key with parents making the choices that work best for them in their unique circumstances, which change over time. Policymakers must provide a level playing field so that choices are supported equally in taxation, allowances, and Child Benefit, recognising that a productive economy relies on an army of invisible carers.

I am a friend of the organisation. I joined and support it because it is one of the few organisations I have found which speaks for me and many other mothers in this country. It is this 'family life cycle' approach which is at the heart of the Purplestockings Movement: the need for respect for families during the time they have care responsibilities; the need for respect for the diversity of women in their aspirations and preferences; and the need to consider children's needs. Peacock states that "in a modern society it's surely time to end the discrimination against caring and unpaid work, for the sake of caregivers as well as the dependants they support". I couldn't agree more.

What differentiates such organisations from, say, political parties which champion the rights of women in the workplace, is the extent to which it places the debate *squarely* within humanity, the need for care and the need for fairness. This is work echoed internationally, for example, by: Canadian-based Motherhood Initiative for Research and Community Involvement (MIRCI); Martha Joy Rose and the Museum of Motherhood, Mamapalooza and The Motherhood Movement; Welfare Warriors; and the Payday Men's Network in the US. Global Women's Strike raise the issue of unwaged and low-paid women under global capitalism. However, the neglect of women's voices when what we say is not what the establishment (now including, of course, the liberal feminist who derides her sisters at home) wants to hear, is a disgrace. It is certainly not feminist. Our disempowerment in society is, it seems, mirrored in the refusal of the political class to listen.

All Mothers Work, a maternal feminist organisation in the UK, is overtly and proudly feminist. Esther Parry, Mother-Sister of the organisation, is absolutely clear about the need for a system which values mothers and rejects the patriarchal oppression of women. All Mothers Work stands for the end of exploitation of women's unpaid labour; fights for radical change; and recognises the power and importance of mothering and caring. To quote Parry:

We reject the patriarchal, androcentric, and capitalist value system which labels caring as worthless, demeaning, and inferior, and we reject the patriarchal model of family. We promote the truth about mothering; that it is strength, power, resilience, and requires endurance, skill, creativity and self-mastery. We believe that the negative way mothering, as 'women's work', is viewed and treated in our society is symbolic of the way in which all women's work is viewed and treated. We insist that mothering be acknowledged as real work, and we call for the introduction of Basic Income to reflect this (as well as destigmatising benefits in general). We believe in the rights of children as full, equal beings, their right to their mothers, and their right to vital attachment and loving, safe, free, innocent, explorative childhoods, free of poverty, abuse, sexualisation, gender stereotyping and adult stresses.

We have to be able to stop and look at the pernicious impact of work culture on our families and home. It is not enough to speak of shared care or maternity leave and universal childcare: we have to see the family as important, care-work as crucial to our societies and the investment of both parents to engage in family life. We need more than lip-service paid to 'care' and 'family'. We need a progressive, radical, humanist, maternal feminism. Parry had this to say at Feminism in London: "By keeping stay-at-home mothers and other carers in a mental and political private sphere, thus silencing and erasing them, and taking them for granted, you are not only doing exactly what patriarchy does to these women, you are condoning, upholding and actively strengthening that oppression, those stereotypes, those lack of rights, visibility, choice and respect." And therein lies the challenge: bring women back into feminism[511] out of the lie that is capitalist emancipation, and bring mothers back in from the cold.

I had great hopes for this coming about in my brief tenure as a founding member, and contributor to policy development, of the UK Women's Equality Party (or WEP). However, experience proved as I had feared when the party first came into existence: *Some women are indeed more equal than mothers.*

In October 2015, WEP — a party essentially formed and dominated by journalists and women of privilege and status — officially launched its policies at Conway Hall in London. I draped my purple tote bag with the words "Every Mother is a Working Mother" over the balcony, in full view of the leader and others on the stage. Above the stage on which they stood and spoke were the words "To Thine Own Self Be True". Amen, to that. With patient reflection since I became involved in the party from its inception and during the policy development process, I have to be true to myself and own my disappointment at the way the party has, like other mainstream parties, missed a trick.

It risks failing women because it seeks only equality, the poorer sister of women's liberation, meekly seeking equality in a system already stacked against women.[512] In fact, I don't think I heard the word 'feminism' mentioned in the leader's speech. Once. It risks failing women because it seeks only equality rather than justice, fairness and true representation of women. And it abjectly fails mothers because it fails to acknowledge them except as in the capacity of employee. It doesn't even mention the word 'mother' once in reference to 'caregiving' in a short section of its manifesto. The leader refused to discuss austerity in an interview on the evening of the launch, despite governmental budget cuts hitting women disproportionately. Come on now, sisters. Pop politics just won't *cut* it.

Moreover, WEP fails to explore radical ways to lessen financial hardship for women from across the social spectrum or to reshape the way we value care and those providing care. Rather, the party was alive with youthful enthusiasm, professional and boardroom concerns, and blinkered talk of workplace equality, with no regard to the complexity and diversity of women's lives and experience and expectations and struggle and desires and strengths and talents. It talks of the unfulfilled potential of half the population: conveniently neglecting the wishes of *many* women.

The fact is that women's equality is only ever going to be a polite nudge, a request within the rules of a previously scripted box which says "this is the game: play it or get out". And my goodness, the WEP really is playing the neoliberal, capitalist game.

So how did I even become involved in this party? After banging on virtual doors since its inception to engage with the party and to invite the party to engage with diverse groups of women, including those which campaign for mothers, single mothers (still the huge majority of lone parents) and women not in professional or elite circles, I was let in. The policy development in the already set brief of 'equality in parenting' (which I immediately challenged as blinkered) was coordinated by an employee of the Fatherhood Institute, and contributed to by men and a small number of women one of whom, let's put it this way, suggested that a mother at home is a "complete waste" and suggested that ideas to support mothers to be with their children were "fascist". Yes. Really. Whilst ostensibly a women's party, it is so busy apologising for its existence that it has blithely held up mothers and their children as sacrificial lambs.

In my experience WEP is giving every impression that women need liberating from full-time mothering, and that only participation in the workplace can lead to 'equality' — a view I cannot share. The feminist message is surely that a mother's place is wherever she wants to be. Not where this party, or that party, or this feminism, or that conservatism says. Being chained to the kitchen sink against our will is just as oppressive as being chained to the workplace when we dream of being with our young children. Feminism and politics must find other ways to lessen the penalties faced by a mother that come from whichever choice she makes.

After suggesting that WEP might wish to expand the diversity of its working group on the 'parenting' issue (although, for a women's party, surely the word 'mother' somewhere, and linked with something positive rather than 'burden' and 'penalty', wouldn't go amiss) no mother's group was brought on board until I insisted that Mothers at Home Matter and Global Women's Strike were brought in. Both represent a significant number of mothers who want to (but are frustrated financially in realising their wishes) or those who do (by choice but at huge financial sacrifice) care for their children themselves. We may as well have stayed silent, like the voices of millions of women busy caring for the families, young and old. Always ignored, often derided, when not patronised or humoured.

Within WEP, mothers are seen as a problem to be solved. The debate is still 'childcare' and effects on equality in the 'workplace' and the 'pay gap' of bearing children. Men, women who pursue the career trajectory rather than the family care line (as is their right) and representatives of father's groups, kept the policy gate on parenting, as though the price to pay for a party seeking to end violence against women is the surrender and trade-off of any 'privilege of motherhood' and the denial of the existence and value of maternal care, for mothers and children, and, indeed, society at large.

In effect, the horse-trading at the heart of a party seeking to champion the rights of women is reinforcing the prevailing and insidious mainstream discourse of disrespect, silencing and devaluing of a mother (and there are many) who wishes not to re-enter the workplace while she has dependent children, and is either struggling by financially to do so, or struggling by emotionally in her job while wishing to be at home instead.

WEP's premise for its policies on women who are mothers can be inferred thus: her 'responsibilities' are decreed to be at home *and* in the workplace (irrespective of her family's wishes, or any wider argument that the work she performs as a mother, raising and caring for her young children, is itself important work of value); her needs and role are to be subsumed into 'parenting'; and a gender split 50:50 in matters of the home as though this is something universally desired by every family, every woman, every man, every child. Someone tell my children, who, until at least two were very often "Daddy? Schmaddy. I want my Mummy".

Democracy in mainstream parties and, now, from all appearances, the WEP, can seem like it is conducted on the basis that the party knows best, that a key vocal and influential elite's interests are the interests of all, that any radical, grassroots reorganisation and re-evaluation is out of the question. Even for a party seeking to present itself as radical. What is a wasted opportunity is the WEP's failure to address or entertain policies which could actually matter to women, such as:

› improved maternity services and investment;

› greater investment in midwifery;

› greater investment in breastfeeding support;

› greater financial support for women and carers;

› greater investment in services to women suffering pregnancy loss;

› greater investment in the availability of legal aid to women in family disputes;

› greater investment in women's refuges so that mothers and children can be protected from violent partners;

› greater investment in maternal mental health services;

› greater investment in community services and projects to support families;

› transferrable tax allowances where one parent cares for the children;

› adjusted pay on return to employment to reflect time out of the workforce to raise children;

› a carer's income or stipend;

› a citizen's or universal basic income;

› reinstatement of the universality of Child Benefit and an increase yearly in line with inflation;

› funded retraining on re-entry to the workplace;

› reduced working week and/or fewer working hours for all to limit the intrusion of the workplace into our lives.

You know, the stuff which might actually protect and support women who are also mothers, the majority of women at some point in our lives. We were all born of our mothers: it is surely a universal concern that those who bring *us* to life are respected, valued and supported.

But despite our efforts, the 'economic' and 'genderless' agenda pushed through as though we were never there. Suddenly, the familiar picture of 'affordable' and 'high quality' childcare and split parental leave took shape as though we had never dared to raise the significant number of families — millions of women — for whom this is not what they would prefer; as though they are an aberration on the image of superficial equality. Yes, women must not be deterred from working outside of the home by extortionate childcare costs: the affordability of substitute care is an important, and feminist, issue. Yet, this does not detract from the cost of raising children and of living, generally. If our governments deem *some* families deserving of assistance with childcare costs, we have to be able to question why comparable assistance is not forthcoming for single-income families which have sacrificed an income to care for the children (and thus have a greater need for assistance) and are taxed disproportionately to boot. In other words, why are some women more equal than others? Well, because full female employment and commodified childcare is the thriving political ideology. Even WEP Leader Sophie Walker, in her speech at the launch, quoted a 'stay at home mother' who wanted help getting back into the workplace, conveniently failing to quote the thousands of us who were contributing to the policy development through their voice-piece Mothers at Home Matter, or the many mothers who contacted WEP on email and social media, or the massive number of mothers who, according to government statistics, would prefer more time, or exclusive time at home with their children.

It repeated the Labour Party's trick after it came into power in 1997 when it completely erased mention of data in an important study,[513] which it itself had commissioned, which showed that a significant number of women actually wished to care for their children (a figure remaining as true today as then) preferring instead to push forward with its version of equality, employment as panacea, and branding women at home just "baking cupcakes".[514] It's a trick which is well tested, and it is such a disappointment to see the WEP ideologically repeating it, in the name of women. I promptly wrote a blog post containing much of what I repeat here. *No, sisters*, I said. *Not in my name.*

A true representation of women must include our diversity, our different needs and wants and circumstances. I do not suggest, and do not believe, that being a mother is the only or true representation of womanhood. Policies are required which enable women to be free of the assumption that childcare responsibilities fall to them as, after all, that works against women who do not want to take on the child-rearing or day-to-day care. However, to confine policies to the model of shared parenting and dual work/care responsibilities does not encompass those very many women for whom this is not preferred or possible. It does not go far enough in extending choice and freedom to choose the form of one's family.

The majority of women in the world become mothers at some point in their lives, or experience pregnancy, or pregnancy loss, for example. A politics which ignores this (instead only addressing motherhood in the context of *burden* and *penalty*) is not going to achieve justice, fairness and true representation of women in all our complexity and different circumstances. It is not politics which serves women. It merely apes political man.

On my lips during the launch of the party was bell hook's question *"ain't I a woman?"* For everything discussed, when we ignore the wider issues relating to mothers (who are women) who want to care for their families, their economic vulnerability and penalties and more, we cannot claim to be a party representing all women. It is a party representing its own preferred model. One which did not include a very large proportion of women. I left the launch knowing that, as I had published in my pamphlet six months before, mothers who mother at home (or who want to) are *personae non grata* in politics. I remain disenfranchised even from the only 'feminist' political party.

As women, we are socialised not to speak up, not to challenge or make a fuss. As I said at the beginning of this book, we may rock the boat (sometimes) but we may not build a new one. The WEP's failure to go far enough demonstrates that all too clearly. I was seasick and so I got off.

THE TIME IS NOW

So here we are. The entire terms of reference, the agenda and rules of modern neoliberal politics and economics, are being set by elite educated white men and professional liberal-feminist women so that families who make, or who yearn to make, the decision that a parent (and it is usually the mother — let us not kid ourselves) stay at home to raise and support the family are entirely neglected by accident or design, depending on the policymaker's whim. In the current climate women do not feel able to say something so unfashionable and so 'retrograde' as: *I wish to devote time to raising my family*; or something so radical and fundamentally important as: *I demand the right to support, recognition, value and equality of treatment in doing so.*

Is it really so controversial to say this? Is it really so outrageous, in 2016, for a woman to dare to: 1. speak in sex-specific terms; 2. point to the fact that a specific branch of feminism has dominated debate so successfully since the 1960s that women are forgetting their own heritage of the inclusive and collaborative nature of the original women's movement, and that feminism has many shades; 3. to recognise that there are many women who wish to relinquish paid employment (or at the very least reduce their hours) during the time of their lives in which they have family responsibilities; 4. to proclaim that there is human, intrinsic value in mothering work and in the raising and nurturing of a family and home life; and, hold on to your hats, 5. that, consequently, mothering and family work should be supported and rewarded rather than penalised and discouraged.

Well, I've said it. Now your turn, sister. The time is now.

We have to be able to speak our needs, in relation to our reproductive bodies, our emotional needs and our labour. We must have the right to stand up for the needs of our children, too. After all, we are looking out for our children, not only for ourselves. We can demand the right to a politics which embraces us, as women and as mothers. So, sisters, Let's join in maternal feminism as an antidote to toxic politics and economics and elements of feminism which are drunk on the neoliberal poison. The time is now.

When we take a look at the history of the women's movement, and some quarters of academic discussion today, it is clear that there is nothing new in these demands. There is nothing outrageous about such claims. There is nothing unrealistic about seeking adequate recognition and support for all citizens involved in productive and valuable work, whether currently deemed worthy of pay or not. As things stand, our societies are freeloading on the unpaid, undervalued and ignored work of mothers. Join the groups which are part of a growing mothers' movement, and start pushing for change. You have a voice. Be *heard*. Join the Purplestockings Movement and march with us. The time is now.

When it comes to politics, the labels of left, right, liberal, Marxist, free-market capitalist, socialist and more, abound. This immediately leads to polarised opinions even where there is significant potential common ground. So when it comes to *my* politics, many would say it's to the left (anti capitalist-accumulation, pro-basic income, remember?). Others would say it is socially conservative (I'm talking about mothers at home, right?). They must have forgotten my views about the limitations of the nuclear family and inclusion of those 'deviant' forms of families. But, really, I'd prefer to decline the labels of left and right. *I'm right here, on the ground.* And we need our grassroots to start to grow. The time is now.

After all, when jobs are being lost to automation; when wealth is accumulating in the 1%; when the workplace increasingly encroaches on family life; and when women remain at higher risk of poverty because they have cared for their families, feminism has to start to ask itself: *are we ever going to find creative ways to protect, support and empower women beyond simply pushing for paid employment?* We must start to recover some of the intellectual and creative verve of the original women's movement: we have to return to discussing redistribution of wealth and the fair organisation of labour. We don't need to agonise over labels of socialism, conservatism, radicalism or whatever. We just need to put *humanity* at the centre. Because the fact is that many mothers remain trapped by the market either as workers or as unwaged carers, and are marginalised by reason of being mothers. *We have to get political.* We need to find ways to value care, to support carers, and put money into the pockets of those who sustain and nourish the human race. At heart, we need to support the right of mothers to frame their lives in the way that is right for *them*: we need to liberate ourselves from conditions which get in the way of this most fundamental of women's rights.

Mothers, our time has arrived.

Part 4

A MOTHER'S HEART

Love

While I loved, and while I was loved,
what an existence I enjoyed!

Charlotte Brontë, *Villette*

BEING LOVED

And so, I have talked about mothers. Our bodies, our minds, and our labour. Yet we have a heart too. The fact is that we have to be able to talk about *love*. The love for our children might well underpin that weak spot of ours, the tiny gap in the blueprint* into which our society can drop the bomb and freeload on our attachment. But it is not just a soft underbelly or Achilles heel. It can be powerful. As bell hooks writes, "love has the potential transformative power for meaningful social change".[515] Yet it is rare to read about it. After all, politics can be dry, detached and distant, the very antithesis of love, care and connection. However, we can *allow* ourselves to see value in humanity and the impact love could have on our societies.

In *The Mommy Brain, How Motherhood Makes Us Smarter*, Katherine Ellison discusses how, for many new mothers, the communion we have with our babies in, say, breastfeeding, where our heartrate slows, our temperature rises and time slows, is unique: "for many new mothers, it's also a potent introduction to a new way of being while they're 'hooked' into strong relationships including and surrounding their child".[516] This resonated with me. I was taken by surprise by the profound relationship with my children in which I could *melt into mothering*. It brought to mind that my mother once sat as I am and I was cradled in *her* arms; soothed, held and loved. Our humanity and our willingness to surrender to our humanity

---

* For Star Wars geeks everywhere.

and vulnerability, to be mindful of the connection at that moment, and to be engaged wholeheartedly in bodily and emotional communion. Being human; being loved.

We know, as mothers and children ourselves, that the mother/child embrace is precious, it is powerful and it has been echoed through time as a central human force. No wonder it has been feared; no wonder it has been envied.

In the modern age, it is increasingly giving way under duress to economic bondage, commodification and disconnection: many of us have neither the time nor the opportunity to embrace our babies and our children as we would like. Our culture is distrustful of love. As blogger and social activist Sophie Christophy puts it, our culture almost believes that, "Too much love is bad for a person — it will make them weak and lesser. A mother's love is suffocating and overbearing. That is the prize jewel belief of the patriarchal mindset. It totally distracts us from the potential of love for liberation."[517] It is this feeling that we have to harness, as mothers, in pushing for a new movement and policies which honour the importance of love, care and nurture. The idea of liberating motherhood has at its core the strength of love we have for our families, and the importance of caring, after all. It is our central value: we must refuse to be marginalised or impoverished for it.

The problem is that, sometimes, our predicament can bring to mind John Lennon's remark that "life is what happens when we are busy making other plans". For mothers who are 'at home' with their children, the message can feel stark: you are missing out, sisters. Life's out there — out there in the 'public sphere'. Out there, you get to be respected as a fully-formed adult human being rather than sneered at as some snot and vomit wiper-upper who sings *Baa Baa Black Sheep* all day and 'wastes her potential'. This misconception has so many threads, to be sure, but it must partly be the result of a very long history in which the talents, the skills and the work of mothers have been disrespected and devalued; and in which women have been segregated into the 'private sphere' to allow the men and fathers to dominate public policy. What's that word again? Patriarchy, was it?

Yet actually, it's the other way around. Life isn't just what happens when we are busy working 'out there', or making plans for something else. Life isn't just what happens when we are busy making money for ourselves or someone else, or building a career. When people suffer, as we all do at some point, we think of the people we love — and plans go out the window.

Being with my children has been the time of my life. I want them to know that. In time. If you are so inclined, being with your children can be the time of your life. So perhaps it might be just as fair to say that life is what is happening when you are with the ones you love. Sisters, mothers, fathers and brothers: we *have* to start allowing ourselves to lean in to life and love.

OUR MOTHERS

It is a timely opportunity now to talk of Our Mothers. My mother, her mother, my father's mother. Working-class women. Women who worked hard every day of their lives — whether in raising their children, working in factories, typing pools, offices, cleaning people's homes, making hats, or selling clothes from a suitcase in the street.

My maternal grandmother is someone who comes alive and alight with love when holding her baby great-grandchildren in her arms; she knitted my children beautiful clothes while I was pregnant; and she gives snippets of wisdom in short, plain, honest speak. I do look to her and know that, at heart, she has light which wants to shine. I am grateful she has lived to see my children and to know that she is loved.

My paternal grandmother, Nanny Lil', passed away when I was 16 and I grieve for the fact that I will never be able to speak to her about her experiences as a young woman and as a mother, grandmother, great-grandmother and great-great-grandmother: she will never see me with my children and treat them to those kisses, those cuddles, or envelope them with one of her deep, cracking laughs. One of the benefits of shared care, where there is willing and available family, is that I had the advantage and joy of having a close relationship with my grandmother — spending hours with my brother and sister at her house before and after school. She was *the* allomother, someone who stepped into my mother's shoes when mum couldn't be there, and gave me milk and sugar.

Something I remember about her, and which is particularly poignant at this time in my life, is that she had a beautiful black and white picture of her own mother as a young woman, in an oval mahogany ornate frame on the wall of her home. Her mother was looking over her, even as she entered her elderly years. Isn't that so very special? A testament to the importance of mothers: even for a woman entering her last years, her own mother long gone. My nan had veiny hands and a warm heart, and was fiery as anything:

the *original* spitfire. She also commanded respect amongst her huge — and colourful — family: my grandad was loved, he was the big man, known down the pub and in the black market; but my nan had clout, grit and strength which her 4 foot 11 frame belied. And so, I frequently thought back to my nan while writing this book. I wonder what she would have made of it all, and where we all are now. If I could only ask her to put on some purple stockings and give Downing Street hell with me with a placard, I know she would have been with me in a flash. So I keep that knowledge with me; knowing that whatever my stature — politically or physically — I can raise the roof if I want to. Dad, your mother was a formidable woman and what a privilege to have known her.

When it comes to my own mother, she has her ways (as all mothers do, for daughters, if we have learned anything from **A Mother's Mind**) to get under my skin, to keep me warm, to drive me nuts and to make it all better: *sometimes all at once.* I saw how she worked extremely hard when I was growing up in the 1980s — a postfeminist success story of full-time work and economic autonomy. Never mind that she would have preferred to be at home, at least for the majority of the week. There had simply come a time, under Thatcher, that working-class families were squeezed so tightly that there was little choice for many, many families. I see the same happening to women, today. Perhaps this is why I resist the script of privileged career women which insists that *all* women must be yearning to get out to do better things and that childcare is the dream ticket. It has its place; but then so does recognising the unique family and the unique woman, and allowing for difference. When it comes to her retirement, I can hardly pin Mum down. She's making up for lost time, after all, to live her life free from the three-hour daily commute and full-time grind. Piano, art, garden, grandchildren, love. *Breathing space.*

Thank you Mum, for teaching me to be a feminist and for imprinting in me the conviction that a man is just as capable of ironing his shirt and cooking a dinner; for encouraging me to use my voice and have faith in my abilities; and for keeping my childhood creative writing all these years. You encouraged my academic success and somehow believed in my abilities when I had no such belief myself. When it comes to mothering — the thing I hold most dear — you must have taught me well what mother love is, while you mothered me as a child, because it somehow poured from me after I too became a mother. I know you always kept us in mind; even if you couldn't be there in person as much as you wanted. I appreciate those times you have said I am a good mother. You might not know this but, despite all appearances in my younger years that I was 'career minded', being a mother is what I have always wanted. My sister, my mother, and me: sisters, daughters and mothers, alike.

MY CHILDREN, MY LOVES

And so, to our children. It has been the persistent call throughout this book: the call to love; the needs of my children; their development and the blossoming of their minds. But overwhelmingly, my children have needed my love. During the editing of this book, I took some extra time to study my children. The way my daughter glances to me, even in a playgroup, or looks up and says "Look Mummy! Look at meeeee!", as she wriggles her bum to the music. I attended a 'Wild Thing' parade at my son's school. He waved, blew kisses and looked over throughout, keen to connect and bask in parental focus. And this brought it all home: why is it that children often look to their parents? Why do they need to feel loved, admired, seen and known? It is the epitome of the dance between parent and child: the basic and real need of children for love and attention. It is in this context that I then reflected on the words of Maurice Sendak, the author of *Where the Wild Things Are*. I wonder whether, perhaps, a child looks for his mother in a crowded audience just to know that he is seen by the person who, in his world, "loved him best of all".

Whilst finishing up the footnotes and bibliography for the book, I celebrated my birthday and, a week before that, my son's birthday too. I told my son that his birthday is *so* special because it is about the day that he came into the world and that we are so grateful that he is here. That we celebrate his joining our family. I told him that the day he was born was one of the happiest days of my life, and that I was so grateful to be his mother. His birthday, after all, was the day that the mother in me was born. So, I nearly cried when my mum gave me a card a week later with the words, "Your birthday will always be special to me, because it's the day you came into my life".

I reflected on this for some time. I had written the chapter on **Maternal Thinking, Maternal Feeling**. I had talked about our emotions as mothers. However, it struck me that *gratitude* is a sentiment that is rarely acknowledged in the debate about motherhood. Yet, I imagine that my mother and I are not the only women to feel that sense of utter thankfulness on our children's birthdays.

A few weeks later, when my daughter sat on my lap, aged two, wearing her glasses for the first time, and gazing at me as though she had truly never focussed on her mother's face close up before, I felt a lump in my throat and tears start to well. I was grateful to her for 'seeing me' and giving me that gift of connection. Her little laugh, a sign that something had 'switched on' for her. I was grateful that we had been able to discount something more serious. I was thankful and utterly relieved. We all have moments like these, throughout our lives with our children, don't we? They weave into our own family's story. They stay with us.

These little events, these fleeting interactions, prompted me to wonder whether perhaps *gratitude* is the sister of mother-love. When expressed, gratitude can be one of the most precious gifts we can give to our children. For them to know they are loved for being themselves and that they have brought their own-shaped joy into the lives of their family.

So it is fitting to sign off this book with these reflections and a message to my children. Thank you both for making me a mother. I was born anew the moment I held each of you in my arms, fresh to this world, close to my heart. I am honoured to be your mother. I am proud to call you my children. My daughter, I love you. I want you to know that you are a worthy human being — of respect, of value and of strength. You have the right to be heard. I hope that, one day, you will read this book — hearing our mothers' stories is a powerful feminist act. Telling our *own* is another. My love, you make my heart sing, you wonderful girl. And my son? Perhaps having a feminist mother and a wonderful sister — who both love you and love your father — will help you to remember, as you grow into a man, that women are human beings too. That you are worthy of the love of a woman if you earn it through decency and respect. And that you are just as capable of care and deserving of the opportunity to care, as women are. Remember always that the hoover is a gender-neutral household appliance. Use it well. You too are a valuable and worthwhile human being. I love you, my son. You are my sunshine, you wonderful boy.

If things continue as they are, society will try to convince you that I wasted my talent, my time and my ambition by giving up my job to look after you, my children. That my time would have been better spent in an office in London, away from you. That you would have been better off looked after by a childcare provider. That I will have viewed being a mother at home as a burden. Don't believe it. I am grateful for you both and the time I spent with you, every day. My ambition had never been for anything but love and doing worthwhile work. *You* brought me *both* these things.

I hope I get to see you grow and live your lives, and I am honoured to have shared this time with you. When I am gone — whenever that might be — if I am in your memories then I will be *with* you even though I cannot be holding your hand.

My tree has fallen; thank you for hearing it.

Glossary of Terms

I'm no Dr Johnson. This is just a low-down on some of the terms I have used in the book, in one place. Some may or may not be dictionary definitions.

AFFECTIVE LABOUR

The 'affective' (as opposed to 'political', 'economic' or 'socio-cultural') relates to relationships of love, care and solidarity. We never hear about it though. Doesn't that tell us something about political priorities?

ALLOMOTHERS/ALLOPARENTS

Allomothers are usually women, often related or otherwise known intimately, trusted to care lovingly and responsively for a child, with whom the child has had ample time to bond and grow familiar.

ANDROCENTRIC

Dominated by or emphasizing masculine interests or a masculine point of view.

BIOLOGICAL ESSENTIALISM

Used to be a core feature of Second Wave feminism: women must not be reduced to our biology. We have minds too! A uterus does not preclude participation in wider society, the arts, the professions or politics! A double -edged sword now that identity politics and liberal feminism have taken this concept a step further to decree that what is between our legs is irrelevant, thereby missing the point about oppression of females based on our biology and reproductive capability.

BLUESTOCKINGS

A collection of educated, intellectual women in the eighteenth century, for example Hannah More (1745–1833).

CARE-WORK

The physical, emotional and relational work of care. Whether care for babies, young children, the sick, the elderly, postpartum mothers, the injured, the dying, care-work is important, it is valuable and it forms the greatest proportion of unpaid work in the UK. You have to be present to do it: there is no care remote control. You have to be a person to do it: we are not yet able to get robots to care.

CAPITALISM

Capitalism is the social, political and economic system in which those who control the means of production (say, the factory and materials) thereby exploit the producers (the workers) of the product and get bloody rich off the back of resulting capital, leading to increased power and influence, *ad infinitum*. So one's shareholders are basically pimps with increasing amounts of bling.

DEPENDENCY

The predicament whereby we are unable to meet our own needs. Babies are dependent. Children are dependent. The sick and infirm are dependent. What deviants, eh? After all, dependency is commonly now associated with moral frailty, felony, fecklessness and addiction. Problem is, none of us is even remotely independent. We all rely on others; we are all dependent in some way to some degree on someone else for *something*.

DUAL-INCOME FAMILIES

A family in which both adults are wage-earners, and childcare is (to greater or lesser degrees depending on whether both are full-time) delegated.

ETHIC OF CARE

Ideas and theories about morals and ethics, particularly in relation to caring for others. There are disagreements about whether women naturally possess an 'ethic of care' or whether this is a stereotypical sexist stick with which to beat us back to the home. Aspects of care include tenderness, responsiveness, attentiveness, consideration, kindness, responsibility, competence and respect.

FAMILY ALLOWANCE/CHILD BENEFIT

A state payment won in 1946 as a result of the work of Eleanor Rathbone in particular, to reflect the unwaged work mothers do in raising their children. Ended up as a nominal sum due to inflation and cost of living, and is no longer a universal benefit. If a wage-earner in the family is a 'higher-rate tax payer' then it is whisked away, even in single-income families. #GoesAgainstEverythingItStoodFor

FEMINISM

Women are people too. We have the right to autonomy and self-determination. You know, the ability to make decisions about our lives and to be free of discrimination, violence or oppression by virtue of little things called uteruses and vaginas.

GASLIGHTING

Derived from Patrick Hamilton's 1938 play *Gas Light* and subsequent film adaptations about a woman whose husband gradually manipulates her into believing that she is going insane. We women may well experience this when we complain about sexual harassment but are told we are being too sensitive or questioned "did he really put his hand up your skirt, or did you just imagine it?", and worse.

GROSS DOMESTIC PRODUCT (GDP)

Calculations undertaken by economists to tell us what is important, valuable and worthwhile. Usually things men have traditionally done. Gives indications of how productive a country is, while excluding a significant part of the population's labour (care). It brings to mind the words of Robert A. Heinlein about theology, namely, the "searching in a dark cellar at midnight for a black cat that isn't there". Given that it excludes some of the most valuable things in humanity — love, maternal care, breastfeeding and happiness, for example — some might say GDP is a similar exercise in futility.

HETERONORMATIVITY

Denoting or relating to a world view that promotes heterosexuality as the normal or preferred sexual orientation.

INCOME SPLITTING

The treatment of the wage-earner's income as notionally being owned by both members of the couple, to rebalance the tax liability of the family where one cares for the children. Similar to transferrable tax allowance. Should be seen as a feminist step as it also goes some way to demonstrate that the wage is jointly owned rather than 'he who earns, owns'. Too scary for 'trickledown' feminists.

LIBERAL FEMINISM

Choice rules OK? Individualism and equality are the pillars upon which this brand of feminism stand. In bed with capitalism and identity politics. Doesn't like radical feminism — *that's* too focused on women, women's reproductive bodies, and our lived experience. And as any good liberal feminist knows, we can't speak about women. It's exclusionary.

LONE PARENTS

The majority of lone parents are women. Mothers. Some are lone parents by choice, others by compulsion, whether as a result of domestic abuse, the death of a partner or desertion. Lone mothers are not deviant. They are no less deserving of a place in maternal feminism.

MANSPLAINING

Often attributed to Rebecca Solnit's essay *Men Explain Things to Me*. The imagery of mansplaining is of a man explaining something to a woman in a condescending or patronising way. If you're a woman, you'll probably know what I'm talking about. If you're a man, I think I'll find that *you* don't tend to mansplain, you just share your superior wisdom and insight on the particular subject at hand. Okay, you're right. Men don't mansplain. Thanks for explaining. Disclaimer: #NotAllMen

MARKET-WORK

Work done for an employer or self-employment. Features wages, tax and GDP.

MARXISM

Socialism on steroids. Not named after one of the Marx brothers. Features words like *accumulation, alienation, surplus labour, surplus value, means of production, Bourgeoisie* and *Proletariat*. Spawned communism, Che

Guevara, and other such stuff of student posters.

Ask some liberal feminists what bourgeois means and they may well answer 'lipstick'. #FeminismNeedsToRecoverItsIntellectualVigour #EmpowermentIsMoreThanSexualisedImage

MATERNAL FEMINISM

The term 'maternal feminism' has been used frequently to describe aspects of the women's movement. Formerly associated with ideas of 'feminine' attributes of care, tenderness and social responsibility; patriarchal values; Christian values; and, latterly, capitalist values. However, I and others use the term to bring it away from the conservative roots and towards greater social justice, recognition of women's needs, desires, preferences and diversity, fair distribution of wealth and labour, and recognition and value of care-work. The term has been used in the more radical sense by others including Anne Manne, Ann Crittenden, Andrea O'Reilly and All Mothers Work, the UK feminist organisation.

MISOGYNY

Sexism. Hatred of girls and women. Violence against girls and women. Discrimination against girls and women. Murder of girls and women. It's everywhere, exemplified by tw*ts on Twitter.

MOTHER-BLAME

If you want to know why that person is a mess, just look at the mother.

MOTHER-WORK

The care and love of children when performed by a mother.

NEOLIBERALISM

Neoliberalism is the prevailing Western capitalist economic ideology in which the markets are allowed to run riot, policy is framed to serve the market, and everything and everyone is reducible to commodity. Privatisation and individualism are central values of this system. Self-sufficiency and self-interest are elevated to virtue, rather than seen as the enemy of community, society, solidarity and compassion. If you don't have a job, or a home, or food on the table it's because you're not working hard enough or are undeserving. The perfect conditions for banking crises. One might say that Margaret Thatcher is the mother (the irony) of this heartless,

SUFFRAGETTE MOVEMENT

Because women were deemed to be the property of their husbands or fathers (remember patriarchy?) and because they were delicate creatures of suspect intelligence, they could not be trusted with the vote or participation in law making. Some women were miffed about this and protested politely with hunger strikes and civil disobedience. When a World War came about, women showed their mettle, and society gave them the vote out of guilt. Or something like that. Favourite colours: purple, green and white.

TRANSITION

The bit before the baby is born when you yell "I want to go home, I can't do this". Even during a home-birth. Intensity city.

TRANSFERABLE TAX ALLOWANCE

Calculating the tax owed by a family more fairly, to take into account the unwaged work of the carer. Under current tax arrangements, each adult has a 'personal allowance' by which they are not taxed for the first, say £10,000 they earn. The result is that a parent who sacrifices an income to care for the children has a personal allowance which gathers dust, but the wage-earner brings home a salary which is taxed as though an individual despite its need for the entire family. As a result, single-income families pay a significantly greater sum than a dual-income family earning the same total wage. #HardWorkingFamiliesIncludeSingleIncomeFamilies

TRICKLEDOWN FEMINISM

The idea that more power at the top for women, the better for all women. A bit like trickledown economics — more wealth at the top means more will trickle down to the masses. Abjectly false.

UNIVERSAL BASIC INCOME

A state payment to every adult citizen. No strings, no means testing and no refunds.

WOMEN

Adult human females. Although making such an apparently innocuous statement can warrant threats from some to "die in a fire cis scum". #ButThat'sForAnotherBook #It'sLikeTheWitchHuntsAllOverAgain #PatriarchyFindsAWay

List of Organisations and Resources

All Mothers Work http://www.allmotherswork.co.uk/

Association for Improvements in the Maternity Services http://www.aims.org.uk/

Attachment Parenting International http://www.attachmentparenting.org/

Basic Income UK http://basicincome.org.uk/

Birthrights http://www.birthrights.org.uk/

Family and Parenting Institute http://www.familyandparenting.org

Feminism in London Conference http://www.feminisminlondon.co.uk/

Gingerbread: Single Parents, Equal Families http://www.gingerbread.org.uk/

Global Women's Strike http://www.globalwomenstrike.net/

International Mothers & Mothering Network
  http://www.internationalmothersandmotheringnetwork.org

Mamapalooza https://mamapalooza.wordpress.com/

MMM Europe — Make Mothers Matter http://www.mmmeurope.org/en

Motherhood Initiative for Research and Community Involvement
  http://motherhoodinitiative.org/

Motherhood Movement, and The Museum of Motherhood
  https://joyrose.wordpress.com/

Mothers at Home Matter http://www.mothersathomematter.co.uk/

Museum of Motherhood Directory http://www.momdirectory.org/

Payday Men's Network http://www.refusingtokill.net/PDindex.htm

Politics of Mothering and Liberating Motherhood
  http://www.politicsofmothering.com

Positive Birth Movement http://www.positivebirthmovement.org/

Save Childhood Movement http://www.savechildhood.net/

Welfare Warriors http://www.welfarewarriors.org/

What About the Children? http://www.whataboutthechildren.org.uk/

Women's Coalition http://www.thewomenscoalitionpac.com/

World Movement of Mothers Europe
  https://www.crin.org/en/library/organisations/world-movement-mothers

Bibliography

Abbey, Sharon and O'Reilly Andrea. *Redefining Motherhood. Changing Identities and Patterns.* Toronto: Second Story Press. 1998.

Adichie, Chimamanda Ngozi. *We Should All Be Feminists.* London: Fourth Estate. 2014.

Appignanesi, Lisa et al. *Fifty Shades of Feminism.* London: Virago. 2013.

Arendt, Hannah. *The Human Condition. Second Edition.* Chicago: University of Chicago Press. 1958.

Asher, Rebecca. *Shattered. Modern Motherhood and the Illusion of Equality.* London: Random House. 2011.

Atwood, Margaret. *The Handmaid's Tale.* London: Vintage. 1996.

Badinter, Elisabeth. *The Conflict. How Overzealous Motherhood Undermines the Status of Women.* New York: Picador. 2011.

Badinter, Elisabeth. *Mother Love. Myth & Reality.* New York: Macmillan Publishing Co. 1981.

Bassoff, Evelyn S. *Mothering Ourselves. Help and Healing for Adult Daughters.* New York: Dutton. 1991.

Baumslag, Naomi and Michels, Dia. *Milk, Money and Madness, The Culture and Politics of Breastfeeding.* Westport: Bergin & Garvey. 1995.

Bell, Diane and Klein, Renate, eds. *Radically Speaking: Feminism Reclaimed.* Melbourne: Spinifex Press. 1996.

Benjamin, Jessica. *The Bonds of Love. Psychoanalysis, Feminism, and the Problem of Domination.* New York: Pantheon Books. 1998.

Benn, Melissa. *Madonna and Child. Towards a New Politics of Motherhood.* London: Jonathan Cape. 1998.

Benn, Melissa. *What Should We Tell Our Daughters? The Pleasures and Pressures of Growing Up Female.* London: John Murray Publishers. 2014.

Bennetts, Leslie. *The Feminine Mistake. Are We Giving Up Too Much?* New York: Hyperion. 2007.

Bergmann, Barbara R. *The Economic Emergence of Women.* 2005. New York: Palgrave Macmillan. 2005.

Berry, Mary Frances. *The Politics of Parenthood. Child Care, Women's Rights, and the Myth of the Good Mother.* New York: Penguin. 1993.

Biddulph, Steve. *Raising Babies. Should Under 3s Go to Nursery?* London: Harper Thorsons. 2005.

Bjornholt, Margunn and McKay, Ailsa. *Counting on Marilyn Waring. New Advances in Feminist Economics.* Bradford: Demeter Press. 2015.

Black, Kathryn. *Mothering Without a Map. The Search for the Good Mother Within.* London: Penguin. 2005.

Bobel, Chris. *The Paradox of Natural Mothering.* Philadelphia: Temple University Press. 2002.

Bock, Gisela and Thane, Pat. *Maternity and Gender Policies. Women and the Rise of the European Welfare States 1880s–1950s.* London: Routledge. 1994.

Bowlby, John. *Attachment.* London: Pelican. 1969.

Boyd, Elizabeth Reid and Letherby, Galye, eds. *Stay-At-Home Mothers. Dialogues and Debates.* Bradford: Demeter Press. 2014.

Brown, Stephanie et al. *Missing Voices. The Experience of Motherhood.* Oxford: Melbourne University Press Australia. 1994.

Buchanan, Andrea J. *Mother Shock. Loving Every (Other) Minute of It.* New York: Seal Press. 2003.

Bunting, Madeline. *Willing Slaves, How the Overwork Culture is Ruling Our Lives.* London: Harper Perennial. 2005.

Burggraf, Shirley. *The Feminine Economy and Economic Man: Reviving The Role of Family in the Postindustrial Age.* Reading, MA: Perseus Books. 1999.

Byrom, Sheena, and Downe, Soo. *The Roar Behind the Silence: Why Kindness, Compassion and Respect Matter in Maternity Care.* London: Pinter & Martin. 2015

Campbell, Beatrix. *End of Equality. The Only Way is Women's Liberation.* Calcutta: Seagull Books. 2013.

Caplan, Paula. *The New Don't Blame Mother. Mending the Mother-Daughter Relationship.* London: Routledge, 2000.

Carter, Pam. *Feminism, Breasts and Breastfeeding.* Basingstoke: Pan Macmillan. 1995.

Chodorow, Nancy J. *The Reproduction of Mothering.* Berkeley: University of California Press. 1999.

Chomsky, Noam. *Profit Over People.* New York: Seven Stories Press. 1998.

Cochrane, Kira, ed. *Women of the Revolution. Forty Years of Feminism.* London: Guardian Books. 2010.

Crittenden, Ann. *The Price of Motherhood. Why the Most Important Job in the World is Still the Least Valued, 10th Anniversary Ed.* New York: Picador. 2010.

Crittenden, Danielle. *What Our Mothers Didn't Tell Us. Why Happiness Eludes the Modern Woman.* New York: Touchstone. 1999.

Cusk, Rachel. *A Life's Work. On Becoming a Mother.* London: Faber and Faber. 2001.

Daly, Mary and Rake, Katherine. *Gender and the Welfare State.* Cambridge: Polity Press. 2003.

Daly, Mary. *Beyond God the Father. Towards a Philosophy of Women's Liberation.* London: The Women's Press. 1986.

Daly, Mary. *Gyn/Ecology, The Metaethics of Radical Feminism.* London: The Women's Press. 1978.

Davis, Angela. *Modern Motherhood, Women and Family in England, 1945–2000.* Manchester: Manchester University Press. 2012.

De Beauvoir, Simone. *The Second Sex.* London: Vintage. 1997.

De Marneffe, Daphne. *Maternal Desire. On Children, Love and the Inner Life*. London: Virago. 2006.

Dinnerstein, Dorothy. *The Mermaid and the Minotaur*. New York: Other Press. 1999.

DiQuinzio, Patrice. *The Impossibility of Motherhood. Feminism, Individualism and the Problem of Mothering*. London: Routledge. 1999.

Dixley, Allison. *Breast Intentions. How Women Sabotage Breastfeeding for Themselves and Others*. London: Pinter & Martin. 2014.

Dodsworth, Laura. *Bare Reality. 100 Women, Their Breasts, Their Stories*. London: Pinter & Martin. 2015.

Douglas, Susan J. *Enlightened Sexism. The Seductive Message that Feminism's Work is Done*. New York: Times Books. 2010.

Douglas, Susan J. *The Mommy Myth. The Idealization of Motherhood and How it Has Undermined All Women*. New York: Free Press. 2004.

Dworkin, Andrea. *Intercourse*. New York: Basic Books. 2007.

Dworkin, Andrea. *Life and Death. Unapologetic Writings on the Continuing War Against Women*. New York: The Free Press. 1997.

Dworkin, Andrea. *Our Blood, Prophesies and Discourses on Sexual Politics*. New York: Perigee Books. 1976.

Dworkin, Andrea. *Pornography: Men Possessing Women*. New York: E.P. Dutton & Co. 1989.

Dworkin, Andrea. *Right-Wing Women. The Politics of Domesticated Females*. London: The Women's Press. 1983.

Dworkin, Andrea. *Woman Hating*. New York: E.P. Dutton & Co. 1974.

Eastman, Crystal. *On Women & Revolution*. Oxford: Oxford University Press. 1978.

Edgell, Stephen et al, eds. *The SAGE Handbook of the Sociology of Work and Employment*. London: Sage Publications. 2016.

Eisenstein, Zillah R. *Capitalist Patriarchy and the Case for Socialist Feminism*. New York: Monthly Review Press. 1979.

Eisler, Riane. *The Chalice and the Blade. Our History, Our Future*. San Francisco: Harper & Row. 1988.

Ellison, Katherine. *The Mommy Brain. How Motherhood Makes Us Smarter*. New York: Basic Books. 2005.

Elshtain, Jean Bethke. *Public Man, Private Woman. Women in Social and Political Thought, Second Edition*. Princeton: Princeton University Press. 1981.

Ennis, Linda Rose. *Intensive Mothering: The Cultural Contradictions of Modern Motherhood*. Bradford: Demeter Press. 2014.

Epstein-Gilboa, Keren. *Interaction and Relationships in Breastfeeding Families, Implications for Practice*. Amarillo: Hale Publishing LP. 2009.

Evans, Mary, ed. *The Woman Question. Readings on the Subordination of Women*. Oxford: Fontana Paperbacks. 1982.

Everingham, Christine. *Motherhood and Modernity. An Investigation into the Rational Dimension of Mothering*. Buckingham: Open University Press. 1994.

Fallows, Deborah. *A Mother's Work*. Boston: Houghton Mifflin Company. 1985.

Faludi, Susan. *Backlash. The Undeclared War Against Women*. London: Vintage. 1992.

Federici, Silvia. *Revolution at Point Zero. Housework, Reproduction and Feminist Struggle*. Oakland: PM Press. 2012.

Federici, Silvia. *Witch-Hunting, Past and Present, and the Fear of the Power of Women. 100 Notes: 100 Thoughts*. Hatje Cantz. 2012.

Fenton Stitt, Jocelyn and Reichert Powell, Pegeen, eds. *Mothers Who Deliver: Feminist Interventions in Public and Interpersonal Discourse*. Albany: State University of New York Press. 2010.

Ferber, Marianne A. and Nelson, Julie A. *Feminist Economics Today, Beyond Economic Man*. London: University of Chicago Press. 2003.

Fine, Cordelia. *Delusions of Gender: The Real Science behind Sex Differences*. London: Icon Books. 2011.

Fineman, Martha Albertson. *The Neutered Mother, The Sexual Family, and Other Twentieth Century Tragedies*. New York: Routledge. 1995.

Firestone, Shulamith. *The Case for Feminist Revolution*. London: Verso. 2015.

Fisher, Elizabeth. *Woman's Creation. Sexual Evolution and the Shaping of Society*. New York: McGraw-Hill Book Company. 1979.

Folbre, Nancy. *The Invisible Heart, Economics and Family Values*. New York: The New Press. 2001.

Folbre, Nancy. *Valuing Children, Rethinking the Economics of the Family*. Cambridge, Massachusetts: Harvard University Press. 2008.

Forster, E.M. *The Machine Stops*. London: Penguin. 2011.

Foster, Dawn. *Lean Out*. London: Repeater Books. 2015.

Fox, Isabelle. *Being There. The Benefits of a Stay-at-Home Parent*. New York: Barron's Educational Series, Inc. 1996.

Francis, Solveig et al. *The Milk of Human Kindness, Defending Breastfeeding From the Global Market and the AIDS Industry*. London: Crossroads Books. 2002.

Fraser, Nancy. *Fortunes of Feminism, From State-Managed Capitalism to Neoliberal Crisis*. London: Verso. 2013.

Frayne, David. *The Refusal of Work, The Theory and Practice of Resistance to Work*. London: Zed Books. 2015.

Freedman, Estelle B. *Feminism, Sexuality & Politics*. Chapel Hill: The University of North Carolina Press. 2006.

Freely, Maureen. *What About Us? An Open Letter to the Mothers Feminism Forgot*. London: Bloomsbury Publishing Plc. 1995.

Friday, Nancy. *My Mother, My Self*. London: Harper Collins Publishers. 1977.

Friedan, Betty. *The Feminine Mystique*. Middlesex: Penguin. 1963.

Friedan, Betty. *The Second Stage*. Cambridge: Harvard University Press. 1998.

Frye, Marilyn. *The Politics of Reality: Essays in Feminist Theory*. California: The Crossing Press. 1983.

Gambotto-Burke, Antonella. *Mama, Love, Motherhood and Revolution*. London: Pinter & Martin. 2015.

Gaskin, Ina May. *Ina May's Guide to Breastfeeding*. London: Pinter & Martin. 2009.

Gaskin, Ina May. *Ina May's Guide to Childbirth*. London: Vermillion. 2008.

Gerhardt, Sue. *Why Love Matters. How Affection Shapes a Baby's Brain*. London: Routledge. 2004.

Gilbert, Neil. *A Mother's Work, How Feminism, The Market and Policy Shape Family Life*. New Haven: Yale University Press. 2008.

Gilligan, Carol. *In a Different Voice. Psychological Theory and Women's Development*. Cambridge: Harvard University Press. 1993.

Gilman, Charlotte Perkins. *Herland*. 1915.

Gilman, Charlotte Perkins. *Women and Economics. A Study of the Economic Relation Between Men and Women as a Factor in Social Evolution*. 1898.

Glenn, Evelyn Nakano et al, eds. *Mothering, Ideology, Experience and Agency*. London: Routledge. 1994.

Glenville, Marilyn. *Overcoming PMS the Natural Way*. London: Piatkus. 2002.

Gonzales, Carlos. *Kiss Me! How to Raise Your Children with Love*. London: Pinter & Martin. 2012.

Gorz, Andre. *Critique of Economic Reason*. London: Verso. 1989.

Green, Fiona Joy and Pelletier, Gary Lee, eds. *Essential Breakthroughs. Conversations about Men, Mothers and Mothering*. Bradford: Demeter Press. 2015.

Greer, Germaine. *Sex and Destiny, The Politics of Human Fertility*. New York: Harper & Row. 1984.

Greer, Germaine. *The Female Eunuch*. London: Flamingo. 2003.

Greer, Germaine. *The Whole Woman*. London: Anchor. 1999.

Grossman, Hildreth Y. and Chester, Nia Lane. *The Experience and Meaning of Work in Women's Lives*. Hillsdale: Lawrence Erlbaum Associates. 1990.

Grosz, Elizabeth. *Volatile Bodies. Toward a Corporeal Feminism*. Bloomington: Indiana University Press. 1994.

Hakim, Catherine. *Models of the Family in Modern Societies*. Aldershot: Ashgate. 2004.

Hakim, Catherine. *Work-Lifestyle Choices in the 21st Century*. Oxford: Oxford University Press. 2000.

Hancock, Emily. *The Girl Within. A Radical New Approach to Female Identity*. London: Pandora Press. 1990.

Hansen, Rick and Hanson, Jan. *Mother Nurture: A Mother's Guide to Health in Body, Mind, and Intimate Relationships*. New York: Penguin. 2002.

Hartsock, Nancy C.M. *The Feminist Standpoint Revisited & Other Essays*. Boulder: Westview Press. 1998.

Hasseldine, Rosjke. *The Silent Female Scream*. Nottingham: Women's Bookshelf Publishing. 2007.

Hayes, Shannon. *Radical Homemakers, Reclaiming Domesticity from a Consumer Culture*. Richmondville: Left to Write Press. 2010.

Hays, Sharon. *The Cultural Contradictions of Motherhood*. Yale: Yale University Press. 1996.

Heffner, Elaine. *Mothering. The Emotional Experience of Motherhood after Feminism.* New York: Doubleday & Company Inc. 1978.

Held, Virginia. *Feminist Morality. Transforming Culture. Society, and Politics.* Chicago: University of Chicago Press. 1993.

Henry, Astrid. *Not My Mother's Sister: Generational Conflict and Third-Wave Feminism.* Bloomington: Indiana University Press. 2004.

Hewlett, Sylvia Ann. *A Lesser Life. The Myth of Women's Liberation.* London: Michael Joseph. 1987.

Hirsch, Marianne and Keller, Evelyn Fox. *Conflicts in Feminism.* London: Routledge. 1990.

Hochschild, Arlie, with Machung, Anne. *The Second Shift, Working Families and Revolution at Home.* London: Penguin Books. 2012.

Hochschild, Arlie. *The Time Bind. When Work Becomes Home and Home Becomes Work.* New York: Henry Hold and Company. 2001.

Hollway, Wendy and Featherstone, Brid. *Mothering and Ambivalence.* London: Routledge. 1997.

hooks, bell. *All About Love, New Visions.* New York: Harper Perennial. 2001.

hooks, bell. *Feminism is for Everybody. Passionate Politics.* London: Pluto Press. 2000.

hooks, bell. *Feminist Theory, From Margin to Center.* Second edition. London: Pluto Press. 2000.

Horwitz, Erika. *Through the Maze of Motherhood: Empowered Mothers Speak.* Bradford: Demeter Press. 2011.

Hrdy, Sarah Blaffer. *Mother Nature, Natural Selection and the Female of the Species.* London: Chatto & Windus. 1999.

Irigaray, Luce. *In the Beginning, She Was.* London: Bloomsbury. 2013.

Irigaray, Luce. *Je, Tu, Nous, Toward a Culture of Difference.* New York: Routledge. 1993.

Irigaray, Luce. *Speculum of the Other Woman.* Ithaca: Cornell University Press. 1985.

Irigaray, Luce. *Thinking the Difference: For a Peaceful Revolution.* London: The Althone Press. 1994.

Irigaray, Luce. *This Sex Which is Not One.* Ithaca: Cornell University Press. 1985.

Jackson, Marni. *The Mother Zone.* Toronto: Canada. 2002.

Jaggar, Alison M. *Feminist Politics and Human Nature.* New Jersey: Rowan & Allanheld. 1983.

James, Oliver. *How Not to F**k Them Up.* London: Vermillion. 2010.

James, Oliver. *Not In Your Genes: The Real Reasons Children are Like their Parents.* London: Vermillion. 2016

James, Selma. *Sex, Race and Class. The Perspective of Winning, A Selection of Writings 1952–2011.* Oakland: PM Press. 2012.

Johnson, Allan G. *The Gender Knot. Unravelling Our Patriarchal Legacy.* Philadelphia: Temple University Press. 2005.

Johnson, Miriam M. *Strong Mothers. Weak Wives.* Berkeley: University of California Press. 1988.

Jones, Bernie D. *Women Who Opt Out. The Debate over Working Mothers and Work-Family Balance.* New York: New York University Press. 2012.

Kawasaki, Mizin Park. *Mothering With Breastfeeding and Maternal Care.* Lincoln: iUniverse. 2006.

Keeton-Digby, Melia. *The Heroines Club: A Mother-Daughter Empowerment Circle.* Cork: Womancraft Publishing. 2016.

Kinser, Amber E. *Motherhood and Feminism.* Berkeley: Seal Press. 2010.

Kiraly, Miranda and Tyler, Meagan, eds. *Freedom Fallacy. The Limits of Liberal Feminism.* Ballarat: Connorcourt. 2015.

Kittay, Eva Feder and Feder, Ellen K. *The Subject of Care, Feminist Perspectives on Dependency.* Maryland: Rowman & Littlefield Publishers Inc. 2002.

Kittay, Eva Feder. *Love's Labor, Essays on Women, Equality and Dependency.* Oxford: Routledge. 1999.

Kitzinger, Sheila. *Ourselves as Mothers, the Universal Experience of Motherhood.* London: Bantam Books. 1993.

Kitzinger, Sheila. *Rediscovering Birth.* London: Little, Brown and Company. 2000.

Kitzinger, Sheila. *The Politics of Birth.* London: Elsevier Butterworth Heinemann. 2005.

Koven, Seth and Michel, Sonya, eds. *Mothers of a New World. Maternalist Politics and the Origins of Welfare States.* London: Routledge. 1993.

Lasch, Christopher. *Haven in a Heartless World, The Family Besieged.* London: W.W. Norton & Company. 1995.

Lasch, Christopher. *Women and the Common Life. Love, Marriage and Feminism.* London: W.W. Norton & Company. 1997.

Lazarre, Jane. *The Mother Knot.* London: Virago Press. 1976.

Lerner, Gerda. *The Creation of Patriarchy.* New York: Oxford University Press. 1986.

Lerner, Harriet. *The Mother Dance. How Your Children Change Your Life.* London: Thorsons. 1998.

Lerner, Sharon. *The War on Moms. On Life in a Family-Unfriendly Nation.* Hoboken: John Wiley & Sons. 2010.

Levy, Jonah D. *The State after Statism: New State Activities in the Age of Liberalization.* Cambridge: Harvard University Press. 2006.

Lorde, Audre. "The Master's Tools Will Never Dismantle the Master's House" 1984 in Berkeley, ed, *Sister Outsider: Essays and Speeches.* CA: Crossing Press. 2007.

Lowinsky, Naomi Ruth. *The Motherline. Every Woman's Journey to Find her Female Roots.* Fisher King Press. 2009.

Lyerly, Anne Drapkin. *A Good Birth: Finding the Positive and Profound in Your Childbirth Experience.* New York: Penguin. 2013.

Lynch, Kathleen et al. *Affective Equality. Love, Care and Justice.* Basingstoke: Palgrave Macmillan. 2009.

Mackay, Finn. *Radical Feminism, Feminist Activism in Movement*. Basingstoke: Palgrave Macmillan. 2015.

Mackinnon, Catharine A. *Feminism Unmodified. Discourses on Life and Law*. Cambridge: Harvard University Press. 1987.

Malos, Ellen. *The Politics of Housework*. 3rd Edition. Cheltenham: New Clarion Press. 1995.

Manne, Anne. *Motherhood. How Should We Care For Our Children?* Crows Nest: Allen & Unwin. 2005.

Marçal, Katrine. *Who Cooked Adam Smith's Dinner? A Story About Women and Economics*. London: Portobello Books. 2015.

Marlow, Joyce, ed. *Votes for Women, The Virago Book of Suffragettes*. London: Virago. 2000.

Matchar, Emily. *Homeward Bound. Why Women Are Embracing the New Domesticity*. New York: Simon & Schuster. 2013.

Maushart, Susan. *The Mask of Motherhood, How Becoming a Mother Changes Our Lives and Why We Never Talk About It*. New York: Penguin. 1999.

McCrobbie, Angela. *The Aftermath of Feminism. Gender, Culture and Social Change*. London: Sage Publications. 2009.

McKay, Ailsa. *The Future of Social Security Policy. Women, Work and a Citizen's Basic Income*. Abingdon: Routledge. 2005.

Menon, Nivedita. *Recovering Subversion. Feminist Politics Beyond the Law*. Urbana: Permanent Black. 2004.

Mies, Maria and Shiva, Vandana. *Ecofeminism*. London: Zed Books. 2014.

Mies, Maria. *Patriarchy and Accumulation on a World Scale*. London: Zed Books. 2014.

Mitchell, Juliet, and Oakley, Ann, eds. *What is Feminism?* Oxford: Basil Blackwell. 1986.

Mitchell, Juliet. *Woman's Estate*. Middlesex: Penguin Books. 1971.

Moberg, Kerstin Uvnas. *The Oxytocin Factor. Tapping the Hormone of Calm, Love and Healing*. London: Pinter & Martin. 2011.

Modleski, Tania. *Feminism Without Women. Culture and Criticism in a 'Postfeminist' Age*. New York: Routledge. 1991.

Mongan, Marie. *Hypnobirthing, The Breakthrough Approach to Safer, Easier, Comfortable Birthing*. London: Souvenir Press. 2005.

Montagu, Ashley. *The Natural Superiority of Women*. London: Rowman & Littlefield Publishers, Inc. 1999.

Moran, Caitlin. *How to be a Woman*. London: Ebury Press. 2011.

Morgan, Robin, ed. *Sisterhood is Forever, The Women's Anthology for a New Millennium*. New York: Washington Square Press. 2003.

Morgan, Robin, ed. *Sisterhood is Powerful. An Anthology of Writings from the Women's Liberation Movement*. New York: Random House. 1970.

Morgan, Robin. *The Demon Lover, The Roots of Terrorism*. New York: Washington Square Press. 1989.

Morgan, Robin. *The Anatomy of Freedom, Feminism in Four Dimensions*. New York: W.W. Norton & Co. 1994.

Napthali, Sarah. *Buddhism for Mothers. A Calm Approach to Caring for Yourself and Your Children*. London: Allen & Unwin. 2003.

Newman, Jack and Pitman, Teresa. *Dr Jack Newman's Guide to Breastfeeding*. London: Pinter & Martin. 2014.

O'Reilly, Andrea, ed. *21st Century Motherhood. Experience, Identity, Policy, Agency*. New York: Colombia University Press. 2010.

O'Reilly, Andrea, ed. *Feminist Mothering*. Albany: State University of New York Press. 2008.

O'Reilly, Andrea, ed. *From Motherhood to Mothering, the Legacy of Adrienne Rich's Of Woman Born*. Albany: State University of New York Press. 2004.

O'Reilly, Andrea, ed. *Maternal Theory, Essential Readings*. Bradford: Demeter Press. 2007.

O'Reilly, Andrea, ed. *Maternal Thinking: Philosophy, Politics, Practice*. Toronto: Demeter Press. 2009.

O'Reilly, Andrea, ed. *Mother Outlaws, Theories and Practices of Empowered Mothering*. Toronto: Women's Press. 2004.

O'Reilly, Andrea, with Porter, Marie and Short, Patricia, eds. *Motherhood, Power and Oppression*. Toronto: Women's Press. 2005.

O'Reilly, Andrea. *Rocking the Cradle. Thoughts on Motherhood, Feminism and the Possibility of Empowered Mothering*. Toronto: Demeter Press. 2006.

O'Reilly, Andrea. *Toni Morrison and Motherhood. A Politics of the Heart*. Albany: State University of New York Press. 2004.

Oakley, Ann and Juliet Mitchell. *Who's Afraid of Feminism? Seeing Through the Backlash*. London: Penguin. 1998.

Oakley, Ann. *Becoming a Mother*. New York: Schocken Books. 1979.

Oakley, Ann. *Gender on Planet Earth*. Cambridge: Polity Press. 2002.

Oakley, Ann. *Housewife, High Value - Low Cost*. London: Penguin. 1974.

O'Brien, Mary. *The Politics of Reproduction*. London: Routledge. 1981.

Odent, Michel. *Birth and Breastfeeding*. East Sussex: Clairview Books. 2003.

Odent, Michel. *Birth Reborn, What Childbirth Should Be*. London: Souvenir Press. 1984.

Palmer, Gabrielle. *The Politics of Breastfeeding, When Breasts Are Bad for Business*. London: Pinter & Martin. 2009.

Palmer, Sue. *Toxic Childhood. How the Modern World is Damaging Our Children and What We Can Do About It*. London: Orion. 2015.

Pankhurst, Emmeline. *Suffragette, My Own Story*. London: Hesperus. 2015.

Parker, Rozsika. *Torn in Two. The Experience of Maternal Ambivalence*. London: Virago. 1995.

Pascall, Gillian. *Social Policy. A New Feminist Analysis*. London: Routledge. 1997.

Pearce, Lucy H. *Burning Woman*. Cork: Womancraft Publishing. 2016.

Pearce, Lucy H. *Moods of Motherhood: The Inner Journey of Mothering*. Cork: Womancraft Publishing. 2014.

Pearce, Lucy H. *Moon Time: Harness the Ever-Changing Energy of Your Menstrual Cycle*. Cork: Womancraft Publishing. 2015.

Peri, Camille, and Moses, Kate, eds. *Mothers Who Think. Tales of Real-Life Parenthood*. New York: Washington Square Press. 1999.

Peskowitz, Miriam. *The Truth Behind the Mommy Wars, Who Decides What Makes a Good Mother?* Emeryville: Seal Press. 2005.

Peters, Joan K. *When Mothers Work. Loving Our Children Without Sacrificing Ourselves*. Reading: Perseus Books. 1997.

Phillips, Anne. *Feminism and Politics*. Oxford: Oxford University Press. 1998.

Phillips, Melanie. *The Ascent of Woman, the History of the Suffragette Movement and the Ideas Behind it*. London: Abacus. 2003.

Phipps, Alison. *The Politics of the Body*. Cambridge: Polity Press. 2014.

Poser, Caroline B. *Mothermorphosis: Vignettes about the Transformation Into and Within Motherhood*. Deadwood: The Mom-Writers Publishing Cooperative. 2006.

Price, Jane. *Motherhood, What it Does to Your Mind*. London: Pandora Press. 1988.

Rabuzzi, Kathryn Allen. *Motherself. A Mythic Analysis of Motherhood*. Bloomington: Indiana University Press. 1988.

Rai, Shirin M, and Georgina Waylen, eds. *New Frontiers in Feminist Political Economy*. London: Routledge. 2014.

Ramazanoglu, Caroline. *Feminism and the Contradictions of Oppression*. London: Routledge. 1989.

Rapley, Gill and Murkett, Tracey. *Baby-led Breastfeeding, How to Make Breastfeeding Work with Your Baby's Help*. London: Vermilion. 2012.

Rathbone, Eleanor. *The Disinherited Family*. Bristol: Falling Wall Press. 1986.

Reddy, Maureen T., with Roth, Martha and Sheldon, Amy, eds. *Mother Journeys, Feminists Write About Mothering*. Minneapolis: Spinsters Ink. 1994.

Redfern, Catherine and Aune, Kristen. *Reclaiming the F Word. The New Feminist Movement*. London: Zed Books. 2010.

Reimer, Vanessa and Sahagian, Sarah, eds. *Mother of Invention. How Our Mothers Influenced us as Feminist Academics and Activists*. Bradford: Demeter Press. 2013.

Reimer, Vanessa and Sahagian, Sarah, eds. *The Mother-Blame Game*. Bradford: Demeter Press. 2015.

Ribbens, Jane. *Mothers and Their Children. A Feminist Sociology of Child-rearing*. London: Sage Publications. 1994.

Rich, Adrienne. *Of Woman Born, Motherhood as Experience and Institution*. London: Virago. 1977.

Richards, Janet Radcliffe. *The Sceptical Feminist, A Philosophical Enquiry*. London: Penguin. 1980.

Roiphe, Anne. *Fruitful*. Boston: Houghton Mifflin. 1996.

Rossi, Alice S., ed. *The Feminist Papers, From Adams to de Beauvoir*. Colombia: Colombia University Press. 1973.

Rothman, Barbara Katz. "Laboring Now: Current Cultural Constructions of Pregnancy, Birth, and Mothering" in *Laboring On: Birth in Transition in the United States*. Simons, Wendy, et al (eds). New York: Routledge. 2007.

Rothman, Barbara Katz. *Recreating Motherhood*. New Brunswick: Rutgers University Press. 2000.

Rowbotham, Sheila. *Hidden From History*. London: Pluto Press. 1973.

Rowbotham, Sheila. *Woman's Consciousness, Man's World*. London: Verso. 2015.

Rowbotham, Sheila. *Women, Resistance and Revolution. A History of Women and Revolution in the Modern World*. London: Verso. 2014.

Rubin, Nancy. *The Mother Mirror. How a Generation of Women is Changing Motherhood in America*. New York: G.P. Putnam's Sons. 1984.

Ruddick, Sara. *Maternal Thinking, Towards a Politics of Peace*. New York: Ballantine Books. 1989.

Sandberg, Sheryl. *Lean In. Women, Work, and the Will to Lead*. London: Ebury. 2015.

Sanders, Darcie and Bullen, Martha M. *Staying Home. From Full-Time Professional to Full-Time Parent*. Boulder: Spencer & Waters. 1992.

Schiller, Rebecca. *All That Matters*. Guardian Shorts. 2015

Schulte Brigid. *Overwhelmed. How to Work, Love and Play When No One Has the Time*. London: Bloomsbury. 2014.

Secunda, Victoria. *When You and Your Mother Can't Be Friends*. Dell Publishing: New York. 1990.

Sennett, Richard. *The Corrosion of Character*. New York: W.W. Norton & Co. 1998.

Sennett, Richard. *The Culture of the New Capitalism*. New Haven: Yale University Press. 2006.

Shaw, Rhonda, and Bartlett, Alison, eds. *Giving Breastmilk, Body Ethics and Contemporary Breastfeeding Practice*. Bradford: Demeter Press. 2010.

Simonds, Wendy, Rothman, Barbara Katz and Norman, Bari Meltzer. *Laboring On: Birth in Transition in the United States*. New York: Routledge. 2007.

Sinnott, Ann. *Breastfeeding Older Children*. London: Free Association Books. 2010.

Slaughter, Anne-Marie. *Unfinished Business*. London: Oneworld Publications. 2015.

Small, Meredith F. *Our Babies, Ourselves. How Biology and Culture Shape the Way We Parent*. New York: Anchor Books. 1998.

Smith, Dorothy E. *The Everyday World as Problematic. A Feminist Sociology*. Boston: Northeastern University Press. 1987.

Smith, Janna Malamud. *A Potent Spell*. Boston: Houghton Mifflin Company. 2003.

Snitow, Ann. *Feminism and Motherhood: An American Reading*. Feminist Review, No. 40 (Spring, 1992), pp. 32–51. Published by: Palgrave Macmillan Journals

Snitow, Ann. *The Feminism of Uncertainty, A Gender Diary*. Durham: Duke University Press. 2015.

Solnit, Rebecca. *Men Explain Things to Me, and Other Essays*. London: Granta Books. 2014.

Sommers, Christina Hoff. *Freedom Feminism, Its Surprising History and Why It Matters Today*. Washington: AEI Press. 2013.

Sommers, Christina Hoff. *Who Stole Feminism? How Women Have Betrayed Women*. New York: Simon & Schuster. 1994.

Spelman, Elizabeth V. *Inessential Woman, Problems of Exclusion in Feminist Thought*. London: The Women's Press. 1990.

Spender, Dale, ed. *Feminist Theorists. Three Centuries of Women's Intellectual Traditions*. London: The Women's Press. 1983.

Spender, Dale. *Women of Ideas, and What Men Have Done to Them*. London: Pandora. 1982.

Srnicek, Nick and Williams, Alex. *Inventing the Future, Postcapitalism and a World Without Work*. London: Verso. 2015.

Stadlen, Naomi. *How Mothers Love, And How Relationships Are Born*. London: Piatkus. 2011.

Stadlen, Naomi. *What Mothers Do, Especially When It Looks Like Nothing*. London: Piatkus. 2004.

Steinberg, Eden. *Your Children Will Raise You. The Joys, Challenges and Life Lessons of Motherhood*. , Boston: Trumpter. 2005.

Steinem, Gloria. *Moving Beyond Words. Age, Rage, Sex, Power, Money, Muscles: Breaking Boundaries of Gender*. New York: Simon & Schuster. 1994.

Steiner, Leslie Morgan, ed. *Mommy Wars. Stay-at Home and Career Moms Face Off on Their Choices, Their Lives, Their Families*. New York: Random House. 2006.

Stephens, Julie. *Confronting Postmaternal Thinking, Feminism, Memory and Care*. New York: Columbia University Press. 2011.

Strong, Shari. Macdonald, ed. *The Maternal is Political. Women Writers at the Intersection of Motherhood and Social Change*. Berkeley: Seal Press. 2008.

Sumner, Penny. *The Fruits of Labour. Creativity, Self-Expression and Motherhood*. London: The Women's Press. 2001.

Suttie, Ian D. *The Origins of Love and Hate*. London: Kegan Paul. 1948.

Tazi-Preve, Mariam Irene. *Motherhood in Patriarchy, Animosity Toward Mothers in Politics and Feminist Theory - Proposals for Change*. Toronto: Barbara Budrich Publishers. 2013.

Thurer, Shari L. *The Myths of Motherhood, How Culture Reinvents the Good Mother*. London: Penguin. 1994.

Torry, Malcolm. *101 Reasons for a Citizen's Income: Arguments for Giving Everyone Some Money*. Bristol: Polity Press. 2015.

Trebilcot, Joyce, ed. *Mothering. Essays in Feminist Theory*. Totowa: Rowman & Allenheld. 1983.

Ungerson, Clare, and Kember, Mary, eds. *Women and Social Policy*. Second Edition. London: Macmillan Press. 1997.

Valenti, Jessica. *Why Have Kids? A New Mom Explores the Truth about Parenting and Happiness*. Las Vegas: Amazon Publishing. 2012.

Van Mens-Verhulst, Janneke et al. *Daughtering & Mothering. Female Subjectivity Reanalysed.* London: Routledge. 1993.

Vandenbeld Giles, Melinda, ed. *Mothering in the Age of Neoliberalism.* Bradford: Demeter Press. 2014.

Walby, Sylvia. *Theorizing Patriarchy.* Oxford: Blackwell Publishers. 1990.

Waldman, Ayelet. *Bad Mother: A Chronicle of Maternal Crimes, Minor Calamities and Occasional Moments of Grace.* London: Two Roads. 2014.

Walker, Barbara G. *The Skeptical Feminist. Discovering the Virgin, Mother & Crone.* San Francisco: Harper San Francisco. 1987.

Waring, Marilyn. *Counting for Nothing, What Men Value and What Women Are Worth, 2nd Edition.* Toronto: University of Toronto Press Inc. 1999.

Warner, Judith. *Perfect Madness, Motherhood in the Age of Anxiety.* London: Vermillion. 2006.

Weeks, Kathi. *The Problem with Work — Feminism, Marxism, Antiwork Politics, and Postwork Imaginaries.* London: Duke University Press. 2011.

Wiessinger, Diane, West, Diana and Pitman, Teresa. *The Womanly Art of Breastfeeding.* London: Pinter & Martin. 2010.

Williams, Joan. *Unbending Gender, Why Family and Work Conflict and What to Do About it.* Oxford: Oxford University Press. 2000.

Wolf, Alison. *The XX Factor. How the Rise of Working Women Has Created a Far Less Equal World.* New York: Crown Publishers. 2013.

Wolf, Naomi. *Misconceptions.* London: Vintage. 2001.

Wolf, Naomi. *The Beauty Myth.* London: Vintage. 1990.

Wollstonecraft, Mary. *A Vindication of the Rights of Woman.* London: Penguin. 2004.

Woolf, Virginia. *A Room of One's Own.* London: Penguin. 2000.

Young, Brigitte et al. *Questioning Financial Governance from a Feminist Perspective.* Abingdon: Routledge. 2011.

References

A MOTHER'S STOCKINGS

1. As bell hooks remarks in *Feminist Theory, From Margin to Center*: "Early feminist attacks on motherhood alienated masses of women from the movement, especially poor and/or non-white women, who find parenting one of the few interpersonal relationship where they are affirmed and appreciated", p 135.

2. See Hochschild, Arlie, with Machung, Anne: *The Second Shift, Working Families and Revolution at Home.*

3. In *The XX Factor, How the Rise of Working Women Has Created a Far Less Equal World*, Alison Wolf discusses some of the studies and changes to men's engagement with domestic work. Things are improving — in some places; for some women; for some chores. Slowwwwwwly.

4. To echo Audre Lorde's observation that "The master's tools will never dismantle the master's house". Lorde, Audre. "The Master's Tools Will Never Dismantle the Master's House" in *Sister Outsider: Essays and Speeches.*

5. For a discussion of the changing socio-economic conditions facing mothers in the UK, see Angela Davis' *Modern Motherhood*. She says, at pp 211–212: "the interviewees did not always think that the lives of women had become easier at the end of the century. The expectations upon women brought new pressures. For example, women who did not want to return to work when their children were school age faced increasing disapproval for not doing so".

6. See the bibliography for further discussions of this concept, particularly the work of Jean Bethke Elshtain in *Public Man, Private Woman* and her essay in *Feminism and Politics*, edited by Anne Phillips, entitled "Antigone's Daughters", pp 363–377. Elshtain is critical of approaches which "have presumed the superiority of a particular sort of public identity over a private one" and discusses how a 'fully public identity for women would require. . . the final suppression of traditional female social worlds", p 363.

7. For a feminist exploration of housewifery, Ann Oakley's *Housewife, High Value - Low Cost*, is worth a read.

8. For discussions by the OECD about women who care for children or who enter low-paid work and the waste of 'human capital', this is an interesting article: http://www.oecdobserver.org/news/archivestory.php/aid/2473/ Babies_and_Bosses:_What_lessons_for_governments_.html

9. For detailed discussion and critique of our economic systems and the problem with the "ideal worker" shaped economy, see Joan Williams' description of the ideal worker and the "full commodification" model in respect of childcare in *Unbending Gender, Why Family and Work Conflict and What to Do About it.*

10. See Laura Bates' important project on women's experiences of sexism and misogyny at http://everydaysexism.com/

11. See Shannon Hayes' *Radical Homemakers, Reclaiming Domesticity from a Consumer Culture*, p 23.

12. See Anne Roiphe's *Fruitful*, p ix.

13. See Adrienne Rich's *Of Woman Born*.

14. See *The Impossibility of Motherhood*, p viii.

15. See Daphne de Marneffe's *Maternal Desire, On Children, Love and the Inner Life*, p 23.

16. Legal scholar Kimberlé Crenshaw discusses why she chose the metaphor of the intersection at http://www.newstatesman.com/lifestyle/2014/04/kimberl-crenshaw-intersectionality-i-wanted-come-everyday-metaphor-anyone-could

17. 'Maternal feminism' has been used frequently to describe aspects of the women's movement. Formerly associated with ideas of 'feminine' attributes of care, tenderness and social responsibility; patriarchal values; Christian values; and, latterly, capitalist values (see Sommer's *Freedom Feminism* and http://sexandthestate.com/christina-hoff-sommers-maternal-feminism-same-old-sexism-new-packaging). However, I use the term to bring it away from the conservative roots and towards greater social justice, recognition of women's needs, desires, preferences and diversity, fair distribution of wealth and labour, and recognition and value of care-work. It is designed to reclaim the word and experience of 'the maternal' in our postmaternal culture (as described by Julie Stephens in her work *Confronting Postmaternal Thinking*). The term 'maternal feminism' has been used in the more radical sense by others including Anne Manne, Ann Crittenden, Andrea O'Reilly and All Mothers Work, the UK feminist organisation.

18. As Nancy Folbre comprehensively argues in *The Invisible Heart*, "children are not pets" and socio-economic policy must reflect that bearing children is not simply a lifestyle choice, pp 109–135.

19. In my research for the pamphlet, I came across Patrice DiQuinzio's *The Impossibility of Motherhood*, which discusses the "paradoxical politics of mothering" (used in a difference sense to my election season focus) in feminist theorising: how to reconcile individualism with the dilemma of difference? According to DiQuinzio, "a paradoxical politics of mothering would take up a wide variety of issues related to conception, pregnancy, birth and child rearing, but it would recognise that it cannot offer a completely coherent and consistent position on these issues", see p 248.

20. See Neil Gilbert's discussion of continuous workplace participation and the occupational elite in *A Mother's Work, How Feminism, The Market and Policy Shape Family Life*.

21. The phrase originates in a controversial article from Felice N. Schwartz, entitled "Management Women and the New Facts of Life" published in Harvard Business Review in 1989.

22. See Joan Williams' *The Maternal Wall* in October 2004, Harvard Business Review.

23. See the bibliography for further reading.

24. As remarked by Andrea Dworkin in *Dworkin on Dworkin*, an interview originally published in *Off Our Backs*, reprinted in *Radically Speaking: Feminism Reclaimed*, edited by Diane Bell and Renate Klein.

25. There are many discussions of sameness and difference throughout feminism. The bibliography contains further reading on these issues.

26. See Eva Feder Kittay's *Love's Labor, Essays on Women, Equality and Dependency*, p 17.

27. For a discussion of standpoint theory, see Nancy Hartsock's *Feminist Standpoint Theory Revisited* and *The Everyday World as Problematic, A Feminist Sociology* by Dorothy E. Smith.

28. See the bibliography for further reading.

29. For critiques of 'boardroom feminism', see Dawn Foster's *Lean Out* and Melissa Benn's *What Shall We Tell our Daughters?* p 157.

30. As exemplified by http://everydayfeminism.com

31. As discussed in *Fifty Shades of Feminism*, edited by Lisa Appignanesi.

32. A sentiment discussed by Anne Manne in *Motherhood*, p 34.

33. See Charlotte Perkins Gilman's *Herland*, which depicts an all-female-society.

34. See comments made by Miriam Clegg, lawyer and wife of former Leader of the Liberal Democrats in the UK: http://www.telegraph.co.uk/news/politics/liberaldemocrats/11144839/Miriam-Clegg-I-dont-want-to-have-it-all-I-just-want-what-men-have.html

35. See her essay "Antigone's Daughters", in *Feminism and Politics*, edited by Anne Phillips, p 364.

36. See Mariam Irene Tazi-Preve's *Motherhood in Patriarchy, Animosity Toward Mothers in Politics and Feminist Theory — Proposals for Change*, p 14.

37. See *The Impossibility of Motherhood*, p xv.

38. Ibid, p 86.

39. To echo Alison Wolf's comments at the Global Women's Strike International Women's Conference in November 2015.

40. As described by Neil Gilbert in *A Mother's Work*.

41. See p 7. This seems to have inspired Anne-Marie Slaughter's title for her work *Unfinished Business*, on women and the issue of care.

42. See the bibliography for further reading, including Christina Hoff Sommer's discussion in *Freedom Feminism* of Hannah More, a Bluestocking who was influential in the early women's movement. See also, the Redstockings Manifesto for the Redstockings women's liberationists, http://redstockings.org/index.php/42-uncategorised/76-rs-manifesto

43. See *Inventing the Future, Postcapitalism and a World Without Work*, by Nick Srnicek and Alex Williams, p 175.

44. To borrow a phrase from Martha Fineman in *The Neutered Mother, The Sexual Family, and Other Twentieth Century Tragedies*, p 2.

45. See Nancy Fraser's article in The Guardian, "How Feminism Became Capitalism's Handmaiden - And How to Reclaim It" Nancy Fraser http://www.theguardian.com/commentisfree/2013/oct/14/feminism-capitalist-handmaiden-neoliberal

46. To echo Silvia Federici and Maria Mies' observations in Maria Mies' *Patriarchy and Accumulation on a World Scale,* that capitalism is "patriarchy's latest manifestation" and shows a parasitic dependence on the "free appropriation of nature and the body and work of women", pp x–xxiv and 1–5.

47. To quote Adrienne Rich in *Of Woman Born,* that the institution of motherhood must be evoked "so that women never again forget that our many fragments of lived experience belong to a whole which is not of our creation. Rape and its aftermath; marriage as economic dependence, as the guarantee to a man of 'his' children; the theft of childbirth from women; the concept of the 'illegitimacy' of a child born out of wedlock; the laws regulating contraception and abortion; the cavalier marketing of dangerous birth control devices; the denial that work done by women at home is part of 'production'; the chaining of women in links of love and guilt; the absence of social benefits for mothers; the inadequacy of childcare facilities in most parts of the world; the unequal pay women receive as wage-earners, forcing them often into dependence on a man; the solitary confinement of 'full-time motherhood'; the token nature of fatherhood, which gives a man rights and privileges over children toward whom he assumes minimal responsibility; the assumption that the mother is inadequate and ignorant; the burden of emotional work borne by women in the family — all these are connecting fibers of this invisible institution . . . ", pp 275–276.

48. http://www.radfemcollective.org/

49. For an exploration of the backlash against feminism, see Susan Faludi's *Backlash*.

50. The 'three ideologies' as explored persuasively by Barbara Katz Rothman in *Recreating Motherhood*: technology, patriarchy and capitalism, pp 13–14.

51. To invoke Virginia Woolf's *A Room of One's Own*. To be fair, I will have referred to this a lot by the end of the book. But it's just so apt. And I really would love a writing shed at the bottom of the garden — that should do it, right? What's the betting my husband hasn't read this far down?
    #AShedOfOne'sOwn #BooksEverywhere #PurpleWallpaper #MyShedMyRules

52. See Anne Manne's *Motherhood*, pp 29–30.

53. bell hooks discusses this issue in *Feminist Theory, From Margin to Center*.

54. For further reading on this subject, see the bibliography, particularly the work of bell hooks.

55. See Catherine Hakim's preference theory and *Work-Lifestyle Choices in the 21st Century*. Hakim writes that "Preference theory is concerned primarily with women's choice between family work and market work: a genuine choice in affluent modern societies", p 1. Hakim surveyed women, including those without children, in various countries about their "work-lifestyle preferences". She found that women tended to fall within three categories, namely, "work-centred", "adaptive" and "home-centred". See also the section Lies, Damned Lies, and Childcare for recent statistics bearing out those findings.

56. For an account of the way in which the Labour Party of the late 1990s and early 2000s reinterpreted statistics and a key study it had commissioned to suit its agenda of full female employment and misrepresentation of mothers, see Catherine Hakim, *Work-Lifestyle Choices in the 21st Century*. She concludes that family and social policies have now focused so far on the 'working mother' that there is now a systemic bias against women who are not in employment. She and Anne Manne (in *Motherhood, How Should We Care for Our Children?*), address the 'Listening to Women' exercise of the Labour Party and the subsequent report *Voices, Turning Listening into Action*, which failed to acknowledge homemakers or full-time parents and which presented no policies to support them, despite the very clear diversity of opinions expressed from mothers, including the fact that many women valued motherhood and "wanted it recognised and supported". See p 106 of *Motherhood*. Manne refers to former Secretary of State Patricia Hewitt's subsequent misgivings about the issue. See Lies, Damned Lies and Childcare in **The Politics of Mothering** chapter for examples from 2016 of similar warping of statistics and political disregard for figures which show a substantial proportion of women would like to care for their children, if only they could afford it.

57. See Betty Friedan's *The Feminine Mystique* for the account of the frustrated housewives screaming silently into their twin tubs.

58. To echo the term used by Ann Snitow in *The Feminism of Uncertainty, A Gender Diary*.

59. To quote the MIRCI in its literature for its 2016 Conference: "Motherhood is the unfinished business of feminism. Motherhood scholars argue that motherhood, as it is currently perceived and practiced in patriarchal societies, is disempowering, if not oppressive, for a multitude of reasons: the societal devaluation of mother-work, the endless tasks of privatized mothering, the incompatibility of waged work and care-work, and the impossible standards of idealized motherhood. Many of the problems facing mothers — whether social, economic, political, cultural, or psychological — are specific to their role and identity as mothers. What is needed therefore is matricentric feminism: a feminism that is fashioned from and for women's particular identity and their work as mothers. This conference positions mothers' needs and concerns as the starting point for a new politic and theory of feminism to empower mothers in Canada and around the world and explores what mothers in the 21st century need to adequately care for their children while living full and purposeful lives. Over the last forty years, motherhood research has focused on the oppressive and empowering dimensions of mothering and the complex relationship between the two. Stemming from the above distinction, the conference will examine 21st century motherhood under four interconnected themes of inquiry: motherhood as experience, identity, agency, and institution". Andrea O'Reilly specialises in the subject of feminist mothering and motherhood and how we must focus on those issues which patriarchal motherhood has traditionally denied women, particularly: "Agency: Having control over their own lives. Authority: The ability to be the author of your own life and to determine your own path. Authenticity: The right to be truthful, to talk about the difficult parts of mothering and to mother according to our own beliefs rather than according to mainstream society's expectations. Autonomy: Being

able to hold into ourselves, rather than sacrificing ourselves and giving up our own lives to be a good mother. Advocacy: Being advocates for each other and for ourselves". See What is Maternal Feminism? by Phd in Parenting, see http://www.care2.com/causes/what-is-maternal-feminism.html

60.   According to O'Reilly, "The chapter on maternal theory examines the central theoretical concepts of maternal scholarship to include Adrienne Rich's distinction between mothering and motherhood, Sara Ruddick's model of maternal thinking and practice and Patricia Hill Collins' concept of othermothering while the chapter on activism considers the 21st century motherhood movement. Feminist mothering is likewise examined as the specific practice of matricentric feminism and this chapter discusses various theories and strategies on and for maternal empowerment. Matricentric feminism is also examined in relation to the larger field of Feminist Theory and Women's Studies" including how "matricentric feminism has been marginalized in feminist scholarship". The book will be published by Demeter Press in October 2016.

61.   See Mary Daly's *Gyn/Ecology, The Metaethics of Radical Feminism*, p 253, for criticism of Carl Jung's theories as they relate to women and mothers.

62.   I have never liked this phrase: I doubt its truth. A mother who is happy yet neglecting her child is not going to produce a happy child. I would much prefer "evidence-based child development practices + empowered mother + financial resources + social support + love = flourishing child", but that's not likely to make its way onto an Internet meme any time soon.

63.   Abraham Maslow's concept of self-actualisation through work clashes with the idea that one can find satisfaction in homemaking and child-rearing.

64.   See Luce Irigaray's *Je, Tu, Nous*, p 20.

65.   See Julie Stephens' *Confronting Postmaternal Thinking*, p 144.

66.   See Juliet Mitchell's *Women's Estate*, p 22.

67.   See, for example, a decision of Ms Justice Russell of the High Court (Family Division) in *H & B v S & M (a Child) (by her Children' Guardian)* [2015] EWFC 36 Case No: FD14P00262. To see the work of international organisation, The Women's Coalition, see http://www.thewomenscoalitionpac.com/

68.   See bell hooks' *Feminist Theory, From Margin to Center*, pp 136–137.

69.   See Helen Lewis' article in *The New Statesman*, "The Motherhood Trap", 16 July 2015: http://www.newstatesman.com/politics/2015/07/motherhood-trap

70.   See Sara Ruddick's *Maternal Thinking, Towards a Politics of Peace*.

71.   This is a key message in the work of psychotherapist and writer Rosjke Hasseldine, see *The Silent Female Scream*, p 41.

72.   A concept explored by Sara Ruddick in *Maternal Thinking*.

73.   For comprehensive analyses of studies around childcare, child development, attachment theory and the Human Genome Project, see variously the work of Oliver James, Steve Biddulph and Anne Manne in the bibliography.

74.   See Jonas Himmelstrand's article in the Institute of Marriage and Family Canada, "Swedish Daycare: International Example or Cautionary Tale?" 10 September, 2015. It addresses: rapidly declining psychological health in youth;

increased sick leave among women; the deteriorating quality of parenthood; highly gender segregated labour market; plummeting school results; and disorder in Swedish classrooms. These are issues which are rarely discussed in the mainstream when politicians promote the 'Swedish Model'.

75. This struck me when reading Anne Manne's *Motherhood* in which she characterises the *child* as other. Saying that, perhaps the mother/child dyad is the *ultimate* Other. So unique. So fragile. So powerful. Yet totally outside the experience of men and of women who are not mothers or who have not enjoyed the mother/child bond and so deemed to be not important.

76. For an exploration of this from the perspective of the Wages for Housework Campaign, see Selma James' *Sex, Race and Class. The Perspective of Winning, A Selection of Writings 1952–2011*.

77. See bell hooks' *Ain't I a Woman?* Sojourner Truth (1796–1883) was born into slavery, was an abolitionist and women's rights activist.

FLESH AND BLOOD

78. From the monologue beginning "All the world's a stage" from William Shakespeare's *As You Like It*.

79. See Luce Irigaray's *Je Tu Nous*, p 108.

80. Ibid, p 109.

81. See Adrienne Rich's *Of Woman Born*, p 11.

82. See Nancy Hartsock's *The Feminist Standpoint Revisited & Other Essays*, p 116.

83. See Julie Stephens' *Confronting Postmaternal Thinking*, p 10.

84. See Mary Daly's *Beyond God the Father, Towards a Philosophy of Women's Liberation*, p 8.

85. See Adrienne Rich's *Of Woman Born*, p 39.

86. See Glosswitch's blog, Glosswatch, *The Worst Thing About Being a Woman*. http://glosswatch.com/2015/11/11/the-worst-thing-about-being-a-woman.

87. Something explored by Shulamith Firestone in *The Dialectic of Sex*.

88. For further reading on patriarchy, see the bibliography, including Gerda Lerner's *The Creation of Patriarchy*.

89. See Maria Mies' *Patriarchy and Accumulation on a World Scale*, p xv.

90. Ibid, p 37.

91. See Andrea Dworkin's "Letters from a War Zone, Writings 1976 to 1989, Part III, I Want a Twenty-Four-Hour Truce During Which There Is No Rape, 1983". http://radfem.org/dworkin/.

92. See the bibliography for further reading. Joan Williams, for example, discusses the drawbacks of dominance theory as a stance in *Unbending Gender*, pp 254–256.

93. See Mary O'Brien's *The Politics of Reproduction*, p 3.

94. See bibliography for further reading.

95.   See the work of Max Dashu and the Suppressed Histories Archive, the work of Amanda Foreman in *The Ascent of Woman*, as well as the bibliography for other books which recount the history of patriarchal suppression of women's narrative and history, for example, Riane Eisler's *The Chalice and the Blade. Our History, Our Future.*

96.   There is a "brutal history of women's silencing" in the making of our culture, art, science, mathematics. See Dorothy E. Smith's *The Everyday World as Problematic, A Feminist Sociology*, p 22.

97.   See Andrea Dworkin's *Our Blood: Prophecies and Discourses on Sexual Politics*, p 78.

98.   See the work of Karen Ingala Smith https://kareningalasmith.com/counting-dead-women, among others.

99.   See Sylvia Walby's *Theorising Patriarchy*, p 178.

100.   See Gloria Steinem's *Moving Beyond Words.*

101.   There are many books on this issue. See the bibliography for further reading, particularly Riane Eisler's *The Chalice and the Blade* and Barbara G. Walker's *The Skeptical Feminist. Discovering the Virgin, Mother & Crone.*

102.   See p 1.

103.   Ibid.

104.   See Shari L. Thurer's *The Myths of Motherhood*, p xxvi.

105.   Ibid, p 25.

106.   See, for example, *Ecofeminism* by Maria Mies.

107.   The theory presented by Mariam Irene Tazi-Preve in her book *Motherhood in Patriarchy.*

108.   See https://www.nationaleatingdisorders.org/get-facts-eating-disorders

109.   See Andrea Dworkin's work *Pornography: Men Possessing Women.*

110.   This is the central proposition of Michel Odent in his work, such as *Birth Reborn, What Childbirth Should Be.*

111.   For an exploration of menstruation and our cycles, see Lucy H. Pearce's *Moon Time.*

112.   However a recent UK company Coexist announced it would introduce policies to accommodate their employees' menstruation and cycles.

113.   I was fortunate to have two lengthy conversations with Rosjke while researching and writing this book. See Rosjke Hasseldine's *The Silent Female Scream.*

114.   See Mariam Irene Tazi-Preve's *Motherhood in Patriarchy*, p 15.

115.   See Barbara Katz Rothman's website http://www.barbarakatzrothman.com/2012/04/surrogacy-israel-hitchens.html and her book *Recreating Motherhood.*

116.   See https://www.byline.com/project/43/article/820

117.   See *Ina May Gaskin's Guide to Childbirth*, p 141.

118.   See, as an example, http://fortune.com/2015/03/03/female-company-president-im-sorry-to-all-the-mothers-i-used-to-work-with

119. See Simone de Beauvoir's *The Second Sex*, p 326.

120. As advocated by Donald Trump in 2016.

121. For an excellent exploration of the need for compassion and humanity in maternity services, see *The Roar Behind the Silence*, edited by Sheena Byrom and Soo Downe.

122. For a discussion of this, see Shelia Kitzinger's *Rediscovering Birth*.

123. See Naomi Wolf's *Misconceptions*, p 173.

124. See Shelia Kitzinger's *Ourselves as Mothers*, p 73.

125. The issue of marriage and the sexual union of adults as forming the basis of the family, as opposed to the horizontal relationships of parent and child or caring relationships is explored by Martha Fineman in *The Neutered Mother*.

126. See Sheila Kitzinger's *The Politics of Birth*, p 1.

127. See Michel Odent's *Birth and Breastfeeding*, p x.

128. See Simone de Beauvoir's *The Second Sex*, p 285.

129. See Nancy Folbre's *The Invisible Heart*, p 109.

130. See Michelle Quashie's blog https://strongsincebirth.wordpress.com/ about her vaginal birth after two caesarean sections.

131. See Sheila Kitzinger's *Rediscovering Birth*, p 73.

132. See Naomi Wolf's *Misconceptions*, p 3.

133. See Barbara Katz Rothman's personal website http://www.barbarakatzrothman.com

134. This is a theme running through Mary Daly's work in *Gyn/Ecology* and *Beyond God the Father*.

135. An organisation with a social media presence which shares powerful images of birth.

136. See Anne Drapkin Lyerly's *A Good Birth: Finding the Positive and Profound in Your Childbirth Experience*.

137. See Nancy Rubin's *The Mother Mirror*, p 185.

138. See Ina May Gaskin's *Guide to Childbirth*, p vii.

139. There is even a petition to have it cancelled from programming, see http://www.fearfreechildbirth.com/blog/one-born-every-minute

140. See Alison Phipps' *The Politics of the Body*.

141. See *Ina May's Guide to Childbirth*, p 131.

142. See Michel Odent's *Birth and Breastfeeding*, p 28.

143. http://womancenteredmidwifery.org/take-action

144. https://www.nice.org.uk/news/press-and-media/midwife-care-during-labour-safest-women-straightforward-pregnancies

145. See http://evidencebasedbirth.com/the-evidence-for-doulas

146. See *Ina May's Guide to Childbirth*, p 141.

147.   See http://www.who.int/mediacentre/factsheets/fs348/en/ Consider, too, the fact that 47,000 women die from complications of unsafe abortion each year. Deaths due to unsafe abortion remain close to 13% of all maternal deaths http://www.who.int/reproductivehealth/topics/unsafe_abortion/magnitude/en/

148.   http://www.telegraph.co.uk/news/uknews/law-and-order/10503079/Alessandra-Pacchieri-Pitiful-tale-of-a-mother-and-her-lost-child.html

149.   See "Any Woman Who Wants a Caesarean on the NHS Should Get One — No Questions Asked", by Milli Hill in The Telegraph, see http://www.telegraph.co.uk/women/health/any-woman-who-wants-a-caesarean-on-the-nhs-should-get-one---no-q/

150.   Such as the baby of Tracey Taylor, baby Kristian, who died following a traumatic delivery and after Taylor's repeated requests for a caesarean had been ignored, see above.

151.   See Milli Hill's article, above.

152.   See the British Pregnancy Advisory Service http://www.reproductivereview.org/index.php/rr/article/1501/

153.   To quote Birthrights, the UK's organisation dedicated to improving women's experience of pregnancy and childbirth by promoting respect for human rights, "We believe that all women are entitled to respectful maternity care that protects their fundamental rights to dignity, autonomy, privacy and equality". See http://www.birthrights.org.uk/

154.   See the work, for example, of the Association for Improvements in the Maternity Services (AIMS), which is "at the forefront of the childbirth movement for more than fifty years. Working towards normal birth. Providing independent support and information about maternity choices. Raising awareness of current research on childbirth and related issues. Protecting women's human rights in childbirth".

155.   The concept of the Iron Maiden in respect of women's bodies is discussed by Naomi Wolf throughout *The Beauty Myth*.

MOTHER'S MILK

156.   See Germaine Greer's *Sex and Destiny, The Politics of Human Fertility,* p 248.

157.   See Germaine Greer's *The Whole Woman*, p 61.

158.   At the heart of it all, objection to or criticism of breastfeeding is misogyny in action, alive and well. It demonstrates a distrust of mothers, an envy of her life sustaining power, and an interference with the mother-child relationship. As Keren Epstein-Gilboa discusses in Breastfeeding Envy, Unresolved Patriarchal Envy and the Obstruction of Physiologically-Based Nursing Patterns in *Giving Breastmilk, Body Ethics and Contemporary Breastfeeding Practice*, edited by Rhonda Shaw and Alison Bartlett, "unresolved envy of nursing is a salient factor with deep historical roots leading to the obstruction of physiologically-based nursing patterns" And this obstruction? Wet nursing, scheduled feedings, formula substitutes, to name three, see pp 205–216.

159.   See the bibliography for further reading, particularly *The Politics of Breastfeeding* by Gabrielle Palmer and *Birth and Breastfeeding* by Michel Odent, for earlier historical practices with regard to colostrum.

160.   See Sarah Blaffer Hrdy's *Mother Nature*, p 131.

161.   In *The Conflict, How Overzealous Motherhood Undermines the Status of Women*, Elisabeth Badinter is scathing about the suggestion of primacy of the mother-child dyad, viewing breastfeeding as a mechanism to deprive women of time (p 107) and status, and is utterly critical of an international organisation which supports mothers in breastfeeding (pp 67–78) as zealous, anti-feminist and essentialist.

162.   For critical feminist discussions of breastfeeding, see the bibliography, in particular, Elisabeth Badinter's *The Conflict* and Pam Carter's *Feminism, Breasts and Breastfeeding*.

163.   See Simone de Beauvoir's *The Second Sex*, p 524.

164.   See Rebecca Asher's *Shattered*, p 49.

165.   In *The Mask of Motherhood, How Becoming a Mother Changes our Lives and Why We Never Talk About It*, Susan Maushart, despite her negative experience of breastfeeding, is right on the money when it comes to the loss of our motherly and womanly narrative, an extremely important influence in our ability to mother. While we cannot be sure of maternal instinct, we can *believe* we have it when we have been surrounded by it, schooled in it and prepared for it socially and by generations of mothers, sisters, aunts and neighbours. To quote Maushart: "we of the present postfeminist generation seem to have lost respect for the wisdom of women who have travelled the path of motherhood before us … to some extent what we don't know about motherhood is what we refuse to hear and refuse to see in the lives of women around us, in the arrogant presumption that we are unique, that we will be different", p 144. In her chapter "Lactation Intolerant, The Worst of Breast is Best" Maushart reflects the fact that if we expect women just "to know instinctively" how to breastfeed, we fail them, p 147.

166.   See Ann Sinnott's *Breastfeeding Older Children* for an exploration of natural term breastfeeding in terms of child development, anthropology and feminism.

167.   Alison Dixley's book, *Breast Intentions, How Women Sabotage Breastfeeding for Themselves and Others*, has an original take on the breastfeeding debate. Her view is that the majority of women are aware that breastfeeding is superior to feeding with substitutes, and that there are many excuses offered, ranging from the physical, to marketing by formula companies. However, she looks to mothers for the reasons why a small percentage of woman are still breastfeeding at, say, three months old. She describes how women undermine each other in their attempts to breastfeed and examines the emotions of early motherhood. Broadly, she explores deception, guilt, excuses, envy, contempt, defensiveness and sabotage. She pulls no punches.

168.   See Gabrielle Palmer's *The Politics of Breastfeeding*, p 23.

169.   See Diane Wiessinger's *The Language of Breastfeeding, Watch Your Language!* Journal of Human Lactation, Vol. 12, No. 1, 1996.

170.   See Sarah Blaffer Hrdy's *Mother Nature*, p 141.

171. Ibid.

172. See Gabrielle Palmer's *The Politics of Breastfeeding*, p 319.

173. See Marilyn Waring, *Counting for Nothing*, p 168.

174. Ibid, p 170.

175. Ibid, p 213.

176. See Francis, Solveig et al's *The Milk of Human Kindness, Defending Breastfeeding from the Global Market and the AIDS Industry*, p 20.

177. Naomi Baumslag and Dia Michels' *Milk, Money and Madness, The Culture and Politics of Breastfeeding*, p xviii.

178. Ibid, p xvii.

179. http://www.theguardian.com/society/2014/may/29/drugs-prostitution-uk-national-accounts

180. For a discussion of mothering at the breast see La Leche League's *The Womanly Art of Breastfeeding* and Karen McBride-Henry and Rhonda Shaw's "Giving Breastmilk as Being-with", p 191 in *Giving Breastmilk, Body Ethics and Contemporary Breastfeeding Practice*.

181. See http://www.hsph.harvard.edu/news/press-releases/mothers-holding-newborns-skin-to-skin-linked-with-lower-death-risk/

182. See Julie Stephens' *Confronting Postmaternal Thinking*, p 134.

183. Ibid, p 135.

184. See Anne Manne's *Motherhood*, p 271.

185. See Julie Stephens' *Confronting Postmaternal Thinking*, p 137.

186. See La Leche League's *The Womanly Art of Breastfeeding*.

187. See Naomi Wolf's *Misconceptions*, p 230.

188. See http://breastfeedingtoday-llli.org/the-work-of-mothering/

189. See Naomi Stadlen's *What Mothers Do* and *How Mothers Love*.

190. See Joan Williams' *Unbending Gender*.

191. See Gabrielle Palmer's *The Politics of Breastfeeding*, p 90.

192. According to the report "Breast Pumps Market - Global Industry Analysis, Size, Volume, Share, Growth, Trends and Forecast 2014–2022", a comprehensive examination of the global breast pumps market.

193. See, for example, the discussion about the focus on the milk — the product — rather the relationship and the process, in Barbara Katz Rothman's *"Laboring Now: Current Cultural Constructions of Pregnancy, Birth, and Mothering"*. In *Laboring On: Birth in Transition in the United States*.

194. See La Leche League's *The Womanly Art of Breastfeeding*.

195. Because breastfeeding is not just for babies. Toddlers, preschoolers and school age children happily nurse at the breast the world over. A special mention for the indomitable and inspiring Denise Sumpter, happily breastfeeding her toddler and seven-year-old, at the time of writing. Recognising that mothers who "feed for longer are often accused of being selfish", she is clear that "there are things I get out of it — like calm, happy children. But I can say with certainty I've done

this entirely for the benefit of my kids". Her children are the picture of health and happiness. As Karleen Gribble notes in her essay "Receiving and Enjoying Milk" in *Giving Breastmilk, Body Ethics and Contemporary Breastfeeding Practice*, edited by Rhonda Shaw and Alison Bartlett, mothers and natural term breastfeeding children know "that there is considerably more to breastfeeding than the supply of food. Children clearly take pleasure, find comfort and relaxation and closeness with their mother" during nursing; and for mothers, "hearing and seeing their child express their pleasure in this intimate and exclusive interaction remains a motivator" to continue to nurse, p 75.

196. Yes, yes, there are tribes where babies suckle for comfort on the male nipple; in some cultures, grandmothers can nurse their grandchildren; and there are individuals who breastfeed using their female anatomy despite personal gender transitions. #Biology #GenderIdentityCulture

197. See Ann Crittenden's *The Price of Motherhood*, p 258.

MATERNAL THINKING, MATERNAL FEELING

198. For an excellent discussion of the 'mask', see Susan Maushart's *The Mask of Motherhood, How Becoming a Mother Changes Our Lives and Why We Never Talk About It.*

199. See Daphne de Marneffe's *Maternal Desire*, pp xi–xii.

200. Ibid, p 25.

201. See Madeline Bunting, *Willing Slaves*.

202. To echo Sharon Hays' *The Cultural Contradictions of Motherhood*.

203. This a theme which runs through Naomi Stadlen's *What Mothers Do*.

204. See Alison Wolf's *The XX Factor. How the Rise of Working Women Has Created a Far Less Equal World*, p 83.

205. See Suzanne Braun Levine's "Parenting: A New Social Contract" in *Sisterhood is for Forever*, edited by Robin Morgan.

206. For discussions of the wider network children crave and need, see the work of Steve Biddulph.

207. See, for example, Joan K. Peters' *When Mothers Work*.

208. See Sarah Blaffer Hrdy's *Mother Nature*, p 5.

209. See Simone de Beauvoir's *The Second Sex*, p 295.

210. See *Your Children Will Raise You. The Joys, Challenges and Life Lessons of Motherhood*, edited by Eden Steinberg, p xiii.

211. See "Realities of Mothers in Europe, A report by World Movement of Mothers Europe (MMMEurope)" Prepared by Joan Stevens, Julie de Bergeyck & Anne-Claire de Liedekerke, p 11. See http://www.mmmeurope.org/ficdoc/FAMILYPLATFORM-Realities-of-Mothers-in-Europe-10-2010.pdf Their report is well worth a read: they are clear that, "It is . . . of vital importance for the sustainability of European society that policy makers acknowledge, value, encourage, and sustain the willing investment in their children by mothers, fathers, and other primary caregivers", p 13. Their recommendations include: "The wellbeing of mothers and fathers and that of their children is

intrinsically linked ... It is important that mothers and fathers are able to create and select conditions that sustain the wellbeing of their family. Parental time spent with children is a non-substitutable form of investment in the future generation. It would not be good to reduce parental effect or substitute for it ... Policy can support actions that help couples prepare for the transition to parenthood. Policy can also support actions that acquaint potential parents with their parental responsibilities and raise awareness of the child's development and needs ... It is important to consider the family not only as a collection of individuals but also as society's multi-generational unit ... It is important that parents have both quality and quantity of time to invest in their children. The right to work in paid employment and the right to engage in unpaid care-work must both be recognised and supported by policymakers. Because of the diversity of conditions and preferences, and because the needs of children and parents change with time, no 'one size fits all' solution can answer the needs of parents better than policies enabling them to make choices appropriate to their unique goals and changing circumstances. Governments must offer choices about family life depending on their season ... There must be support for mothers who wish to care for their family full-time: Cash benefits for children, not dependent on parents' work status, could be used to purchase the kind of childcare the parents select such as external day-care solutions, internal in-house services or replacing part of foregone income if parents wish to invest personally in rearing their children at home ... Unpaid work should rightly be recognised for social security coverage and pension entitlement ... Help mothers return to work after they rear their children. Research seems to indicate that children — hence society at large — largely benefit from a 'stay at home' parent who directly invests in children's development. Our society should assist and help these parents. This could be done through household tax relief", pp 40–41.

212. See Anne Manne's *Motherhood*, p 50.

213. See Andrea O'Reilly's *Toni Morrison and Motherhood: A Politics of the Heart*, p 19.

214. See, for example, http://www.renegademothering.com/2013/02/09/i-became-a-mother-and-died-to-live/

215. See Caroline Poser's book *Mothermorphosis, Vignettes about the Transformation Into and Within Motherhood*.

216. See Sara Ruddick's *Maternal Thinking*, p 17.

217. Ibid. p 24.

218. For more discussions on 'mothering' as done by fathers, see the work of Sara Ruddick, Barbara Katz Rothman and Joanne S. Frye's "Parental Thinking What Does Gender Have to Do with It?" In *Essential Breakthroughs. Conversations about Men, Mothers and Mothering*, edited by Fiona Joy Green and Gary Lee Pelletier, p 14.

219. See http://breastfeedingtoday-llli.org/the-work-of-mothering/

220. Ibid.

221. See http://www.telegraph.co.uk/news/health/children/10391131/The-rise-of-Motherism-prejudice-against-stay-at-home-mums.html

222. See Naomi Stadlen's *What Mothers Do* discussion of the state of being interruptible at any time, pp 54–59.

223. See Betty Friedan's *The Feminine Mystique*.

224. See Ann Crittenden's *The Price of Motherhood*, p 4.

225. See Sarah Blaffer Hrdy for a discussion of maternal intelligence and its part in evolution, in *Mother Nature*.

226. See Katherine Ellison's *The Mommy Brain, How Motherhood Makes Us Smarter*.

227. Ibid, p 8.

228. See http://www.telegraph.co.uk/women/family/why-its-time-to-ditch-the-baby-brain-myth-for-good/ and http://www.telegraph.co.uk/news/health/12087502/Baby-brain-is-a-myth-as-having-a-baby-turns-women-into-better-workers-study-claims.html

229. See Adrienne Rich's *Of Woman Born*.

230. See Naomi Stadlen's *What Mothers Do, Especially When it Looks Like Nothing*.

231. See Shari L. Thurer's *The Myths of Motherhood* and Susan Maushart's *The Mask of Motherhood*.

232. See Jessica Benjamin. *The Bonds of Love. Psychoanalysis, Feminism, and the Problem of Domination*.

233. For a beautiful account of the *Moods of Motherhood*, see Lucy H. Pearce's book of the same name.

234. See the bibliography for more discussion about maternal ambivalence, particularly Rozsika Parker's *Torn in Two. The Experience of Maternal Ambivalence* and Wendy Hollway and Brid Featherstone's *Mothering and Ambivalence*.

235. See Joan K. Peters' *When Mothers Work*, p 60.

236. See Sheryl Sandberg's *Lean In*.

237. See http://everyonesbusiness.org.uk/

238. See https://blogs.canterbury.ac.uk/discursive/all-in-the-brain/

239. See http://www.theguardian.com/commentisfree/2016/feb/26/mental-illness-misery-childhood-traumas echoing words of mental health activist Eleanor Longden.

240. See http://mobile.nytimes.com/blogs/opinionator/2016/03/15/why-therapists-should-talk-politics/

241. For a discussion of 'depleted mother syndrome' see Rick and Jan Hanson's *Mother Nurture: A Mother's Guide to Health in Body, Mind, and Intimate Relationships*.

242. For discussions about this, see the bibliography, in particular, Sheila Kitzinger's *Ourselves as Mothers*, p 13, and Naomi Stadlen's *What Mothers Do*.

243. See Mia Scotland's blog https://mindfulmiablog.wordpress.com/2015/12/08/torturing-new-mothers-and-then-wondering-why-they-get-mentally-ill/

244. See Sheryl Sandberg's *Lean In*.

245. See Sarah Blaffer Hrdy's discussion on allomothers in *Mother Nature*, p 267.

246. My emphasis. See Eva Feder Kittay's *Love's Labor*, p 107.

247. See Adrienne Rich's *Of Woman Born*, p 276.

248. For example, see http://newsroom.ucla.edu/releases/stress-hormone-foreshadows-postpartum-243844.

249. See Germaine Greer's *The Whole Woman*, p 249.

250. See Naomi Wolf's *Misconceptions*, pp 193–194.

251. See Janna Malamud Smith's *A Potent Spell*, p 46.

252. See Betty Friedan's *The Feminine Mystique*.

253. Ibid, p 13.

254. Ibid. Friedan discussed the emptiness women had expressed, the lack of fulfilment in 'waxing the kitchen floor' (p 17) and described vividly the lack of autonomy, the discontent and depression, early marriage, early motherhood in their late teens or early twenties, (contrasting with today's 30 for first-time motherhood in the UK) increasing birth rates, and mothers' little helpers (p 28) (no, not the pixie-eared variety). Women were expected, according to Friedan, to be 'Happy Housewife Heroines' (p 30), whose commitment must be the fulfilment of their own femininity (p 38). She makes it clear that these women lose all sense of self, existing only for and through her husband and children (p 42).

255. See Rosjke Hasseldine's *Silent Female Scream*.

256. Ibid, p 13.

257. Ibid, p 37, 41 and 189. See also Brigid Schulte's *Overwhelmed. How to Work, Love and Play When No One Has the Time*.

258. See bell hooks' *All About Love*, pp 130–132.

259. See Arlie Hochschild's, *The Time Bind. When Work Becomes Home and Home Becomes Work*.

260. See Naomi Stadlen's *What Mothers Do*.

261. Ibid, pp 54–59.

262. See, for example, *Feminist Mothering*, edited by Andrea O'Reilly.

A MOTHER'S PLACE IS IN THE WRONG

263. See *The Mother-Blame Game*, edited by Vanessa Reimer and Sarah Sahagian.

264. I use the term 'matraphobic' as a collective term for fear of becoming one's mother; fear of other mothers; distrust of mothers' powers and general mother-blame behaviour. Others use different spellings depending on meaning. See bibliography for further reading.

265. See Paula Caplan's *Don't Blame Mother* in *Maternal Theory*, edited by Andrea O'Reilly, p 37.

266. See Adrienne Rich's *Of Woman Born*, p 226.

267. See Shari L. Thurer's *The Myths of Motherhood*, p xxi.

268. See Sharon Hays', *The Cultural Contractions of Motherhood*.

269. See the poem of Coventry Patmore.

270. See Shari L. Thurer's *The Myths of Motherhood*.

271. See Paula Caplan's *The New Don't Blame Mother*, p 23, quoting Judith Herman and Helen Lewis.

272. See the bibliography for further reading on this issue, particularly the work of Sara Ruddick in *Maternal Thinking*; and Dorothy Dinnerstein's *The Mermaid and the Minotaur*. Dinnerstein discusses, in particular, the results and implications of "female dominated childcare", p 93.

273. See Paula Caplan's *The New Don't Blame Mother*, p 30.

274. Ibid, p 36.

275. Ibid.

276. For a discussion of intergenerational conflict in feminism, see Astrid Henry's *Not My Mother's Sister: Generational Conflict and Third-Wave Feminism*.

277. See Sara Ruddick's *Maternal Thinking*, p 29.

278. See Noam Chomsky's *Profit Over People*.

279. See Shari L. Thurer's *The Myths of Motherhood*, p xxiii.

280. See Miriam Peskowitz's *The Truth Behind the Mommy Wars, Who Decides What Makes a Good Mother?*, see pp 16 and 19.

281. See Vanessa Reimer and Sarah Sahagian's *The Mother-Blame Game*, p 5.

282. Ibid, p 5.

283. See *Of Woman Born*, p 276.

284. Ibid p 32.

285. See Rosjke Hasseldine's *The Silent Female Scream*.

286. See Shari L. Thurer's *The Myths of Motherhood*.

287. For a discussion of the 'new momism' see Susan J. Douglas' *The Mommy Myth. The Idealization of Motherhood and How it Has Undermined All Women*. For further discussion about motherhood and maternal practices, see Elisabeth Badinter's *The Conflict. How Overzealous Motherhood Undermines the Status of Women;* Sharon Hays' *The Cultural Contradictions of Motherhood*; Chris Bobel's *The Paradox of Natural Mothering: Stay-At-Home Mothers, Dialogues and Debates*, edited by Elizabeth Boyd and Gayle Letherby; and *Intensive Mothering: The Cultural Contradictions of Modern Motherhood*, edited by Linda Rose Ennis.

288. See Laurie Penny in *The New Statesman*, 26 October 2016 http://www.newstatesman.com/politics/feminism/2015/10/women-can-t-have-it-all-because-game-rigged

289. Individualism is a significant problem when it comes to mothers and feminism. As Patrice DiQuinzio notes in *The Impossibility of Motherhood*, "feminism has found it impossible to theorize mothering adequately in terms of an individualist theory of subjectivity", see p xii.

290. See article by Nikita Redkar in Everyday Feminism, *5 Sexist Assumptions We Feminists Need to Stop Making About Stay-At-Home Moms*, March 18, 2016.

291. See Sheila Kitzinger's *Ourselves as Mothers*.

292. For an excellent discussion of this issue see Sarah Ditum's article "Feminism and the Mummy Mystique: Why being a mother isn't the 'full stop' on my life", *The New Statesman*, 11 November 2013. See http://www.newstatesman.com/society/2013/11/feminism-and-mummy-mystique-why-being-mother-isnt-full-stop-my-life

293. Ibid.

294. See *Fruitful*, pp 200–201.

295. See Nancy Rubin's *The Mother Mirror*, p 268.

296. See http://www.allmotherswork.co.uk/

297. See Sheila Kitzinger's *Ourselves as Mothers*, p 8.

298. Ibid, p 1.

299. Ibid, p 3.

300. See Melissa Benn's *What Shall We Tell Our Daughters?*, p 192.

301. See Sheila Kitzinger's *Ourselves as Mothers*, p 3.

302. Ibid, p 5.

303. Buddhism and early Chinese philosophy discuss the drawbacks of our attachment to some kind of concrete, authentic, 'self'. We have to ask whether the pain of trying to retain a 'pre-baby' us is a significant cause of unhappiness in mothers who have been led to believe under Western culture that we all have a core, fixed, 'self'. The realisation of impermanence, change and growth certainly helped me embrace my new identity as a mother — and led to doing things which I would never have had the guts to do, like 'put myself out there' in this book.

304. See, for example, Elisabeth Badinter's *The Conflict*.

305. See Sara Ruddick's *Maternal Thinking*, p 111.

306. See Joan Williams' *Unbending Gender*, p 40.

307. See Mariam Irene Tazi-Preve's *Motherhood in Patriarchy*, p 100.

308. To borrow Martha Fineman's phrase. See *The Neutered Mother*.

309. See Germaine Greer's *The Female Eunuch*.

310. See the bibliography for further reading, particularly Elisabeth Badinter's *Mother Love*.

311. To reflect Gloria Steinem's observations that women were becoming the men they wanted to marry.

312. For example, see *The Meaning and Experience of Work in Women's Lives*, edited by Hildreth Y. Grossman and Nia Lane Chester.

313. An example of financial investment by the state where the result — rising female employment — is one which is desired by neoliberal ideology.

314. Exemplified by the notion of 'meternity': the claim by novelist Meghann Foye that women without children deserve a period of leave for themselves because, like, mothers get time off with babies to just swan about, get manicures, have a 'break' from work and not suffer with incontinence, vaginal tears, lack of sleep, exhaustion or keep babies alive, warm, sheltered and fed. They have the temerity to leave work at 6pm to get home to their damn kids when they should

be working to the bone in the office like everyone else. A prime example of the 'children as pets' mentality: maternity leave is a holiday and care-work is not work.

CARE-WORK IN A POSTMATERNAL CULTURE

315. For an exploration of the 'postmaternal' concept, see Julie Stephens' *Confronting Postmaternal Thinking*.

316. See the keynote speech delivered by Gloria Steinem at the 3rd Annual Women & Power Conference organized by Omega Institute and V-Day in September 2004.

317. See the essay by Alice Rossi, "Eros and Caritas: A Biopsychosocial Approach to Human Sexuality and Reproduction", as discussed by Anne Manne in *Motherhood*, p 57.

318. See Margaret Atwood's *The Handmaid's Tale*.

319. See Julie Stephens' *Confronting Postmaternal Thinking*, p 136.

320. In 2016, Erika Edwards Decaster and Carolina-Kawika Allen, along with a delegation of 20 other women, attended the United Nations Commission on the Status of Women representing maternal feminism. They describe frequent belittling and dismissal, by other women, when representing maternal feminism and mothers, as though even the term 'mother' is regressive. Many of us activists have experienced similar mockery, derogatory comments, dismissal or even plain anger, from professed feminists and politicians and policy-makers. Enough's enough.

321. Ibid.

322. See Jonah Levy's *The State after Statism: New State Activities in the Age of Liberalization*.

323. To echo Audre Lorde's observation that "The master's tools will never dismantle the master's house". Lorde, Audre. "The Master's Tools Will Never Dismantle the Master's House" in *Sister Outsider: Essays and Speeches*.

324. See Naomi Ruth Lowinsky's *The Motherline*, p xi.

325. See Adrienne Rich's *Of Woman Born*, p 127.

326. See the work of Julie Stephens, Barbara Katz Rothman and Maria Mies in particular for further discussions about patriarchy, technology and capitalism. See bibliography for further reading.

327. I am grateful to Frances Hutchinson for introducing me to *The Machine Stops* in the course of writing this book, and for her time in conversation about the issues arising in this book and the social credit movement.

328. A key message in Marilyn Waring's *Counting for Nothing*, see pp 7–8, and 135–152.

329. For examinations of studies of childcare, group daycare, and childhood wellbeing — including the professional reputations and difficulties of those who go against the accepted line, see Anne Manne's *Motherhood*, Oliver James' *They F**k You Up*, and Steve Biddulph's *Raising Babies*.

330. See Anne Manne's *Motherhood*, p 295.

331. See Robin Morgan's *The Demon Lover, The Roots of Terrorism.*

332. See her TED Talk about vulnerability, https://www.ted.com/talks/brene_brown_on_vulnerability?language=en

333. See Eva Feder Kittay's *Love's Labor.*

334. For a comprehensive discussion of dependence, see, in particular, Martha Fineman's *The Neutered Mother.*

335. For a discussion of this see Nancy Fraser and Linda Gordon's essay *A Genealogy of Dependency: Tracing a Keyword of the US Welfare State,* in *The Subject of Care, Feminist Perspectives on Dependency,* edited by Eva Feder Kittay and Ellen Feder p 14.

336. When politicians talk about "hard-working families", the crucial role of families in providing care fades into the background. See Madeline Bunting's article, "Who Will Care For Us In the Future? Watch Out for the Rise of the Robots", in which she wrote, "the historical undervaluing of care as women's work has been recharged by a contemporary culture of disdain for those human experiences of dependence, commitment and need". http://www.theguardian.com/commentisfree/2016/mar/06/who-will-care-for-us-in-the-future-robots-outsourcing-humanity

337. For the discussion of "inevitable" dependence and "derivative" dependence, see Martha Fineman's *The Neutered Mother,* pp 161–163.

338. Ibid.

339. See Anne-Marie Slaughter's *Unfinished Business,* pp 78–79.

340. In the UK, recognition is granted in divorce settlements to a spouse who has sacrificed an income to raise the children, and the courts will usually take a starting point of 50:50 ownership of marital assets. However, the popular view persists and is rampant across social media and in conversation — just take a listen or raise the question and just *hear* what people say about 'lazy' wives.

341. See Eva Feder Kittay and Ellen Feder's *The Subject of Care, Feminist Perspectives on Dependency.*

342. See Eva Feder Kittay's *Love's Labor,* p 182.

343. Ibid, p 5.

344. Ibid, p 182.

345. See Anne Manne's *Motherhood, How Should We Care for Our Children?* p 5.

346. As discussed by, for example, Susan J. Douglas and Sharon Hays in their work.

347. See Anne Manne's *Motherhood,* p 9.

348. Ibid, p 128.

349. See the bibliography for further reading.

350. For further reading, see bibliography. See also organisations such as Save Childhood Movement and What About the Children?

351. See *Affective Equality, Love, Care and Justice by* Kathleen Lynch and others, p 12.

352. See "Realities of Mothers in Europe, A report by World Movement of Mothers Europe (MMMEurope)" Prepared by Joan Stevens, Julie de Bergeyck & Anne-Claire de Liedekerke, p 11. See http://www.mmmeurope.org/ficdoc/ FAMILYPLATFORM-Realities-of-Mothers-in-Europe-10-2010.pdf., p 20.

353. See Oliver James' *How Not to F**k Them Up* and *Not in Your Genes: The Real Reasons Children Are Like their Parents*.

354. See Steve Biddulph's *Raising Babies*.

355. See Ian Suttie's *The Origins of Love and Hate*.

356. See Elaine Heffner's, *Mothering. The Emotional Experience of Motherhood after Feminism*, p 35.

357. Carlos Gonzales, *Kiss Me! How to Raise Your Children With Love*.

358. As explored by Mary Ainsworth, see Anne Manne's discussion of her work in *Motherhood*, p 138.

359. See Anne Manne's *Motherhood*, p 9. At p 184, she questions why we "read of the 'cult of motherhood' and of the psychologically vulnerable child as artefacts of their time, but never of our own ideologies of the 'cult of quality childcare' and the 'independent, resilient and competent child'. We avoid examining the ways in which our contemporary ideas about motherhood and childhood might also — to use Marx's sense of ideology — be representing and concealing an interest".

360. See Anne-Marie Slaughter's *Unfinished Business,* p 231.

361. Kathleen Lynch notes that "verbal utterances of affection, care or solidarity (which may be valuable in and of themselves) become empty forms of rhetoric when they are not complemented by undertakings on behalf of others", see *Affective Equality*, pp 35–66.

362. For an examination of care, the ethic of care and affective labour, see Eva Feder Kittay's *Love's Labor*, and Kathleen Lynch's *Affective Equality*, p 35.

363. See Madeline Bunting's article in the Guardian, "Who Will Care for Us in the Future? Watch Out for the Rise of the Robots", http://www.theguardian. com/commentisfree/2016/mar/06/who-will-care-for-us-in-the-future-robots-outsourcing-humantiy?CMP=share_btn_fb

364. As Kathleen Lynch and Judy Walsh discuss in *Love, Care and Solidarity: What is and is Not Commodifiable* in Affective Equality, p 35.

365. See Anne Manne's *Motherhood*, p 8.

366. Many feminist, psychoanalytic writers and thinkers, and others, have addressed the sharing of care — between mothers, fathers, grandparents and institutional childcare and nurseries. The theory seems to persist that a mother caring for her child is an aberration, tending to neurosis and other psychological conditions or vulnerabilities, and that we need to abolish exclusive motherhood. For some further reading on this, see Dorothy Dinnerstein's *The Mermaid and the Minotaur* and Nancy Chodorow's *The Reproduction of Motherhood*. Some feminists recognise that many mothers may well be alarmed and distressed by the notion that they may not care for their own children exclusively or predominantly: in *Feminism and Motherhood*, Ann Snitow says "We're talking

about a slow process of change when we talk about motherhood; we're talking about social divisions which are still fundamental. Giving up the exclusivity of motherhood is bound to feel to many like loss", p 43.

367. See http://www.aontas.com/download/pdf/cr_women_learning.pdf

368. See Martha Fineman's *The Neutered Mother*, p 9. Martha Fineman's case is that the state should look to care relationships as being the representative of 'what family is' in politics, economics and law, rather than the horizontal sexual relationships of adults, exemplified by the husband and wife heterosexual marriage. Now, we remember marriage don't we? You know, the stark representation of patriarchy in its historical transaction transferring property of women from father to husband. You were thinking 'cake', weren't you? Told you I was 'not the fun kind'. Fineman is clear that state subsidy and protection should not focus on the sexual union — itself tenuous, easily dissolved, and harbouring less of a tie than the parent/child relationship — but, rather, the relationship of care, in terms of the vertical bond exemplified by the metaphor of the mother/child relationship. Hers is a radical and refreshing take — and one which even professed 'feminist politicians' show little willingness even to debate, despite the fact that it places women and the core relationships in which care and love feature highly, at the core of policy and which would abolish a system which prioritises the notion of the 'male head of the family' within a patriarchal institution.

369. See Kathleen Lynch's *Affective Equality*, p 12.

370. The Yahoo CEO took two weeks after having twins.

371. For further reading on care, see the bibliography.

372. See Sharon Hays' *The Cultural Contradictions of Motherhood*.

373. See Joan K Peter's *When Mothers Work*, pp 131–166.

374. In *Stay at Home Mothers, Dialogues and Debates*, edited by Elizabeth Boyd and Gayle Letherby, p 218.

375. See *The Politics of Housework*, edited by Ellen Malos.

376. See Oliver James' take on group daycare in *How Not To F**k Them Up*.

377. See bell hooks' *All About Love* for a discussion of extended families and the importance of community, beyond the 'nuclear family'.

378. See Eva Feder Kittay's *Love's Labor*, p 107

379. See Shari L. Thurer's *The Myths of Motherhood*, p xiii.

380. See Sara Ruddick, *Maternal Thinking*, p 29 and *Motherhood, Power and Oppression*, edited by Andrea O'Reilly et al for further readings

381. See Sara Ruddick's *Maternal Thinking*, p 35.

382. See *The Politics of Housework*, edited by Ellen Malos.

383. To quote Ellen Malos, "what we still have to do is to combat attempts to make [allowances or domestic work's inclusion in GDP] the measure of a woman's worth to society, or to narrow her potential to the pursuit of homely virtues and the service of husband, children and family". Ibid, p 217.

384. See *The SAGE Handbook of the Sociology of Work and Employment*, edited by Stephen Edgell, Heidi Gottfried, Edward Granter, p 83. There have been slow improvements in the greater participation in the home, albeit not universally and not in respect to all chores. For a recent study, see Alison Wolf's *The XX Factor*.

385. See the bibliography for further reading, for example, Shannon Hayes' *Radical Homemakers* and Shari L. Thurer's *The Myths of Motherhood*.

386. See Shannon Hayes' *Radical Homemakers*, p 250.

387. Ibid, p 13.

388. See Emily Matchar's *Homeward Bound*, p 11.

389. Ibid, p 15.

390. See Shannon Hayes' *Radical Homemakers*, p 14.

391. See Simone de Beauvoir's discussion of married women and mothers in *The Second Sex*, pp 445–542.

392. See Christina Hoff Sommer's *Who Stole Feminism? How Women Have Betrayed Women*, p 257.

393. See Leslie Bennett's *The Feminine Mistake. Are We Giving Up Too Much?* p xxvii.

394. See Barbara Bergmann's *The Economic Emergence of Women*, p 152.

395. http://www.theatlantic.com/politics/archive/2012/06/1-wives-are-helping-kill-feminism-and-make-the-war-on-women-possible/258431/

396. It is not lost on us that many liberal feminists, while supporting the 'labour rights' and agency of women to, say, 'sell sex' or be 'a surrogate', fail to show the same support for women whose exercise of their agency takes them home to their children. Might this be because, at heart, liberal feminism is actually patriarchal capitalism, the market and individualism with make-up on? A debate to be had, for sure. Just not here — I've got a book to write.

397. In *The Price of Motherhood*, Ann Crittenden acknowledges the fear of many feminists that if we make the 'job' of motherhood easier, by investing in support of carers, that women will "drift back into domestic subservience", see p 7. There are many examples throughout feminist literature about the fear that women will choose to raise their children, if given the chance, and let the whole side down. See the bibliography for further reading.

398. As recounted by Shannon Hayes in her discussion of Betty Friedan. See *Radical Homemakers*, p 249.

399. See Maureen Freely's *What About Us? An Open Letter to the Mothers Feminism Forgot*.

400. Indeed, 'work' is a controversial term, and not just within feminism or in relation to unwaged domestic labour. For an interesting discussion of the 'invention of work' and how it became separate from life, I recommend that you take a read of Andre Gorz's *Critique of Economic Reason* — and stop and think about 'work' and the issue of innate value of market-work. Kathi Weeks asks us to think about *The Problem with Work*. David Frayne explores *The Refusal of Work*. Nick Srnicek and Alex Williams discuss full automation and redistribution of wealth in *Inventing the Future, Postcapitalism and a World Without Work*.

401. See *Feminism is For Everybody*, p 53.

402. See Nancy Folbre's *The Invisible Heart*, p xi. She also quotes Robert Kuttner's *Everything for Sale, The Virtues and Limits of Markets:* "When everything is for sale, the person who volunteers time, who helps a stranger, who agrees to work for a modest wage out of commitment to the public good, who desists from littering even when no one is looking, who forgoes an opportunity to free-ride, begins to feel like a sucker". Ain't that the truth. Now, we're not suckers. We're mothers. Let's get moving. #Purplestockings

403. For a comprehensive, global assessment of the divide between what has traditionally 'counted' and what has not, see Marilyn Waring's *Counting for Nothing*.

404. See "Realities of Mothers in Europe, A report by World Movement of Mothers Europe (MMMEurope)" Prepared by Joan Stevens, Julie de Bergeyck & Anne-Claire de Liedekerke, pp 21–22.

405. For an insightful take on home education, see the books and blog of Ross Mountney https://rossmountney.wordpress.com/

406. See bell hooks' *All About Love*, p 108.

407. ""I can see mass unemployment on the horizon as the robotics revolution takes hold," said Noel Sharkey, a professor emeritus of robotics and artificial intelligence at the University of Sheffield in the UK. Sharkey recently started the Foundation for Responsible Robotics to help us avoid the "potential societal and ethical hazards" from the widespread application of autonomous robots." Source http://www.theguardian.com/technology/2016/mar/19/robot-based-economy-san-francisco.

408. See *The Social Artist* (incorporating The Social Crediter) The Journal of the Social Credit Secretariat, Quarterly Review for Economic Democracy, Autumn 2015 Vol.3, No.3, ISSN: 2053-5236 (online 2053-5244), p 47.

409. See Adrienne Rich's *Of Woman Born*, p 13.

410. See *A Feminism Where 'Lean In' Means Leaning on Others*, by Gary Gutting and Nancy Fraser in *The New York Times*, 15 October 2015, http://opinionator.blogs.nytimes.com/2015/10/15/a-feminism-where-leaning-in-means-leaning-on-others/?_r=1 . This is a concept also explored by, for example, Marie Mies in *Patriarchy and Accumulation on a World Scale*: when one group of women improve their conditions, another group of women face the strain.

411. See http://www.theguardian.com/commentisfree/2013/oct/14/feminism-capitalist-handmaiden-neoliberal

412. See Silvia Federici's foreword to *Patriarchy and Accumulation on a World Scale*, p ix.

413. See Melissa Benn's *What Shall We Tell our Daughters?* p 133.

414. See Dawn Foster's *Lean Out*, p 45. Reni Eddo-Lodge discusses this briefly, too, in her Guardian video, "Why women should stop striving for equality" http://www.theguardian.com/commentisfree/video/2015/jul/08/why-women-should-stop-striving-for-equality-video.

THE INVISIBLE HAND THAT ROCKS THE CRADLE

415. Often attributed to Rebecca Solnit's essay *Men Explain Things to Me.* The imagery of mansplaining is of a man explaining something to a woman in a condescending or patronising way.

416. A term coined by Jocelyn Fenton Stitt in *Mothers Who Deliver,* p 165.

417. See Joan Williams' *Unbending Gender* for a comprehensive discussion of the ideal worker.

418. See Anne-Marie Slaughter's *Unfinished Business.*

419. See excellent article by George Monbiot for further reading http://www.theguardian.com/books/2016/apr/15/neoliberalism-ideology-problem-george-monbiot

420. See the bibliography for further reading, including Arlie Hochschild's work. For a good exploration of this concept, see also *Willing Slaves,* by Madeleine Bunting, p 208.

421. The UN estimates that "More than 1 billion in the world today, the great majority of whom are women, live in unacceptable conditions of poverty, mostly in the developing countries. Poverty has various causes, including structural ones. Poverty is a complex, multidimensional problem, with origins in both the national and international domains", see http://www.un.org/womenwatch/directory/women_and_poverty_3001.htm

422. See Kathleen Lynch's *Affective Equality,* and *Mothering in the Age of Neoliberalism,* edited by Melinda Vandenbeld Giles for further discussions in this theme.

423. As Beatrix Campbell notes in *End of Equality,* p 4: "an ugly name for an ugly deal".

424. The OECD (Organisation for Economic Co-operation and Development) defines GDP as "an aggregate measure of production equal to the sum of the gross values added of all resident institutional units engaged in production (plus any taxes, and minus any subsidies, on products not included in the value of their outputs). The sum of the final uses of goods and services (all uses except intermediate consumption) measured in purchasers' prices, less the value of imports of goods and services, or the sum of primary incomes distributed by resident producer units". Yes, I know. Clear as mud.

425. See Shirley Burggraf's *The Feminine Economy and Economic Man: Reviving The Role Of Family In The Postindustrial Age,* p 10, and Ann Crittenden's *The Price of Motherhood,* p 65.

426. To echo Nancy Folbre's *The Invisible Heart.*

427. See bell hooks' *Feminism is For Everybody,* pp 4–5.

428. See Nancy Fraser's *The Fortunes of Feminism.*

429. See with Marianne Ferber and Julie Nelson's *Feminist Economics Today, Beyond Economic Man,* p vii.

430. http://progress.unwomen.org/en/2015/

431. http://www.theatlantic.com/business/archive/2016/03/unpaid-caregivers/474894/

432. See Katrine Marçal's *Who Cooked Adam Smith's Dinner?* p 186.

433. Ibid, p 17.

434. See *The Great Transition: Social Justice and the Core Economy* by Anna Coote, Head of Social Policy at nef, with additional input from Professor Neva Goodwin, Co-Director of the Global Development & Environment Institute, Tufts University. NEF is the "UK's leading think tank promoting social, economic and environmental justice. Our aim is to transform the economy so that it works for people and the planet. The UK and most of the world's economies are increasingly unsustainable, unfair and unstable. It is not even making us any happier — many of the richest countries in the world do not have the highest wellbeing". See http://www.neweconomics.org/publications/entry/the-great-transition-social-justice-and-the-core-economy.

435. See Office for National Statistics, Household satellite accounts: 2005 to 2014. https://www.ons.gov.uk/economy/nationalaccounts/satelliteaccounts/compendium/householdsatelliteaccounts/2005to2014

436. See Shirley Burggraf's *The Feminine Economy and Economic Man: Reviving The Role Of Family In The Postindustrial Age*, p ix.

437. Ibid, p x.

438. See Katrine Marçal's *Who Cooked Adam Smith's Dinner?* p 197.

439. The notion that women will necessarily speak for women in all sections of society is, perhaps, one of the reasons why a gender split of 50:50 in the UK Parliament, for example — while important as a matter of fairness, decency, justice and democracy — would hardly necessarily and *of itself* lead to greater representation of women. Similarly, more women 'at the top' of business would, as Dawn Foster notes in *Lean Out*, hardly lead to greater promotion of the diversity of women's interests and needs, as it neglects "competing interests", as well as being insulting, p 79.

440. In *Counting for Nothing: What Men Value and What Women Are Worth*, Marilyn Waring echoed the line of the movement in which Selma James was involved: *All women count*. Waring addressed the place of women in the world economy and the then UN System of National Accounts which neglected women's work and worth. As Gloria Steinem says of Waring's work, "Homemakers in industrial countries and women who do most of the agricultural work in the Third World will be equally grateful to this book for putting an end to their shared semantic slavery: no reader should refer to such workers as 'women who don't work' ever again ... the double standard that calls what happens to men 'politics', but what happens to women 'culture', is permanently broken", p xii (Steinem's introduction to *Counting for Nothing*).

441. See Mary Daly and Katherine Rake's *Gender and the Welfare State*, p 172.

442. Ibid, p 175.

443. Maria Mies is clear that increased technology — so that automation performs the work — is not going to lead to human liberation. After all, it is not 'work' which is oppressive, it is the social structure of exploitation. As with E.M. Forster's *The Machine Stops*, technology is not going to liberate us if we continue to serve the machine and not our humanity; and even less so where the technology we worship is destructive to life and the environment. One interesting aspect of Mies' work is that she challenges people to give up their idea that more money

will bring them happiness or a better life. Mies calls this the "subsistence perspective". See Maria Mies' *Patriarchy and Accumulation on a World Scale*, p xxiii.

444. In her essay, "The Care-Centered Economy: Rediscovering What Has Been Taken for Granted", Ina Praetorius asks "if equal opportunity is not the solution: what other policy is necessary to correct the mistakes not only of economics but of the entire symbolic order of which Western economics and economic science ... are a part so all people can live together on peaceful and beneficial terms?" http://us.boell.org/sites/default/files/the_care-centered_economy.pd

445. http://www.theguardian.com/world/2015/nov/08/women-gender-roles-sexism-emotional-labor-feminism?CMP=share_btn_fb

446. See Melissa Benn's *Madonna and Child*, p 19.

447. Silvia Federici notes that capitalism is a parasite, depending on "free appropriation of nature and the body and work of women", p x Maria Mies' *Patriarchy and Accumulation on a World Scale*. This message must be spoken loud and clear and feminism must be prepared to listen: our systems rely on exploitation of workers and women. Our labour, sisters, is being exploited. Just as it has always been.

448. See Nancy Fraser's *The Fortunes of Feminism*, p 1.

449. See http://www.theguardian.com/commentisfree/2013/oct/14/ feminism-capitalist-handmaiden-neoliberal?CMP=share_btn_fb

450. Ibid.

451. Ibid.

452. Silvia Federici, one of the key figures in the Wages for Housework Campaign in the US, acknowledges this, too, in *Revolution at Point Zero: Housework, Reproduction and Feminist Struggle*, she criticises the institutionalisation of feminism and the "reduction of feminist politics to instruments of the neoliberal agenda of the United Nations", p 11. One might say that UN Women has capitalist equality at its heart. No room for the heartspace for our children. UN Women and equality are practically unquestioned as benign, and so I am aware that I risk pointing out that there really is no Easter Bunny; but it bears some consideration: yes, international work seeking to ensure fair and equitable access to education and resources is important. UN Women does immensely important work. Yet most of the 'economic empowerment' business is predicated on neoliberalist 'economic participation': women are kept poor because care-work prevents them from 'working' and enjoying full human rights. If the focus is on employment, rather than other ways to support women, then the financial implications of care-work will continue to work against women.

453. See Anne Manne's *Motherhood*.

454. How has this happened? In *The Fortunes of Feminism*, Nancy Fraser is clear that feminism has contributed to the rise of neoliberalism in a number of ways 1) its critique of the family wage and the breadwinner/dependant male/female ideal model which, Fraser explains, was central to a "state-organised capitalism"; 2) in politicising the personal, which expanded the political agenda to challenge the hierarchies in status, themselves based on gender stereotypes and perceived gender differences (which, lo, worked to the detriment of women who couldn't

possibly work as a civil engineer because, like, maths n' stuff); and 3) its critique of the notion of "paternalism" in welfare states as though the State putting money in the purse of women is an act of bribery to sit tight, like a good girl and stay in the kitchen where you belong.

455.   See Chimamanda Ngozi Adichie's *We Should All Be Feminists*, p 46.

456.   There are studies and theories about the improved financial positions of mothers and the way in which mothers tend to use their resources for the good of their young and their prospects, see the bibliography for further reading, for example, Sarah Blaffer Hrdy's *Mother Nature*.

457.   See Selma James' *Sex, Race and Class*, p 29.

458.   Colloquially known as 'glory labour'.

459.   See Selma James' *Sex, Race and Class*, p 44.

460.   See Ann Crittenden's *The Price of Motherhood*, p 9.

461.   For the perspective of a key figure in the women's movement in the UK, see Eleanor Rathbone's *The Disinherited Family*. See the bibliography for further reading.

462.   See Suzie Fleming's introduction to *The Disinherited Family* for a comprehensive examination of Family Allowance and the work of Eleanor Rathbone.

463.   See the bibliography for further reading on relative poverty within families.

464.   See Ann Crittenden's *The Price of Motherhood*, p 274.

465.   I like this quote from Richard Buckminster Fuller: "We must do away with the absolutely specious notion that everybody has to earn a living. It is a fact today that one in ten thousand of us can make a technological breakthrough capable of supporting all the rest. The youth of today are absolutely right in recognizing this nonsense of earning a living. We keep inventing jobs because of this false idea that everybody has to be employed at some kind of drudgery because, according to Malthusian-Darwinian theory, he must justify his right to exist. So we have inspectors of inspectors and people making instruments for inspectors to inspect inspectors. The true business of people should be to go back to school and think about whatever it was they were thinking about before somebody came along and told them they had to earn a living". See "The New York Magazine Environmental Teach-In" by Elizabeth Barlow in New York Magazine (30 March 1970), p. 30.

466.   http://basicincome.org.uk/

467.   Ibid.

468.   See Douglas Social Credit for a history of the movement, including *The Social Artist* publication. http://socialcredit.schooljotter2.com/

469.   http://www.bbc.co.uk/news/business-35339475?ocid=wsnews.chat-apps.in-app-msg.whatsapp.trial.link1_.auin

470.   See p 122.

471.   See p 31.

472.   See p 41.

473.   See bell hooks' *Feminism is for Everybody*, p 49.

474. See bibliography for further reading, particularly Ailsa McKay's *The Future of Social Security Policy. Women, Work and a Citizen's Basic Income* and Malcolm Torry's *101 Reasons for a Citizen's Income: Arguments for Giving Everyone Some Money.*

475. See, for example, Ann Crittenden's *The Price of Motherhood*, p 110.

476. See Ailsa McKay's *The Future of Social Security Policy. Women, Work and a Citizen's Basic Income*, pp 1 and 2.

477. Ibid.

478. Ibid, p 3.

479. Ibid, p 2.

480. Ibid.

481. See Silvia Federici's *Revolution at Point Zero. Housework, Reproduction and Feminist Struggle*, p 57.

482. See bell hooks' *Feminist Theory, From Margin to Center*, p 134.

483. See Kathi Weeks' *The Problem with Work*, p 230.

484. Ibid.

485. See the bibliography for further reading.

486. Ibid.

487. See http://www.imfcanada.org/issues/swedish-daycare-international-example-or-cautionary-tale

488. See http://www.economist.com/blogs/economist-explains/2015/05/economist-explains-12?fsrc=scn%2Ffb%2Fwl%2Fee%2Fst%2Fwhysomanydutchpeopleworkparttime

489. The city of Utrecht is planning a form of basic income. http://www.theguardian.com/world/2015/dec/26/dutch-city-utrecht-basic-income-uk-greens?CMP=fb_gu

490. To quote Christopher Lasch in *Women and the Common Life*, "A strategy more consistent with the original aims of the feminist movement . . . would challenge the prevailing definition of success. It would challenge the separation of home and the workplace . . . instead of acquiescing in the family's subordination to the workplace, it would seek to remodel the workplace around the needs of the family. It would question the ideology of economic growth and productivity, together with the careerism it fosters. A feminist movement that respected the achievements of women in the past would not disparage housework, motherhood, or unpaid civic and neighbourly services. It would not make a paycheck the only symbol of accomplishment. It would demand a system of production for use rather than profit . . . Instead of seeking to integrate women into the existing structures of the capitalist economy, it would appeal to women's issues in order to make the case for a complete transformation of those structures. It would reject not only the 'feminine mystique' but the mystique of technological progress and economic development. It would no longer care about showing how 'progressive' it was. By rejecting 'progress', of course, it would put itself beyond the pale of respectable opinion — which is to say, it would become as radical as it now merely claims to be", pp 119–120.

491. See Adrienne Rich's *Of Woman Born*, p 285.

492. See the bibliography for further reading.

493. See Anne Manne's *Motherhood*, p 99.

494. See https://www.gov.uk/government/uploads/system/uploads/ attachment_data/file/504782/SFR09-2016_Childcare_and_ Early_Years_Parents_Survey_2014-15_-_report.pdf

495. See Catherine Hakim's preference theory and *Work-Lifestyle Choices in the 21st Century*. Hakim writes that "Preference theory is concerned primarily with women's choice between family work and market work: a genuine choice in affluent modern societies", p 1.

THE POLITICS OF MOTHERING

496. See Department for Education's *Childcare and Early Years Survey of Parents 2014* and *Office for National Statistics report on Overview of UK Labour Market, March 2015*.

497. Office for National Statistics, Household Satellite Accounts, Valuing Informal Childcare in the UK, 2010. http://webarchive.nationalarchives.gov. uk/20160105160709/http://www.ons.gov.uk/ons/dcp171766_300224.pdf

498. *The Family Test, Guidance for Government Departments.* Department for Work and Pensions, October 2014.

499. The European Union Council has described the high numbers of mothers in part-time employment or none at all as a "social challenge" requiring urgent attention. See "Brussels, 13.5.2015 com (2015) 277 final Recommendation for a Council Recommendation on the 2015 National Reform Programme of the United Kingdom and delivering a Council opinion on the 2015 Convergence Programme of the United Kingdom", http://ec.europa.eu/europe2020/pdf/ csr2015/csr2015_uk_en.pdf

500. See http://www.telegraph.co.uk/women/mother- tongue/10971560/Average-age-of-mothers-hits-30.html

501. See Mary Daly's *Beyond God the Father. Towards a Philosophy of Women's Liberation*, p 8.

502. Indeed, bell hooks criticises the lack of "mass-based feminist protest challenging the government's assault on single mothers and the welfare system. Privileged women, many of whom call themselves feminists, have simply turned away from the 'feminization of poverty'. hooks characterises this as a profound betrayal. See *Feminism is For Everybody*, p 42.

503. See the bibliography for further reading, for example, Sylvia Ann Hewlett's *A Lesser Life*.

504. The Conservative Chancellor, George Osborne's go-to phrase to describe the nature of a mother's decision to care for her children. http://www.telegraph. co.uk/news/politics/10223383/Fury-over-George-Osbornes-snub-to-stay-at- home-mums.html

505. After all, the UK Government cuts are disproportionately affecting women.

506. See the bibliography for further reading, including the work of Catherine Hakim, Ann Crittenden and Anne Manne.

507. See http://www.info4migrants.com/finland/en/information/child-home-care-allowance

508. See Catherine Hakim's paper presented at the Presidential Conference on Parental Childcare and Employment Policy: Collision or Complementarity?, held in Prague, 5–6 February 2009, "Should Social Policy Support Parenthood and Family Work?". According to Hakim, both these policies "comply with the argument from preference theory that policy must now be even-handed between the three groups of women (home-centred, work-centred, and adaptive) instead of always being biased in favour of only one group (usually careerist women)".

509. For a breakdown of these statistics, see Mothers at Home Matter's *Who Cares About The Family?* http://www.mothersathomematter.co.uk/

510. The Universal Declaration of Human Rights (UDHR) was proclaimed by the United Nations General Assembly in Paris on 10 December 1948.

511. See Tania Modleski. *Feminism Without Women. Culture and Criticism in a 'Postfeminist' Age* for an interesting discussion about women's visibility.

512. Reni Eddo-Lodge discusses liberation v equality in her Guardian video, "Why women should stop striving for equality" http://www.theguardian.com/commentisfree/video/2015/jul/08/why-women-should-stop-striving-for-equality-video

513. See endnote 37 for Catherine Hakim's discussion of the study and its failure to acknowledge the diversity in women's wishes and failure to suggest policies to support family care.

514. See Oliver James' *How Not to F**k Them Up*, for a revealing comment made by Harriet Harman which demonstrates the contempt with which some feminist politicians hold mothers at home and homemakers. James quotes Harman as saying: "I suppose we have to give mothers a choice. If they want to hang about at home all day doing nothing, well, it's up to them", see p 38. In the 2015 General Election campaign, the Labour Party launched its 'Women's Manifesto' at a children's nursery. Says it all. In the US, Hillary Clinton gave a similar impression during campaigning for her husband's political career, thus: "I suppose I could have stayed home, baked cookies and had teas". Clinton had been a lawyer and activist. Clearly, nappies, baking and nursery rhymes were the equivalent of imbibing a cup of cold vomit. Well, hopefully, the Presidency will present more opportunities to avoid the baking. If she got it.

LOVE

515. See bell hooks' *All About Love, New Visions*.

516. Ibid.

517. https://sophiechristophy.wordpress.com/2016/03/17/fear-of-women-attachment-to-schooling/

Index

ABOUT THE AUTHOR

V ANESSA OLORENSHAW is a mother of two, activist, breastfeeding counsellor, and former barrister, law reporter and trade union rep from the South East of England. Always intellectually curious and raised — unwittingly, she suspects — to be a feminist within her leftie working-class family.

A revolutionary type of spirit, she has spoken at conferences about maternal feminism, motherhood and the socio-economic situation in which women are expected to raise their families in twenty-first century Western culture.

In March 2015, she published *The Politics of Mothering*, a pamphlet for the UK General Election. She was a founding member-cum-agitator of the Women's Equality Party UK and contributed to policy development on parenting.

Vanessa adores being with her children (they're brilliant, you know) and her husband (she is married to a pretty decent bloke). She balances her hippie tendencies with black outfits and Doc Martens.

She tweets at @VOlorenshaw.

https://politicsofmothering.wordpress.com/

https://www.facebook.com/Politics.of.Mothering/

#MothersOfTheWorldUnite

#LiberatingMotherhood

#Purplestockings

Also from Womancraft Publishing

Burning Woman by Lucy H. Pearce

The long-awaited new title from Amazon bestselling author Lucy H. Pearce. *Burning Woman* is a breath-taking and controversial woman's journey through history — personal and cultural — on a quest to find and free her own power.

Uncompromising and all-encompassing, Pearce uncovers the archetype of the Burning Women of days gone by — Joan of Arc and the witch trials, through to the way women are burned today in cyber bullying, acid attacks, shaming and burnout, fearlessly examining the roots of Feminine power — what it is, how it has been controlled, and why it needs to be unleashed on the world during our modern Burning Times.

With contributions from leading burning women of our era: Isabel Abbott, ALisa Starkweather, Shiloh Sophia McCloud, Molly Remer, Julie Daley, Bethany Webster . . .

A must-read for all women! A life-changing book that fills the reader with a burning passion and desire for change.
Glennie Kindred, author of *Earth Wisdom*

Moon Time: harness the ever-changing energy of your menstrual cycle, by Lucy H. Pearce

Hailed as 'life-changing' by women around the world, *Moon Time* shares a fully embodied understanding of the menstrual cycle. Full of practical insight, empowering resources, creative activities and passion, this book will put women back in touch with their body's wisdom. Amazon #1 bestseller in Menstruation.

Lucy, your book is monumental. The wisdom in Moon Time sets a new course where we glimpse a future culture reshaped by honoring our womanhood journeys one woman at a time.
ALisa Starkweather, founder of the Red Tent Temple Movement

The Heroines Club: A Mother-Daughter Empowerment Circle
by Melia Keeton-Digby

The Heroines Club offers nourishing guidance and a creative approach for mothers and daughters, aged 7+, to learn and grow together through the study of women's history. Each month focuses on a different heroine, featuring athletes, inventors, artists, and revolutionaries from around the world – including Frida Kahlo, Rosalind Franklin, Amelia Earhart, Anne Frank, Maya Angelou and Malala Yousafzai as strong role models for young girls to learn about, look up to, and be inspired by.

Offering thought-provoking discussion, powerful rituals, and engaging creative activities, The Heroines Club fortifies our daughters' self-esteem, invigorates mothers' spirits, and nourishes the mother-daughter relationship. In a culture that can make mothering daughters seem intimidating and isolating, it offers an antidote: a revolutionary model for empowering your daughter and strengthening your mother-daughter relationship.

The Heroines Club is truly a must-have book for mothers who wish to foster a deeper connection with their daughters. As mothers, we are our daughter's first teacher, role model, and wise counsel. This book should be in every woman's hands, and passed down from generation to generation.
Wendy Cook, founder of Mighty Girl Art

The Other Side of the River: Stories of Women, Water and the World
by Eila Kundrie Carrico

A deep searching into the ways we become dammed and how we recover fluidity. It is a journey through memory and time, personal and shared landscapes to discover the source, the flow and the deltas of women and water.

Part memoir, part manifesto, part travelogue and part love letter to myth and ecology, *The Other Side of the River* is an intricately woven tale of finding your flow . . . and your roots.

An instant classic for the new paradigm.
Lucia Chiavola Birnbaum, award-winning author and
Professor Emeritus

Reaching for the Moon: a girl's guide to her cycles by Lucy H. Pearce

The girls' version of Lucy H. Pearce's Amazon bestselling book *Moon Time*. For girls aged 9–14, as they anticipate and experience their body's changes. *Reaching for the Moon* is a nurturing celebration of a girl's transformation to womanhood.

A message of wonder, empowerment, magic and beauty in the shared secrets of our femininity ... written to encourage girls to embrace their transition to womanhood in a knowledgeable, supported, loving way.
thelovingparent.com

The Heart of the Labyrinth by Nicole Schwab

Reminiscent of Paulo Coelho's masterpiece *The Alchemist* and Lynn V. Andrew's acclaimed *Medicine Woman* series, *The Heart of the Labyrinth* is a beautifully evocative spiritual parable, filled with exotic landscapes and transformational soul lessons.

Once in a while, a book comes along that kindles the fire of our inner wisdom so profoundly, the words seem to leap off the page and go straight into our heart. If you read only one book this year, this is it.
Dean Ornish, M.D., President, Preventive Medicine Research Institute, Clinical Professor of Medicine, University of California, Author of *The Spectrum*

Moods of Motherhood: the inner journey of mothering by Lucy H. Pearce

Moods of Motherhood charts the inner journey of motherhood, giving voice to the often nebulous, unspoken tumble of emotions that motherhood evokes: tenderness, frustration, joy, grief, anger, depression and love.

Lucy's frank and forthright style paired with beautiful, haunting language and her talent for storytelling will have any parent nodding, crying and laughing along — appreciating the good and the bad, the hard and the soft, the light and the dark. A must-read for any new parent.
Zoe Foster, *JUNO* magazine

Womancraft
PUBLISHING

Life-changing, paradigm-shifting books
by women, for women

Visit us at www.womancraftpublishing.com
where you can sign up to the mailing list for
discounts and samples of our forthcoming titles
before anyone else.

(f) Womancraft Publishing

(•) WomancraftBooks

(◎) Womancraft Publishing

If you have enjoyed this book, please leave a
review on Amazon or Goodreads.

CPSIA information can be obtained
at www.ICGtesting.com
Printed in the USA
BVHW040452250221
601054BV00004B/19